# BETWEEN FAULT LINES AND FRONT LINES

# BETWEEN FAULT LINES AND FRONT LINES

## Shifting Power in an Unequal World

Edited by
**Katja Hujo and Maggie Carter**

BLOOMSBURY ACADEMIC
LONDON • NEW YORK • OXFORD • NEW DELHI • SYDNEY

BLOOMSBURY ACADEMIC
Bloomsbury Publishing Plc
50 Bedford Square, London, WC1B 3DP, UK
1385 Broadway, New York, NY 10018, USA
29 Earlsfort Terrace, Dublin 2, Ireland

BLOOMSBURY, BLOOMSBURY ACADEMIC and the Diana logo are trademarks of
Bloomsbury Publishing Plc

First published in Great Britain 2022

Copyright © United Nations Research Institute for Social Development 2022

Katja Hujo and Maggie Carter have asserted their right under the Copyright, Designs and
Patents Act, 1988, to be identified as Editors of this work.

Cover design by Daniel Benneworth-Gray
Cover image © Rawpixel

A catalogue record for this book is available from the British Library.

A catalog record for this book is available from the Library of Congress.

ISBN: HB: 978-1-3502-2903-7
PB: 978-1-3502-2902-0
ePDF: 978-1-3502-2905-1
eBook: 978-1-3502-2904-4

Typeset by Deanta Global Publishing Services, Chennai, India
Printed and bound in Great Britain

# CONTENTS

## Part I
## INEQUALITIES IN CONTEXT

## Part II
## ENGINES OF INEQUALITY: INSTITUTIONS, POLITICS AND POWER

# ILLUSTRATIONS

## Figures

## Tables

# FOREWORD

Economic inequality has been high at previous points in modern human history but never before has this inequality constrained the well-being and opportunities of so many billions of people. Never before has it threatened the very existence of the planet on which we live.

Even as governments and aid agencies named poverty reduction as the primary "development" objective for the new millennium, we knew that higher rates of inequality would slow the rate at which economic growth could reduce poverty. The main conclusion drawn at that time by policy makers was not that inequalities in society should be reduced, but rather that countries needed to deliver more economic growth. A focus on reducing inequalities in and of themselves was seen as contrary to the natural order and working against free market forces. Globalization was expected to flatten disparities, and inequalities would become extinct in a connected world of more opportunities.

Some countries did indeed grow faster than others, at least until the global economic and financial crisis checked that pathway. China in particular did the heavy lifting that allowed the world to claim that extreme monetary poverty had been halved. But inequality stunted the progress that could have been made and now it acts as a brake on progress across the full suite of Sustainable Development Goals.

Like poverty, which we understand as multidimensional, there are many inequalities that exist and combine to limit capabilities and opportunities. Vertical inequalities describe those relating to income and wealth, while horizontal inequalities serve as the basis for discrimination against and exclusion of certain groups or communities. Often they reinforce each other, with marginalized groups around the world being poorer and unable to access jobs, services and resources.

Inequalities are a problem now not only because fewer people are connected to growth and economic security, but because the world is steadily being oriented to those who are already well-off. The rules of the game have been subtly rewritten to protect the wealth of the rich and in doing so limit the opportunities of everyone else. Inequalities have become self-sustaining while social mobility has been choked. This slow creep is expressed through the policies and institutions that leaders and officials put in place.

The policies and institutions that are keeping the rich rich are the same ones that exert an inexorable gravitational pull toward unsustainable development and crises, felt most acutely through the destruction of the climate, ecosystems and biodiversity. Economic power has traditionally been synonymous with political power—indeed, by 2020 half the members of the US Congress were millionaires. The powerful will tend to look after themselves first.

To understand the impact that inequalities have on our prospects for human progress and planetary survival, and their root causes, we need to look at not just the very poor but also the very rich. That is where this book comes in, focusing squarely on how economic and political elites keep the balance of the world tilted to their benefit. It uncovers how they lobby for favorable tax treatment or contracts and ensure that their wealth can be passed down the family tree like an inherited title.

Even 20 years ago, the various injustices that inequalities breed could remain largely hidden. Now, an internet connection in the poorest place on the planet can expose the consumerist excesses in the richest. And that, in turn, is energizing a new movement and quest for a fairer and more sustainable world. Through research and advocacy, UNRISD supports this movement. This book showcases many examples of how less powerful people organize, build alliances and successfully claim their rights. UNRISD explores inequalities through all our research programs, and our policy recommendations point to the need to develop new contracts that combine ecological and social rights and responsibilities—or eco-social contracts—that by necessity emphasize solidarity and sustainability in the face of exclusion and injustice.

Many argue, correctly, that some inequalities are innate and inevitable. They can be created by different talents and even luck. But an evolved humanity should seek to level up and maximize opportunities for all, guaranteeing that everyone can live a dignified life and enjoy fundamental human rights. That can only be done if we strip back the entrenched and ossified inequalities that characterize our world today and which have been slowly put in place by privileged elites.

Paul Ladd, Director, UNRISD
Geneva, August 2021

# PREFACE

Inequality as a social, political and development issue has risen toward the top of public agendas, with its damaging impacts on social, environmental and economic sustainability and its links to poverty, insecurity, crime and xenophobia now widely demonstrated and acknowledged. This was crystalized with the inclusion of a stand-alone goal on inequalities in the 2030 Agenda for Sustainable Development in 2015. However, despite this prominence in both national and global development agendas, the conversation largely revolves around the bottom of the inequality pyramid—the poorest of the poor—with little attention paid to the drivers of inequality and structures that reproduce and reinforce it.

Building on its long-standing body of work on the subject, the United Nations Research Institute for Social Development has sought to shift the debate, exploring the drivers and consequences of inequalities and how people, communities, social relationships and institutions are adapting and innovating in response to them. Following an international conference, "Overcoming Inequalities in a Fractured World: Between Elite Power and Social Mobilization," that UNRISD convened in November 2018, this book pulls together many strands of research presented as papers and speeches by an interdisciplinary and regionally diverse group of scholars, activists and practitioners.

In the book, we interrogate the roles that elites and institutions of power play in the deepening of social and economic cleavages across the globe. We also explore how inequalities manifest themselves and what their impacts are, from a historical macroeconomic perspective, in spatial and intergenerational terms, in policies and institutions, and in different sectors such as the hedge fund industry or the gig economy. The volume thus aims to uncover the intersectional nature of economic and group-based inequalities, such as those related to gender, race, ethnicity, age, sexual orientation, citizenship or labor market status, disability or other markers of disadvantage. And finally, we seek to bring to global attention recent case studies from different countries that analyze how people have been mobilizing and taking action creatively to overcome structural barriers and push for equality and social justice. Ultimately, the volume is situated in the sites of fracture wrought by inequality—the fault lines—and the sites of struggle where those in power come face to face with those working for a more just future—the front lines.

Since our work on this book began, the world has entered more deeply into crisis. From the Covid-19 pandemic, to accelerating climate crisis and related natural disasters, to violent conflicts and state collapse, as we have seen recently in Afghanistan, Ethiopia, Haiti, Lebanon and Myanmar, the prospects for the future seem ever darker. These crises have also shown how our unequal world undermines solidarity and resilience, and is therefore ill-prepared to cope with crisis and to protect the most vulnerable groups. Those people who were already at the bottom of the pyramid in terms of power and resources have fallen further behind at the same time as several of the richest men and corporations in the world have multiplied their wealth.

Understanding the drivers and consequences of inequality, how to rein in elite power, and learning from successful political and social movements and reforms that address inequality and social injustice are therefore imperative if we want to emerge from these present crises into a more livable, resilient and just future.

This book would not have come to fruition without the support of many people. First and foremost we would like to thank all the chapter authors for their contributions, which they prepared in challenging times of Covid infections, lockdowns and increased care burdens while balancing professional and personal responsibilities.

We would also like to thank those people who supported the 2018 conference and the various activities that followed: UNRISD interns Alberto Parmigiani, Martyna Linartas, Tejal Ambardekar and Paul Scharfenberg; the Friedrich-Ebert-Stiftung Geneva office, in particular former director Hubert Schillinger, current director Hajo Lanz and Yvonne Bartmann, who provided generous funding and support; and partners at the University of Geneva, in particular Professor Jonas Pontusson. This volume also benefited from all those who helped steer the direction of the project by providing useful feedback on the inequalities research program and the various initiatives that have come out of it, including Yusuf Bangura, Daniel Beland, Sarah Cook, Enrique Delamonica, Andrew Fischer, Terence Gomez, Evelyne Huber, Ganga Jey Aratnam, Gabriele Köhler, Rubén Lo Vuolo, Henning Melber, Ananya Mukherjee Reed, Ben Phillips, James Putzel, Nitya Rao, Andrew Rosser, Aaron Schneider, Jojo Nem Singh, Peter Utting and Imraan Valodia.

Within UNRISD we are especially grateful for the leadership, enthusiasm and support of our Director Paul Ladd, who contributed to this project in many important ways, from his firm belief that we needed to bring the issue of elite power and wealth concentration onto UN agendas to his active participation and interest in all phases of this work.

This book would not be in your hands today without the support of the UNRISD Communications and Outreach team, including Joannah Caborn Wengler, who has supported the project in all aspects of communications with both attention to detail and a flair for nuance; Sergio Sandoval, whose arresting and impactful graphic design work has left a lasting impression on the project and those who have engaged with it; and finally our chief of communications, Jenifer Freedman, who consistently lends her considerable skills and insight to push our work to new levels.

This book benefited from the meticulous copyediting of Elizabeth Stone at Bourchier, which we gratefully acknowledge.

We would also like to thank the editorial team at Zed/Bloomsbury Publishing for their excellent advice and support during the production process, as well as an anonymous peer reviewer for very insightful comments.

Last but not least, on behalf of UNRISD we would like to take this opportunity to thank our funding partners. As is the case with all UNRISD work, this important research would not have been possible without the core institutional support received from the governments of Sweden, Switzerland and Finland.

Katja Hujo and Maggie Carter
Geneva, August 2021

# ABBREVIATIONS AND ACRONYMS

| | |
|---|---|
| ADESP | Asociación de Empleadas del Servicio Doméstico del Paraguay (Paraguayan Association of Domestic Service Employees) |
| AIM | American Indian Movement (United States) |
| ANC | African National Congress (South Africa) |
| ASHA | Accredited Social Health Activist (India) |
| BPP | Black Panther Party (United States) |
| CDE | Centro de Documentación y Estudios (Center for Documentation and Studies) (Paraguay) |
| CNT | Central Nacional de Trabajadores (National Workers' Union) (Paraguay) |
| CODEFAT | Conselho Diretor do Fundo de Amparo ao Trabalhador (Council of the Fund for Workers' Support) (Brazil) |
| CUT-A | Central Unitaria de Trabajadores-Auténtica (Authentic Sole Workers' Union) (Paraguay) |
| DA | Democratic Alliance (South Africa) |
| DFID | Department for International Development (United Kingdom) |
| FAO | Food and Agriculture Organization |
| FDI | Foreign direct investment |
| FNRU | Fórum Nacional para Reforma Urbana (National Forum for Urban Reform) (Brazil) |
| FSU | Former Soviet Union |
| GDP | Gross domestic product |
| GMO | Genetically modified organisms |
| HNT | HomeNet Thailand |
| ILO | International Labour Organization |
| IMF | International Monetary Fund |
| IPR | Intellectual property rights |
| LAC | Latin America and the Caribbean |
| LACCU | Liga de Amas de Casa y Consumidores del Uruguay (Uruguayan Housewives' and Consumers' League) |
| LAC-Py | Liga de Amas de Casa del Paraguay (Paraguayan Housewives' League) |
| LAMATA | Lagos Metropolitan Area Transport Authority |
| LHF | Local Health Fund (Thailand) |
| LSSM | Lok Swasthya SEWA Mandali (India) |
| MBO | Membership-based organization |
| MENA | Middle East and North Africa |
| MNRU | Movimento Nacional de Reforma Urbana (National Movement for Urban Reform) (Brazil) |
| MO | Medical officer |
| NGN | Nigerian naira |

| | |
|---|---|
| NGO | Nongovernmental organization |
| NHSO | National Health Security Office (Thailand) |
| NLP | National Land for People (United States) |
| NOLA | Networks of Labor Activism |
| OECD | Organisation for Economic Co-operation and Development |
| PAIF | Programa de Assistência Integral a Famílias (Program for Integral Assistance to Families) (Brazil) |
| PAS | Programa de Avaliação Seriada (Serial Evaluation Program) (Brazil) |
| PBF | Programa Bolsa Família (Bolsa Família Program) (Brazil) |
| PHC | Primary health care |
| PIT-CNT | Plenario Intersindical de Trabajadores—Convención Nacional de Trabajadores (Inter Trade Union Plenary—National Workers' Convention) (Uruguay) |
| PNSIPN | Política Nacional de Saúde Integral da População Negra (National Program for Integral Health Care of the Black Population) (Brazil) |
| PPP | Purchasing power parity |
| PT | Partido dos Trabalhadores (Workers' Party) (Brazil) |
| RKS | Rogi Kalyan Samiti (India) |
| SDGs | Sustainable Development Goals |
| SEC | Securities and Exchange Commission (United States) |
| SEWA | Self Employed Women's Association (India) |
| SINTRADI | Sindicato de Trabajadoras Domésticas de Itapúa (Itapúa's Domestic Workers' Union) (Paraguay) |
| SINTRADOP | Sindicato de Trabajadoras Domésticas del Paraguay (Paraguayan Domestic Workers' Union) |
| SSA | Sub-Saharan Africa |
| SSK | SEWA Shakti Kendra (India) |
| SUAS | Sistema Único de Assistência Social (National Social Assistance System) (Brazil) |
| SUTD | Sindicato Único de Trabajadoras Domésticas (Single Domestic Workers' Union) (Uruguay) |
| TRIPS | Trade-Related Aspects of Intellectual Property Rights |
| UCLG | United Cities and Local Governments |
| UFW | United Farmworkers' Union (United States) |
| UNCTAD | United Nations Conference on Trade and Development |
| UNDP | United Nations Development Programme |
| UNESCO | United Nations Educational, Scientific and Cultural Organization |
| UNICEF | United Nations International Children's Emergency Fund |
| UNRISD | United Nations Research Institute for Social Development |
| USD | United States dollar |
| WIEGO | Women in Informal Employment: Globalizing and Organizing |
| WTO | World Trade Organization |
| WW2 | Second World War |

# CONTRIBUTORS

**Laura Alfers** is Director of Social Protection at the global action-research-policy network Women in Informal Employment: Globalizing and Organizing (WIEGO) and is Research Associate in the Department of Sociology, Rhodes University, South Africa. Her research interests sit at the intersections of labor, urban and social policy, with a focus on understanding how organizations of informal workers are working to influence those policies.

**Maggie Carter** is Senior Research Analyst in the Transformative Social Policy Programme at the United Nations Research Institute for Social Development (UNRISD), where she co-coordinates the projects "Overcoming Inequalities in a Fractured World: Between Elite Power and Social Mobilization" and "From Science to Practice: Research and Knowledge to Achieve the SDGs." She is co-author of the UNRISD 2022 Flagship Report, "Overcoming Inequalities in Times of Crisis—Towards a New Eco-Social Contract." Her research focuses on spatial inequality, citizenship and social policy.

**Katja Hujo** is Senior Research Coordinator in the Transformative Social Policy Programme at UNRISD. Katja's academic work focuses on social policy, poverty and inequality and socioeconomic development. She coordinates the research project "Overcoming Inequalities in a Fractured World: Between Elite Power and Social Mobilization" and has recently guest-edited a themed section "Social Protection and Inequality in the Global South: Politics, Actors and Institutions" in *Critical Social Policy* 41(3). She is lead author of the UNRISD 2022 Flagship Report, "Overcoming Inequalities in Times of Crisis—Towards a New Eco-Social Contract."

**Tom Lavers** is Senior Lecturer at the University of Manchester's Global Development Institute. His research focuses on the political economy of development, in particular land, agrarian transformation, infrastructure and social policy.

**Matias López** is a postdoctoral researcher at the Albert Hirschman Centre on Democracy at the Graduate Institute of International and Development Studies in Geneva, Switzerland. His research, which focuses on how inequality affects democratic stability and policy making, has been published in recent editions of *Socio-Economic Review, American Behavioral Scientist, PS: Political Science and Politics* and *Sociology Compass*.

**Julie MacLeavy** is Professor at the School of Geographical Sciences, University of Bristol. Her research interests lie in the field of economic geography, particularly in welfare state restructuring, labor market transitions and urban policy reforms.

**David Manley** is Professor at the School of Geographical Sciences, University of Bristol, and Honorary Fellow of OTB Research for the Built Environment, Delft University of Technology. He has written extensively across urban issues, including segregation and contextual effects relating to place.

**Kate Meagher** is Associate Professor in Development Studies at the Department of International Development, London School of Economics and Political Science. She has published widely on the informal economy and economic change, including "Working in Chains: African Informal Workers and Global Value Chains" (*Agrarian South: Journal of Political Economy*, 8(1-2), 2019). Her current research interests include labor informalization, the gig economy, informality and the social contract and the hybrid assemblages of economic inclusion.

**Megan Tobias Neely** is Assistant Professor in the Department of Organization at Copenhagen Business School and coauthor of *Divested: Inequality in the Age of Finance* (2019). Her recent book *Hedged Out: Inequality and Insecurity on Wall Street* (2022) explains why the US hedge fund industry generates extreme wealth, why mostly white men benefit and why reforming Wall Street will create a more equal society.

**Fritz Nganje** lectures in the Department of Politics and International Relations at the University of Johannesburg. His primary areas of research include the foreign relations of subnational governments, decentralized cooperation, local peacebuilding, as well as South Africa's foreign policy and diplomacy in Africa.

**Roberto Pires** is Researcher and Professor at the Institute for Applied Economic Research (Ipea) and at the National School of Public Administration, Brasília, Brazil. His main research interests include policy implementation, social inequalities and state-society relations.

**Vladimir Popov** is a principal researcher in the Central Economics and Mathematics Institute of the Russian Academy of Sciences. He is also Professor Emeritus at the New Economic School in Moscow and Adjunct Research Professor at the Institute of European and Russian Studies at Carleton University in Ottawa. He worked as Senior Economic Affairs Officer and Inter-regional Adviser at UNDESA (2009–2015). He has published extensively on world economy and development issues, most recently *When Life Expectancy is Falling: Mortality Crises in Post-Communist Countries in a Global Context* (2020).

**Elisa Reis** is Professor of Political Sociology at the Federal University of Rio de Janeiro, where she is also Chair of the Interdisciplinary Research Network for the

Study of Social Inequality. She is a member of the Brazilian Academy of Sciences and of the Academy of Science for the Developing World. Her work focuses on elite perceptions of poverty and inequality and on evolving patterns of interaction between state, market and civil society. She is the author of more than 100 articles published in Brazil and elsewhere.

**Antonio Roman-Alcalá** is an educator, researcher, facilitator and organizer whose work focuses on food, farming and building grassroots power. He has founded urban farms, grassroots coalitions, policy-focused networks and scholar-activist collectives, and currently teaches in community and university contexts (including at the University of California Santa Cruz) while researching collaborative efforts to improve social movement effectiveness.

**Raquel Rojas Scheffer** is a postdoctoral researcher at the Institute for Latin American Studies at the Free University of Berlin. She holds a PhD in Sociology from the Free University of Berlin and an MA in Social Sciences from the Humboldt University of Berlin. Raquel is originally from Paraguay, where she earned a Specialist Degree in Social Development from the Latin American Social Sciences Institute (FLACSO) and a BA in Social Sciences from the National University of Asunción. Her research focuses on inequalities, social movements, labor relations, social policies and political systems.

**Jeremy Seekings** is Professor of Political Studies and Sociology, and Director of the Centre for Social Science Research at the University of Cape Town. His recent and current work focuses on the history and politics of social policy as well as parties, elections and voting, with a primary focus on Southern Africa.

**Vandana Shiva** is a physicist and world-renowned environmental thinker and activist, as well as a leader in the International Forum on Globalization and of the Slow Food Movement. She is Director of Navdanya and of the Research Foundation for Science, Technology and Ecology. She is author of numerous influential books, including *Making Peace with the Earth* (2012), *Soil Not Oil* (2009), *Staying Alive* (1988/2010), *Globalization's New Wars* (2005), *Earth Democracy* (2005) and *Oneness vs. the 1%* (2018). Among her many awards are the Right Livelihood Award (also known as the Alternative Nobel Prize), the UNEP Global 500 Award and the MIDORI Prize for Biodiversity. *Forbes* magazine identified her as one of the top seven most powerful women on the globe in November 2010.

**Graziella Moraes Silva** is Associate Professor in Anthropology and Sociology at the Graduate Institute of International and Development Studies in Geneva, Switzerland. Other affiliations include the Interdisciplinary Network for the Study of Inequality at the Federal University of Rio de Janeiro and the Center for Social Development in Africa at the University of Johannesburg. She is a coauthor of *Getting Respect: Dealing with Stigmatization and Discrimination in the United States, Brazil and Israel* (2016) and has authored articles in *Socio-Economic Review,*

*Ethnic and Racial Studies* and *Journal of Latin American and Caribbean Ethnic Studies.*

**Jomo Kwame Sundaram** is Senior Adviser at the Khazanah Research Institute, Fellow of the Academy of Science, Malaysia, Emeritus Professor at the University of Malaya and Visiting Fellow at the Initiative for Policy Dialogue, Columbia University. He was Founder-Chair of International Development Economics Associates (IDEAs), UN Assistant Secretary General for Economic Development (2005–2012) and Assistant Director General, Food and Agriculture Organization (FAO) (2012–2015). He received the 2007 Wassily Leontief Prize for Advancing the Frontiers of Economic Thought.

**Chana Teeger** is Assistant Professor in the Department of Methodology and a faculty associate of the International Inequalities Institute at the London School of Economics. She is also Senior Research Fellow in the Sociology Department at the University of Johannesburg, South Africa. Her work focuses on race, inequality, education, elites and collective memory, and has appeared in *American Sociological Review*, *Social Forces*, *Sociology of Education* and *Socio-Economic Review*.

# Part I

## INEQUALITIES IN CONTEXT

# Chapter 1

## INTRODUCTION

### BETWEEN FAULT LINES AND FRONT LINES: SHIFTING POWER IN AN UNEQUAL WORLD

Katja Hujo and Maggie Carter

*Understanding Inequality: A Power-Centered Approach*

Reducing poverty has long been on the agenda of policy and development actors the world over, culminating in its inclusion as the first of the United Nations Millennium Development Goals in 2000. In discussions about poverty and its many ills, however, the relationship with inequality historically has received scant attention. Yet in recent years, the focus has begun to shift from the bottom of the pyramid to the top. "Inequality" has become the word on all our lips, the ugly exposed truth of a world in which growth trickles upwards to the few, whereas the many are deprived of basic needs and life chances, a world in which 22 men own more wealth than all the women in the continent of Africa (Oxfam 2020). At the heart of this relationship is a gross imbalance of power, driven by economic dominance. This shift in how we understand the massive disparities of our time— typified by the inclusion of inequality as the 10th of 17 Sustainable Development Goals (SDGs) in 2015—opens the door for, even compels, investigation into the inner workings of these power imbalances: Who and what drive these inequalities? Which beliefs, policies and institutions produce and reproduce them? What are the consequences for economies, societies, nature and people? And what can be done about it? These are some of the questions this book aims to address.

Inequality is highly detrimental for our societies and economies, undermining well-being and health, democracy and participation, as well as social, environmental and economic sustainability (e.g., Chancel 2017; Stiglitz 2012; Therborn 2013; UNDP 2019; UNRISD 2010; Wilkinson and Pickett 2009). Not all inequalities are a problem, but at least three factors indicate when inequalities have become an issue of economic and social justice:[1] first, when inequality is the result of discrimination

---

1. As the UK Commission on Social Justice established as one of its principles, not all inequalities are unjust, but unjust inequalities should be reduced and where possible eliminated (Commission on Social Justice 1993: 16).

and systematic disadvantage such as fewer opportunities and lack of access to essential services, basic living standards, decent work or meaningful participation in public life; second, when inequalities are growing at exponential rates, leading to power concentration on the one hand and disempowerment on the other, creating multiple fractures and biases in our political and economic systems which undermine societal progress; and third, when social discontent and sentiments of unfairness are expressed in (violent) protest, political radicalization and "Othering" (see Roman-Alcalá in this volume), posing a threat to social cohesion and democracy.

The inequalities that shape our current times meet these three criteria: they reveal deep-seated power asymmetries and patterns of exclusion; economic inequalities have risen steadily in most places over four decades, with no turning point in sight; and people are increasingly raising their voices against them, claiming justice.

The chapters in this volume were first presented and discussed at the international conference "Overcoming Inequalities in a Fractured World: Between Elite Power and Social Mobilization," convened by the United Nations Research Institute for Social Development (UNRISD) in November 2018 (Hujo and Carter 2018). In a context where the international development community had agreed, for the first time in the history of the United Nations (Freistein and Mahlert 2016; Köhler 2015), to reduce inequalities within and between countries as well as other forms of inequality, such as gender disparities, in the context of the SDGs (UN 2015), the key objective of the conference was to better understand the political economy of inequality. This was motivated by the fact that development actors, at least in their official discourse, tend to ignore questions of power and politics in their problem analysis, leading to apolitical and technocratic approaches and a focus on poor populations, whereas the role of the rich and powerful remains unexplored and unaddressed.

Contrary to this, our approach puts power at the center of analysis, both the power of elites and the counterpower of those who organize collectively to redress social injustices. The focus on poor and vulnerable people and the silence on elites in current development approaches evoke notions of charity and the attempt to explain inequalities through agentless processes such as globalization or the (in-)famous invisible hand of the market (see Meagher in this volume). However, as Dorling states, "growing inequality is not an unfortunate by-product of highly efficient competitive markets, but the end product of subtle rises in protectionism" (Dorling 2019: 57). A social justice approach, on the other hand, requires that actors and relationships be made explicit. This volume approaches inequality as a product of entrenched power structures, in which a small group of people have highly disproportionate control over and access to resources, and understands that, inversely, inequality is essential for the maintenance of these structures.

In this volume we explore the ways in which:

- global inequalities are in large part reproduced and compounded by elite capture of economic and political power, and the growing concentration of income and wealth;

- the same power asymmetries that drive inequality tend to inhibit policy and institutional change that are needed to address it;
- recent global crises such as the Great Recession and the Covid-19 pandemic have exacerbated inequalities, while opening up discursive space and highlighting the value and urgency of alternative policy pathways and broad coalitions for egalitarian change;
- combating elite power and reducing inequality require reimagining paths to social change through collective mobilization and strategic alliances, in a complex context of shifting class structures and identities, new forms of citizenship and social contracts, the changing world of work and technological change, increased connectivity and restricted mobility.

Authors contributing to this volume engage with these themes while following their own intellectual paths grounded in diverse disciplines such as anthropology, economics, geography, international relations, political science, public administration, public policy and sociology. Hence, the chapters in the book address the theme of inequality and power in different and sometimes contradicting ways, applying various analytical lenses and methodological approaches ranging from historical analysis, to political economy, to structuralism, to actor- or agency-centered analyses, with entry points such as ideas/ideology, behaviors and perceptions. Finally, some contributions also reflect scholar-activist perspectives that transcend academic boundaries, as exemplified most strongly in the epilogue to this volume. While this diversity arguably stands in the way of a more consistent and sustained perspective, it reflects the plurality of relevant critical research in this field, a plurality which is often ignored in decision-making circles dominated by one-size-fits-all methods and "randomista economics" (Kabeer 2020) but which can equally fall victim to siloed thinking and paradigmatic warfare in academia. To help the reader navigate this complex field of research, this introduction aims to make sense of not only the different approaches and cases, highlighting the connections and complementarities, but also contradictions that naturally emerge from an interdisciplinary engagement of the multiple linkages between inequality and power in the age of contested hyper-globalization.

## Inequality and Its Discontents: A Brief Historical Overview

The belief that inequalities—those which impede people from developing their capabilities and full potential, and limit social mobility across class, identities and space—must be reduced was a fundamental pillar of the postwar multilateral order in which most countries in the world committed to international norms of human rights, peace, security, development and international cooperation (UN 1946, 1948).

Nevertheless, inequality, in particular economic inequality, did not receive much attention during the early period of postwar development when inequalities in wealth and income were actually decreasing (Piketty 2014, 2019), and a rising tide of economic growth seemed to lift all boats. States were eager to establish comprehensive social security systems such as pensions, unemployment insurance or social assistance that would maintain social peace and act as automatic stabilizers in times of economic downturns. Investments in education, health, social housing and public transport created synergies between the interests of employers to access "human capital," workers who saw their social wage and purchasing power increase and governments that reaped benefits in terms of increased tax revenue and electoral gains. During the same period, equality of rights improved dramatically, in particular with regard to political rights and antidiscrimination law, which made great progress during the wave of democratization and decolonization, culminating in the 1990s, as well as regarding women's rights and greater equality of rights for Indigenous peoples and disabled persons (UN DESA 2006).

This twentieth-century social contract associated with democratic welfare states in the global North, combining growth, redistribution and expansion of social rights, started to unravel with fiscal crises and stagflation in the 1970s. Its dissolution continued when a new paradigm of neoliberal globalization gained ground in the 1980s, the negative results of which are well known: the end of the developmentalist social contract in the global South during the lost decade of austerity policies and structural adjustment (Ocampo 2014; see Meagher in this volume), jobless growth, rising precarity and an increasing share of national income accruing to capital compared with labor in the global North (ILO 2016; Standing 2011), and rising inequalities and environmental destruction worldwide. These problems have worsened over the last two decades or so during a period that economists such as Piketty call "hyper-capitalism" and that the United Nations Conference on Trade and Development (UNCTAD) calls "hyper-globalization"— the dominance of capital owners, private finance and large corporations increasingly capturing markets and engaging in rent-seeking activities, leading not only to previously unseen levels of inequalities and climate crisis but also to extreme levels of debt, heightened insecurity, and stalling of investment and structural change (Hujo 2021; Piketty 2019; UNCTAD 2020).

During the first phase of neoliberal globalization, and in particular after the demise of socialism in Eastern Europe and the former Soviet Union (Piketty 2019), inequality was not a policy issue despite the fact that it was increasing: when unleashed market forces, technological change and reduced redistribution had negative effects on income equality in the 1980s, it was argued that efficiency was more important than equity (Le Grand 1990; Okun 1975). Growth, assumed to be driven by high savings rates of the rich channeled into investment, was supposed to automatically trickle down to the poor, whereas large-scale redistribution through state policies was considered detrimental for employment creation and growth. This perspective is not as monolithic as it used to be following mounting criticism of the free market ideology and its adverse ecological, social and economic impacts (Stiglitz 2002; UNRISD 1995), but it is still the dominant discourse of a significant proportion of elite actors (see Moraes Silva et al. in this volume).

Jomo Kwame Sundaram and Vladimir Popov delve more deeply into these issues in Chapter 2, arguing that the growth performances in developing countries have been uneven and the few successes of catching up cannot be linked to free market ideology, a narrative that was, for example, promoted by the World Bank to explain the so-called East Asian miracle (World Bank 1993). Historically, the multiplicity of developmental trajectories suggests that there are no universal recipes for rapid catch-up growth, while the managed development approach of Asian countries became increasingly popular. Nor is the inequality picture clear-cut: the chapter unpacks the paradox of inequality among countries reducing in aggregate measures, while within most countries income and wealth inequalities have been increasing. According to Jomo and Popov, the data suggest that rising inequality is due to rising profit rates, as the income shares of the richest have been growing for decades. The authors contend that such increases in wealth concentration will be difficult to reverse despite pressures for progressive redistribution, due to the prevailing neoliberal economic ideology, declining fiscal space and the concentration of political power skewed toward the benefit of the wealthy. They nevertheless consider that reversing this pattern is key: beyond the moral imperative to reduce inequality, high inequality hinders growth, weakens political institutions, reduces social mobility and increases social tension.

These insights explain why, in the most recent period of hyper-globalization, inequality has finally taken center stage in public debates. Interestingly, this discussion is not only led by progressive political, academic and civil society actors but also by business-friendly circles such as the World Economic Forum, which focuses on adverse impacts on business and sustainable development, or economists within the International Monetary Fund or the World Bank, who consider inequality as detrimental for achieving development goals such as poverty reduction and growth (Lakner et al. 2019; Ostry et al. 2018; WEF 2014).[2]

Whether judged from an intrinsic or instrumental perspective, the multiple expressions of inequality are a symptom that something is profoundly wrong with our global development model. Its steady increase indicates no change of direction after the global financial crisis in 2008, generating outrage and motivating protesters in New York City to set up an encampment in the city's Financial District, launching the Occupy Wall Street movement and coining the slogan "We are the 99 percent." It also shows how far offtrack the promises of the 2030 Agenda for Sustainable Development are, "to leave no one behind" and to reduce inequality within and between countries (SDG 10) as well as gender inequality (SDG 5) (UN 2015, 2020a). The Covid-19 pandemic has added insult to injury: people with low incomes, precarious livelihoods and other social markers of disadvantage are disproportionately affected by the devastating health and socioeconomic impacts the crisis has triggered, whereas the rich have become richer (Bottan et al. 2020; Oxfam 2021).

2. An argument put forward by Persson and Tabellini (1994: 617) that "income inequality is harmful for growth, because it leads to policies that do not protect property rights and do not allow for full [sic] appropriation of returns from investment" is still visible in the new IMF papers on inequality, for example Ostry et al. (2018).

## This Is What Inequality Looks

*Economic inequality at a glance*

According to Oxfam, the world's 2,153 billionaires now own the same wealth as 60 percent of the global population or 4.6 billion people (Oxfam 2020). Income and wealth inequality continues to increase at an alarming rate (despite the fact that some of the fastest growing countries in Asia have reduced the gap with developed economies since the late 1980s; see Jomo and Popov in this volume). The global top 1 percent of earners captured 27 percent of real income growth between 1980 and 2016, more than twice the amount of the bottom 50 percent (World Inequality Lab 2018). In addition, during the peak of the global Covid-19 pandemic the world's billionaires became 27.5 percent richer (UBS 2020), and at the same time more than 120 million people are estimated to have fallen into extreme poverty (Kharas 2020).

While extreme poverty continues to affect more than 9 percent of the global population (World Bank 2020), in 2018 some 1.3 billion people in 105 countries lived in households with overlapping deprivations regarding basic needs such as health, education, access to water and sanitation, electricity or cooking fuel. About 84.3 percent of people classified as poor with regard to multiple dimensions (health, education, standard of living) live in sub-Saharan Africa (558 million) and South Asia (530 million) (UNDP and OPHI 2020). In addition, half of the global population has no access to essential health services, and two-thirds of the global population has no or only partial social protection coverage (ILO 2017; WHO and World Bank 2017). A significant proportion of the population in rich countries such as the United Kingdom suffer basic deprivations such as food insecurity (Dorling 2019). And such vulnerabilities are made all the more disastrous during times of crisis. For example, the ability to shield oneself from the most brutal effects of climate change is often directly related to socioeconomic status—as well as race, ethnicity, gender and citizenship status—and in fact the impacts of climate change tend to exacerbate these inequalities. Those least responsible for global warming incur the highest social cost and further are often either left out of or negatively impacted by policies meant to stem the impacts of climate change. This "triple injustice" is directly correlated to various forms of inequality, which affect where one lives, one's access to social services necessary to cope, one's community's resilience to shocks and one's ability to influence policy (Cook et al. 2012; UNRISD 2016). Such inequalities are also to blame for the vastly unequal distribution of the impacts of the Covid-19 pandemic, both within countries—in terms of job security, access to health care, access to technology, ability to continue working/attending school remotely, safe and socially distanced housing, citizenship status and so on—and between countries, as weaker health systems, fraying social safety nets and lack of fiscal resources are making the challenge of tackling Covid in the global South even harder, and prospects for a quick recovery much bleaker, with the vaccine still far out of reach for most developing countries (Bottan et al. 2020; ILO 2020).

*Inequality compounded*

In addition to the economic (or "vertical") inequalities described earlier, inequality also manifests horizontally (Stewart 2013), as people's capabilities and life chances are deeply affected by their gender, age, skin color, religion, sexual orientation, gender identity, citizenship status and other characteristics. Vertical inequalities and horizontal inequalities reinforce each other, resulting in entrenched structures of stratification, segregation and discrimination which constrain people's aspirations, life choices and well-being.

In the case, for example, of women and girls, there remain persistent and protracted gaps in achieving women's rights and realizing tangible progress on the ground, especially regarding labor rights, equal pay and a fair distribution of unpaid care work (UN Women 2015; UNRISD 2016). Women tend to cluster in lower-paying jobs, notably in the informal sector (see chapters by Alfers and Rojas Scheffer in this volume) (and on the flip side of that, are often excluded from certain high-paying jobs, as described by Neely in this volume), and are more likely to work in part-time jobs or interrupt careers due to care responsibilities. Women are spending on average three times as many hours as men on unpaid care and domestic work, a care burden which is exacerbated by a lack of access to basic infrastructure and health and education services (Esquivel and Kaufmann 2017).

These inequalities also have a transnational dimension: the internationalization of care and domestic work through employment of female migrant workers (Kofman and Raghuram 2010). Care-related migration is one example of the gendered patterns of international migration, often performed by domestic workers, characterized by intersecting inequalities related to gender, class and race/ethnicity (see Rojas Scheffer in this volume).

Intersecting inequalities are also highly visible at the local level. Economic inequality determines where and in what conditions one lives (which has impacts for health and safety, mobility, access to green space, availability of local services, etc.), forming exclusions that are compounded by social inequalities, such as poor public education and health systems, imbalance in access to public resources between rural and urban areas, insufficient social protection systems and low-paid low-quality jobs. These spatial divisions can be mapped on to social inequalities such as race, ethnicities and gender, for example the way in which a combination of displacement, exclusion and segregation has relegated communities of color, including migrants, to areas of deprivation and closed off pathways to securing incomes and assets. Further, such divisions cement themselves over time, as possibilities for redistribution are undermined by the intergenerational transfer of capital (MacLeavy and Manley in this volume). The current crises also present new ways for understanding these overlaps, for example, the increased incidence of domestic violence in the case of women and LGBTQI+ persons confined to homes with violent family members (UN 2020; UN Women 2020), as well as the higher rate of infection and death among communities of color, which is largely linked to the forms of exclusion and their consequences for quality of life laid out earlier (Covid Tracking Project 2020; Oxfam 2021; Platt and Warwick 2020; Sze et al. 2020).

Further, these compounding inequalities tend to be transferred across generations, as the chapter by MacLeavy and Manley shows, whereas accumulated privilege—a combination of gender, race and income—allows rich elites and their offspring to occupy privileged spaces in urban environments and labor markets amplifying their influence and power. An example can be found in the case of one of the most profitable economic sectors, hedge funds, as described in the chapter by Neely.

*Fault lines: Fractures wrought by growing inequality*

While such inequalities as described previously are not new, they are growing more dramatic, girded by neoliberal policies and compounded by a number of factors: corporate capture of political processes and state institutions, lax global and national tax governance, rapid technological change and new digital divides, the financialization of the global economy and the erosion of labor rights, to name a few, resulting in new "expulsions"—of migrants from their countries, of farmers from their land, of urban-dwellers from public and private spaces, of workers from their rights and protections, of communities from access to resources (Sassen 2014; Standing 2019). And while austerity measures that have become a hallmark of cyclical adjustments in the age of neoliberalism (Ortiz et al. 2020) have been temporarily suspended in many places in response to the pandemic, fiscal stimulus has been highly unequal, as low-income countries lack fiscal space (ILO 2020).

As a result, society is fracturing in ways that are becoming more and more tangible, with the growing divide between the privileged and the rest dramatically rearranging both macro structures and local lifeworlds. In the context of these compounding global crises, those with means have made use of them to shield themselves from the worst effects of poverty, inequality, environmental degradation and disruption, violence and insecurity, often creating walled off private worlds (Caldeira 2001; Forrest et al. 2017). Those without have been left to get by with underfunded and under-functioning public services, administered by states growing less and less accountable to their citizens. These cleavages have eroded social cohesion, citizenship practices and trust in public institutions, leaving deep fault lines that manifest economically, politically, socially and spatially. As a consequence, governments are increasingly perceived to lack capacity to foster inclusive development and to protect the well-being and rights of their citizens and residents in a rapidly changing and increasingly uncertain world.

One of the most acutely felt outcomes of this perceived lack of capacity is the rise of political polarization and extremism, in some cases instigated by political leaders themselves, in most cases undermining trust in political leaders and democracy in general. One much cited manifestation of this trend is Trumpism, referred to in Roman-Alcalá's chapter in this volume as an example of "Othering," a process of engendering inequalities and marginality based on group identity (powell and Menendian 2016). Trumpism relied on the vilification of "other" groups and association with a common identity of nonelites to garner support for an agenda that "extended neoliberal assaults on the poor, the working class and the environment," favoring elite interests to the detriment of citizens (p. 193). The Trump administration is not the only example of the radicalization of political leaders and the entry of far-right political parties into power. Other examples come from countries such as Poland, Hungary, India and Brazil, which have seen conservative-religious or ethno-nationalist political forces winning elections and embarking on strategies of Othering, and the rise of right-wing parties in several European countries such as France, Germany, Italy, the Netherlands and the Scandinavian countries.[3] As institutions representing the public good and universal values are increasingly disempowered or co-opted, with meaningful spaces of civic engagement supplanted with divisive populist rhetoric, collective visions of social justice and equity are increasingly sidelined, with huge consequences for all people, regardless of which side of the political spectrum they fall.

## *The Reproduction of Inequality: Place, Power and Institutions*

In 2011, the Occupy Wall Street movement created a new narrative for how we talk about inequality, that of the 1 percent and the 99 percent (see also Dorling 2019; Weeks 2014; and Shiva in this volume). By pointing to the massive disparity represented in these numbers and juxtaposing these two groups as forces positioned against each other, it made a clear argument: the inequalities we are facing globally, regionally, nationally and locally are not a natural and unavoidable reality of our world order, but rather a result of choices made within entrenched power structures and global economic systems. This is where a select few, the 1 percent, have highly disproportionate control over and access to resources, and therefore over decisions. This situation is reinforced by the current economic order, which distributes gains toward capital owners to the detriment of labor and the environment (UNCTAD 2020; Jomo and Popov in this volume). As elites gain a prominent foothold in political processes, whether directly or indirectly, they often act to preserve and perpetuate a system that benefits the few at the expense of the many, halting the possibilities for equitable redistribution. Drawing on case studies from North America, Latin America, Africa and Europe, Part II of this volume reveals the various ways in which inequality is a compounding and self-reproducing process and explores the power imbalances, girded by economic dominance, that are at the heart of this cycle, from the very local to the transnational levels.

---

3. In Europe, the average vote share of populist parties has increased continuously since the 1980s, from 10.1 percent in 1980 to 11.3 percent in 2000 to 18.4 percent in 2017. Populist parties are currently represented in nine governments and hold 17.5 percent of all seats within European national parliaments (see UN 2017).

Inequalities often come to a head most visibly at the local level, spaces in which those at either end of the spectrum engage with each other on a daily basis, mediated through various forms of power relations and social, spatial and economic barriers. In Chapter 3, Julie MacLeavy and David Manley explore the intergenerational transmission of inequalities from a geographical perspective. The chapter offers insights into the production and reinforcement of spatial divides between and within population groups in Western postindustrial nations. It outlines how transfers of wealth, as well as broader social and cultural factors, enable more advantaged members of society to isolate themselves in the most privileged locations, while those from disadvantaged backgrounds—in particular populations with inherited disadvantage linked to intersectional inequalities based on gender, sexuality, race/ethnicity, age, disability and religion—are relegated to areas of deprivation. The authors emphasize the importance of applying the relational concept of inequality: "circumstances of those at the bottom end of the income distribution are produced as the result of the intense and increasing concentrations of wealth that do not trickle down, but instead yield further inequalities because the concentration 'floods upwards'" (p. 55). They explain that "striving for equality of opportunity is, in itself, insufficient because the ability to take advantage of the opportunities is not equally spread," creating obstacles to upward social mobility (p. 55). Developing an understanding of the intergenerational processes that refract stratification processes is seen as vital to understanding the continual rise in inequalities and its myriad effects in the current Covid-19 crisis.

MacLeavy and Manley reveal the ways in which those with privilege build borders around their worlds, to keep out the majority and maintain control over the processes of wealth production, divisions that restrict social mobility and limit access to small elite groups of people. In Chapter 4, Megan Tobias Neely explores this phenomenon on a micro scale with her investigation into hedge funds, an industry where those with access to economic and political power wield it in order to "hoard access to resources, protect their interests, and drive top incomes ever further upward" (p. 62) with ramifications that echo far beyond Wall Street. Neely explores the everyday practices that concentrate capital among Wall Street's working rich, revealing the ways in which the hedge fund industry operates through a patrimonial system relying on elite social ties and industry networks. In this gendered, racialized and class-based system, white men, using their access to resources, support and opportunities, act as gatekeepers of the industry, which concentrates wealth from one generation to the next and widens inequalities. Neely's analysis illustrates how the reproduction of inequality within the industry, leaving women and persons of color at disadvantage, has ramifications that extend well beyond it, given the amount of influence hedge funds wield in the global economy, creating instability, driving down wages, bankrupting companies and playing a key role in the shrinking of the middle class.

Looking at the other side of the coin, the new working precariat, Kate Meagher (Chapter 5) shows the way new regimes of labor, designed to adapt to and compensate for the staggering insecurity and vulnerability of the current globalized neoliberal era, are in fact reproducing inequality in new ways. Exploring the rise of digital employment platforms in Africa, a region plagued by high levels of informality, unemployment and rapid population growth, Meagher looks beyond the techno-solutionist hype to explore how the gig economy is reshaping livelihood opportunities and reformatting processes of social and economic inclusion among digital taxi ride-hailing workers in Nigeria. Amid calls for a new social contract in order to facilitate the creation of quality employment, the chapter asks whether these proposed changes actually address the problems of precarity and disaffection among Nigerian gig workers or if they consolidate a new regime of accumulation around the digital incorporation of precarious labor. The chapter examines the quality of the livelihoods created by the gig economy and the limitations of digital employment in promoting sustainable livelihoods and services of public value. The case of Nigerian digital workers informs a consideration of whether this particular vision of a new social contract represents a mechanism of economic inclusion or adverse incorporation for Nigeria's informal labor force, focusing attention on the requirements for a more inclusive social contract in the post-Covid era.

In the three chapters discussed earlier, an underlying thread is the role of institutions. Inequalities and unequal power relations are maintained and reinforced through formal and informal institutions ranging from electoral rules to education systems, family structure, labor practices, property rights, urban planning, access to finance and capital and social norms, among others. The chapter by Roberto Pires (Chapter 6) explores the role of government institutions in reproducing social inequalities during policy implementation. It identifies different mechanisms through which the day-to-day operations of government, and the encounters between public service workers and users, may engender risks of inequality reproduction. Implementation processes take place in the hidden recesses of routine or in the obscure actions and inactions of public agents. Beyond contributing to fulfillment of the formal objectives of social policies, the chapter argues that policy implementation processes also produce other non-intended effects on service users and recipients. These effects may contribute to the persistence of social inequalities by producing the accumulation of material and symbolic disadvantages for already vulnerable social groups. The chapter presents an analytical framework that helps to unpack inequality-increasing mechanisms related to institutional design and governance and to street-level interactions and practices, and it provides concrete examples from Latin American case studies. The author concludes that recognizing these mechanisms is an important step toward making social policies and services more effective in the pursuit of inclusion and equality.

Like Pires, Fritz Nganje (Chapter 7) reveals how interventions meant to stem inequalities are often either directly co-opted by elite actors or are by design vulnerable to their interests. In this chapter, Nganje draws on the example of partnerships between Brazilian and Mozambican cities to critique attempts to democratize urban governance and development through city-to-city cooperation. As an expression of the notion of technical cooperation among developing countries, city-to-city cooperation in the global South has the potential to catalyze inclusive urban governance and development by exposing local authorities and communities to useful experiences, best practices and innovative ideas. However, the author argues that the predominantly technocratic and depoliticized approach to city-to-city cooperation reflected in the exchanges between Brazilian cities and their Mozambican counterparts is incapable of inducing the kind of urban transformation inspired by Henri Lefebvre's notion of a "right to the city." When city partnerships are designed and implemented in a manner that fails to challenge unequal power relations and to empower poor urban residents, the urban elite tend to use their position as gatekeepers of the institutional landscape of cities to determine which foreign ideas are localized and how, undermining the transformative potential of city-to-city cooperation. In the worst cases, city-to-city cooperation can become a tool to reinforce the disenfranchisement of marginalized urban communities. The author concludes by making the case for re-politicizing city-to-city cooperation in the global South, in particular through incorporation of non-state actors and diverse stakeholders into exchanges and cooperation, in order to unlock its transformative capacity.

## Elite Motives, Perceptions and Preferences Driving Inequality

As explored in the chapters summarized previously, power relations are at the heart of inequality and its reproduction, and the driving force is the actors behind it: elites. Elites constitute a unique social group defined by their disproportionate control over resources—be they economic, political, cultural—and their ability to translate those resources into power, influence and other forms of capital (Khan 2012). They are often linked much more closely to each other across linguistic, cultural and geographic divides than to citizens of their own nations. Elites play an important role in determining the policy agendas that either reduce or increase inequality. Some business elites have gained a prominent foothold in political processes, often serving to preserve and perpetuate a system that benefits the few at the expense of the many (Cárdenas and Robles-Rivera 2020; Delamonica et al. 2020). Their influence extends from media to elections to policy making, from the local to the transnational level, standing in the way of more equitable redistribution (Cárdenas and Robles-Rivera 2020; Parmigiani 2022). Backed up by theories and narratives of market liberalism and meritocracy, they are proving less and less willing to accept anything more than voluntary standards (Atria et al. 2021; Utting 2007; Weeks 2014; see also MacLeavy and Manley, and Neely in this volume). Tax evasion and avoidance persists by wealthy individuals and global companies alike, with an estimated 10 percent of global wealth held in tax havens (Credit Suisse 2017).

Part III zeroes in on elites themselves, offering insights into their role in perpetuating or reducing inequality through different channels of influence and institutional arrangements, asking specifically how their motives, ideologies, perceptions and preferences drive processes of disenfranchisement and marginalization and what opportunities exist to gain their explicit or tacit support for egalitarian change. The chapters explore different roles of elites, from political to business actors, to external donors. Insights into elite perceptions about social policy and redistribution are compared across regions and between elites and popular sectors.

In Chapter 8, Tom Lavers asks under what circumstances political elites take action to address forms of inequality and what motivates their decision to do so. Contrary to structuralist approaches highlighted in some of the preceding chapters, he argues that ideas are a key factor in shaping the structures that produce inequality—from intra-elite power relations to institutions—and that ideational change can play an important role in tackling inequality, including by shaping patterns of accumulation, redistribution and recognition. The chapter proposes an adapted framework to political settlements theory (Khan 2010), which hitherto has emphasized explanations based on the material interests of elites, paying little attention to the causal role of ideas. Lavers illustrates his approach of bringing in an ideational dimension into the theory with a range of country examples representing different types of power balances among elite groups and between elite and nonelite factions. The author finds that a better understanding of the particular role ideas play in political settlements allows for the alignment of change strategies and policy proposals with the ideational commitments and perceived interests of key decision makers. Crises and moments of instability and uncertainty such as the Covid-19 pandemic are understood as windows of opportunity to shift paradigmatic ideas beyond the more pragmatic goal of ideational influencing.

If, by definition, elites concentrate power and resources, it follows that the design and implementation of redistributive policies depend largely on their preferences. Understanding such preferences, as well as the conditions and reasons for them, is thus key for understanding how inequality is reproduced or can be transformed. In Chapter 9, Graziella Moraes Silva, Matias López, Elisa Reis and Chana Teeger explore Brazilian and South African elite preferences about redistribution by presenting the results of a survey on perceptions of inequality. The research relies on random samples of economic, political and bureaucratic (top-tier civil servants) elites in Brazil and South Africa, unpacking the concept of elite and showing its heterogeneity, with interesting findings on elite characteristics such as educational background, parental education, gender and race. The chapter finds significant country and sector diversity in elite perceptions, in particular regarding their views on the relationship between economic growth, redistribution and inequality and their preferred solutions to address these issues. Elites are not automatically opposed to redistribution. According to the authors, "the implicit assumption that elites will always benefit from inequality ignores the fact that—unless due to exogenous shocks such as war or epidemics—redistribution necessarily follows some kind of elite action, engagement or tacit approval" (p. 152). The results show that in both Brazil and South Africa elites believe inequality to be a problem because of its externalities such as violence, political patronage or loss of human capital. However, these perceptions and policy preferences vary across sectors of elites, in particular between business elites on the one hand and political and bureaucratic elites on the other, which raises questions about intra-elite bargains and their outcomes.

In Chapter 10, Jeremy Seekings takes this discussion further by analyzing elite perceptions of poverty and inequality in Africa and how these perceptions shape their attitudes toward social protection. The chapter posits that ideology matters, in conjunction with other factors including material and institutional interests, and political and fiscal opportunities and constraints. Seekings argues that the persistence of poverty and inequality in the continent is in large part due to the ambivalence or hostility of political elites to the kinds of redistributive policies associated with the welfare state across much of northwest Europe. This attitude, he suggests, is rooted in the conservative ideology that predominates among African political elites. Whatever their views on democracy and the role of the state in economic development, most members of the political elite distinguish between "deserving" and "undeserving" poor people, are averse to "dependency" on "handouts" and worry about the effects of government interventions (including social cash transfers) on productivity and morality. On the other hand, Seekings finds that this does not entirely preclude reforms that benefit poor people. Across much of the region some members of the political elites recognize that the state should take over the responsibility for the poor (or, at least, the deserving poor) previously shouldered by kin or community. The chapter also analyzes popular attitudes toward poverty, inequality and social protection, finding general support for existing social protection programs, but also a clear perceived hierarchy of desert for receiving support. The author concludes that it is not clear that the norms and values of elites across most of Africa are out of line with popular norms and values, which implies that conservative social protection policies such as conditional cash transfers or workfare aligning both with social norms and elite ideology are more likely to be politically successful, though unlikely to be successful in addressing the root causes of inequality and poverty.

## At the Front Lines: Propelling Progressive Change

The chapters described paint a mixed if not troubling picture of a system in which those with power and resources wield them to block pathways for progressive change, for example in terms of progressive taxation and rights-based social policies. In the past, progressive policy change in industrialized democracies was often steered by broad cross-class coalitions between popular and middle classes that effectively pressured elites; in countries of the global South, enlightened leaders and liberation movements often played a similar role, providing broad access to health, education and political participation as part of nation building. Since the 1980s, however, we have witnessed the slow but continuous unraveling of these twentieth-century social contracts (UNRISD 2021). The neoliberal turn, globalization, structural adjustment, austerity, authoritarian politics and multiple crises go a long way to explaining why social contracts have broken down, exposing increasing inequalities and fault lines between capital and labor, ruling elites and citizens, rich and poor. The social and economic forces that underpinned the progressive policy change of the past take a very different shape today, as economic systems have evolved, identities have shifted, new forms of politics have unfolded and new conceptions of class have arisen (Crouch 2004; Esping-Andersen 1990; Lentz 2015; Standing 2011).

And while such spaces for progressive change have been closed, new ones are constrained by a range of factors: as laid out earlier, governments with a developmental and redistributive stance are increasingly stripped of resources and policy space in the context of neoliberal globalization and recurrent crises; middle classes are either moving toward precarity or increasingly aligned with elite interests, opting out of processes for the public good, motivated by various incentives including political stability, security and access to better life opportunities (Crouch 2004; Lentz 2015; Nicolas 2020); identity groups among popular and middle classes consistently fail to mobilize around deeply shared interests, and are instead pitted against each other by nationalist and xenophobic discourses; the voice of the demos has begun to weigh less and less as the overwhelming economic dominance of elite sectors takes hold of political processes (Bartels 2008; Cárdenas and Robles-Rivera 2020; Gilens 2012).

In response, new forms of social movements, alliances and coalitions are emerging to counteract these tendencies. Marginalized groups of workers are cooperating and collaborating in new ways, applying multiple strategies to stabilize their livelihoods in a rapidly changing environment. Communities, social relationships and institutions are shifting in response to growing inequalities and the lack of tools to combat them, adapting and innovating (Köhler 2020). In Part IV of the book, we present a few examples that may give us some reasons to be guardedly optimistic about the possibilities for positive change.

In Chapter 11, Antonio Roman-Alcalá draws lessons from historical examples of cross-sector alliances in the United States. He seeks to understand through historical research and conceptualization how movements composed of marginalized groups have sought to counter "Othering"—the undermining of their humanity in order to maintain group-based social stratification. In focusing on acts of solidarity as key features of movement success, the chapter outlines three major strategies used by movements: assimilation, valorization and differencing. Through historical vignettes from twentieth-century California involving Black agrarians, Indigenous people and migrant farmworkers, the chapter unpacks how assimilation, valorization and differencing have intersected with Othering and solidarity, and from this identifies lessons that might help researchers and activists better grasp the dynamics of change over time. It finds that assimilation and valorization are helpful but insufficient to ensure change, as they do not enlarge the circle of "we," which is necessary to mount successful challenges to elite power. Differencing, in contrast, is the pivotal strategy to counter "Othering" among various Others and overcome lines of difference between them. His analysis is keenly attentive to the way in which this "Othering" continues to shape US politics nationally. With this chapter, Roman-Alcalá aims to put forward research that is actionable and that can be a useful source of knowledge for future movements to draw on. This chapter therefore sits at the intersections of research and action.

Raquel Rojas Scheffer (Chapter 12) focuses on the collective action of paid domestic workers in Paraguay and Uruguay to access basic social rights such as minimum wages, maximum working hours and social security. Domestic work, a highly feminized occupation with high shares of migrant labor, is characterized by the intersections of various axes of inequality related to gender, citizenship, race and ethnicity, and type of employment, constituting an occupational group which "has been historically discriminated against, both in law and in practice" (p. 209). Confined to a private workplace, collective organization has been a challenge. Nonetheless, domestic worker organizations in Uruguay and Paraguay have built networks with different types of actors within and across national borders, for example trade unions and the national association of housewives in the case of Uruguay, and women's groups and international organizations such as the International Labour Organization (ILO) and UN Women in the case of Paraguay. These two cases provide examples of how different actors who "share an interest in subverting power hierarchies, be they based on regimes of gender, class, ethnicity and/or citizenship," can come together to form networks of activism (p. 221). The chapter explores various contexts that may promote or inhibit this, which strategies are most effective and the complexity of building alliances between ideologically and structurally distinct groups.

In Chapter 13, Laura Alfers explores how organizations of informal workers—as a specific type of social movement—are attempting to influence the provision of health services from below. The study offers a new perspective for two important reasons: first, social policy scholarship tends to be dominated by institutionalist approaches which favor top-down explanations of policy development; and second, while there has been a growing academic focus on organizing in the informal economy and the interactions between the state and informal workers, very little of this has had an explicit focus on social policy. The chapter, which includes two case studies—a health cooperative in India and an organization of home-based workers in Thailand—focuses at the level where national or local social policies and practices of the state meet the ground and where these are contested, engaged with and transformed by informal workers. It looks particularly at how informal workers' organizations have become involved in the provision of social services—something that is often termed "co-production." Debates on the co-production of services within social policy have centered around the dilemma of task-shifting onto poorer women or overburdening them with unpaid care work and low-paid work. The chapter examines the tension between this concern and a less-considered aspect of co-production: the way it is being used by organizations as a political strategy to shift relations of power between the state, owners of capital and poorer informal women worker-citizens to influence the shape and nature of policy, and ultimately to reimagine a social compact for the twenty-first century.

The volume concludes with an epilogue by one of today's most salient critical voices, Vandana Shiva, who makes an impassioned call to decolonize knowledge, disperse power and build inclusive democracies, and suggests tools with which to do so. Shiva analyzes the multiple crises and destructive forces brought about by the 1 percent economy, juxtaposing it with a "one earth" and "one human community" model. Her condemnation of the mega-rich and their pursuit of profit, both poignant and powerful, explores how the system they have put in place and fought to preserve has undemocratically enforced uniformity and monocultures, division and separation, monopolies and external control—over finance, food, energy, information, health care and even relationships. Shiva, along with the other authors featured in Part IV of this volume, suggests tools with which to counter elite influence and interests and reduce inequality. Many lessons can be drawn from these examples of peaceful processes of policy change that have made societies greener and more socially just, leveled out social stratification, and devolved power and resources from elites to nonelites, or toward marginalized or discriminated groups. As a way forward, she highlights the need to revalorize and center traditional forms of knowledge, echoing Roman-Alcalá, another scholar-activist voice in this volume, in order to bring our global systems into harmony with the planet.

By way of conclusion, we acknowledge that this volume might raise more questions than it answers on the relationship between inequalities and power and the interplay between the diverse mechanisms of markets, institutions, policies, norms and ideas that drive and reproduce inequality. The volume aims to contribute new empirical analysis that helps us to understand, on the one hand, the various fractures wrought by inequalities in different contexts, the political drivers of inequality, and the role of powerful elites in producing and maintaining these inequalities, and, on the other hand, the agency of marginalized actors, their collective action and cross-class alliances, which can lead to incremental transformative changes that level out some inequalities. It illustrates the diversity of experiences and sheds light on both how elites think and strategize, and how those at the bottom of the pyramid act creatively to defend their rights. To truly achieve social justice requires an approach that attacks inequality at the structural level, addresses root causes and rearranges power structures.

Indeed, there is no shortage of knowledge on economic models and policies that can successfully reduce inequalities and promote inclusive and sustainable development (UNRISD 2016, 2010). They range from universal social policies and fundamental rights at work, progressive taxation, business and market regulation, gender equality policies, antidiscrimination legislation, human rights and equal opportunities policies, as well as affirmative action for disadvantaged groups (Hujo and Carter 2019). The question is how these policies get onto political agendas and under what conditions and how they are implemented. The volume shows that egalitarian policy change requires collective action, instigated by progressive political leaders and parties, supported by international commitments and rights frameworks, and driven by civil society alliances and social movements. The recent Covid-19 pandemic with its devastating and highly unequal effects has strengthened calls for transformative change and greater social justice. It has certainly led to some reshuffling of power structures, triggered unprecedented fiscal policy responses and raised the voice of the demos, while it also led to further income and wealth concentration at the top. If crises present an opportunity to change entrenched norms, policies and institutions reproducing inequality and exclusion, perhaps the time has come to finally move from the reign of the 1 percent to the one human community.

## References

Atria, Jorge, Julius Durán and Simón Ramírez. 2021. "Consent to Pay Taxes and Expectations of the State: Perceptions of the Chilean Economic Elite." *Occasional Paper: Overcoming Inequality in a Fractured World No. 14*. Geneva: United Nations Research Institute for Social Development.

Bartels, Larry M. 2008. *Unequal Democracy: The Political Economy of the New Gilded Age*. New York: Russell Sage Foundation and Princeton University Press.

Bottan, Nicolás L., Diego A. Vera-Cossio and Bridget Hoffmann. 2020. "The Unequal Impact of the Coronavirus Pandemic: Evidence from Seventeen Developing Countries." *IDB Discussion Paper No. 785*. Washington, DC: The Inter-American Development Bank.

Caldeira, Teresa. 2001. *City of Walls: Crime, Segregation and Citizenship in São Paulo*. Berkeley: University of California Press.

Cárdenas, Julián and Francisco Robles-Rivera. 2020. "Business Elites in Panama: Sources of Power and State Capture." *Occasional Paper: Overcoming Inequality in a Fractured World No. 12*. Geneva: United Nations Research Institute for Social Development.

Chancel, Lucas. 2017. *Insoutenables Inégalités: Pour une Justice Sociale et Environnementale*. Paris: Les Petits Matins.

Commission on Social Justice. 1993. *The Justice Gap*. London: Institute for Public Policy Research.

Cook, Sarah, Kiah Smith and Peter Utting. 2012. "Green Economy or Green Society? Contestation and Policies for a Fair Transition." *Occasional Paper: Social Dimensions of Green Economy and Sustainable Development No. 10*. Geneva: United Nations Research Institute for Social Development.

Covid Tracking Project. 2020. *The COVID Racial Data Tracker*. Washington, DC: The Atlantic Monthly Group.

Credit Suisse. 2017. *Global Wealth Report and Global Wealth Databook*. Zurich: Credit Suisse AG, Research Institute.

Crouch, Colin. 2004. *Post-Democracy*. Cambridge: Polity Press.

Delamonica, Enrique, Jamee K. Moudud and Esteban Pérez Caldentey. 2020. "Power and Politics: Taxation, Social, and Labour Market Policies in Argentina and Chile, 1990–2010." In *The Politics of Domestic Resource Mobilization for Social Development*, edited by Katja Hujo, 207–236. Basingstoke: Palgrave Macmillan and the United Nations Research Institute for Social Development.

Dorling, Daniel. 2019. *Inequality and the 1%* (3rd edition). London: Verso.

Esping-Andersen, Gøsta. 1990. *The Three Worlds of Welfare Capitalism*. Cambridge: Polity Press.

Esquivel, Valeria and Andrea Kaufmann. 2017. *Innovations in Care: New Concepts, New Actors, New Policies*. Bonn: Friedrich-Ebert-Stiftung, Global Policy and Development.

Forrest, Ray, Sin Yee Koh and Bart Wissink (eds.). 2017. *Cities and the Super-Rich: Real Estate, Elite Practices and Urban Political Economies*. New York: Palgrave Macmillan.

Freistein, Katja and Bettina Mahlert. 2016. "The Potential for Tackling Inequality in the Sustainable Development Goals." *Third World Quarterly*, 37(12):2139–2155.

Gilens, Martin. 2012. *Affluence and Influence: Economic Inequality and Political Power in America*. New York: Russell Sage Foundation and Princeton University Press.

Hujo, Katja. 2021. "Social Protection and Inequality in the Global South: Politics, Actors and Institutions. Editorial Introduction to Themed Section on Social Protection and Inequality in the Global South: Politics, Actors and Institutions." *Critical Social Policy*, 41(3):343–363.

Hujo, Katja and Maggie Carter. 2018. *Call for Papers and Conference: Overcoming Inequalities in a Fractured World: Between Elite Power and Social Mobilization*. Geneva: United Nations Research Institute for Social Development.

Hujo, Katja and Maggie Carter. 2019. "Overcoming Inequalities in the Context of the 2030 Agenda for Sustainable Development." *Issue Brief No. 10*. Geneva: United Nations Research Institute for Social Development.

ILO (International Labour Organization). 2016. *Wage Inequality in the Workplace: Global Wage Report 2016/17*. Geneva: ILO.

ILO (International Labour Organization). 2017. *World Social Protection Report 2017–19: Universal Social Protection to Achieve the Sustainable Development Goals*. Geneva: ILO.

ILO (International Labour Organization). 2020. *ILO Monitor: COVID-19 and the World of Work—Sixth Edition. Updated Estimates and Analysis*. 23 September. Geneva: ILO.

Kabeer, Naila. 2020. "Women's Empowerment and Economic Development: A Feminist Critique of Storytelling Practices in 'Randomista' Economics." *Feminist Economics*, 26(2):1–26.

Khan, Mushtaq. 2010. *Political Settlements and the Governance of Growth-Enhancing Institutions*. Unpublished working paper. London: School of Oriental and African Studies (SOAS).

Khan, Shamus. 2012. "The Sociology of Elites." *Annual Review of Sociology*, 38:361–377.

Kharas, Homi. 2020. "The Impact of COVID-19 on Global Extreme Poverty." *Future Development Blog*. 21 October. Brookings Institution. https://www.brookings.edu/blog/future-development/2020/10/21/the-impact-of-covid-19-on-global-extreme-poverty/.

Kofman, Eleonore and Parvati Raghuram. 2010. "The Implications of Migration for Gender and Care Regimes in the South." In *South-South Migration: Implications for Social Policy and Development*, edited by Katja Hujo and Nicola Piper, 46–83. Basingstoke: Palgrave Macmillan and the United Nations Research Institute for Social Development.

Köhler, Gabriele. 2015. "Seven Decades of 'Development,' And Now What?" *Journal of International Development*, 27: 733–751.

Köhler, Gabriele. 2020. "Creative Coalitions in a Fractured World: An Opportunity for Transformative Change?" *Occasional Paper: Overcoming Inequality in a Fractured World No. 4*. Geneva: United Nations Research Institute for Social Development.

Lakner, Christoph, Daniel Gerszon Mahler, Mario Negre and Espen Beer Prydz. 2019. "How Much Does Reducing Inequality Matter for Global Poverty?" *Policy Research Working Paper No. 8869*. Washington, DC: World Bank.

Le Grand, Julian. 1990. "Equity versus Efficiency: The Elusive Trade-Off." *Ethics*, 100(3): 554–568.

Lentz, Carola. 2015. "Elites or Middle Classes? Lessons from Transnational Research for the Study of Social Stratification in Africa." *Working Paper No. 161*. Mainz: Johannes Gutenberg University Mainz.

Nicolas, Alrich. 2020. "Le Processus d'Appauvrissement des Classes Moyennes en Haïti et ses Conséquences Economiques et Sociales." *Occasional Paper: Overcoming Inequality in a Fractured World No. 6*. Geneva: United Nations Research Institute for Social Development.

Ocampo, José Antonio. 2014. "The Latin American Debt Crisis in Historical Perspective." In *Life after Debt: The Origins and Resolutions of Debt Crisis*, edited by Joseph Stiglitz and Daniel Heymann, 87–115. Basingstoke: Palgrave Macmillan.

Okun, Arthur Melvin. 1975. *Equality and Efficiency: The Big Tradeoff*. Washington, DC: Brookings Institution Press.

Ortiz, Isabel, Matthew Cummins, Jeronim Capaldo and Kalaivani Karunanethy. 2020. "The Decade of Adjustment: A Review of Austerity Trends 2010–2020 in 187 Countries." *ILO Extension of Social Security Series No. 53*. Geneva: International Labour Organization.

Ostry Jonathan D., Andrew Berg and Siddharth Kothari. 2018. "Growth-Equity Trade-offs in Structural Reforms." *IMF Working Paper 18/05*. Washington, DC: International Monetary Fund.

Oxfam. 2020. "Time to Care: Unpaid and Underpaid Care Work and the Global Inequality Crisis." *Oxfam Briefing Paper*. Oxford: Oxfam International.

Oxfam. 2021. "The Inequality Virus: Bringing Together a World Torn Apart by Coronavirus through a Fair, Just and Sustainable Economy." *Oxfam Briefing Paper*. Oxford: Oxfam International.

Parmigiani, Alberto. 2022. "The Political Power of Economic Elites in Contemporary Western Democracies." *Occasional Paper: Overcoming Inequality in a Fractured World No. 13*. Geneva: United Nations Research Institute for Social Development.

Persson, Torsten and Guido Tabellini. 1994. "Is Inequality Harmful for Growth? Theory and Evidence." *The American Economic Review*, 84(3): 600–621.

Piketty, Thomas. 2014. *Capital in the Twenty-First Century*. Cambridge, MA: Harvard University Press.

Piketty, Thomas. 2019. *Capital et Idéologie*. Paris: Editions du Seuil.

Platt, Lucinda and Ross Warwick. 2020. *Are Some Ethnic Groups More Vulnerable to COVID-19 than Others?* London: Institute for Fiscal Studies.

powell, john a. and Stephen Menendian. 2016. "The Problem of Othering." *Othering and Belonging: Expanding the Circle of Human Concern*, 1: 14–40.

Sassen, Saskia. 2014. *Expulsions: Brutality and Complexity in the Global Economy*. Cambridge, MA: The Belknap Press of Harvard University Press.

Standing, Guy. 2011. *The Precariat: The New Dangerous Class*. London and New York: Bloomsbury Academic.

Standing, Guy. 2019. *Plunder of the Commons: A Manifesto for Sharing Public Wealth*. London: Pelican Books.

Stewart, Frances. 2013. "Approaches towards Inequality and Inequity: Concepts, Measures and Policies." *Discussion Paper: Perspectives on Equity*. Florence: UNICEF Office of Research.

Stiglitz, Joseph. 2002. *Globalization and Its Discontents*. London: Penguin Books.

Stiglitz, Joseph. 2012. *The Price of Inequality: The Avoidable Causes and Invisible Costs of Inequality*. New York: Norton.

Sze, Shirley, Daniel Pan, Clareece R. Nevill, Laura J. Gray, Christopher A. Martin, Joshua Nazareth, Jatinder S. Minhas, Pip Divall, Kamlesh Khunti, Keith R. Abrams, Laura B. Nellums and Manish Pareek. 2020. "Ethnicity and Clinical Outcomes in COVID-19: A Systematic Review and Meta-Analysis." *EClinicalMedicine*, 29: 100630.

Therborn, Göran. 2013. *The Killing Fields of Inequality*. Cambridge: Polity Press.

UBS. 2020. "Riding the Storm: Market Turbulence Accelerates Diverging Fortunes." Zurich: UBS and PwC Switzerland. https://www.ubs.com/content/dam/static/noindex/wealth-management/ubs-billionaires-report-2020-spread.pdf.

UN (United Nations). 1946. *Statute of the International Court of Justice*. San Francisco: UN.

UN (United Nations). 1948. "Universal Declaration of Human Rights." *Resolution 217 A*. New York: UN.

UN (United Nations). 2015. *Transforming Our World: The 2030 Agenda for Sustainable Development*. New York: UN.

UN (United Nations). 2017. "Report of the Special Rapporteur on Contemporary Forms of Racism, Racial Discrimination, Xenophobia and Related Intolerance." *A72/287*. New York: UN.

UN (United Nations). 2020a. *The Sustainable Development Goals Report 2020*. New York: UN.

UN (United Nations). 2020b. "Violence and Discrimination Based on Sexual Orientation and Gender Identity during the Coronavirus Disease (COVID-19) Pandemic." *Report of the Independent Expert on Protection against Violence and Discrimination Based on Sexual Orientation and Gender Identity, Victor Madrigal-Borloz. A/75/258*. New York: UN.

UN DESA (United Nations Department of Economic and Social Affairs). 2006. "Social Justice in an Open World: The Role of the United Nations." *The International Forum for Social Development*. New York: UN DESA.

UN Women. 2015. *Progress of the World's Women 2015–2016: Transforming Economies, Realizing Rights*. New York: UN Women.

UN Women. 2020. *Covid-19 and the Care Economy: Immediate Action and Structural Transformation for a Gender-Responsive Recovery*. New York: UN Women.

UNCTAD (United Nations Conference on Trade and Development). 2020. *Trade and Development Report—From Global Pandemic to Prosperity for All: Avoiding Another Lost Decade*. Geneva: UNCTAD.

UNDP (United Nations Development Programme). 2019. "Beyond Income, Beyond Averages, Beyond Today: Inequalities in Human Development in the 21st Century." *Human Development Report 2019*. New York: UNDP.

UNDP (United Nations Development Programme) and OPHI (Oxford Poverty and Human Development Initiative). 2020. *Global Multidimensional Poverty Index 2020—Charting Pathways Out of Multidimensional Poverty: Achieving the SDGs*. New York and Oxford: UNDP and OPHI.

UNRISD (United Nations Research Institute for Social Development). 1995. *States of Disarray. The Social Effects of Globalization*. Geneva: UNRISD.

UNRISD (United Nations Research Institute for Social Development). 2010. *Combating Poverty and Inequality: Structural Change, Social Policy and Politics*. Geneva: UNRISD.

UNRISD (United Nations Research Institute for Social Development). 2016. *Policy Innovations for Transformative Change. Implementing the 2030 Agenda for Sustainable Development*. Geneva: UNRISD.

UNRISD (United Nations Research Institute for Social Development). 2021. "A New Eco-Social Contract—Vital to Deliver the 2030 Agenda for Sustainable Development." *Issue Brief*. Geneva: UNRISD.

Utting, Peter. 2007. "CSR and Equality." *Third World Quarterly*, 28(4): 697–712.

Weeks, John. 2014. *Economics of the 1%: How Mainstream Economics Serves the Rich, Obscures Reality and Distorts Policy*. London: Anthem Press.

WEF (World Economic Forum). 2014. *Outlook on the Global Agenda 2015*. Geneva: WEF.

WHO (World Health Organization) and World Bank. 2017. *Tracking Universal Health Coverage: 2017 Global Monitoring Report*. Geneva: WHO.

Wilkinson, Richard and Kate Pickett. 2009. *The Spirit Level: Why Greater Equality Makes Societies Stronger*. New York: Bloomsbury Press.

World Bank. 1993. *The East Asian Miracle: Economic Growth and Public Policy*. Washington, DC: World Bank.

World Bank. 2020. "COVID-19 to Add as Many as 150 Million Extreme Poor by 2021." *Press Release*, 7 October. Washington, DC: World Bank.

World Inequality Lab. 2018. *World Inequality Report*. Paris: World Inequality Lab.

# Chapter 2

## GLOBAL ECONOMIC INEQUALITIES

### TRENDS AND DRIVERS[1]

Jomo Kwame Sundaram and Vladimir Popov

### Introduction

Most contemporary discussions of economic inequality focus on household or personal income differences at the national level. There have been few efforts to look at household income inequality at the world level. One major issue is whether to compare incomes using exchange rates or purchasing power parity (PPP). Despite very high levels of income inequality in some countries, world inequality is even higher.

We try to use different sources to ascertain trends in economic inequality at the global and national levels as well as economic disparities among countries. We also look at labor and capital income shares to understand trends in income and wealth distribution in addition to revisiting the relationship between economic inequality, investment and growth.

The chapter begins with a brief outline of the history of inequality in the world, showing how inequality among countries has grown over the centuries and that some degree of convergence occurred relatively recently. This apparent inter-country convergence is then analyzed in the subsequent sections, bringing to light some intra-country trends. We then consider how concerns about growth and poverty affect discussions of inequality. Finally, we look at some political questions surrounding the debate on inequality.

1. This chapter is revised from the working paper "Accelerating Growth and Reducing Inequality: Trends and Policy Approaches" prepared by the authors in 2018 for the Working Paper Series on Growth and Reducing Inequality, a joint effort of the G-24 and Friedrich-Ebert-Stiftung New York. We are grateful to Nazran Zhafri Ahmad Johari for his assistance in finalizing this chapter.

## Inequalities in Historical Perspective

Long-term trends suggest that income and wealth inequality increased from the 1500s, and more sharply from the early nineteenth century, before reaching an all-time peak in the early twentieth century (Table 2.1). In the West, they started to decline after the First World War and the 1917 Russian Revolution. But for the world as a whole, changes after the Second World War (WW2) have been far more significant.

Angus Maddison has estimated incomes in different parts of the world for the last two millennia. He suggests that for the first one and half millennia, average incomes were roughly similar in the world. Differences began about five centuries ago, from the time of the Iberian voyages of exploration and conquest. The Maddison Project (2013) estimated the ratio of average per capita income in Western Europe to other countries at approximately 1:1 around 1500. The income and wealth gaps between the rich or "advanced" countries of the global North and the developing countries of the global South have been growing for half a millennium, from around 1500, and began accelerating about two centuries ago.

However, the gap between the contemporary global North and South, or between developed (Western Europe, its mainly Anglophone settler colonies in North America and Australasia, and Japan) and developing countries, widened more rapidly from around two centuries ago, as the Industrial Revolution and imperialism increased differences in productivity, output and incomes.

During Hobsbawm's "short twentieth century" from the 1920s to the 1980s, increasing income and wealth inequalities were temporarily interrupted (Hobsbawm 1995 [1994]). Greater egalitarianism in the West began with the emergence of socialist countries with lower levels of inequality (with Gini coefficients between 25 percent and 30 percent on average), spreading checks to inequalities in capitalist industrial economies due to the spread of and mobilization by socialist and even populist—including fascist—movements, as well as the impact of the 1929 financial crash and the subsequent Great Depression (Figure 2.1). The evidence from the Great Depression of the 1930s and in the post–WW2 period has been quite mixed, with some evidence suggesting that inter-country gaps have started to close.

**Table 2.1** Historical Gini coefficients in some Western locations (%)

| Years | 14 | 1000 | 1290 | 1550 | 1700 | 1750 | 1800 | 2000 |
|---|---|---|---|---|---|---|---|---|
| Rome | 39 | | | | | | | |
| Byzantium | | 41 | | | | | | |
| Holland | | | | 56 | | 63 | 57 | 30.9 |
| England | | | 36.7 | | 55.6 | 52.2 | 59.3 | 37.4 |
| Old Castile/Spain | | | | | | 52.5 | | 34.7 |
| Naples/Italy | | | | | | | 28.1 | 35.9 |
| France | | | | | | | 55 | 33 |

*Source:* Authors' elaboration based on Milanovic et al. (2007); some data for 2000 from World Development Indicators database (WDI, n.d.).

*Note:* A perfectly equal group scores 0, while an absolutely unequal one scores 1, or 100 percent.

The European colonization of sub-Saharan Africa (SSA), Latin America and, to a lesser extent, South and Southeast Asia led to the transformation and exploitation of their economies through their subordination to Western domination. By 1900, the ratio of average per capita incomes in the West (Western Europe and the British dominions, former settler colonies in North America and Australasia) compared with the global South (developing countries) stood at 6 to 1 and remained thereabouts at the end of the twentieth century. If China is excluded, the ratio of average per capita incomes in rich countries to poor countries has increased since the end of WW2 but not as rapidly as before WW2 (Popov and Jomo 2017; Wade 2004).

At the global level, "catching up" among countries since the late 1980s, especially the rapid growth of large, populous economies such as China and India, has led to some income convergence between developed and developing nations, or the global North and South respectively, lowering overall global inequality (Milanovic 2016). This U-turn to the great North–South divergence since the Industrial Revolution two centuries ago has been slowed during the post–WW2 Keynesian and postcolonial "Golden Age," and by growth accelerations, mainly in some populous Asian economies, since the late twentieth century (see Figure 2.1).

National-level inequalities have increased and remain high in SSA, Latin America and the former Soviet Union (FSU), where institutional continuity was interrupted and institutional capacity weakened. Regressions—relating Gini coefficients of income distribution to per capita GDP (gross domestic product), population density, urbanization and colonial status—suggest that colonialism greatly increased inequality: colonies had Gini coefficients nearly 13 percentage points higher than non-colonies (Williamson 2009). In Latin America, inequality increased from an estimated 22.5 percent in 1491 to over 60 percent in 1929.

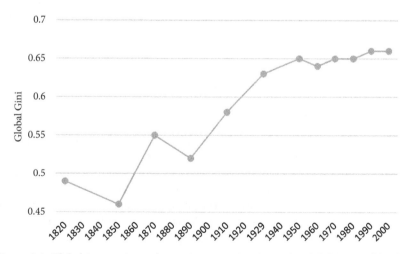

**Figure 2.1** Global income inequality, 1820–2000. *Source*: Authors' elaboration based on Moatsos et al. (2014). Note: The global Gini coefficient is measured by global interpersonal inequality rather than at the inter-country level.

These broad global trends obscure considerable variations across regions and countries, especially in the South. Since the 1980s about half the countries in the world have recorded increases in national inequality, with Gini coefficients rising over two percentage points (IMF 2017). This has been the case for most advanced economies of the North where increasing income inequality was largely driven by the accelerated growth of the incomes of their top 1 percent, related in turn to growing wealth and power concentration. Piketty (2014) noted that while national income inequalities were largely checked in the North before and after WW2, the decades since the 1980s have seen its resurgence. Since 1980, the income share of the top 1 percent has grown most in Australia, Canada, the United Kingdom and the United States, with wealth concentration rising even faster.

The collapse of world output by 3.4 percent in 2009, following the severe international financial crisis of 2008, was the largest decline in the last seven decades—much greater than the 1.4 percent fall in 1982, the 0.4 percent decline in 1974 and the 0.8 percent reduction in 1975 (Popov and Jomo 2015). However, the 2008–2009 global financial crisis does not seem to have been a turning point for inequality trends comparable to the Great Depression of the 1930s (Eichengreen and O'Rourke 2009) and certainly not unique in terms of recent financial and stock market collapses (Popov and Jomo 2015).

Wealth distribution is even more unequal, with the greatest concentration at the top, accelerating in recent years as suggested by the latest annual series of Oxfam reports to the World Economic Forum. Total global wealth reached USD 255 trillion in 2016, with more than half belonging to the richest 1 percent of the world's population. In 2018, 26 people owned the same amount of wealth as the 3.8 billion people who make up the poorer half of humanity, down from 43 people in 2017 (Oxfam 2019). A third of the world billionaires' wealth was inherited, while another 43 percent can be attributed to cronyism, involving mainly political connections. The super-rich and big corporations have accelerated wealth concentration by evading taxes, minimizing costs and influencing relevant policies and regulations (Hardoon 2017).

### Global inequality and national inequalities

Aggregate measures of differences in incomes of individuals or households in the world can be analyzed to differentiate between inequality *among* and *within* countries. Thus, overall global inequalities can be decomposed to distinguish between "within country" and "among countries" components as inequality within a country is part of but cannot be equated with global inequality. However, aggregate measures of overall inequality obscure various, often contradictory, trends. This section intends to distinguish "internal" national inequalities from the effects of divergence among countries, the latter not considering such inequalities. Milanovic (2005) and Sutcliffe (2004) consider both national inequalities and inter-country disparities together.

Growing inequalities within countries and decreasing disparities between North and South have shaped global inequalities since the 1970s (Figure 2.2). Global inequalities among individuals or households were probably growing in the 1980s

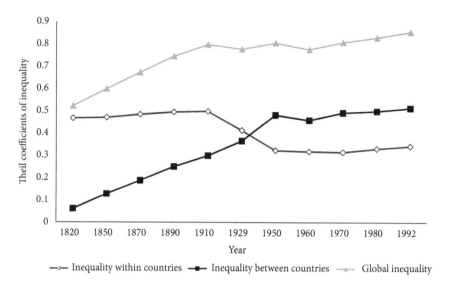

**Figure 2.2** Theil global coefficients of income inequality, 1820–1992. *Source*: Authors' elaboration based on Bourguignon and Morrisson (2002).

and 1990s as declining disparities among countries exacerbated rising in-country inequalities until around the turn of the century. Overall world inequality—among the people of the world—is higher than inequality found even within the most unequal countries. In other words, the level of overall global income inequality is greater than national-level income inequalities. Milanovic (2005) has shown that about two-thirds of overall world inequality is due to inter-country disparities, namely political geography rather than intra-country inequality, implying that location is more significant than class.

With the growth slowdown since the 2008–2009 global financial crisis that mostly affected developed countries, the North–South gap continued to close as many developing countries, including in SSA, continued to grow faster than developed countries. This was largely thanks to increased mineral and other primary commodity prices, due to continuing demand growth from other industrializing countries in the South. However, over the last four decades of the twentieth century, the already huge differences in output between the 20 richest and 20 poorest countries actually increased (ILO 2004).

*Inter-country disparities*

The world economy has grown very significantly over the last half century, but income data shows how uneven this growth has been. Despite growth accelerations in some developing countries from the late twentieth century, world income inequality continued to increase during much of this period, as Milanovic (2009) has shown.

Figures 2.3 and 2.4 show these trends among countries by income as well as by region. Only a handful of developing countries grew fast enough to join the

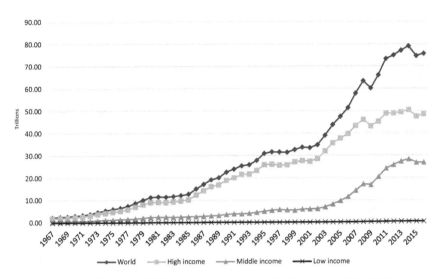

**Figure 2.3** GDP (current USD) by country income level group, 1967–2015. *Source*: Authors' elaboration based on data from WDI (n.d.).

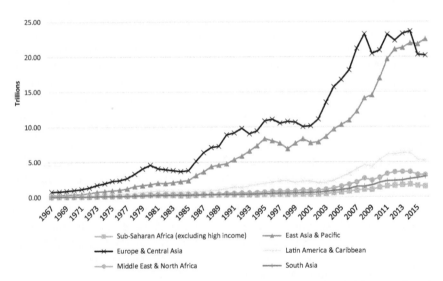

**Figure 2.4** GDP (current USD) by region, 1967–2015. *Source*: Authors' elaboration based on data from WDI (n.d.).

ranks of the high-income countries. From around the turn of the century, middle-income countries have grown faster, on average, than rich countries, reducing overall world income inequality, especially inter-country disparities. Growth in East Asia, India, Latin America and even mineral-rich countries in SSA account for these trends, but overall growth rates have declined since 2014. If we compare the periods 1960–1962 and 2000–2002, the development of per capita income in the 20 poorest countries and the 20 richest countries shows increasing disparities: while per capita income in the poorest countries remained almost the same, increasing from USD 212 to USD 267, the richest countries almost tripled per capita GDP from USD 11,417 to 32,339 (ILO 2004).[2]

The world may continue to experience gradual global convergence in average national income levels, such that the gap between the North and the South will continue to narrow over the twenty-first century (Figure 2.3). But this outcome is not assured as there is no reason to assume that recent trends will necessarily continue. Moreover, many developing countries have not been catching up, and all too many "growth accelerations" have not been sustained (Reddy and Minoiu 2009a). Some economies with high or higher per capita incomes have become rich due to mineral wealth and relatively small populations, while many other developing countries have not been able to sustain growth and industrialization, and in many cases have experienced "premature deindustrialization." The World Bank and others refer to being stuck in this apparent development cul-de-sac as the "middle-income country trap."

The decades since 1950 have seen developing countries increasing their shares of world income and population. Developing countries now also account for larger shares of international trade, international investment, industrial production and manufactured exports than ever before. Developing countries can only sustain this if economic growth, human development and social progress rise together.

Such growth accelerations in some developing countries, mainly involving populous Asian countries, have reversed the Great Divergence between the industrialized countries and the developing countries of the South at an aggregate level. But growth so far has been uneven among countries and over time, with relatively few, albeit large, developing countries sustaining high growth over several decades to bring about overall North–South convergence (Nayyar 2013).

With much of the rest of the world left behind, or unable to sustain growth beyond brief spurts, disparities within the South continue to grow (Popov and Jomo 2017). Various regions in the global South—especially SSA, but also much of Latin America—as well as Eastern Europe and the FSU have not been catching up since the 1970s. Others have fallen further behind, especially much of Africa during the last two decades of the twentieth century, Latin America during the 1980s (Ocampo et al. 2007) and the FSU in the 1990s.

Declining overall North–South income disparities point to slow and uneven economic convergence, despite several reversals, following Asian and African decolonization after WW2. Per capita national incomes had diverged considerably in the period between 1820 and 1950, before converging modestly after WW2 until the 1960s. Nevertheless, most countries in the North have stayed rich, whereas much of the South has stayed relatively, if not absolutely, poor, with average per capita incomes below half the North's.

---

2. In constant 1995 USD, simple averages.

Hence, North–South disparities have started to decline, reversing the previous divergence in per capita income levels (UN 2014). The gaps in economic development and average income levels between North and South have continued to close, with the widespread developed country slowdown following the 2008 global financial crisis and the commodity price boom that lasted until 2014, largely benefiting the global South in relative terms. Even if China is excluded from consideration, as it accounts for much of the reversal of the Great Divergence in the last four decades, the disparity between North and South rose modestly from the 1950s to the 1970s, before rising faster from the 1980s, and then declining early in the twenty-first century (Milanovic 2009).

## *Inter-Country Convergence*

Sustaining rapid growth at the national level is complicated, typically requiring various crucial inputs—infrastructure, human resources, strong institutions and economic stimuli, among other things. There are no universal recipes for rapid catch-up growth as one-size-fits-all solutions do not exist. After all, reforms needed for success are not the same in different contexts (Polterovich and Popov 2005a, 2006). Determining why some countries grow faster than others is arguably the main analytical challenge for development economics. This is a variation of Smith's question about the nature and sources of the wealth of nations (Smith 1776).

Various economists claim that economic success stories prove what they have been arguing. Hausmann et al. (2005) propose "growth diagnostics" to overcome "binding constraints" holding back economic growth. Such constraints may be due to "incomplete" markets; lack of state capacity, appropriate human resources or infrastructure; or other relevant factors, including international trends and constraints.

Some favor more liberalized or privatized economies, associated with the Washington Consensus,[3] while others prefer more centralized and (government) interventionist ones as in East Asia. The Washington Consensus strongly promoted greater individual freedom, trade and financial liberalization, extending private

---

3. The Washington Consensus was principally reflected in the main neoliberal policy conditionalities and advice of the World Bank and International Monetary Fund (IMF), especially during the 1980s. Some World Bank research publications of the mid-1990s suggest a broader range of perspectives. For example, while *The East Asian Miracle* (1993) acknowledged the role of the state and "functional" policy interventions in the region's rapid growth, the 1996 *World Development Report* (World Bank) argued that consistent "neoliberal-light" policies, combining liberalization of markets, trade and new business entry with reasonable price stability, could achieve much, even in countries lacking clear property rights and strong market institutions. The following *World Development Report* (World Bank 1997), entitled "The State in the Changing World," emphasized the importance of state institutions for growth.

property rights and "entrepreneurship." The Washington Consensus has been dominant since the 1980s, while East Asian experiences have been commonly misrepresented and misinterpreted in the context of this narrative. Privatization of state-owned enterprises, freer trade, financial liberalization and democratic political institutions were said to be prerequisites for successful development by the Washington Consensus.

Economic liberalization is said by neoliberals to be the basis for rapid growth. However, the 1980s, the first decade of the Washington Consensus, resulted in a "lost decade" of development in Latin America as well as in SSA. This has led to more emphasis being put on "good governance" and cross-border economic liberalization, often referred to as globalization, since the 1990s. Governance thus became a convenient means to excuse the failure of the Washington Consensus.

In the course of the second half of the twentieth century, some countries in Latin America, Africa and the Middle East experienced growth spurts and seemed to be catching up for a while. However, most such growth spurts did not last (Reddy and Minoiu 2009b), losing momentum after the early 1980s' debt crises, resulting in the aforementioned "lost decade" in Latin America (1980s) and an even longer stagnation in Africa for a quarter century from the late 1970s.

In Eastern Europe, economic liberalization undermined excessively bureaucratic and centralized planning, and sometimes involved pragmatic privatization, for example, to stakeholders already directly engaged in enterprise operations. However, in SSA and Latin America, modest state capacities and interventions were often done away with, with mixed consequences, sometimes setting back economic growth and development. Foreign direct investment (FDI) was expected to fill the gap, but rarely did so, with the shortfall typically blamed on the inadequacy of government reforms. Governments were then pressured to further diminish their already limited capacities and capabilities, ostensibly to advance economic liberalization measures to "liberate" forces expected to accelerate investment and growth.

In contrast, others have credited progress in East Asia to policy interventions, including industrial policy. For others, FDI is considered essential for developing country growth (although FDI was not significant for late industrialization in Japan, South Korea, Taiwan or perhaps even pre-1990s China). It is also moot whether foreign aid boosts growth or crowds out domestic savings and investment (Channing et al. 2010; UNCTAD 2003). Besides, many policy options used by the now rich countries in the nineteenth and twentieth centuries are no longer available to most poor countries today (Reinert 2007).

There have been several major attempts at catch-up development since the twentieth century. Failures as well as successes can be instructive. Japan, South Korea, Taiwan, Hong Kong and Singapore grew rapidly for much of the second half of the twentieth century, becoming the only economies to have successfully caught up with the West enough to be considered developed. As with the US Marshall Plan in Western Europe from the late 1940s, rapid postwar growth in Northeast Asia was helped by US anticommunist priorities in Asia. Generous aid and policy and fiscal space were crucial for accelerating economic growth and structural transformation in these economies.

Despite increasing income inequality since the 1980s in many countries, improved growth in developing countries in the first decade of the twenty-first century, at least until the commodity price collapse in 2014, has accelerated the decline in overall global income inequality.

From the 1970s and 1980s, countries in Southeast Asia, China, India and elsewhere have been "catching up" as well. China resumed growth and structural transformation in the 1950s, accelerating from the 1980s onwards, while Malaysia, Thailand and Indonesia accelerated, albeit less consistently, in the 1970s, and Vietnam followed with pragmatic "Chinese-style" market-oriented reforms from the mid-1980s. The rise of East Asia, and especially of China, in the last few decades has made (state) interventionist or *dirigiste* catch-up development models and strategies more attractive. However, these economies are widely presented and increasingly seen as special cases, not suitable for emulation by others.

Nevertheless, successful catch-up development cases grew in number in the second half of the twentieth century. With growth accelerations in India, Bangladesh, Ethiopia and some other developing countries, the Great Divergence appears to have come to an end, helped by the lackluster performance of many richer countries since the 2008–2009 Great Recession following the global financial crisis. The North–South gap in average per capita incomes has not only stopped widening but also started to close.

The trend had begun as accelerated growth in Asia, especially from the 1980s, when it spread to the more populous economies. Increasing demand from these newly industrializing economies contributed to rising primary commodity prices. Higher employment in the southern cone of Latin America as well as better social provisioning also reduced national-level inequalities, although these trends have partly been reversed in recent years.

Since early this century and at least until 2014, Eastern Europe, the FSU, LAC (Latin America and the Caribbean), the Middle East and North Africa (MENA) and SSA were experiencing faster per capita output growth than rich country members of the Organisation for Economic Co-operation and Development (OECD) for the first time in decades (Figure 2.4). Most of LAC, SSA, Eastern Europe and the FSU have not been catching up as impressively as most of East Asia, and some countries even fell behind, especially in the 1980s and 1990s (Ocampo et al. 2007) and, most recently, since 2014, after oil and other primary commodity prices collapsed.

### National or Intra-Country Inequalities

In the 1970s, Western capitalism seemed under threat from within and without. High inflation and economic slowdowns in major Western countries followed the two oil price shocks in 1974 and 1979. This unexpected stagflation seemed unresponsive to traditional Keynesian fiscal and monetary policy measures.

The neoliberal reaction in the Anglophone West, led by the UK and US governments of Thatcher and Reagan in the 1980s, soon followed, weakening, if not reversing, policies for progressive redistribution. Government spending, including social spending, stopped growing, as many social security programs were cut, and unemployment rose sharply as trade unions were defeated in their industrial actions and union membership fell. The top income tax rates dropped sharply (Popov and Jomo 2016), while income and wealth inequalities have risen in many Western countries since.

National income shares accruing to capital increased at the expense of labor, with rentier shares—for example accruing to finance or intellectual property rights—growing much more than the real economy. Whereas in the 1950s and 1960s generally high profit margins allowed social welfare programs to expand, mitigating income inequalities, increased profit margins since 1990 have been reflected in rising income inequalities.

If producers are mainly wage earners, income distribution will be influenced by the nature of wage determination rather than simply by changes in productivity or input and output prices, and hence, costs. Where unemployment is high and incomes low, for example, workers are generally more willing to accept lower wages. But where labor is better organized and wage determination more regulated, wages are more likely to rise with productivity increases.

As China's rapid growth and increased inequalities have significantly affected world trends, it is important to consider these trends and some of their consequences. Income inequalities in China have also increased considerably since the 1980s, but this did not create strong resistance as income and welfare levels have risen significantly over the last four decades. Some also suggest that the country's large population may have mitigated the significance of such inequalities (Popov 2014; 2021). For several decades, living standards in China did not rise as much as productivity, but in recent years, wages and living standards have risen faster as employers face labor shortages and need greater employee skills and productivity. Moreover, with improved social protection and provisioning (public health, education, housing) after earlier marketization reforms had undermined social benefits, the social wage increased more than the money wages or even the real wages workers receive.

### Economic Inequality, Poverty and Growth

In analyzing how best to reduce extreme poverty, Lakner, Mahler, Negre and Prydz (2019) use data from 164 countries, accounting for 97 percent of the world's population, to compare the relative efficacy of either increasing growth or reducing inequality. The study finds that lowering a country's Gini coefficient for inequality by 1 percent every year has a bigger impact on global poverty than raising a country's annual growth rate by one percentage point above International Monetary Fund (IMF) forecasts.

Lakner and his colleagues (2019) project that in 2030 there will be 550 million people living in extreme poverty, that is, people living on less than USD 1.90 a day, if current inequality levels do not change and per capita GDP grows as projected by the IMF. It then simulates the impact of reducing the Gini coefficient by 1 percent or 2 percent every year, between 2018 and 2030.[4] The study projects that over 100 million fewer people would be living in extreme poverty by 2030 with a 1 percent annual reduction in the Gini coefficient.

The period since the 1980s has seen greater wealth and income inequality in many, though not all, societies. Social provisioning has declined not only in many welfare states but also where governments offer tax-financed social provisioning. Such social provisioning has also declined in China, Russia and many other economies in transition. Hence, individuals and families depend much more on their own assets and incomes.

Growth in recent decades appears to be associated with decreased income inequality, while countries with greater increases in their Gini coefficients in the period 1990–2008 had lower per capita GDP growth rates. The empirical evidence suggests that developing countries with high income inequalities are more likely than others to end up in vicious cycles of poor-quality institutions, low growth, limited social mobility and higher social tensions and conflicts.

It is often the case that major transformations, while disruptive, are necessary to break out of such vicious cycles:

> The frequent claim that inequality promotes accumulation and growth does not get much support from history. On the contrary, great economic inequality has always been correlated with extreme concentration of political power, and that power has always been used to widen the income gaps through rent-seeking and rent-keeping, forces that demonstrably retard economic growth. (Milanovic et al. 2007: 29–30)

As Stiglitz notes:

> widely unequal societies do not function efficiently, and their economies are neither stable, nor sustainable in the long run.... When the wealthiest use their political power to benefit excessively the corporations they control, much needed revenues are diverted into the pockets of a few instead of benefiting society at large.... That higher inequality is associated with lower growth—controlling for

---

4. The World Bank's Global Shared Prosperity Database's historical data shows a consistent change of 1 percent yearly in national Gini measures in about half the countries. A 2 percent yearly change was found only in 15 percent of cases. If a country had an income inequality Gini coefficient of 0.40 in 2018 (similar to that of the United States), with a reduction of 2 percent each year, its Gini coefficient should decline to 0.31 by 2030 (similar to Germany's now). But with a 1 percent reduction annually, its Gini coefficient would be 0.35 (similar to the UK's) by 2030.

all other relevant factors—has been verified by looking at the range of countries and looking over longer periods of time. (Stiglitz 2012: 83, 117)

Latin American countries, he continues, present a grim picture of where other states with growing inequalities could end up:

> The experience of Latin American countries, the region of the world with the highest level of inequality, foreshadows what lies ahead. Many of the countries were mired in civil conflict for decades, suffered high levels of criminality and social instability. Social cohesion simply did not exist. (Stiglitz 2012: 84)

### Inequality, Growth, Politics

Redistribution has long been portrayed and perceived as harmful for growth. The median voter theorem claims that the tax rate selected by a government is that preferred by the median voter; this view has become influential in discussions of elections, inequalities, redistribution and growth. Higher income inequality is believed to encourage consideration of redistribution options as an alternative to promoting growth with the expectation of "lifting all boats." It is argued that for the poor majority, losses due to economic growth slowdowns or stagnation can be more than offset by redistribution (Alesina and Rodrik 1994).

Alesina and Rodrik (1994) argued that redistribution measures are more likely to be adopted in democracies than under authoritarian regimes where governments can politically afford to ignore the poor. Democracies with higher income inequalities will face greater pressures for income redistribution in favor of the poor and are more likely to redistribute progressively, which will adversely affect economic growth. However, there is little actual evidence that there is indeed more redistribution going on in democracies with high inequalities (e.g., Perotti 1996).

On the contrary, Polterovich and Popov (2005b) offered evidence to argue that democratization leads to slower, not faster, growth of government revenue as a share of GDP. Nor is there strong evidence that less redistribution, other things being equal, leads to higher growth. The ratio of government revenue/ spending to GDP, or even the amount of transfers, is not necessarily a good indicator of redistribution, as tax systems and government spending may be more or less progressive and may benefit certain influential lobbies more than others (Milanovic 2000).[5]

Besides ideological or cultural preferences, formal as well as informal institutions and processes have similar redistributive effects as government-

---

5. Milanovic (2000) identified data problems and showed why many tests of the redistributive impact of income inequalities in democracies have not produced meaningful results.

led redistribution efforts. In countries where democratic transition undermines traditional redistributive mechanisms, without creating alternative, democratic mechanisms, the net impact of democratization may even increase income inequalities that eventually undermine growth (see Polterovich and Popov 2005b).

Milanovic, Lindert and Williamson (2007: 29) argued that "great economic inequality has always been correlated with extreme concentration of political power, and that power has always been used to widen the income gaps." Economic and political inequality reinforce each other; thus, national and international policies tend to benefit the—increasingly transnational—wealthy. Reforms to reduce these inequalities are therefore essential for moving forward.

Rising inequality has likely played a role in the ethno-cultural populist-nationalist movements sweeping much of the world today. To be sure, in many developing countries, especially in Africa and Asia, ethno-populisms have been encouraged by imperial powers to enable "divide and rule" since colonial times. The failure of Western social democracy and associated movements to successfully cope with the neoliberal resurgence from the 1980s, the postindustrial postmodern turn to identity politics and the end of the Cold War have enabled successful populist mobilization against the "Other" in the form of immigration and foreign economic competition.

Inequalities may also influence growth via political instability. Alesina and Perotti (1996) argue that high income inequality leads to greater political instability, which worsens investment conditions with adverse consequences for growth. Statistical evidence supports both their hypotheses: of links between inequality and political instability, and between investment climate and growth. While there is no evidence that higher inequalities cause greater (state) redistribution or that greater redistribution negatively impacts growth, the evidence is strong that high inequality hinders growth.

Correct diagnosis of the relationship between inequality and growth is crucial for finding the appropriate policy remedies. If inequality damages growth by causing political instability, the negative impact of inequalities should be found, not only in democracies but also in autocracies, where reducing income inequalities should also reduce instability and increase incentives, investments and growth. But if the contrary holds true, and redistributive interventions disrupt growth, and some inequality increases investment and growth, autocracies may have some advantages over democracies. However, so-called autocracies are often less unequal than supposed democracies. Thus, former and current "socialist" countries—China,[6] Cuba, Vietnam, North Korea—had the lowest inequalities in the world during their socialist regimes. Particular voting arrangements may also be more conducive than others to limit inequality and promote growth in certain circumstances.

---

6. China has a relatively high Gini coefficient of income distribution (over 40 percent), but if controlled for the size and the level of development of the country it is in fact rather low (Popov 2021).

## Concluding Remarks

The new conventional wisdom is that excessive economic inequality of outcome can cause social and political instability and hurt growth. While some inequality in outcomes is said to be unavoidable due to variations in ability, talent, initiative and fortune, current inequalities and disparities enjoy little such legitimacy. Excessive inequality and exclusion undermine social cohesion, exacerbate social and political polarization and hamper economic growth (Berg and Ostry 2011; Rodrik 1999).

However, attempting to equalize societies is likely to be difficult and resisted, especially by the privileged. Undoubtedly, some societies are more tolerant of inequality than others, according to the extent to which prevailing ideologies legitimize differences. Unequal economic distribution may be more acceptable if the distribution of opportunities is seen as fair, allowing for social mobility. Hence, some argue that ensuring equality in opportunity is more feasible than equality of outcome and likely to be legitimate.

Broadly speaking, inter-country disparities have declined since the 1990s, while intra-country inequality has often increased. However, closer examination reveals how declining inter-country inequality has primarily been driven by Asia, especially China's growth in recent decades. For other developing countries, catch-up growth has been uneven or unsustainable at best, but reducing inequality and accelerating growth are not necessarily contradictory. Beyond the moral imperative to ensure equity, addressing within-country inequality could, in fact, promote social progress, more stable political institutions and economic growth.

## References

Alesina, Alberto and Roberto Perotti. 1996. "Income Distribution, Political Instability, and Investment." *European Economic Review*, 40: 1203–1228.

Alesina, Alberto and Dani Rodrik. 1994. "Distributive Politics and Economic Growth." *Quarterly Journal of Economics*, 109: 465–490.

Berg, Andrew G. and Jonathan D. Ostry. 2011. "Inequality and Unsustainable Growth: Two Sides of the Same Coin?" *IMF Staff Discussion Note DN/11/08*. Washington, DC: International Monetary Fund.

Bourguignon, François and Christian Morrisson. 2002. "Inequality among World Citizens: 1820–1992." *American Economic Review*, 92(4): 727–744.

Channing, Arndt, Sam Jones and Finn Tarp. 2010. "Aid, Growth, and Development: Have We Come Full Circle?" *Journal of Globalization and Development*, 1(2).

Eichengreen, Barry and Kevin H. O'Rourke. 2009. "A Tale of Two Depressions." *Vox CEPR Policy Portal*, 6 April.

Hardoon, Deborah. 2017. "An Economy for the 99%." *Oxfam Briefing Paper*. Oxford: Oxfam International.

Hausmann, Ricardo, Dani Rodrik and Andrés Velasco. 2005. *Growth Diagnostics*. Cambridge, MA: Harvard Growth Lab.

Hobsbawm, Eric. 1995 (1994). *The Age of Extremes: The Short Twentieth Century, 1914–1991*. London: Abacus.

ILO (International Labour Organization). 2004. *A Fair Globalization: Creating Opportunities for All*. Geneva: ILO.

IMF (International Monetary Fund). 2017. *IMF Fiscal Monitor: Tackling Inequality. October 2017*. Washington, DC: IMF.

Lakner, Christoph, Daniel Mahler, Mario Negre and Espen Prydz. 2019. "How Much Does Reducing Inequality Matter for Global Poverty?" *Policy Research Working Paper No. 8869*. Washington, DC: World Bank.

Maddison Project. 2013. *Maddison Project Database*. Groningen, Netherlands: University of Groningen. Accessed 22 August 2019. https://www.rug.nl/ggdc/historicaldevel opment/maddison/releases/maddison-project-database-2013.

Milanovic, Branko. 2000. "The Median-Voter Hypothesis, Income Inequality, and Income Redistribution: An Empirical Test with the Required Data." *European Journal of Political Economy*, 16: 367–410.

Milanovic, Branko. 2005. *Worlds Apart: Measuring International and Global Inequality*. Princeton, NJ: Princeton University Press.

Milanovic, Branko. 2009. "Global Inequality Recalculated: The Effect of New 2005 PPP Estimates on Global Inequality." *MPRA (Munich Personal RePEC Archive) Paper No. 16538*. Munich: University Library of Munich.

Milanovic, Branko. 2016. *Global Inequality: A New Approach for the Age of Globalization*. Cambridge, MA: Harvard University Press.

Milanovic, Branko, Peter H. Lindert and Jeffrey G. Williamson. 2007. "Measuring Ancient Inequality." *Policy Research Working Paper No. 4412*. Washington, DC: World Bank.

Moatsos, Michael, Joery Baten, Peter Foldvari, Bas van Leeuwen and Jan Luiten van Zanden. 2014. "Income Inequality since 1820." In *How Was Life? Global Well-being since 1820*, edited by Jan Luiten van Zanden, Joerg Baten, Marco Mira d'Ercole, Auke Rijpma, Conal Smith and Marcel Timme, 199–215. Paris: OECD.

Nayyar, Deepak, ed. 2013. *Catch Up: Developing Countries in the World Economy*. New Delhi: Oxford University Press.

Ocampo, José Antonio, K. S. Jomo and Rob Vos. 2007. "Explaining Growth Divergences." In *Growth Divergences: Explaining Differences in Economic Performance*, edited by José Antonio Ocampo, K. S. Jomo and Vos Robert, 1–24. London: Zed Books.

Oxfam. 2019. "Public Good or Private Wealth." *Oxfam Briefing Paper*. Oxford: Oxfam GB.

Perotti, Roberto. 1996. "Growth, Income Distribution, and Democracy: What the Data Say." *Journal of Economic Growth*, 1(2): 149–187.

Piketty, Thomas. 2014. *Capital in the Twenty-First Century*. Cambridge, MA: Harvard University Press.

Polterovich, Victor and Vladimir Popov. 2005a. "Appropriate Economic Policies at Different Stages of Development." *MPRA (Munich Personal RePEC Archive) Paper No. 20066*. Munich: University Library of Munich.

Polterovich, Victor and Vladimir Popov. 2005b. "Democratization, Quality of Institutions and Economic Growth." *NES Working Paper No. 2006/056*. Moscow: New Economic School.

Polterovich, Victor and Vladimir Popov. 2006. "Stages of Development, Economic Policies and New World Economic Order." *Paper presented at the Seventh Annual Global Development Conference*, St. Petersburg, 19–21 January. https://ssrn.com/abstract =1754382.

Popov, Vladimir. 2014. *Mixed Fortunes: An Economic History of China, Russia and the West*. New York: Oxford University Press.

Popov, Vladimir. 2021. "Why Europe Looks So Much Like China: Big Government and Low Income Inequalities." *Paper No. 106326*. Munich: Munich Personal RePEc Archive.

Popov, Vladimir and K. S. Jomo. 2015. "Income Inequalities in Perspective." *Development*, 58(2–3): 196–205.

Popov, Vladimir and K. S. Jomo. 2016. "Increasing Economic Inequality Not Inevitable." *Inter Press Service*, 13 May.

Popov, Vladimir and K. S. Jomo. 2017. "Convergence? More Developing Countries Are Catching Up." In *The Rest beyond the West*, edited by Piotr Dutkiewicz and Vladimir Popov, 7–23. Cheltenham: Edward Elgar.

Reddy, Sanjay G. and Camelia Minoiu. 2009a. "Development Aid and Economic Growth: A Positive Long-Run Relation." *Working Paper No. 09/118*. Washington, DC: IMF.

Reddy, Sanjay G. and Camelia Minoiu. 2009b. "Real Income Stagnation of Countries: 1960–2001." *Journal of Development Studies*, 45(1): 1–23.

Reinert, Erik S. 2007. *How Rich Countries Got Rich . . . And Why Poor Countries Stay Poor*. London: Constable.

Rodrik, Dani. 1999. "Where Did All the Growth Go? External Shocks, Social Conflict, and Growth Collapses." *Journal of Economic Growth*, 4(4): 385–412.

Smith, Adam. 1776. *An Inquiry into the Nature and Causes of the Wealth of Nations*. London: W. Strahan.

Stiglitz, Joseph E. 2012. *The Price of Inequality: How Today's Divided Society Endangers Our Future*. New York: W. W. Norton.

Sutcliffe, Bob. 2004. "World Inequality and Globalization." *Oxford Review of Economic Policy*, 20(1): 15–37.

UN (United Nations). 2014. "World Economic and Social Survey 2014: Reducing Inequality for Sustainable Development." *Economic and Social Council Report E/2014/50*. New York: UN.

UNCTAD (United Nations Conference on Trade and Development). 2003. *World Investment Report 2003—FDI Policies for Development: National and International Perspectives*. Geneva: UNCTAD.

Wade, Robert Hunter. 2004. "Is Globalization Reducing Poverty and Inequality?" *World Development*, 32(4): 567–589.

Williamson, Jeffrey G. 2009. "History without Evidence: Latin American Inequality since 1491." *Discussion Paper No. 3*. Göttingen, Germany: Georg-August-Universität.

World Bank. 1993. *The East Asian Miracle*. New York: Oxford University Press.

World Bank. 1996. *World Development Report 1996: From Plan to Market*. Washington, DC: World Bank.

World Bank. 1997. *World Development Report 1997: The State in the Changing World*. Washington, DC: World Bank.

World Development Indicators (WDI). n.d. "WDI Database." Washington, DC: World Bank. Accessed 22 August 2019.

## Part II

ENGINES OF INEQUALITY: INSTITUTIONS, POLITICS AND POWER

# Chapter 3

## SOCIO-SPATIAL INEQUALITIES AND INTERGENERATIONAL DEPENDENCIES

### Julie MacLeavy and David Manley

#### Introduction

There has long been substantial interest in societal inequalities and the extent to which they may result from economic or social and cultural factors. The consequences of a group or individual's unequal access to resources, privilege, power and control in a society have been explored, particularly how and why disadvantage can combine and accumulate not only over a single life course but also over multiple generations to influence income, education and occupational status. The OECD (2015) has reported work on income inequality and segregation, and multiple Western governments have sought to identify interventions at various societal levels that will be effective in reducing and ultimately eliminating inequalities given documentation of the long-run impacts of children growing up poor. Although economic growth has done much to improve material conditions across Western postindustrial nations, research has shown the life-diminishing effects of prioritizing growth over equality as inequalities develop and serve to reduce access to a broad range of societal resources and opportunities required for upward mobility. Epidemiologists Richard Wilkinson and Kate Pickett's (2009) book *The Spirit Level* highlights the long-term consequences of exposure to adversity, including the negative social processes that widening disparities produce for nation-states. Similarly, economist Thomas Piketty's (2014) book *Capital in the Twenty-First Century* considers both how and why nations become unequal as disparities between economic and social classes sustain and reinforce advantage and disadvantage over time.

This chapter explores the intergenerational transmission of inequalities from a geographical perspective. In particular, it outlines how intergenerational inheritances, including both wealth transfers—intentional and unintentional—and the transmission of broader social and cultural class dimensions from one generation to the next, are projected across space. Building on existing research documenting how intergenerational relations are exacerbating existing spatial divides between population groups, while also forging new factions within population groups (e.g., Sharkey 2013; van Ham et al. 2014), it explains how inequalities become embedded through a range of processes enacted at multiple sites and scales. Within the geographic context in which individuals live, the spatial expressions of social inequalities are commonly viewed through the lens of residential segregation. Here, concern is directed at the potential for individuals to live separate lives so that while individuals may live in the same city, their places of residence, schooling and wider everyday life activities may be spatially distinct (see Cantle 2001; Casey 2016). It is important to note that residential segregation has persisted in spite of the fact that, broadly speaking, at a national level, diversity has risen so there is greater potential for individuals from different cultural, religious or ethnic backgrounds to meet in the course of day-to-day life. Moreover, Western cities have become increasingly culturally and racially diverse (Catney 2016; Harris 2017; Zwiers et al. 2018). Therefore, as population-level economic inequality increases, there is a simultaneous macro-scale decrease in spatial inequality that is not evident at the neighborhood scale. Despite this, the neighborhood remains a critical site in which groups and individuals can be located and place-based remedies installed. Segregated communities prevent investment; mixed communities allow partnerships and integration. In what follows, we suggest that concern therefore needs to shift away from the cultural toward the economic and its social outcomes. In many Western countries, the gap between the extremes of the income distribution has increased and become embedded in and through residential location and inhabitants' daily activity patterns (Ohlsson et al. 2009; Piketty 2014). Thus, when we view the world at meso and micro scales, we see that the concentration of wealth within society and spatially within cities through segregation is increasing such that individuals within one socioeconomic group are less likely to live in proximity to and come into contact with individuals from other socioeconomic groups, regardless of any shared religious or racial characteristics (Kukk et al. 2019). The "class" dynamics of residential segregation are cumulative and self-reinforcing.

We propose that segregation is, at least in part, the spatial expression of wealth and income inequalities. Linking inequalities to intergenerational class mobility, we further suggest that a key concern in terms of understanding individual barriers to upward mobility lies in understanding how individuals sort into and out of social and residential spaces. If sorting is a benign or even random process without structure, then access to resources and both social and place advantages is not problematic—each individual or household regardless of their origin class has an equal opportunity to gain access to certain destinations. If, on the other hand, sorting is even slightly structured, then understanding the processes behind that structure and the key determinants that give rise to the outcomes we view is crucial (Manley and van Ham 2011; Hedman and van Ham 2012). In this instance, the continual rise of income and wealth inequalities is of wider interest because of the spatial fixity that appears alongside it. What much of the current literature lacks is a longitudinal connection that integrates into accounts of the relationship between inequalities and mobility the sorting of people into socioeconomically distinct neighborhoods over the life course. With an increased distance between the top and bottom ends of the distribution being repeatedly identified as a barrier to mobility in society (Blanden et al. 2005; Breen 2004; Lamont et al. 2014; Nunn et al. 2007), the place connectivity between and through generations has been underplayed. One of the few authors to identify and analyze the intergenerational transmission of advantages and disadvantages is David Willetts (2011) in *The Pinch*. Willetts shows how those located toward the upper end of the middle classes are tightening their grip on the opportunities available for the next generation, negatively affecting the chances of upward mobility for those without equal access to such parental resources (see also Friedman and Laurison 2019). Building on this, we are particularly concerned with the significance and value of connections forged through place and how increasing disparities between residential groups are generative of economic and social disparities within generations.

We start by charting the macro structures through which individuals access their places of residence and other spaces, which ultimately lock in the "spatial opportunity structures" that they experience (Galster and Sharkey 2017: 1). The overarching rationale is to encourage a consideration of (a) the structures that govern differences in space such that *where* an individual lives conditions many of the opportunities they can access and (b) the intergenerational structures that govern the spatiality of individual life courses such that who is able to access different spaces is not even. This latter concern necessarily encompasses an interest in the extent to which the intergenerational production of inequalities may be stratified according to gender, sexuality, race/ethnicity, age, disability and religion, as it is clear that the transmission of advantages and disadvantages from one generation to the next is part of a broader complex of inheritances that can differentiate impacts at the level of the individual. We then reflect upon the life-diminishing consequences of the resultant spatial differentiation: how the greater ability of advantaged individuals and households to maintain (or improve) their position by setting their superior resources against any perceived threats causes adverse effects for those less able to adapt, as exemplified by the current pandemic. Just like the Spanish Flu pandemic in the early 1900s, the Covid-19 pandemic has been extremely spatialized (Bambra et al. 2020). Not only have the changes it has provoked been experienced in a spatially differentiated way, but they have also shed light on the extent to which growing inequalities matter to the health and well-being of the collective.

## Macro Inequalities

At the macro level, the story of household income and wealth is one of divergence. In some of the richest countries, the gap between those who are at the top end of the distribution and those who are not has been growing substantially over many decades (Dorling 2014; Stiglitz 2011). A brief hiatus in the initial aftermath of the global financial crisis that saw population level inequalities fall—through the drop in financial returns on investments, rather than as a result of wage growth for those at the bottom end of the income distribution—has been superseded by a continuation of earlier increases in inequalities between economic and social classes (Onaran and Guschanski 2016). More critically, the rank order of the population is unchanging. Those at the top of the distribution remain at the top. Those at the bottom of the distribution also remain in position. If one of the overall goals of government policy is to secure a means through which a fairer and more just society can be formed, then the presence of elastic inequalities (i.e., inequalities whereby the distribution remains regardless of the stretch) should be of political concern (MacLeavy and Manley 2018). Any action needs to take account of the application of neoliberal policies that have contributed to the destructive structural effects of globalization, for this is also a story set in the context of long-term changes in the global economy. Focusing on the long-term decline of manufacturing, economists Patricia Rice and Anthony Venables (2020) note that patterns of inequality are largely set by social and institutional mechanisms. As such, industry once in decline has struggled to adjust to successive economic shocks, with persistent underdevelopment resulting in spillover effects between firms causing economic activity to cluster elsewhere. As a result, industrial decline has led to entrenched place-based exclusion for almost 60 years: the consequence of this is that, once in decline, it is very difficult to change the course of neighborhoods and current patterns of inequality are persistent.

However, exploring the distribution of income and wealth at the macro level does not provide a nuanced picture of the processes or outcomes that individuals will experience, as institutional, cultural and sociohistorical variables can produce different outcomes for different cities and different groups. At the city level, increases in inequalities can be driven by major economic dynamics associated with the shift from industrial to postindustrial labor markets. Toward the end of the twentieth century, sociologist Saskia Sassen (1990; see also 2001) reasoned that an emergent trend in the major cities of the world would be the increased polarization of groups along social and economic lines. The reduction in manufacturing employment and the rise of the postindustrial economy, she predicted, would result in a "hollowing out" of the middle groups, with rises in employment for both the well-qualified professionals and managers, and the expansion of employment for the low skilled and less well educated as providers of the services underpinning the "new economy." In the years after the publication of the *Global City* thesis, the academic literature has debated the effectiveness of this theory. Early geographical interlocutors such as Chris Hamnett (1994, 1996) found that this polarization had not transpired in London. Two decades later, David Manley and Ron Johnston (2014) followed up this analysis with a demonstration that the "professionalization" of the workforce had still not transpired, and had in fact halted, during the 2000s. However, more recent research has found that in all three of the cities that were the focus of Sassen's work there has been a move toward professionalization, with the changes in New York being the greatest, then London and finally Tokyo. Thus, even in a globalized world where everything appears interconnected and dependent, local contexts influence social relationships and structures (Manley et al. 2015; van Ham et al. 2020).

Expanding from these case studies, an exploration of Western capital cities has provided a more nuanced picture of contemporary urban dynamics. Although they do not conform perfectly to Sassen's theory, there is evidence of increasing social polarization in many capitals including Madrid, Tallinn, Oslo and Stockholm, which is leading to the increased spatial segregation of different income groups (van Ham et al. 2016). Cross-national comparison reveals the extent to which this process is mediated by geographical and historical place-specific factors, including different welfare state structures that yield different labor markets and rates of participation for migrant workers (Esping-Andersen 1990, 1993). Even within the same country, cities have their own specific social and economic histories, and within cities there are different types of neighborhoods, both of which lead to differences in their characters and social compositions. Applying this directly to labor markets, we observe relative homogeneity in job opportunities in neighborhoods within the "old" industrial cities and the neighborhoods around the old factory locations, which contrasts with relative diversity of opportunities in those cities that have regenerated and are more service sector-oriented. Thus, as economic restructuring and labor market differentiation progresses, it alters the social and economic structures and the distribution of the population within cities, albeit at different rates. The impact of this differentiation leads to exclusionary access to employment, and these differences both within and between cities can produce differences in outcomes for the residents—the so-called neighborhood effects argument (van Ham et al. 2012). This means, then, there is a case for exploring the spatiality of economic transitions on residents and their life courses.

## Meso-Level Inequalities

The neighborhood effects literature suggests that the residential context in which individuals live can have a substantial impact on their life course outcomes (Manley et al. 2013; van Ham et al. 2012). Effects have been identified on many dimensions of individual outcomes including health, education, employment and social attitudes. Successive Western governments have sought to invest in places through area-based regeneration, either through the renewal or mixing of housing stock or through larger-scale labor market interventions. Within the context of this chapter particular interest is paid to the identification of the neighborhood as one of the sites through which the later life success of children can be influenced. The key insight is that if segregation is the spatial expression of societal inequalities and the neighborhood can impact individual outcomes, then the societal inequalities can directly *and* indirectly impact individuals. Through the neighborhood, inequalities can become a (further) barrier to social mobility and later life achievement. Sociologist John Logan's (1978) analysis of the stratification of place implies that local areas confer a set of advantages and disadvantages to residents that become ever greater over time. Furthermore, recent research in Canada has shown that the neighborhood context in which individuals are born can have a long and lasting impact on their life course outcomes, even if they depart from that neighborhood relatively early in life (Glass and Bilal 2016).

Similarly, research in Sweden (van Ham et al. 2014), the Netherlands (de Vuijst et al. 2017) and the United States (Sharkey 2013) has demonstrated that there are spatial inheritances relating to the neighborhood context in which an individual grows up and the subsequent neighborhood career they go on to experience. Geographer Maarten van Ham and colleagues (2014) used Swedish register data to explore the reproduction of neighborhood context in a cohort of home leavers in 1990. Following their subsequent life course, they determined that the neighborhood in which an individual grows up is highly predictive of the type of neighborhood that they will go on to live in later in life. Of course, there are many processes that can lead to this outcome, and in some cases it is likely to be driven by homophily—people actively seek out others who are similar to them for positive interactions (Dean and Pryce 2017). However, it is likely that some of the reproduction of the "truly disadvantaged" (Wilson 1987) is a consequence of negative externalities accrued during childhood in neighborhoods with fewer resources. This is seen in the relative difficulty with which individuals from the poorest neighborhoods achieve later life access to the wealthiest neighborhoods (de Vuijst et al. 2017; Manley et al. 2020; van Ham et al. 2014). Using internationally comparative data and methods to analyze the socio-spatial transitions in England, Sweden, Estonia and the Netherlands, Nieuwenhuis and colleagues (2017) also confirm these findings. In the US context, the work of sociologist Patrick Sharkey (2013) has demonstrated that over a long period of time those individuals who grow up in a deprived neighborhood are much more likely to themselves live in a deprived neighborhood as adults. As a result, their children will also grow up in a deprived neighborhood, reproducing the spatial inequality. Moreover, if the adults had parents who also grew up in poverty, then their life chances are further diminished with lower educational success and employment opportunities. What this literature points to is a locking into place of disadvantage so that groups are circulating in different, albeit often similarly located but socially distinct, residential locations.

Of course, the neighborhood is not the only spatial context that individuals experience: van Ham and Tammaru (2016) highlight that there is a multitude of sites at which context can have influence including the workplace, leisure spaces, cultural spaces and the schools that children attend. Manley and colleagues (2020) highlight a further influence through research that compares the contribution of the household to the neighborhood of residence. Using data from Sweden and comparing siblings who grow up in the same neighborhood and household, with individuals who grow up in the same neighborhood but in separate households, they demonstrate that the local household environment has a substantial impact on the subsequent spatial career of individuals, relegating the neighborhood to a secondary position. Thus, it is at the micro scale where we need to investigate the impact of stratification and the interpersonal interactions that write into individual life courses how individuals are affected by inequalities.

## Micro Inequalities

Moving from the neighborhood to the individual involves a shift in focus from the residential mobility literature to the scaffolding of support that individuals receive and experience from parents, wider family members and friends. This includes the role of money, as well as time or expertise in helping individuals to navigate the labor market, housing market or other significant socioeconomic spheres. Many accounts of the postindustrial economy position growing disparities of income and wealth as the consequence of contemporary labor market demands for not only high-skilled service workers but also a vast array of unskilled laborers (e.g., Holmes and Mayhew 2015). However, work at the micro scale has drawn attention to the supply side processes underlying the socio-spatial patterns that are now emerging between and within cities (e.g., McDowell 2003). An empirical focus on the groups employed within different niches of the labor market can therefore be useful in highlighting the role of social and cultural capital in reproducing and deepening inequalities in comparative life chances of specific urban populations. Building on aforementioned accounts of the importance of place in analyzing and explaining inequalities, such research points to the role of community and family networks in mediating the life chances of individuals inhabiting a specific local context, as well as the intergenerational (dis)continuities between those who conform to the path suggested by their neighborhood origin and those who are footloose. It demonstrates that while the social networks and cultures pertaining to different neighborhoods can affect the labor market positions of residents, intergenerational relations are able to disrupt and alter the trajectories of individuals within these particular social and spatial contexts by creating different capacities to cope with disadvantages being wrought by global processes of economic restructuring.

Geographer Rory Coulter's (2016) work in the United Kingdom, for instance, details how intergenerational transfers of wealth from parents to children for the purchase of housing can bestow a form of privilege that increases the recipient's chances of upward social mobility when compared with those without the equivalent means of financial support (see also Galster and Wessel 2019). Unable to benefit from the substantial house price inflation resulting from the shift toward pro-market, homeownership-oriented housing policies in this context, low-income renters, whose parents were also renters, find their education and job opportunities are restricted by their inability to draw on or build up an asset base (Forrest and Hirayama 2009). The concurrent revival of private landlordism through the growth of precarious financial products intended to induce investment in housing has also shaped the opportunity structures for younger generations by facilitating new intragenerational relationships between landlord and tenant: in the United Kingdom it is increasingly common for private renting to involve peer-to-peer arrangements, with payments made by renters to their owner-occupying peers for a room within a mortgaged property (Walker and Jeraj 2016). In Japan, where similar policy orientations have not yielded the same growth in property values, housing also continues to be unaffordable for many renters. Coupled with growing job insecurity, those without access to parental wealth in Japan's younger generation are unable to afford their own homes (Forrest and Hirayama 2009).

With housing options becoming more dependent on family background, so too are the life trajectories of young people. While home ownership helps some to insulate themselves in the most privileged locations, those from more disadvantaged backgrounds can find themselves clustered in areas with greater deprivation, where there is a "spatial mismatch" (Kain 1968) between the education or skills of residents and the types of jobs available locally. An immediate response to this problem has often been to suggest that the unemployed should "get on their bike" to find work (see, e.g., Ashmore 2017). However, the spatial mismatch highlights the wider problem within more specialized labor markets whereby when large employers or industries shift, the skills of the remaining workforce are not as transferrable as they once were or the distance to the next suitable employer is simply too great. An exemplar here is in the gradual removal of heavy industry in the north of England or the closure of the Honda factory in Swindon in 2021, resulting in 3,000 workers directly losing their jobs in manufacturing. This can create an unemployed "underclass," which then serves as an abjectifying category that has a further and lasting effect on individual opportunities and job prospects. Thus, housing operates as a generator of inequalities not only because owner-occupancy typically reduces lifetime housing costs while providing security, tax advantages, collateral and the opportunity to accumulate and release equity, but also because those without the means to purchase are more vulnerable to indirect forms of economic, social and cultural disadvantage: it is easier to leverage assistance when individuals can group and pull on their collective experiences. For instance, efforts to protect existing greenbelts from new housing developments tend to be more successful when located in areas of wealth (see Merry et al. 2016). Similarly, it is striking that in the United Kingdom the 2013–2014 flooding of the Somerset Levels resulted in substantial investment in flood protection and mitigation measures, whereas more deprived communities in the north of England (notably Doncaster) that have experienced more frequent flood events have not managed to successfully engage government or resources in their defense provisions, despite having a greater population at risk of inundation. In the formation of community housing tenure can also shape personal attributes (knowledge, social networks, skills and experience) that can further affect labor market participation and career progression (Ermisch and Halpin 2004).

The point is not (just) that rich and poor people are prone to live in different places through processes of sorting within the housing and labor markets; nor is it simply that space and place help to create wealth and poverty in a manner that sustains the cultural reproduction of economic inequalities. It is that the processes and reproductions that result from the uneven fortunes of individuals are the product of intergenerational transfers that intersect with the power of place to produce positive or negative associations. This is particularly evident in nations where state welfare programs have been retrenched and in their place the family framed as the foundation of all social assistance (see, e.g., Cameron 2015). Feminist scholars have long highlighted the negative impacts of an emphasis on familial forms of welfare in terms of a reliance on unpaid domestic labor and its typical performance by women. Yet there are further consequences of assuming that all families are equally well resourced and able to support their kin. While some may be able to secure or even advance the social position of their offspring, an increasing number of others are now finding themselves subject to successive waves of economic and social pressure reducing their capacity to support family members. Those in the middle of the income distribution are particularly feeling the squeeze resultant from the neoliberal ethos of meritocratic advancement and finding their prospects—and those of their children—are shrinking as a result of their inability to individually counteract the effects of depressed wage levels, decreased job security and a steep rise in the number of hours worked for wages per household (MacLeavy and Manley 2018; see also Fraser 2013). Although targeted interventions to break cycles of family poverty have had some success in deprived geographical areas, recent reviews suggest vulnerable populations may benefit more from inclusion in mainstream provisions as mainstreaming reduces the stigma associated with targeting while also increasing coverage.

The intergenerational production of inequalities may be further stratified at the individual level according to gender, sexuality, race/ethnicity, age, disability and religion. These axes of social differentiation remain relatively underexamined in debates about intergenerational transmissions owing to a tendency to assume they are socially ascribed characteristics that may enable or constrain individuals in different places in different ways. Yet an intersectional approach provides an important means of examining how class and nonclass differences articulate. An intersectional approach is important for both ethnographic and statistical analyses into the households, neighborhoods and urban spheres facing the impact of growing disparities of fortune, as well as the feelings of discontent with which these have recently been associated. Building on qualitative research interrogating the interrelationships between class and other forms of social hierarchy and division, quantitative work has begun to address the issue of intersectionality and acknowledge that binary categories of belonging are not sufficient for understanding the complexities of modern society (see, for instance, Green et al. 2017; Jones et al. 2018; Wemrell et al. 2017). By directing attention toward the substantial differences that may exist within families and households, an intersectional framework can illuminate the diversity of embodied inequalities that are implicated in systems of social stratification. Recent studies of work and employment, for instance, have shown us that men and women experience the postindustrial economy differently, with young men from Black and minority ethnic backgrounds often found to be most at risk of unemployment as a consequence of contemporary labor market transitions (Trust for London 2020). Similarly, state welfare provisions may entrench rather than mitigate forms of gender, race and age inequality. While the postwar consensus was based on the principles of full (male) employment with a package of policies that reinforced traditional gender roles, more recent reforms have divided women, providing support for those from low-income households to enter the labor market, while constraining women with a high-earning husband or partner (MacLeavy 2011). There are also reported Black–white differences in women's welfare-to-work transitions (Brush 2011). Such work underlines the danger in thinking about various forms of difference in isolation. We need to compare and link inherited disadvantage to intersectional inequalities based on gender, sexuality, race/ethnicity, age, disability and religion. It is at the level of the individual that the relations between the macro, meso and micro are established. The dynamics of the postindustrial economy do not impinge in a direct way upon the individual, but rather are brought about by variables that mediate place-specific factors and sociocultural differences between groups.

### Intergenerational Transmission as a Geographical Process

By linking together research from multiple national contexts, the importance of inequalities for individuals and their ability to achieve successful life course outcomes becomes clear. Inequalities are growing and the reproduction of those inequalities is extending through generations, so that those individuals growing up in less well-off circumstances are more likely to be living in similar, less well-off places when they transition into their own independent life course. By contrast, those who are brought up in wealthier neighborhoods appear to have stronger buffering so that they are less likely than their poorer cohort partners to be exposed to less well-off neighborhoods later in life. This suggests that inequalities are increasingly manifest in spatial divides, which, in turn, yield unequal differentiated access to the means and mechanisms for upward social mobility. In short, the access to as well as distribution of the social, political, economic and cultural resources available in a society is becoming increasingly uneven over time. In this regard, it is essential to understand the close relationship between economic inequality and residential segregation as spatial fixity is part of the story behind reduced social mobility. Within a meritocratic society, an individual's success, in terms of their employment or social status, should be a function of their abilities, not their background. However, when children grow up without the opportunity, for instance, to access quality schooling—such as when the school is unable to provide sufficient equipment for learning or more recently when school closures in response to Covid-19 resulted in unequal access to learning as many families did not have sufficient computing or internet access—the possibility for an individual to realize their potential is restricted and their overall performance lower than it could otherwise have been. In these circumstances, the meritocratic outcomes are no longer a function of ability alone but equally a function of other external influences.

It is also important to consider how structures are reinforced over generations so that people repeat the spatial exposures in their adult life that they had in their childhood. Analyzing the relationship between financial hardship, cultural marginalization and residential segregation in a single period gives only a limited perspective on the problem. Individuals need to be followed over time and through space to understand all the influences that act upon them. These include socioeconomic factors that can generate spatial divides—work, education and access to material goods, products and services—as well as social and cultural characteristics such as gender, sexuality, race/ethnicity, age, disability and religion with which these factors intersect. These intersections show the importance of subjective and intersubjective experiences of disparity, demonstrating that inequality is a complex, evolving and multifaceted phenomenon.

Recognition and demonstration of the fact that those who have advantages (in the labor or housing market, for instance) are able to use them to benefit further is necessary to shift the public and political dialogue around the meritocratic ideal. By underlining the persistence of inherited hierarchies, a longitudinal approach may—for instance—provide support for egalitarian policies. The emerging view of economic status and power as "fortresses of privilege" (Appiah 2018) is driven by a sense that class hierarchies have been resistant to postwar welfare policies that were intended to protect and support members of the working classes and allow some of their offspring to progress in the areas of education, employment or housing. Moreover, while these mechanisms of mobility are being steadily dismantled, the derision and scorn accorded to those who find themselves unable to move up the hierarchy of occupations and income remain (Valentine and Harris 2014). Rather than operating as equalizers, educational institutions from schools to universities continue to support the stratification of society, with affluent parents using their financial resources to secure advantages for their children—through extra private tuition or coaching for entrance exams to work experience only accessible via personal social networks—as a means of ensuring their continued access to society's power and wealth. Although (limited) provisions are made for those from the very poorest backgrounds, as well as to promote diversity through the greater inclusion of minority groups, the opportunity hoarding of the most privileged is disregarded: the focus is on providing ways for (some) individuals to progress without addressing the long-running processes that drive inequality.

Sociologist Charles Tilly's (2000) "relational nature of inequality" is rooted in understanding the value of adopting an empirical focus that goes beyond the study of people who live in circumstances of poverty and disadvantage. This is not simply because those experiencing economic and other forms of marginality do not always group together, as they may equally be scattered or rootless as a result of life circumstances, or unable to coalesce in a virtual or physical movement for social and economic justice or participatory democracy. It is also because the circumstances of those at the bottom end of the income distribution are produced as the result of the intense and increasing concentrations of wealth that do not trickle down, but instead yield further inequalities because the concentration "floods upwards." Thus, striving for equality of opportunity is, in itself, insufficient because the ability to take advantage of the opportunities is not equally spread. Policy focus needs to shift toward explicit interventions to bolster the opportunities for those less able to the exclusion of the advantaged. It also needs to be matched by efforts to alleviate poverty. After all, a more rigorous effort to achieve true meritocracy would still result in a class-based system, with rewards for those at the top in marked contrast to those afforded to persons not in possession of the talents or capacity to succeed.

### Conclusion: Covid-19 Reflections on Intergenerational Inheritances

Contemporary research suggests people are unequal because extreme disparities lead to structural barriers to prosperity that exacerbate existing spatial divides between groups while also forging new factions within a population inhabiting the same residential space. In this discussion we have sought to recognize the continuum between positive and negative experiences of intergenerational transfer, as well as the possibilities of disenfranchisement and disillusionment related to shifting labor market demands (based on the observation that opportunities available to some groups in society do not reflect differences in education or training, but rather physical attributes and associated behavioral traits or, to put it differently, forms of discrimination). When uneven development is put into play with ethnic and gender disparities, inequalities become clearer. We have sought to articulate the need to develop a geographical understanding of the intergenerational relations that compound inequalities because there are distinct spatialities to inequalities—to where is and where is not (dis) advantaged—which connect strongly to who is and who is not (dis)advantaged. It is not until this spatial structure of inequalities has been recognized and acknowledged that we will be able to move forward with suitable place-based remedies that may serve to ameliorate some of the greater injustices. In short, just as we recognize there are social biases and injustices so too are there spatial biases and injustices.

In closing, we reflect on the themes we have raised in relation to the social determinants and impacts of the Covid-19 pandemic. The health, economic and social challenges it has raised have clearly been experienced in a spatially differentiated way: taking the example of the United Kingdom there is a clear macro-level geography where regions are experiencing different rates of infection, different versions of the lockdown restrictions and, as a result, different short- and long-term consequences, which are felt within the four constituent states as well as between them. Within those macro regions, at the meso level, the legacy of deindustrialization and historical underinvestment is apparent (Rice and Venables 2020): while many London residents have been able to work from home and socially distance within parks and as a household unit, in parts of the north of England where there is more contact-intensive industry, where housing is often older or lacks regeneration and reinvestment, and where the co-dependencies between households are larger, efforts to suppress the virus have been less successful as a result of structural constraints rather than individual activities.

Turning to the micro level, within the larger macro regions there are population groups for whom the government restrictions resulting from the pandemic may not have been wholly negative. Indeed, physical distancing and related restrictions may have delivered some short-term positive impacts for those who can work from home, whose occupations are no more precarious now than they were at the start of 2020; who can avail themselves of home delivery networks for food and luxury purchases; and who are able to use their back gardens or who have access to open public spaces where distancing is more easily achieved.

For others, some restrictions could be offset—those whose schooling either continued without disruption or were able to access the technological means to learn by switching between online and in person as needed. The groups for whom this was possible predominantly were those who already had advantages, wealth and connectivity. By contrast, those families supplying services, through either precarious employment or secure employment where working from home was not a possibility and therefore experienced the lockdowns and restrictions as a constraint through which they have had to keep going, have been further disadvantaged. Those disadvantages could have been manifest in the home, but the local community was influential in the clustering of infection rates, and the ability to cope with the impacts of the pandemic (Mikolai et al. 2020). If a household did not have access to online resources, or the mode of access was through a phone or tablet, engagement with and access to support became more difficult and inequalities were further amplified. The time lost within the schooling system will in some cases be difficult to make up and leave those already experiencing disadvantages continuously restricted (Burgess and Sievertsen 2020; Major et al. 2020).

What we have seen during this period is an amplification of longer-term trends, with increased divergence between those succeeding and others struggling. The differences that have emerged out of the actions taken to ameliorate the pandemic—lockdowns, travel restrictions, working from home and so on—have not themselves instigated new trends but have amplified those already present, although until now less visible. The increased reliance on food banks (Power et al. 2020), the failure of shops and business, and the cementing of the online into the everyday all point to the acceleration of some serious economic restructuring. In the residential domain, there are also signs that those who can move to more spacious surroundings are leaving the cities. This could be the start of a long-term trend reversing the recent decades of exclusionary inner-city developments and super gentrifications. It is not, however, the death of the city. Urban areas are likely to remain key locations for the super-rich and the well-connected (Atkinson 2020). As archivist Euan Roger (2020) highlights, the Plague in Tudor London resulted in similar, albeit short-term, tendencies. The realization and progression of existing trends and the real consequences of life with limited resources along with the reliance of modern Western society on (key) workers in precarious employment conditions may—we hope—provide the impetus to reconsider the social relations across society, as the well-being of one group depends on the well-being of all the others.

## References

Appiah, Kwame Anthony. 2018. "The Myth of Meritocracy: Who Really Gets What They Deserve?" *The Guardian*, 19 October.

Ashmore, John. 2017. "Norman Tebbit Does Not Like Being Told to Get on His Bike." *Total Politics*, 22 February.

Atkinson, Rowland. 2020. *Alpha City: How London Was Captured by the Super-Rich*. London: Verso.

Bambra, Clare, Paul Norman and Niall Philip Alan Sean Johnson. 2020. "Visualising Regional Inequalities in the 1918 Spanish Flu Pandemic in England and Wales." *Environment and Planning A: Economy and Space*, December: 1–5.

Blanden, Jo, Paul Gregg and Stephen Machin. 2005. "Intergenerational Mobility in Europe and North America." *Report Supported by the Sutton Trust*. London: Centre for Economic Performance, LSE.

Breen, Richard. 2004. *Social Mobility in Europe*. Oxford: Oxford University Press.

Brush, Lisa D. 2011. *Poverty, Battered Women and Work in US Public Policy*. Oxford: Oxford University Press.

Burgess, Simon and Hans Henrik Sievertsen. 2020. *Schools, Skills, and Learning: The Impact of COVID-19 on Education*. London: Vox, CEPR Policy Portal.

Cameron, David. 2015. "Speech on Opportunity by then Prime Minister David Cameron." *Transcript*, 22 June 2015. https://www.gov.uk/government/speeches/pm-speech-on-opportunity

Cantle, Ted. 2001. *Community Cohesion: A Report of the Independent Review Team*. London: Home Office.

Casey, Louise. 2016. *The Casey Review: A Review into Opportunity and Integration*. London: Department for Communities and Local Government.

Catney, Gemma. 2016. "Exploring a Decade of Small Area Ethnic (De-)Segregation in England and Wales." *Urban Studies*, 53(8): 1691–1709.

Coulter, Rory. 2016. "Parental Background and Housing Outcomes in Young Adulthood." *Housing Studies*, 33(2): 201–233.

de Vuijst, Elise, Maarten van Ham and Reinout Kleinhans. 2017. "The Moderating Effect of Higher Education on the Intergenerational Transmission of Residing in Poverty Neighbourhoods." *Environment and Planning A*, 49(9): 2135–2154.

Dean, Nema and Gwilym Pryce. 2017. "Is the Housing Market Blind to Religion? A Perceived Substitutability Approach to Homophily and Social Integration." *Urban Studies*, 54(13): 3058–3070.

Dorling, Danny. 2014. *Inequality and the 1%*. London: Verso.

Ermisch, John and Brendan Halpin. 2004. "Home Ownership and Social Inequality in Britain." In *Home Ownership and Social Inequality in Comparative Perspective*, edited by Karin Kurz and Hans-Peter Blossfeld, 255–280. Stanford: Stanford University Press.

Esping-Andersen, Gøsta. 1990. *The Three Worlds of Welfare Capitalism*. Cambridge: Polity.

Esping-Andersen, Gøsta (ed.). 1993. *Changing Classes: Stratification and Mobility in Post-Industrial Societies*. London: Sage.

Forrest, Ray and Yosuke Hirayama. 2009. "The Uneven Impact of Neoliberalism on Housing Opportunities." *International Journal of Urban and Regional Research*, 33(4): 998–1013.

Fraser, Nancy. 2013. "How Feminism Became Capitalism's Handmaiden—and How to Reclaim It." *The Guardian*, 14 October.

Friedman, Sam and Daniel Laurison. 2019. *The Class Ceiling: Why It Pays to be Privileged*. Bristol: Policy Press.

Galster, George and Patrick Sharkey. 2017. "Spatial Foundations of Inequality: A Conceptual Model and Empirical Overview." *RSF: The Russell Sage Foundation Journal of the Social Sciences*, 3(2): 1–33.

Galster, George and Terje Wessel. 2019. "Reproduction of Social Inequality through Housing: A Three-Generational Study from Norway." *Social Science Research*, 78: 119–136.

Glass, Thomas A. and Usama Bilal. 2016. "Are Neighborhoods Causal? Complications Arising from the 'Stickiness' of ZNA." *Social Science & Medicine*, 166: 244–253.

Green, Mark A., Clare R. Evans and S. V. Subramanian. 2017. "Can Intersectionality Theory Enrich Population Health Research?" *Social Science & Medicine*, 178: 214–216.

Hamnett, Chris. 1994. "Social Polarization in Global Cities: Theory and Evidence." *Urban Studies*, 31: 401–425.

Hamnett, Chris. 1996. "Social Polarization, Economic Restructuring and Welfare State Regimes." *Urban Studies*, 8: 1407–1430.

Harris, Richard. 2017. "Measuring the Scales of Segregation: Looking at the Residential Separation of White British and Other School Children in England Using a Multilevel Index of Dissimilarity." *Transactions of the Institute of British Geographers*, 42(3): 432–444.

Hedman, Lina and Maarten van Ham. 2012. "Understanding Neighbourhood Effects: Selection Bias and Residential Mobility." In *Neighbourhood Effects Research: New Perspectives*, edited by Maarten van Ham, David Manley, Nick Bailey, Ludi Simpson and Duncan Maclennan, 79–99. Dordrecht: Springer.

Holmes, Craig and Ken Mayhew. 2015. "Have UK Earnings Distributions Polarised?" *INET Oxford Working Paper No. 2015-02*. Oxford: Institute for New Economic Thinking, Oxford University.

Jones, Kelvyn, Ron Johnston, James Forrest, Christopher Charlton and David Manley. 2018. "Ethnic and Class Residential Segregation: Exploring Their Intersection—a Multilevel Analysis of Ancestry and Occupational Class in Sydney." *Urban Studies*, 55(6): 1163–1184.

Kain, John F. 1968. "Housing Segregation, Negro Employment, and Metropolitan Decentralization." *Quarterly Journal of Economics*, 82(1): 175–197.

Kukk, Kristiina, Maarten van Ham and Tiit Tammaru. 2019. "EthniCity of Leisure: A Domains Approach to Ethnic Integration during Free Time Activities." *Tijdschrift Voor Economische en Sociale Geografie*, 110(3): 289–302.

Lamont, Michèle, Stefan Beljean and Matthew Clair. 2014. "What Is Missing? Cultural Processes and Causal Pathways to Inequality." *Socio-Economic Review*, 12(3): 573–608.

Logan, John R. 1978. "Growth, Politics and the Stratification of Places." *American Journal of Sociology*, 84(2): 404–416.

MacLeavy, Julie. 2011. "A 'New Politics' of Austerity, Workfare and Gender? The UK Coalition Government's Welfare Reform Proposals." *Cambridge Journal of Regions, Economy and Society*, 4(3): 355–367.

MacLeavy, Julie and David Manley. 2018. "(Re)discovering the Lost Middle: Intergenerational Inheritances and Economic Inequality in Urban and Regional Research." *Regional Studies*, 52(10): 1435–1446.

Major, Lee Elliot, Andrew Eyles and Stephen Machin. 2020. "Generation COVID: Emerging Work and Education Inequalities." *Paper No. CEPCOVID-19-011*. London: Centre for Economic Performance, LSE.

Manley, David and Ron Johnston. 2014. "London: A Dividing City, 2001–11?" *City*, 18(6): 633–643.

Manley, David, Kelvyn Jones and Ron Johnston. 2015. "Occupational Segregation in London: A Multilevel Framework for Modelling Segregation." In *Socio-Economic Segregation in European Capital Cities*, edited by Tiit Tammaru, Szymon Marcińczak, Maarten van Ham and Sako Musterd, 54–78. London: Routledge.

Manley, David and Maarten van Ham. 2011. "Choice-Based Letting, Ethnicity and Segregation in England." *Urban Studies*, 48(14): 3125–3143.

Manley, David, Maarten van Ham, Nick Bailey, Ludi Simpson and Duncan Maclennan (eds.). 2013. *Neighbourhood Effects or Neighbourhood Based Problems? A Policy Context*. Dordrecht: Springer.

Manley, David, Maarten van Ham and Lina Hedman. 2020. "Inherited and Spatial Disadvantages: A Longitudinal Study of Early Adult Neighborhood Careers of Siblings." *Annals of the American Association of Geographers*, 110(6): 1670–1689.

McDowell, Linda. 2003. *Redundant Masculinities? Employment Change and White Working Class Youth*. Oxford: Blackwell.

Merry, Michael S., David Manley and Richard Harris. 2016. "Community, Virtue and the White British Poor." *Dialogues in Human Geography*, 6(1): 50–68.

Mikolai, Júlia, Katherine Keenan and Hill Kulu. 2020. "Intersecting Household-Level Health and Socio-Economic Vulnerabilities and the COVID-19 Crisis: An Analysis from the UK." *SSM-Population Health*, 12:100628.

Nieuwenhuis, Jaap, Tiit Tammaru, Maarten van Ham, Lina Hedman and David Manley. 2017. "Does Segregation Reduce Socio-Spatial Mobility? Evidence from Four European Countries with Different Inequality and Segregation Contexts." *IZA Working Paper 2017/10*. Bonn: IZA.

Nunn, Alex, Steve Johnson, Surya Monro, Tim Bickerstaffe and Sarah Kelsey. 2007. "Factors Influencing Social Mobility." *Research Report No. 450*. London: Department for Work and Pensions.

OECD (Organisation for Economic Co-operation and Development). 2015. *In It Together: Why Less Inequality Benefits All*. Paris: OECD.

Ohlsson, Henry, Jesper Roine and Daniel Waldenström. 2009. "Long Run Changes in the Concentration of Wealth: An Overview of Recent Findings." In *Personal Wealth from a Global Perspective*, edited by James B. Davies, 42–63. Oxford: Oxford Scholarship Online.

Onaran, Özlem and Alexander Guschanski. 2016. "Rising Inequality in the UK and the Political Economy of Brexit: Lessons for Policy." *Greenwich Papers in Political Economy 15630*. London: University of Greenwich, Greenwich Political Economy Research Centre.

Piketty, Thomas. 2014. *Capital in the Twenty-First Century*. Harvard: Harvard University Press.

Power, Maddy, Bob Doherty, Katie Pybus and Kate Pickett. 2020. "How COVID-19 Has Exposed Inequalities in the UK Food System: The Case of UK Food and Poverty". *Emerald Open Research*, 2:11.

Rice, Patricia G. and Anthony J. Venables. 2020. "The Persistent Consequences of Adverse Shocks: How the 1970s Shaped UK Regional Inequality." *Oxford Review of Economic Policy*, 37(1): 13–151.

Roger, Euan C. 2020. "'To Be Shut Up': New Evidence for the Development of Quarantine Regulations in Early-Tudor England." *Social History of Medicine*, 33(4): 1077–1096.

Sassen, Saskia. 1990. *The Global City: New York, London, Tokyo* (1st Edition). Princeton: Princeton University Press.

Sassen, Saskia. 2001. *The Global City: New York, London, Tokyo* (2nd Edition). Princeton: Princeton University Press.

Sharkey, Patrick. 2013. *Stuck in Place: Urban Neighborhoods and the End of Progress Toward Racial Equality*. Chicago: University of Chicago Press.

Stiglitz, Joseph E. 2011. "Of the 1%, by the 1%, for the 1%." *Vanity Fair*, 31 March.

Tilly, Charles. 2000. "Relational Studies of Inequality." *Contemporary Sociology*, 29: 782–785.

Trust for London. 2020. *UK Youth Unemployment Rate Continues to Rise; Young Black Men Are Particularly Affected*. London: Trust for London.

Valentine, Gill and Catherine Harris. 2014. "Strivers vs Skivers: Class Prejudice and the Demonisation of Dependency in Everyday Life." *Geoforum*, 53(1): 84–92.

van Ham, Maarten, Lina Hedman, David Manley, Rory Coulter and John Östh. 2014. "Intergenerational Transmission of Neighbourhood Poverty: An Analysis of Neighbourhood Histories of Individuals." *Transactions of the Institute of British Geographers*, 39(3): 402–417.

van Ham, Maarten, David Manley, Nick Bailey, Ludi Simpson and Duncan Maclennan (eds.). 2012. *Neighbourhood Effects Research: New Perspectives*. Dordrecht: Springer.

van Ham, Maarten and Tiit Tammaru. 2016. "New Perspectives on Ethnic Segregation over Time and Space: A Domains Approach." *Urban Geography*, 37(7): 953–962.

van Ham, Maarten, Tiit Tammaru, Elise de Vuijst and Merle Zwiers. 2016. "Spatial Segregation and Socio-Economic Mobility in European Cities." *IZA DP No. 10277*, October. Bonn: IZA Institute of Labor Economics.

van Ham, Maarten, Masaya Uesugi, Tiit Tammaru, David Manley and Heleen Janssen. 2020. "Changing Occupational Structures and Residential Segregation in New York, London and Tokyo." *Nature Human Behaviour*, 4(11): 1124–1134.

Walker, Rosie and Samir Jeraj. 2016. *The Rent Trap*. London: Pluto Press.

Wemrell, Maria, Shai Mulinari and Juan Merlo. 2017. "An Intersectional Approach to Multilevel Analysis of Individual Heterogeneity (MAIH) and Discriminatory Accuracy." *Social Science & Medicine*, 178: 217–219.

Wilson, William Julius. 1987. *The Truly Disadvantaged: The Inner City, the Underclass, and Public Policy*. Chicago: University of Chicago Press.

Wilkinson, Richard and Kate Pickett. 2009. *The Spirit Level: Why Equality Is Better for Everyone*. London: Allen Lane.

Willetts, David. 2011. *The Pinch: How the Baby Boomers Took Their Children's Future—And Why They Should Give It Back*. London: Atlantic Books.

Zwiers, Merle, Maarten van Ham and David Manley. 2018. "Trajectories of Ethnic Neighbourhood Change: Spatial Patterns of Increasing Ethnic Diversity." *Population, Space and Place*, 24(2): 1–11.

# Chapter 4

## KEEP IT IN THE FAMILY

### INEQUALITY IN ACCESS TO CAPITAL ON WALL STREET[1]

Megan Tobias Neely

## *Introduction*

Wall Street elites' economic and political might allows them to hoard access to resources, protect their interests and drive top incomes ever further upward (Lin and Neely 2020; Tomaskovic-Devey and Lin 2011). This is no more evident than in the enormous payouts in the hedge fund industry. Hedge fund moguls may take home over USD 1 billion in any given year, and the threshold for the 25 highest-paid hedge fund managers is USD 225 million (Moyer 2018; Picker and Faber 2019). Portfolio managers at established hedge funds garner average compensations of USD 2.4 million, and analysts, a junior position, collect nearly USD 680,000 on average (Institutional Investor 2019). For reference, the top 1 percent of US *households* earned an average of USD 845,000 in total annual income (Yavorsky et al. 2019).

Hedge funds reflect the new class of salaried top earners that Thomas Piketty (2014) coined the "working rich" and thus, as a case, capture the consequences for inequality when privately owned capital engenders patrimonialism (Neely 2018), a system of inherited advantage among men (Adams 2007). Scholars have identified how financial elites form close networks (Godechot 2016), navigate tumultuous careers (Ho 2009), preserve the fortunes of the global rich (Harrington 2016) and mediate gendered global capital flows (Hoang 2020). Less examined are the everyday practices that concentrate capital among Wall Street's working rich and how these widen the divide between the haves and the have-nots.

1. I thank the editors Katja Hujo and Maggie Carter, as well as Kate Henley Averett, Shelley Correll, Alison Dahl Crossley, James Galbraith, Jennifer Glass, Ken-Ho Lin, Shamus Khan, Michela Musto, David Pedulla, Cecilia Ridgeway, Sharmila Rudrappa, Katherine Sobering and Christine Williams for their thoughtful comments on previous versions of this chapter. "Keep It in the Family: Inequality in Access to Capital on Wall Street" is adapted from Megan Tobias Neely, "Reaching the Top" in *Hedged Out: Inequality and Insecurity on Wall Street,* 178–201. Berkeley, CA: University of California Press, 2022.

A key to understanding the outcomes of extreme financial power and economic inequality lies in the work of the so-called winners of inequality. Hedge fund founders are a case of the working rich who have benefited from rising inequality. How do these founders launch firms that can net profits in the millions and billions? Moreover, what do the accounts of hedge fund founders tell us about how elites reproduce inequality?

I investigate the resources that hedge fund founders draw on to access capital from elite networks. Starting a hedge fund requires considerable resources afforded by social networks, which is also the case for other small businesses, entrepreneurial endeavors and family enterprises (Bessière 2014; Lane 2011; Viscelli 2016). In this context, however, the entrepreneurial risks people take provide them with even larger sums of money made possible by elite networks. The enormous scale amplifies the potential payoffs and the founder's ability to pass along wealth. Thus, the founder becomes a patron in a gendered, racialized and classed system that underpins the industry and its outsized incomes (Neely 2018). But income inequality isn't the only social problem at hand. It is a product of systemic inequality that compounds over time, as the beneficiaries concentrate their power and resources from one generation to the next.

I interviewed 48 industry insiders and observed 13 workplaces and 22 industry events such as conferences, panels and social hours. Data collection took place over six years, from 2013 to 2019, in New York, Texas and California, which have the highest concentration of hedge funds in the United States (Preqin 2019). In this chapter, I focus on the 17 people who founded a hedge fund (Table 4.1), although I also draw on other people I interviewed and spoke to at events. Of the 17, 11 people

**Table 4.1** List of founder interviewees

| Name | Age | Gender | Race/Ethnicity | Education | Founder role |
|------|-----|--------|----------------|-----------|--------------|
| Albert | 46 | Man | White | PhD | Chief investment officer |
| Brian | 54 | Man | White | MBA | Chief investment officer |
| Cynthia | 59 | Woman | White | BA | Chief operating officer |
| Deborah | 53 | Woman | White | PhD | Chief investment officer |
| Diane | 53 | Woman | White | BA | Chief investment officer |
| Farrah | 48 | Woman | Middle Eastern American | BS | Chief operating officer |
| Jamie | 33 | Man | Multiracial | JD | Chief investment officer |
| Jeffrey | 52 | Man | White | BA/BS | Chief investment officer |
| Jerry | 26 | Man | Latinx | BS | Chief investment officer |
| Justin | 47 | Man | White | MBA | Chief investment officer |
| Ken | 49 | Man | White | BA/BA | Chief investment officer |
| Linda | 39 | Woman | Asian American | BA | Chief operating officer |
| Margaret | 29 | Woman | Asian American | BS | Founding partner, investments |
| Scott | 44 | Man | White | JD | Chief operating officer |
| Sharon | 44 | Woman | White | MBA | Chief operating officer |
| Vincent | 54 | Man | White | JD | Chief investment officer |
| Wayne | 48 | Man | Asian American | PhD | Chief investment officer |

served as the primary investment decision maker (chief investment officer)—the most powerful position—at their respective hedge fund: Albert, Brian, Jamie, Jeffrey, Jerry, Justin, Ken, Vincent, Wayne, Diane and Deborah. Only the latter two were women. The remaining six founders, who cofounded the firms, were head of operations and business development: Cynthia, Farrah, Margaret, Sharon, Linda and Scott, the only man. Eleven founders were white and 10 were men. I overrepresented for women and racial minority men, who combined account for leaders in firms that manage only 3 percent of hedge fund assets (Barclays Global 2011; Kruppa 2018).

## Social Inequality in Access to Capital

In 2016, 27 million people in the United States founded a new business, but it was on an uneven field (Cheng 2018; Lange et al. 2017). For instance, while women own four out of every 10 US businesses, men are more likely to start the businesses that garner big, private investments. Women, penalized by the gender biases of investors and their networks, instead tend to rely on small business loans (with their more stringent requirements), and their entrepreneurial endeavors are accordingly smaller and less profitable over time (Ewens and Townsend 2020; Kanze et al. 2018; Settembre 2019; Thébaud 2015).

Scholars have shown, time and again, how deeply held and socially constructed status beliefs cast men, particularly white class-advantaged men, as better entrepreneurs and more worthy of funding (stereotypes that are heightened in times of uncertainty like the Great Recession, when trust is paramount) (Bielby 2012; Lyons-Padilla et al. 2019; Thébaud 2015; Thébaud and Sharkey 2016). For example, in experimental studies, women, Sarah Thébaud (2015) establishes, are seen instead as relatively less capable, their businesses less viable, while others point out that, in finance specifically, asset allocators consistently hold Black fund managers, even those with strong performance records, to a higher standard than their white peers when making their investment decisions (Lyons-Padilla et al. 2019). Thus, gender, race and social class play a crucial role when it comes to who is recognized as an entrepreneur and how they obtain financing (Knight 2006; Wingfield and Taylor 2016).

Overall, entrepreneurs who receive funding are more likely to be white men from higher-income families, whose upbringing has afforded them a consistent safety net and therefore the ability to engage in riskier endeavors (Levine and Rubinstein 2017). In fact, they report having histories of engaging in disruptive, illicit activities as teens but also having higher self-esteem than others. By adulthood, it appears these entrepreneurs feel more comfortable taking the professional risk of launching a business venture. Gender dynamics in heterosexual families shape these outcomes, given that sons remain more likely to inherit family businesses than daughters, who are less likely to be recognized for, let alone encouraged in, building their leadership skills (Bessière 2010; Byrne et al. 2019; Lane 2011; Rao 2020). Heterosexual couples tend to maintain breadwinner ideas for men, casting women's entrepreneurial endeavors as sources of supplementary income (Yang and Aldrich 2014). This gendered conditioning continues in workplaces, where white men incur fewer penalties than women and racial minority men for taking risks, and sometimes for failing, too (Fisk and Overton 2019; Nelson 2017; Wingfield 2013).

Moreover, structural inequalities according to race, class and gender both in households and on Wall Street enrich upper-class white men, making them more likely to hold and allocate capital. The top 1 percent of US earners are largely white men, because of durable inequality in the education system and labor market (Connell 1987; Lipsitz 1998; Tilly 1999). Women account for only 16 percent of the 1 percent, despite accounting for nearly half of the labor force (Keister 2014; Piketty et al. 2018; Yavorsky et al. 2019), and the households earning the highest 10 percent are over 90 percent white (Manduca 2018). In the financial sector, white men garner the highest incomes and hold the jobs that allocate capital (Bielby 2012; Lin and Neely 2017; Roth 2006). Since elite networks among the wealthy and on Wall Street tend to be segregated by gender, race and class (McDonald 2011; McGuire 2000, 2002), gender and racial disparities in who holds personal wealth and who allocates institutional capital impact the likelihood that entrepreneurs without race, class and gender privilege can get access to funding.

Consistent with the existing literature, founding a hedge fund requires considerable social, familial and institutional forms of support. The enormous volume of capital in this industry has a snowballing effect that funnels the transfer of wealth into the hands of a small and privileged network. This happens because hedge funds are private financial firms that pool large amounts of money from wealthy investors to invest in the stock market. The average US hedge fund spends USD 75,000 in startup costs and USD 100,000 in operational costs over its first year (Grant Thornton 2014). To become *profitable*, hedge funds require an average of USD 85 million in assets from high-net-worth client investors (GPP and AIMA 2018).

The US Securities and Exchange Commission (SEC) requires that to become accredited client investors in registered hedge funds (all funds with over USD 100 million in assets under advisement are required to register) individuals must meet a financial threshold: a minimum net worth of USD 1 million (excluding their primary residence) and an annual income of USD 200,000 (SEC 2019). Accredited investors are understood as having lower financial risk and warranting less regulatory protection than other investors, and only 13 percent of the US population qualifies (up from 2 percent in the 1980s). This would indicate that very few individuals could invest in hedge funds, but institutional investors—pensions, governments, universities and other nonprofit endowments—comprise over half of client investments, demonstrating how a wide segment of society has a stake in hedge funds (Preqin 2019).

Made possible by financial sector deregulation, the hedge fund industry grew over the past 30 years because it provided investors with a less regulated and more lucrative alternative to investment banking. Traditionally, the wealthy were the primary investor base and still compose 8 percent of investors today

(Preqin 2019). Most operate through "family offices," which are family estate and trust investment funds that fund philanthropic endeavors or establish intergenerational wealth. Since 1990, family offices, as an asset class, have increasingly transferred their money from traditional investments to hedge funds (Mallaby 2011).

For the affluent, of course, accredited client investor status is an upper-class signifier, as visible as a private jet. As Cynthia, a white woman who was chief operating officer for her first hedge fund, launched in the mid-1990s, and a second founded in the early 2000s, said: "By the time 2002–2003 came around, the biggest thing you could do when you went to a cocktail party is say, 'I'm a hedge fund investor,' because that meant you were accredited and had a lot of money."

Not only does starting a hedge fund require access to these elite social worlds, it also requires entrance into and success within a patrimonial system that provides access to tremendous amounts of capital (see also Neely 2018). Max Weber (1922) defined patrimonialism as a gendered and racialized organization of authority in which a leader assumes power through networks based on trust, loyalty and tradition. Most hedge fund founders procure seed money from these wealthy investors, usually through elite networks and professional mentors. The industry terminology for early-stage investments—"seed" funding—even carries a distinctly reproductive connotation, reflecting the transfer of inherited family wealth. For white men, gaining these networks' support involves entering another privileged "family" support system that cushions risk, amplifies financial rewards and ensures successful founders' ability to pass along their own wealth and reputation.

Attracted by the prospect of making higher investment returns and diversifying their portfolios, wealthy investors, elite networks and professional mentors provide founders with the seed money to launch hedge funds. In what follows, I examine three factors that shaped how the founders in my research gained access to such patrimonial capital. The first features a manager providing both training and funding, and the second requires personal ties to wealthy investors. The third is a precipitating crisis, such as a poorly performing investment portfolio or a stock market crash, which provides an opportunity to spin off a business unit into an independent hedge fund. These paths aren't mutually exclusive, and several founders benefited from access to more than one.

## Elite Social Ties

The "friends and family round" of funding is the first phase of starting a hedge fund. White men from elite backgrounds, such as Ken, tended to take their proximity to such affluent, amenable networks for granted, framing this initial round of funding as a time of proving themselves in dogged trading with limited funds until they could amass enough capital to court institutional investors. Echoing other founders' stories, he told me, "It's that critical first USD 20 million then USD 50 million then USD 100 . . . only then you can approach institutional investors.

Before that, I call it 'nickel and diming' it. You have to put your head down. . . . It's a long haul to do it."

Several founders recounted how their families and personal networks provided the initial investments. Despite these wealthy connections, it was common for founders, especially the elite white men, to downplay their access to first-round funding; instead, they emphasized the hard work that had gotten them where they were. Brian, who ran his own hedge fund with USD 200 million under management, started his career in the early 1990s at a large investment firm. He spent a few years there in an introductory analyst job, stock picking, then left to launch his hedge fund. Despite having an MBA from an Ivy League university, Brian described himself at that point as a total industry outsider: "I didn't have the contacts in finance. I didn't know anybody."

Yet Brian's perceived lack of contacts did not prevent him from recruiting investors: he raised USD 2 million in early investments from his personal and professional networks (including, he mentioned, a former girlfriend's father and "connections through my [other] exes") as well as seed funding from his previous boss at the investment firm. His family and religious networks from his childhood community in the South, his graduate school contacts, a colleague's father and his poker friends all invested in Brian's friends and family round, in his view because he was so "trustworthy." After our interview, I read in a news article that Brian's father had an over 20-year tenure as the CEO of a public company and "plenty of friends in the business community" in Brian's hometown. I don't doubt his sincerity, but the fact that Brian perceived his vast wealthy networks as lower status than those in the industry captures how commonly those with race, class and gender privilege take its relative ease for granted.

Other founders were able to tap into transnational flows of capital from personal networks that extended abroad. In the 1990s, Jeffrey cofounded a hedge fund with a client base of affluent European families. He recounted, "My partners were very, very wealthy European families that were plugged into that world." Without his partners' family connections, Jeffrey stressed, "There was no way you or I or anybody was going to pick up the phone and [just] call these families." He referred to using the "network effect" to access these ultra-high-net-worth investors but consistent with how whiteness is often left unmarked, didn't mention they were white families, a detail that I verified through additional research into his firm.

Funding from a wealthy family provided Sharon, who is white, her first opportunity to start a hedge fund in the 1990s. At first, she and two colleagues— one a well-known portfolio manager with connections—invested money for a large family office. Then, the hedge fund built a track record and recruited other investors. Sharon recounted: "We went to large institutions, we went to consultants, went to other families and foundations." Sharon attributed their ability to raise funds to networking: "If you come out of the institutional business, you understand the process of who are the gatekeepers and who are the direct buyers, so we just used our Rolodexes and started calling . . . we would get on panels. That's how you build your business." In another moment during Sharon's account, she shared a time earlier in her career when she was building that Rolodex of social capital and her boss denied her a client account, because the client did not like "women" or "Jews." She recounted how he said to her, "I don't think you should cover them. I don't think it's a good mix." The experiences of Sharon and other interviewees reveal how race, class and gender structure family and institutional networks.

In several cases, racial minority men and women demonstrated how access to wealthy networks abroad could counteract the dominant racial hierarchies within US financial services. Jerry, who is Mexican American, provided an exceptional case that counters the norm of affluent white networks. Jerry founded a hedge fund using skills he developed at an investment bank to grow his inheritance from his father. Jerry stressed the importance of his access to foreign assets, specifically through family ties on both sides of the US–Mexico border. Jerry said he took a cautious approach to money management and market analysis, because his client investors—whom he called his "partners"—were from his family's social networks. He felt both a personal and professional responsibility to do well.

Eileen, too, had international networks to thank for her hedge fund's capital base. At one investment conference, I met Eileen, who is Chinese and ran her own hedge fund out of New York and Shanghai, dividing her time between locations. After graduating with an MBA from an Ivy League school, she began her career in investment banking and then specialized in Chinese equities at several hedge funds. Over the past decade, Chinese markets had opened up to foreign investors, which she called a tremendous opportunity. But, Eileen said, US investors were reluctant to invest in Chinese stocks and bonds because of the perceived lack of transparency: "There are corporate governance issues and fraudulent companies coming out of China, which leads all investors to [either] assume all Chinese companies are fraudulent, or trust them all because they have no benchmarks for evaluating corporate governance." Eileen's extensive networks with Chinese executives and government officials gave her insight into investment opportunities and enabled her to assuage xenophobic fears of US investors and overcome their reticence to invest in foreign funds.

Although whiteness is associated with the dominant category of elites on Wall Street specifically, people of color with elite networks that extend abroad show how foreign investors can help to challenge white supremacy in finance. Such transnational elites capture the increasing global impact of financial investors in places like China, Hong Kong and Singapore, as Kimberly Hoang's (2015, 2018) research demonstrates. The United States remains the center of the hedge fund industry, managing three-fourths of assets under management worldwide (Preqin 2019), but the funds' investors are increasingly global. In Asia today, high-net-worth individuals have double the wealth claimed by high-net-worth North Americans (PwC 2020). The association with whiteness among US financial elites may become more tenuous, even disappear, in coming years.

While in some cases people who are racial minorities profited from their access to wealthy transnational networks from places such as Mexico, India and China, it was far more common for founders to describe white-dominated networks. My sample has a lower proportion of white people—11 out of 17 founders (33 out of

48 total interviewees)—than in the industry (Barclays Global 2011; Kruppa 2018). I intentionally oversampled for people of color to understand how race impacts access to capital. Most were from upper-middle-class and upper-class backgrounds. Of the founders of color, only Wayne, Jamie and Farrah had a middle- or working-class upbringing. Drawing from the broader group of people whom I encountered during fieldwork, these founders did not represent the norm.

While some interviewees of color benefited from wealthy social connections abroad, others identified access to rich networks as a major barrier to advancing in the industry. Matthew, who wasn't among the founders in my sample but was one of the more senior Black men I met, gave the example of two people—one white and one Black—with the same idea for a hedge fund. Matthew said: "One of them is going to have access to people with capital. The other will not. And that's the difference between who can start a hedge fund and who can't. I think it flows from there. It's access to capital."

Matthew and the other Black men I met in hedge funds did eventually leave their firms, but as consultants or contractors—not to start their own funds. Matthew said his trading style had become obsolete, yet I couldn't help but wonder if his path would have been different if he were white. Matthew's account supports previous research that documents how Black financial professionals struggle to access white wealth. In a study of a performance-based pay system, William Bielby (2012) found that Black financial advisers earned one-third to 40 percent less than their white colleagues. These gaps were, in part, attributed to Black workers' difficulty in generating commissions from white households, especially since personal referrals and social networks were a key mechanism in building a client base early on, and the gaps widened over the course of their careers. Other research identifies how even high-performing Black fund managers are held to a higher standard of "success" than their white counterparts, revealing and resulting in racial biases in asset allocation (Lyons-Padilla et al. 2019). I expect similar dynamics are at work at hedge funds, which require founders to have considerable personal financial capital to sustain themselves through the startup period and access to affluent investor networks that, in the US context, are predominantly white. Because of systemic racism, the amount of domestic wealth available from the networks of nonwhite investors is far lower. Thus, even though upper-class Matthew had vast networks built through his Ivy League education and long years working at elite financial firms, he never seriously considered launching a hedge fund.

The majority of my interviewees had access to elite networks through either their families or universities. Yet Sasha provided one of several exceptions to this rule. A Black woman and first-generation immigrant raised in a working-class family, Sasha said: "I didn't get here because of my networks. I'm from Jamaica. My parents' networks aren't going to help me here." Sasha said she struggled to build networks in this industry, recounting how people rarely responded to her emails after networking events. She perceived the networks that were more accessible to her—often through gender- and race-based professional associations—as deemed to be of less value in the industry. Unlike the majority of my interviewees who attended elite universities, Sasha got her MBA at a state school: "Not everybody can go and pay fifty thousand a year." A headhunter recruited her to work as an accountant in the back office, a less prestigious and lower-paying department, at a hedge fund. Later, she made her way into a higher-paying job in client services. Sasha perceived her lack of access to affluent family and school networks as a primary barrier to her advancement that made it unlikely for her to become a hedge fund founder.

Some founders lacking class-privileged backgrounds relied on financial support from spouses. Justin's wife's income and benefits from a well-paid corporate job enabled him to take the risk of starting a hedge fund. Similarly, Wayne timed his departure from a stable job at an investment firm for when his wife's benefits started at her job. Jamie also said his wife's financial support allowed him to start a hedge fund. While both Justin and Wayne raised investor funds through their professional networks in financial services, Jamie worked in the nonfinancial corporate sector before starting a hedge fund. Jamie said his middle-class upbringing and nonelite education did not provide opportunities to find investors, unlike founders who rely on social ties to elite networks.

Whether through professional or personal ties, access to wealthy networks and personal capital are necessary for launching a hedge fund. Initial investors are often located through familial, racial, ethnic and religious networks, which reflect patrimonial structures enabled by trust networks and a shared sense of loyalty among families, friends and colleagues. These patrimonial structures are predominantly organized around gendered and racialized relationships such that the nonwhite men as well as women founders are relatively rare among hedge funds.

### Cultivated Firms

Hedge fund founders provide valuable forms of mentorship, training and seed funding to a select group of trustworthy, loyal protégés. Should a protégé go on to start their own hedge fund, the apprentice–master relationship may lead to the transfer of large sums of seed money, cementing the familial—generally patrilineal and racialized—relationship while allowing the original founder to diversify investments and increase profits. A hedge fund founder may even seed a lineage of affiliated firms guided by shared investment principles and professional guidance, as the Tiger Cub firms evidence so clearly (see later). Because another hedge fund seeds the firm and grooms its founder, I call these "cultivated firms."

At age 18, Ken, introduced earlier, started his first hedge fund. White and class-privileged, he told me that gathering seed funding was quite organic and spontaneous, as though the opportunity arose through sheer good luck, though his initial pool of USD 200,000 included USD 25,000 from each of several of his father's friends, an unspecified amount from his father (the dean of a business school who ran a hedge fund on the side) and USD 10,000 each from his mother and grandparents. It was too little money for him to need to register his hedge fund with the SEC, but it grew as he set a track record. By his early 20s, Ken had been featured in the *Wall Street Journal*, which called him the leading fund in his strategy and printed his phone number. Soon it was "ringing off the hook" and he had tens of millions in assets under management. When he hit 25 employees, Ken said, "Raising the capital was difficult," so he hired outside marketers to reach the "big investors"—large institutional investors.

The strategy the *Wall Street Journal* referred to was once a niche investment path that Ken's father had developed. "My dad just had a philosophy that he came up with," Ken remembered. Today, Ken and his father's practice is a mainstream investing strategy, but they are known as the progenitors. Ken received other mentorship from his father's friends and contacts, including several traders—all white men—who would become hedge fund billionaires. Ticking off names I regularly see in *Forbes* and *New York Times* headlines, Ken told me, "I had the opportunity to invest with some of the greatest commodities traders and meet them and learn the industry professionalism from them." Without seeming self-conscious, he mentioned, "I met them when I was very young, one after the other." As a young teenager, Ken had observed well-established traders as they worked, asked them for tips and read the books they suggested. Back in the 1980s, he recalled, a trader who is now a billionaire had just USD 10 million under management and would allow a rapt Ken to watch him in action, "trading and doing all this crazy yelling while he's doing stuff in the markets." Ken's narrative started out suggesting that he had almost stumbled into becoming a hedge fund founder, yet even at age 18 he had all the hallmarks of a typical founder: elite upper-class white networks saturated with money and trust, and experienced mentors eager to train him in an investment tradition. His apparently exceptional backstory masks what was actually a quite standard cultivated firm.

Owing to the large sums of money involved, extraordinarily successful hedge fund managers who were nearing retirement groomed their sons to take on the family business. Examples include top hedge fund managers such as George Soros, Warren Buffet and Andrew Marks. Although there are many cases of founders, like Ken's father, who either invest in or pass down their businesses to a son (Copeland 2014), I found only one anecdotal record of this being done for a daughter (Kruppa 2018). Justin, a white man, provides insight into why. He has two adult daughters, one of whom works in finance, yet expressed ambivalence about them following his path: "I don't know [if I want them to], because it's very much an old boys' industry. Sooner than later I would want them to get out on their own so that they don't have a boss. Then they don't have to get along with anyone, and they are not in a subservient position, except with investors." Justin apparently didn't consider training his daughters to take over *his* firm, which would have obviated his concerns about them working for men in the industry.

Most protégés get access to mentorship, training and networks on the job, rather than through their own family. Additionally, because a small asset base better sustains some investment strategies, larger hedge funds can gain new opportunities for revenue generation by seeding small firms. The most notorious example is Julian Robertson of Tiger Management, the "Wizard of Wall Street," who has seeded an estimated 120 affiliated, protégé-founded firms known as the Tiger

Cubs and Grand Cubs (Altshuller et al. 2014). The total assets under management of just the 62 Cub firms registered with the SEC is over USD 250 billion (implying that the Tiger family's wealth is substantially larger). That these firms feature similar investment philosophies, strategies and performance outcomes suggests that Robertson groomed their founders to perform according to his model. In other words, they feature a shared investment tradition. Since 2006, Robertson's protégés have outperformed the Standard & Poor's 1500 Index by 53.9 percent, bolstering Robertson's wealth and status beyond his own firm.

While I did not interview the founders of the Tiger Cub firms, I spoke with several hedge fund founders who received partial or full seed funding from a previous hedge fund boss, past colleague or a family member who worked in the industry. The hedge fund where Linda worked shut down when the founder transitioned to managing his own wealth, but not before investing some USD 50 million in seed money to support his employees' launch of their own new firm. Linda recounted that the new cofounders were "a team that was contributing a lot to the performance and kind of holding the [previous] firm up and together, so it made more sense, and the owner was ready to move on to his next chapter." In addition, she said, "some of the old investors from the prior firm came over as well." When we met, a few years later, Linda's new firm managed a couple of billion in assets—the support from their previous firm's founder, in financial and social capital, had enabled the firm to fundraise successfully.

As with Julian Robertson's Tiger Cubs, the previous firm's founder trusted Linda and her cofounders to invest his money because he had trained them into a particular investment tradition and business model that he endorsed. Of the transition, Linda said: "He supported us. It was a very unique transition because we took his people, the firm, the employees, as well as he gave us the equipment, the computers, even the leases, we took over. Some of the technology contracts . . . and so we were able to work together immediately." Building the firm out of an established model helped to ensure it ran smoothly. Linda identified the human and social capital of the employees as an important part of what made the transition feasible.

Farrah, who is of Middle Eastern descent and one of the hedge fund cofounders who went on to hold a client-services role at her fund, also partnered with colleagues from a previous hedge fund and raised funds from investors out of the client base she had built there and throughout her career. The fact that her cofounder, the portfolio manager, had a strong reputation and track record that investors trusted eased the path to Farrah convincing people to provide early-stage funding. Interestingly, the dynamic between Farrah and her partner matched the common gendered division of labor at hedge funds: women are tracked into client-facing positions while men work as investment decision makers, and this may indicate that it's easier for a woman to become a hedge fund founder if she is willing to serve in those client-services roles. That said, Farrah's career took a major hit on account of this decision when her fund eventually went under.

After five years, the fund's performance dropped and the firm went under. That was when Farrah saw the consequences of the gendered division of labor, in which she, a founder, took a feminized, role in client services. While her colleagues on the investment management side of the business could go on to manage their own money, Farrah struggled to find a comparable position at another firm. First, she settled for a less senior position at another smaller firm, then, after the 2008 financial crisis, cycled through a series of short-term jobs in small, struggling firms. Farrah lamented how if she had Ivy League credentials or wealthy family ties, she would be able to find a better job. Instead, Farrah had grown up in the South and, the first in her family to graduate from college, attended a local state school. Without an elite background, Farrah took a less senior role at an investment bank, with a salary half what she'd previously commanded. When I asked if she would start a hedge fund again, she responded, "No. Would I go to a startup? Never." Because she lacked an elite background and held roles gender-typed as feminine that did not afford her the money or training to manage her own investments, Farrah did not have the same long-term success as her former hedge fund partners.

Hedge funds rely on an apprenticeship style of education, allowing employees to build strong bonds with one another and their manager. This system of education presents opportunities to venture out and start one's own firm, especially when a former employer provides the seed funding. When employees are groomed into an investment tradition, over time they receive access to training and investor funds that may enable them to start their own hedge funds. Yet for those more often hedged out—in Farrah's case a racial minority woman in a client-services rather than a portfolio manager position—attaining and losing founder status can seem like proof that elite white men are better suited to those top roles.

### Financial Distress

A third context in which founders typically launch their own firms is a counterintuitive one: financial distress at their previous firm, as in the event of a financial crisis. For potential founders, leveraging a crisis involves reducing the distressed firm's operating load by departing and taking some or all of the business unit and customer base to start a new fund. It can be quite seamless, because the new founder has access to the previous firm's wealthy investors in order to recruit new client investors.

Vincent told me that founding his own hedge fund "was very opportunistic." He was working at a large investment bank, where he had created a new business unit: "I started in this firm and within 18 months, I was running a desk [a business unit]. So, it was a rapid ascent. I started something they didn't have. I used my legal skills to expand on a concept." This novel investment business within the investment bank would become the foundation for his hedge fund when the opportunity arose with the Russian debt crisis in 1998. When management asked for voluntary resignations, Vincent "took a long shot and said, 'Would you be upset if I took this team out and created my own thing? I'll take care of all the clients. You'll never have a client issue. Clients love me. They'll travel.'" The bank didn't formally approve Vincent's plan, demurring "'Well, we can't say yes.' But they winked or blinked or whatever and I did it." Looking the other way freed the investment bank from a source of financial distress, and it allowed Vincent to move his business unit "out of the investment bank, joined with a competitor, made a twice as large-sized firm." Over an eight-year period, Vincent's firm grew from USD 50 billion to over USD 200 billion in assets.

The financial crisis of 2008 provided many such founding opportunities. Two people in my study followed Vincent's path, with Deborah and Albert taking business platforms they ran at investment banks and spinning them off into independent hedge funds. A white woman, Deborah started her own hedge fund after decades of experience on Wall Street. After completing a doctorate in statistics at the University of Chicago, Deborah moved to New York: "At that point in the mid-'80s, there were a lot of jobs available. Everyone was looking for people with my skillset as well as many other skillsets. It was just a boom time in the business." She started in research and modeling, which diverted her from the more popular trading path but prepared her for portfolio management. After a decade, she moved into and eventually ran the proprietary trading unit, overseeing the firm's money rather than investors' money. This appointment, she recalled, was "meant to be an honor [the firm] gave people to prepare them to go to hedge funds." In 2008, the bank was forced to downsize, and Deborah was, in fact, ready to start a hedge fund:

> Luckily at [the investment bank], it was a very entrepreneurial, aggressive place, so I had been basically running my own business for a long time. Not just trading, but actually managing the expense side of the equation as well and hiring, so it wasn't that huge of a step to go to a hedge fund, but it's all incremental. It's kind of all an evolution of one's career.

Like Vincent, Deborah had first become an internal entrepreneur, building a business unit, then spun off the business as a separate hedge fund.

Feeling frustrated with the political dynamics of investment banking, Albert decided to capitalize on the skill set he had developed by leading business units using hedge fund strategies within investment banks as well as the regulatory changes that came after the financial crisis. The "permanent reduction in risk capital on the part of the banks," he explained, opened up investment opportunities he felt ready to grasp. "In my mind, if there was ever a time to really take the gamble and see if you could build something by yourself, then it was then." Whereas the financial crisis provided an opportunity for Vincent and Deborah to leave firms in distress, Albert left to capitalize on investments related to the banks' exposure to risky capital and those underlying risky assets.

For founders like these, financial distress and crisis provided an opportunity to start their own firms. However, these openings may have set them off on a less secure path, especially in the case of Deborah and Albert who launched during a recession. In general, women and racial minority men are more likely to assume leadership positions in organizations facing instability or crisis, which often sets them up to fail—a phenomenon called the "glass cliff" (Cook and Glass 2013; Ryan and Haslam 2007). While I did not interview enough founders to discern whether people of color and white women were more likely to stay at failing companies but assume leadership roles or to leave to start their own hedge funds, it is certain that the founder's route is especially challenging for those without access to wealthy networks.

## Conclusion

Hedge fund founders often attribute their success to having a high tolerance for risk and strong drive to succeed. Yet I found that success is most closely associated with the social, familial and institutional forms of support typical of America's elite upper class, particularly white-dominant elite networks. Three influential factors shaped how the hedge fund founders that I interviewed gained access to investment capital: having personal ties to wealthy investors, having a founder at a previous employer who provides training and funding, and/or having an opportunity arise from a previous employer's financial distress. The importance of familial and family-like ties that provide resources, training and other forms of support categorizes these firms as "cultivated firms," grown within the patrimonial structure of high finance and furthering the transfer of US wealth among relatively closed networks.

Put differently, the paths that hedge fund founders take to entrepreneurship reflect the privileges more often afforded to elite white men by the gatekeepers who recruit and reward the people who "look like them." Whether it be through grooming practices, friends and family money or a wife's support, upper-class white men more easily accessed the resources, support and opportunities that enabled them to launch their own firms in the top position of chief investment officer.

Not everyone can become a finance capitalist (Collins et al. 2013; Fridman 2017), so what happens to everyone else, especially the have-nots? And what are the costs of finance-driven inequality to society as a whole? Hedge funds make investments that can collapse company share prices, throw entire industries into turmoil and drive down currencies and economies worldwide, as occurred in the economic crises in Asia in the 1990s (Pitluck 2014). Consequently, hedge funds have increased systemic risk and volatility in financial markets (Elyasiani and Mansur 2017), as in the 2008 financial crisis that created instability for populations around the world and devastated the savings of average workers (Grusky et al. 2011; Lewis 2011). More recently, hedge funds profited by betting that the stock market would crash in March 2020 because of the Covid-19 crisis (Neely and Carmichael 2021).

Moreover, hedge fund investors often invest in corporations and put pressure on the executives to restructure their workforces to boost the company's share value. In this way, the work of hedge fund investors has been tied to layoffs and stagnant wages at corporations, a source of the shrinking middle class and impoverished working class (Brav et al. 2015; Jung 2015; Zorn et al. 2006). Hedge fund founders not only make investment decisions that bolster their own coffers, their investments also determine the well-being and livelihoods of workers throughout the class distribution. Thus, hedge funds are a key and understudied piece of how the financial sector has exacerbated inequality since the 1980s by disempowering workers while enriching those at the top.

## *References*

Adams, Julia. 2007. *The Familial State: Ruling Families and Merchant Capitalism in Early Modern Europe*. Ithaca, NY: Cornell University Press.

Altshuller, Stan, Joe Peta, and Christopher Jordan. 2014. "Like Tiger, Like Cub." *Novus Research*.

Barclays Global. 2011. *Affirmative Investing: Women and Minority Owned Hedge Funds*. Boston: Capital Solutions Group.

Bessière, Céline. 2010. *De Génération en génération: Arrangements de famille dans les entreprises viticoles de Cognac*. Paris: Raisons d'agir.

Bessière, Céline. 2014. "Female and Male Domestic Partners in Wine-Grape Farms (Cognac, France): Conjugal Asymmetry and Gender Discrimination in Family Businesses." *The History of the Family*, 19(3): 341–357.

Bielby, William. 2012. "Minority Vulnerability in Privileged Occupations." *The ANNALS of the American Academy of Political and Social Science*, 639(1): 13–32.

Brav, Alon, Wei Jiang and Hyunseob Kim. 2015. "The Real Effects of Hedge Fund Activism: Productivity, Asset Allocation, and Industry Concentration." *The Review of Financial Studies*, 28(10): 2723–2769.

Byrne, Janice, Salma Fattoum and Sarah Thébaud. 2019. "A Suitable Boy? Gendered Roles and Hierarchies in Family Business Succession." *European Management Review*, 16(3): 579–596.

Cheng, Michelle. 2018. "Why Minority Women Now Control Nearly Half of All Women-Run Businesses." *Inc.*, 6 November.

Collins, Randall, Michael Mann and Craig Calhoun. 2013. *Does Capitalism Have a Future?* Oxford: Oxford University Press.

Connell, Raewyn W. 1987. *Gender and Power: Society, the Person, and Sexual Politics*. Stanford, CA: Stanford University Press.

Cook, Alison and Christy Glass. 2013. "Glass Cliffs and Organizational Saviors: Barriers to Minority Leadership in Work Organizations?" *Social Problems*, 60(2): 168–187.

Copeland, Rob. 2014. "Financial Elite's Offspring Start Their Own Hedge Funds." *Wall Street Journal*, 22 September.

Elyasiani, Elyas, and Iqbal Mansur. 2017. "Hedge Fund Return, Volatility Asymmetry, and Systemic Effects: A Higher-Moment Factor-EGARCH Model." *Journal of Financial Stability*, 28(February): 49–65.

Ewens, Michael and Richard R. Townsend. 2020. "Are Early Stage Investors Biased against Women?" *Journal of Financial Economics*, 135(3): 653–677.

Fisk, Susan R. and Jon Overton. 2019. "Who Wants to Lead? Anticipated Gender Discrimination Reduces Women's Leadership Ambitions." *Social Psychology Quarterly*, 82(3): 319–332.

Fridman, Daniel. 2017. *Freedom from Work: Embracing Financial Self-Help in the United States and Argentina*. Stanford, CA: Stanford University Press.

Godechot, Olivier. 2016. *The Working Rich: Wages, Bonuses and Appropriation of Profit in the Financial Industry*. London: Routledge.

GPP (Global Prime Partners) and AIMA (Alternative Investment Management Association). 2018. "Making It Big." *Hedge Fund Manager Survey 2018*. London: AIMA.

Grant Thornton. 2014. "Hedge Funds 101 for Emerging Managers." Grant Thornton LLP.

Grusky, David, Bruce Western and Christopher Wimer. 2011. *The Great Recession*. New York: Russell Sage Foundation.

Harrington, Brooke. 2016. *Capital without Borders: Wealth Managers and the One Percent*. Cambridge, MA: Harvard University Press.

Ho, Karen. 2009. *Liquidated: An Ethnography of Wall Street*. Durham, NC: Duke University Press.

Hoang, Kimberly Kay. 2015. *Dealing in Desire: Asian Ascendancy, Western Decline, and the Hidden Currencies of Global Sex Work*. Berkeley, CA: University of California Press.

Hoang, Kimberly Kay. 2018. "Risky Investments: How Local and Foreign Investors Finesse Corruption-Rife Emerging Markets." *American Sociological Review*, 83(4): 657–685.

Hoang, Kimberly Kay. 2020. "Engendering Global Capital: How Homoerotic Triangles Facilitate Foreign Investments into Risky Markets." *Gender & Society*, 34(4): 547–572.

Institutional Investor. 2019. "All-America Buy-Side Compensation." Institutional Investor LLC.

Jung, Jiwook. 2015. "Shareholder Value and Workforce Downsizing, 1981–2006." *Social Forces*, 93(4): 1335–68.

Kanze, Dana, Laura Huang, Mark A. Conley and E. Tory Higgins. 2018. "We Ask Men to Win and Women Not to Lose: Closing the Gender Gap in Startup Funding." *Academy of Management Journal*, 61(2): 586–614.

Keister, Lisa A. 2014. "The One Percent." *Annual Review of Sociology*, 40(1): 347–367.

Knight, Mélanie. 2006. "The Production of the Female Entrepreneurial Subject: A Space of Exclusion for Women of Color?" *Journal of Women, Politics & Policy*, 27(3–4): 151–159.

Kruppa, Miles. 2018. "The 'David' Problem." *Absolute Return*, 7 September.

Lane, Carrie M. 2011. *A Company of One: Insecurity, Independence, and the New World of White-Collar Unemployment*. Ithaca, NY: Cornell University Press.

Lange, Julian E., Abdul Ali, Candida G. Brush, Andrew C. Corbett, Donna J. Kelley, Phillip H. Kim and Mahdi Majbouri. 2017. *Global Entrepreneurship Monitor: United States Report 2017*. Babson Park, MA: Babson College.

Levine, Ross and Yona Rubinstein. 2017. "Smart and Illicit: Who Becomes an Entrepreneur and Do They Earn More?" *The Quarterly Journal of Economics*, 132(2): 963–1018.

Lewis, Michael. 2011. *The Big Short: Inside the Doomsday Machine*. New York: W. W. Norton & Company.

Lin, Ken-Hou, and Megan Tobias Neely. 2017. "Gender, Parental Status, and the Wage Premium in Finance." *Social Currents*, 4(6): 535–555.

Lin, Ken-Hou and Megan Tobias Neely. 2020. *Divested: Inequality in the Age of Finance*. Oxford: Oxford University Press.

Lipsitz, George. 1998. *The Possessive Investment in Whiteness: How White People Profit from Identity Politics*. Philadelphia: Temple University Press.

Lyons-Padilla, Sarah, Hazel Rose Markus, Ashby Monk, Sid Radhakrishna, Radhika Shah, Norris A. "Daryn" Dodson and Jennifer L. Eberhardt. 2019. "Race Influences

Professional Investors' Financial Judgments." *Proceedings of the National Academy of Sciences*, 116(35): 17225–17230.

Mallaby, Sebastian. 2011. *More Money Than God: Hedge Funds and the Making of a New Elite*. New York: Penguin Books.

Manduca, Robert. 2018. "Income Inequality and the Persistence of Racial Economic Disparities." *Sociological Science*, 5(March): 182–205.

McDonald, Steve. 2011. "What's in the 'Old Boys' Network? Accessing Social Capital in Gendered and Racialized Networks." *Social Networks*, 33(4): 317–330.

McGuire, Gail M. 2000. "Gender, Race, Ethnicity, and Networks: The Factors Affecting the Status of Employees' Network Members." *Work and Occupations*, 27(4): 501–524.

McGuire, Gail M. 2002. "Gender, Race, and the Shadow Structure: A Study of Informal Networks and Inequality in a Work Organization." *Gender & Society*, 16(3): 303–322.

Moyer, Liz. 2018. "Four Hedge Fund Managers Top $1 Billion in Pay." *CNBC*, 30 May.

Neely, Megan Tobias. 2018. "Fit to Be King: How Patrimonialism on Wall Street Leads to Inequality." *Socio-Economic Review*, 16(2): 365–385.

Neely, Megan Tobias, and Donna Carmichael. 2021. "Profiting on Crisis: How Predatory Financial Investors Have Worsened Inequality in the Coronavirus Crisis." *American Behavioral Scientist*, 65(12): 1649–1670.

Nelson, Julie A. 2017. *Gender and Risk-Taking*. New York: Routledge.

Picker, Leslie, and David Faber. 2019. "Hedge Fund Returns in 2018: The Good, the Bad, the Ugly." *CNBC*, 7 January.

Piketty, Thomas. 2014. *Capital in the Twenty-First Century*. Cambridge, MA: Belknap Press.

Piketty, Thomas, Emmanuel Saez and Gabriel Zucman. 2018. "Distributional National Accounts: Methods and Estimates for the United States." *The Quarterly Journal of Economics*, 133(2): 553–609.

Pitluck, Aaron Z. 2014. "Watching Foreigners: How Counterparties Enable Herds, Crowds, and Generate Liquidity in Financial Markets." *Socio-Economic Review*, 12(1): 5–31.

Preqin. 2019. *Global Hedge Fund Report*. New York: Preqin Ltd.

PwC. 2020. *Asset Management 2020: A Brave New World*. London: PwC.

Rao, Aliya Hamid. 2020. *Crunch Time: How Married Couples Confront Unemployment*. Berkeley, CA: University of California Press.

Roth, Louise Marie. 2006. *Selling Women Short: Gender and Money on Wall Street*. Princeton, NJ: Princeton University Press.

Ryan, Michelle K. and S. Alexander Haslam. 2007. "The Glass Cliff: Evidence That Women Are Over-Represented in Precarious Leadership Positions." *British Journal of Management*, 16(2): 81–90.

SEC (US Securities and Exchange Commission). 2019. "Accredited Investors." *Investor Bulletin. Press Release*. Washington, DC: U.S. Securities and Exchange Commission, 31 January.

Settembre, Jeanette. 2019. "Venture Capitalists Still Give Most of Their Money to White Men, Study Finds." *MarketWatch*, 13 February.

Thébaud, Sarah. 2015. "Status Beliefs and the Spirit of Capitalism: Accounting for Gender Biases in Entrepreneurship and Innovation." *Social Forces*, 94(1): 61–86.

Thébaud, Sarah and Amanda J. Sharkey. 2016. "Unequal Hard Times: The Influence of the Great Recession on Gender Bias in Entrepreneurial Financing." *Sociological Science*, 3(January): 1–31.

Tilly, Charles. 1999. *Durable Inequality*. Berkeley, CA: University of California Press.

Tomaskovic-Devey, Donald and Ken-Hou Lin. 2011. "Income Dynamics, Economic Rents, and the Financialization of the U.S. Economy." *American Sociological Review*, 76(4): 538–559.

Viscelli, Steve. 2016. *The Big Rig: Trucking and the Decline of the American Dream.* Berkeley, CA: University of California Press.

Weber, Max. 1922. *The Theory of Social and Economic Organization.* Edited by Talcott Parsons. Mansfield Centre, CT: Martino Fine Books.

Wingfield, Adia Harvey. 2013. *No More Invisible Man: Race and Gender in Men's Work.* Philadelphia: Temple University Press.

Wingfield, Adia Harvey and Taura Taylor. 2016. "Race, Gender, and Class in Entrepreneurship: Intersectional Counterframes and Black Business Owners." *Ethnic and Racial Studies*, 39(9): 1676–1696.

Yang, Tiantian and Howard E. Aldrich. 2014. "Who's the Boss? Explaining Gender Inequality in Entrepreneurial Teams." *American Sociological Review*, 79(2): 303–327.

Yavorsky, Jill, Lisa Keister, Yue Qian and Michael Nau. 2019. "Women in the One Percent: Gender Dynamics in Top Income Positions." *American Sociological Review*, 84(1): 54–81.

Zorn, Dirk, Frank Dobbin, Julian Dierkes and Man-shan Kwok. 2006. "Managing Investors: How Financial Markets Reshaped the American Firm." In *The Sociology of Financial Markets*, edited by K. Knorr-Cetina and A. Preda, 269–289. Oxford: Oxford University Press.

# Chapter 5

## REWIRING THE SOCIAL CONTRACT

### ECONOMIC INCLUSION AND THE GIG ECONOMY IN NIGERIA

Kate Meagher

*Introduction*

The rise of digital employment platforms across the globe has been accompanied by a demand for a "new social contract" suited to the changing nature of work in the twenty-first century. New digital arrangements for linking workers to employers have brought the promise of modernization and expanding job creation, along with the threat of increased precarity of employment as existing systems of labor protection are rendered obsolete. The risks of digital employment are particularly acute for workers in sub-Saharan Africa, who are caught between vast informal economies that employ 77 percent of workers outside agriculture and rising youth unemployment, which is highest among graduates (AfDB/OECD/UNDP 2012; World Bank 2018). Despite Africa's economic resurgence, levels of informal and vulnerable labor are increasing as the paradox of "jobless growth" confronts a demographic tsunami. Over 10 million new workers enter African labor markets each year, while only 3.2 million jobs are created (AfDB 2017). Finding adequate employment for Africa's underemployed masses has become a key security as well as social issue. A 2018 African Economic Outlook (AfDB/OECD/UNDP 2018: xv) report notes that "In the face of rapidly growing populations and heightened risks of social unrest or discontent, jobless growth is the most serious concern for African policy makers."

Digital employment, widely referred to as the gig economy, has been portrayed as the path to a brighter future of work for Africa's marginalized and informal workers (World Bank 2018; Rockefeller Foundation 2014). By connecting marginalized workers with improved technology, resources and markets, digital jobs offer to "bring informal workers out of the shadows and into the mainstream" (Grunewald 2017). The opportunity for rapid generation of modern employment holds great appeal for workers and policy makers alike, and the framing of a new social contract to address the vulnerabilities of widespread informality holds similar political appeal. Can online employment platforms deliver on their promise to create modern, good-quality jobs for Africa's underemployed masses? What kind of social contract is needed to turn potentially precarious employment into decent work, work that is fairly remunerated, guarantees social protection and fundamental rights at work (ILO 1999). Do these changes offer a prospect for the transformation of informal employment into sustainable livelihoods for expanding young populations across the African continent?

Drawing on recent research on digital ride-hailing services in Nigeria, this chapter examines what the gig economy can contribute to the task of decent employment generation in contemporary Africa. A first section considers why the rise of the gig economy has triggered a demand for a new social contract and explores requirements of a social contract that is fit for purpose. A subsequent section examines evidence from digital ride-hailing in Nigeria, offering an assessment of the quality of livelihoods created through new forms of digital employment platforms and the limitations of digital employment in promoting decent work and social stability, particularly in the wake of Covid-19. Evidence from Nigeria informs a consideration of whether the prevailing vision of a new social contract represents a mechanism of economic inclusion or adverse incorporation for informal workers, followed by a reflection on the parameters of a sustainable social contract for gig workers in a post-pandemic world.

## A Social Contract for the Gig Economy

Persistent poverty, jobless growth and expanding informal economies across the developing world have widely been decried as the signs of a broken social contract (Jütting and de Laiglesia 2009; Perry et al. 2007; World Bank 2018). In the face of globalization, rapid technological change and weak institutions, the state has been charged with failing to deliver on the conventional social contract based on stable employment and social welfare provision (Medina et al. 2017; Stanford 2017; UNRISD 2016). Worse still, there is increasing disquiet about the fairness of the prevailing social contract in developing countries, particularly in Africa and South Asia, where the majority have never held a formal job and cannot qualify for social protection. Where precarious employment is the norm rather than the exception, notions of a just social contract are increasingly focused on the need to distribute social benefits more equally rather than protecting a small share of formal jobs in a sea of precarity (Ferguson 2015; Jütting and de Laiglesia 2009; Lund 2009; Neilson and Rossiter 2008; World Bank 2018).

Conversely, digital employment platforms are increasingly celebrated for their ability to expand employment into deprived areas, helping unemployed and underemployed workers leverage access to the formal economy. Known variously as the "on-demand economy," the "gig economy," the "sharing economy" or the "platform economy," digital employment is seen as the key to job creation and growth owing to its ability to link workers to opportunities and shorten periods of unemployment. According to the 2019 World Development Report (World Bank 2018: 3), *The Changing Nature of Work*, the gig economy uses new technology to bring "quality jobs" to millions of people trapped in marginalized informal livelihoods and creates new pathways out of informality. Tens of thousands of digital jobs have been created across Africa by platforms such as Uber, Digital Divide Data and Jumia, which promise higher earnings than many formal sector jobs (Connectivity at the BoP Forum 2017; Hunt and Machingura 2016; World Bank 2018). Gig employment platforms are also known for scaling up quickly owing to the role of financialization in driving rapid investment and innovation in promising digital businesses (Stanford 2017; World Bank 2018). Uber spread to over 80 countries in under a decade, and Alibaba took only two years to reach 1 million users. Graham et al. (2017: 137) contend that many marginalized workers see "outsourced digitally mediated work as a way to transcend some of the constraints of their local labour markets," using new technologies to tap into the global economy.

Proponents of the gig economy emphasize the need for a new social contract appropriate to the more flexible labor needs of digital employment (McKinsey Global Institute 2018; World Bank 2018). The Adecco Group, the world's largest temporary staffing agency, highlights the significant gaps in social protection for gig workers and embraces the call for a twenty-first-century social contract that is "fit for purpose" (Adecco Group 2017). Reaping the benefits of technological change is said to demand a move away from narrow twentieth-century models of social protection to the creation of a new social benefit system extended to all workers regardless of employment status and funded through general taxation (Perry et al. 2007; World Bank 2018). Yet the futuristic aura surrounding the notion of a new social contract has tended to overwhelm more measured assessments of whether the proposed changes actually improve the welfare of marginalized workers. More reflection is needed on what a social contract does and whether the new social contract envisioned for the gig economy offers a more effective means of creating jobs, reducing informality and protecting workers in developing countries.

### What is the purpose of a social contract?

Understanding the potential of a new social contract to improve the lot of informal workers requires a more critical consideration of what the concept means. A number of scholars have shown that there is no single definition of the social contract (Boucher and Kelly 1994; Hickey 2011; Nugent 2010). The term can be used to serve a variety of political purposes, ranging from affirming natural rights, rational bargains to better support the common good or a legitimating device to establish the fairness of a new arrangement (Boucher and Kelly 1994). Both Hickey (2011) and Nugent (2010) make the point that social contracts are not necessarily progressive; they can be elitist bargains to legitimate inequalities. Using examples from Botswana and South Africa, Hickey (2011) argues that social protection measures have been used to support different kinds of social contracts, making side-payments to the excluded without addressing their exclusion or effecting a more generalized redistribution of resources and economic empowerment.

Proponents of a new social contract tend to put forward a rather stylized view of what a social contract entails. The proposed contract for the gig economy focuses only on a dyadic contract between citizens and the state, evaluates distributive "fairness" in terms of inequalities between workers and represents the unraveling of the old social contract as a product of agentless forces of progress. The role of capital is largely airbrushed out of the discussion. The 2019 World Development Report (World Bank 2018: 125) contends that "[a] social contract envisions the state's obligations to citizens and what the state expects in return," and expresses concerns about the "fairness" of a social contract that protects formal work in societies where most work informally. This ignores the underlying meaning of the social contract, which is about supporting the common good and ensuring distributive justice, not just between citizens and the state or between formal and informal workers but between capital and labor. Breman and van der Linden (2014: 934) contend that "the minimum requirement of a social contract is for the state to hold capital accountable for contributing to decent and dignified work for the labouring masses," a position also reflected in the United Nations Research Institute for Social Development 2016 Flagship Report (UNRISD 2016) and the International Labour Organization's (ILO) (2019) Global Commission on the Future of Work report.

In developing countries in particular, the argument that the existing social contract is unfair in places where informality is the norm misrepresents the nature of the developmental social contract. Scully (2016) points out that for workers in the global South, the postindependence social contract was not built around social protection but around the promise of national development from which all would benefit over time (see also Mustapha and Whitfield 2009). Security and economic stability are not viewed as entitlements of citizenship but as future benefits to be attained in the course of national development. In a report on nonstandard employment, the ILO (2016) argues that the standards of formal employment are not irrelevant to countries where precarity is the norm, since such standards are the basis of labor law and underpin the commitment to promoting decent work as the economy develops by resisting tendencies toward labor informalization or jobless growth. The failure to expand decent work despite strong economic growth across much of Africa raises questions about distributive fairness in the growth process, rather than signaling problems of fairness in the allocation of social protection.

The demand for a new social contract calls for closer attention to what went wrong with the old social contract. The contention that the twentieth-century social contract disintegrated in the face of unstoppable processes of globalization and technological change is challenged by Nugent (2010) and others, who highlight the ways in which it was actively dismantled by neoliberal market reforms (Lee and Kofman 2012; Meagher et al. 2016; Mkandawire and Soludo 1999; Stanford 2017). A range of political and economic actors were at work in the processes of rolling back the state, deregulating labor markets and creating systems of outsourcing to evade labor regulations. As Lee and Kofman (2012: 405) put it, "precarity, in short, is not a mechanical and inevitable outcome of an innocent and agentless global process." It is worth considering whether calls for a new social contract are as benevolent as they first appear, given that many of those involved in demolishing the old social contract are central to the call for a new one, including the World Bank, the International Monetary Fund and large corporate interests (Adecco Group 2017; Shafik 2018; World Bank 2018). Questions need to be asked about whether the kind of social contract envisioned to support the gig economy through access to low-level benefits has the interests of labor at its heart or represents an effort to rewire the social contract in the interest of corporate profit rather than the public good. Attention to the nature of labor relations in the gig economy will highlight whether calls for a new social contract are driven by the needs of labor or capital.

*Back to the future?*

The gig economy is widely being touted as a central aspect of the "future of work" owing to its technically advanced, flexible and accessible character. But a closer look at the nature of the gig economy reveals social arrangements that have more in common with the past than the future of work. A growing number of critical voices have noted that the gig economy has much in common with the putting-out systems of early capitalism (Bellace 2016; Stanford 2017). The practices of casualization, piecework, reliance on the worker's own capital equipment, coordination by intermediaries and lack of job security are all more reminiscent of work in the nineteenth rather than the twenty-first century. The only thing new is the use of digital connections to source and monitor labor. Bellace (2016) argues that looking to the past offers a useful reminder that this is not the first time that society has faced the collapse of the preexisting social contract in the face of rapid technological change and market deregulation (see also Hickey 2011). She suggests that refocusing on the principles that guided past solutions may help to point the way forward (Bellace 2016). The challenge is to build a social contract that upholds the rights of working people to a decent standard of living, while maintaining the focus on distributive justice between capital and labor, rather than between formal and informal workers, employees and employers or older and younger generations.

Cutting through the futuristic rhetoric surrounding the gig economy requires a closer look at the evidence. What is the basis of the claim that the gig economy is the future of work? What evidence is there that the gig economy makes a positive contribution to employment generation and reducing informality? Is the call for a new social contract based on a clear understanding of the regulatory needs of the gig economy, and how have these needs been affected by the Covid-19 pandemic?

The gig economy is said to be spreading rapidly across the world, particularly since the onset of Covid-19, but it still accounts for a modest share of workers. Statistics on the size of the gig economy, referring to platform-based digital employment, indicate that just before the pandemic it accounted for 0.5–5 percent of the labor force in the United States and EU, and less than 0.3 percent in developing countries (Adecco Group 2017; Askitas et al. 2018; World Bank 2018). More exuberant statistics on the size of the gig economy from the US Bureau of Statistics involve a more expansive definition of the gig economy, including non-digital contingent, temporary and employment agency workers (Risher 2020).

Statistics from the same source indicate that platform-based employment in the United States amounts to only 3 percent of this more widely defined gig economy (Lavietes and McCoy 2020). Despite enthusiastic accounts of its expansion, digital employment in the global South remains even more limited. Digital development scholar Richard Heeks (2019) estimated that in 2019 there were 30–40 million platform-based gig workers in the global South, amounting to some 1.5 percent of the workforce. Even significant increases under Covid-19 still offer very limited contributions to employment generation in the face of limited skills, double-digit unemployment and vast informal economies.

In addition to generating very limited levels of employment, questions have been raised about how much new or good-quality employment the platform-based gig economy creates. A McKinsey Global Institute report (2018: 65) acknowledges that digital employment platforms "have a relatively modest impact on employment" and do as much to eliminate and informalize jobs as to create them. The report estimates a contribution to job creation of 0.4 percent per year. An EU report (Askitas et al. 2018) on appropriate regulation for online employment platforms similarly notes that there is little evidence the gig economy improves access to quality jobs or contributes to the formalization of employment, despite widespread claims that digital linkages should contribute to greater formalization and professionalization of informal work. On the contrary, there is a significant risk that gig work may crowd out the creation of formal jobs by undermining the viability of existing formal employment in various industries, as well as creating incentives to evade payment of social benefits through misclassification of workers as independent contractors, referred to as "bogus self-employment" (Askitas et al. 2018: 84; Johnston and Land-Kazlauskas 2018; Meagher 2020).

Equally problematic for the development of an equitable social contract, the gig economy is associated with the blurring rather than the sharpening of regulatory obligations. Disputes over the employment status of gig workers and the sectoral regulations governing online platforms have given rise to persistent regulatory "gray areas" that stifle effective regulatory responses despite the availability of appropriate regulatory options (Askitas et al. 2018; Stanford 2017: 385). These gray areas have allowed online employment platforms to sidestep employment obligations to workers, and licensing as well as taxation obligations to the state owing to the hesitation of regulators to stifle innovation and financialized investment flows. Far from clarifying the requirements for more equitable employment regulation, proponents of gig economy seem committed to clouding the regulatory issues at stake, while calling for a new social contract to plug the social welfare gaps created in the process.

These observations highlight the need to ensure that discussions about a new social contract are asking the right questions and clarifying the real issues at stake. Can the gig economy really create as many "quality" jobs as proponents claim? Is the digital character of jobs obscuring wider questions of decent work? New questions are being asked about whether digital connections enhance or undermine economic inclusion from the perspective of labor. There are also growing concerns about how the gig economy affects the financing of services and social protection.

How does the notion of a new social contract funded by taxation and extended across the informal economy reshape resource flows between capital, labor and the state? While calls for a new social contract to support the gig economy have been exacerbated in the context of the Covid-19 pandemic, the pandemic period has also afforded a clearer glimpse of the problematic power and distributive relations underpinning the gig economy, prompting a closer examination of who gains and who loses from the social bargain being proposed to enable this form of digital employment (Katta et al. 2020; Masiero 2021).

## Digital Taxis and the New Social Contract

An analysis of the role of digital ride-hailing companies in Nigeria will be used here to ground debates about the gig economy and appropriate changes in the social contract. Digital ride-hailing services, referred to henceforth as digital taxis, account for a significant share of online employment across the globe. In the EU, digital taxi drivers make up two-thirds of gig workers. Uber, the lead digital taxi company, has grown from its inception in 2009 to operate in 80 countries at its peak, including eight African countries, and despite financial stresses still operates in 69 countries across the world. Uber's main competition, Bolt (formerly Taxify), now operates in 35 countries, including seven African countries (Malinga 2020; Mohammed 2018). Nigeria is regarded as an important market for both companies, owing to its vast population of some 200 million, chaotic urban transport systems and high levels of unemployment, particularly among graduates (Cenfri 2020).

Digital taxi companies make lavish claims about their capacity for job creation, improved incomes, passenger convenience, improving the efficiency of urban transport and reducing congestion (Adepoju 2017; Houeland 2018). At the same time, digital taxis have been associated with a range of problems in the cities in which they operate, including protests by regular as well as digital taxi drivers over unfair competition and low incomes, and conflicts with urban authorities over evasion of license fees and taxes, resulting in outbreaks of violence and the banning or partial banning of Uber in seven countries. A focus on digital taxis in Nigeria will serve to explore whether digital taxis offer reliable prospects for the rapid creation of quality jobs and the kind of social contract best suited to supporting livelihoods in the digital taxi sector.

### Digital taxis in Nigeria

Digital taxis came to Nigeria in 2014 when Uber started up operations in Lagos, the country's sprawling commercial capital. Taxify (now rebranded as Bolt) came to Lagos in 2016, and Uber extended its operations to the national capital, Abuja, in the same year, with Taxify/Bolt hard on its heels. Currently, Uber and Bolt are the leading digital taxi companies in both cities, although a local company, Oga Taxi, runs a distant third in Lagos and Abuja. Some 10 to 15 other Nigerian digital taxi startups are also operating in various Nigerian cities, mostly in Lagos, but none of them have captured a significant or stable share of the market (Ama Nti Osei 2018; Weiner 2015). This chapter draws on fieldwork conducted from June to August 2018 in Lagos and Abuja, with desk-based follow-up in 2021, focusing on the effect of digital taxis on economic inclusion and urban transport. Numerous interviews were conducted with digital, standard taxi and executive car hire drivers, government officials in relevant ministries, officials in Bolt and Oga Taxi, and labor union representatives. Interviews were followed up by a survey of 200 digital taxi drivers evenly distributed between Lagos and Abuja, involving rides initiated from peripheral as well as central areas of both cities. Evidence from the Nigerian digital taxi sector challenges the idea that the gig economy is an expanding source of quality jobs and indicates problematic effects on public transport and urban planning that the proposed new social contract is unlikely to resolve.

## Job creation and incomes

Despite impressive claims about potential job creation and high incomes, the benefits of digital taxi driving have been relatively modest in Nigeria. Uber claims to have created 9,000 jobs by 2017, and Bolt, currently the leading digital taxi employer in the country, claims to have over 10,000 drivers, while Oga Taxi claims to have about 10 percent of the market (Interview, Oga Taxi, 4 July 2018; Interview, Taxify/Bolt, 4 July 2018; *Vanguard* 2018). But the total of some 21,000 jobs is dramatically reduced by the realities of pluriactivity in local livelihood strategies. Digital taxis represent a second income rather than a "job" for 38.5 percent of drivers, while 58.8 percent of the full-time drivers work for two or more digital taxi companies simultaneously in order to maximize incomes, reducing actual creation of new jobs from 21,000 across the three main digital taxi companies to just 7,388 in a country of 200 million people.

In the process, digital taxis also displace other livelihoods, particularly regular taxis in Lagos and executive car hire in Abuja. Digital taxi fares are nearly half those of regular taxis in Lagos and less than half the cost of car hire services. In Abuja, regular taxis remain competitive with digital taxi fares, but executive car hire firms in Abuja indicated a decline in business of 40–60 percent since 2016. With more than 15,000 taxis and car hire drivers operating across Lagos alone, it is not clear that digital taxis offer net job creation. Furthermore, digital taxi drivers were already complaining widely of lack of customers and falling incomes by 2018, indicating market saturation and weak prospects for future job creation in Nigeria's two most dynamic digital taxi markets.

Income levels are also well below advertised levels of NGN 200,000 per month, owing to the many "hidden costs" of being a digital taxi driver (Rogers 2015; Weiner 2015). Aside from the commission, which is 25 percent for Uber and 15 percent for Bolt and Oga Taxi, tempting income projections do not include the cost of petrol, maintenance and repairs, mobile phone data and mandatory insurance. Tempting income projections also ignore the fact that 50.5 percent of drivers do not own the car they drive and have to make heavy weekly returns to the car owner on a worker, rental or hire purchase basis. Returns to car owners, which involve a flat rate negotiated between the owner and driver, averaged 25.1 percent, on top of commission payments averaging 19.4 percent and petrol costs of 23.2 percent of average takings.

Taking these various issues into account, monthly earnings of full-time digital taxi owner-drivers averaged NGN 111,272, while full-time drivers who did not own their cars earned only NGN 22,746 per month, barely above the derisory minimum wage in mid-2018 and well below the current minimum wage of NGN 30,000 per month. Drivers worked extremely long hours to generate even this level of income. Owner-drivers averaged 68 hours per week, while non-owner drivers averaged 76.2 hours owing to the additional pressure of having to make returns to the car owner. Those who had been doing digital taxi driving for some time noted that incomes used to be better but had been seriously eroded by fare cuts, reductions in vehicle standards and the entry of too many drivers as the digital taxi companies battle each other for market share.

*Employment status*

The vexed question of the employment status of digital taxi drivers revolves around the claim of digital taxi companies that they "disintermediate" relations between drivers and customers, turning gig drivers into independent contractors. However, a growing number of studies has established that gig economy platforms do not liberate drivers from an employer but create new forms of digital intermediation that allow the platforms to control the labor of drivers while evading economic obligations to workers (Askitas et al. 2018; Graham et al. 2017; Murphy and Carmody 2015).

Digital taxi companies refer to drivers as "partners" rather than employees but use corporate regulation and algorithms to exert considerable control over the activities and incomes of drivers. Drivers have no control over fares or vehicle specifications, are not allowed to see where customers are going before accepting a trip and are subject to disciplinary algorithms via customer and activity ratings, which penalize drivers for cancelling rides, working shorter hours or failing to please customers. In May 2017, Uber slashed fares by 40 percent, triggering a drivers' strike in Lagos, while low fares triggered a strike in Abuja in October 2016 (Kazeem 2016). Further strike action took place in 2018 and again in 2020. According to one disgruntled driver, "They don't even consult with us. What is the essence of a partnership if decisions are one way?" (NUPEDP Facebook page, 3 March 2018).

Regular taxi and executive car hire drivers in Nigeria also dispute the view of digital taxis as "disintermediated." As an official from a car hire company in Abuja explained, the relationship between driver and customer is independent of the car hire agency, while this is not the case with digital taxis (Interview, JVJ Car Hire, 28 June 2018). Digital taxi drivers are not allowed to build up independent customer lists or to negotiate independently with customers. Moreover, digital taxi drivers are subject to additional employment intermediaries in cases where the driver does not own the car, a practice common across all the digital taxi companies. As noted in the previous section, vehicle owners—largely formal sector employees, businesspeople and civil servants—consume an even larger share of the gains than the digital taxi companies themselves, with some operating fleets of digital taxis that generate a considerable income stream. Far from being independent, digital taxi drivers operate within multiple layers of employment relations with limited space for agency except through extreme self-exploitation.

In addition to suffering from a lack of autonomy and labor protection, drivers also lack social protection. Some digital taxi platforms offer social benefit packages via commercial insurance arrangements operated by third-party companies. Bolt offers optional health insurance and Oga Taxi offers optional health and pension packages for drivers willing to have premiums deducted from their pay. The closest thing to an employment benefit is Bolt's offer of one month's free health insurance if drivers complete 200 trips in a month while maintaining a high driver rating. However, this is only available to the first 1,000 qualifying drivers, in line with a gamification ethos that turns social benefits into a prize rather than a social right (Interview, Lagos, 18 August 2018; van Doorn and Chen 2021).

Digital taxi work also ignores the class character of decent work. Given the language and IT skills required, 59 percent of digital taxi drivers in Nigeria are university graduates. However, commercial driving is a low-status activity in Nigeria, and graduates find it demeaning to be treated as lowly household drivers by customers who are often younger and less educated. While the income of owner-drivers can be twice as high as the salary of entry-level graduate jobs, the lack of benefits, pressure to work long hours, low job status and lack of progression opportunities undermine any sense of inclusion. Only 41.4 percent of digital taxi drivers regarded the activity as a "job," falling to 35.4 percent among owner-drivers and 32.8 percent among graduates. The majority saw it is as a stopgap or source of extra income. Similarly, only 25 percent of drivers considered digital taxi driving a "formal" activity, owing to its low status, insecurity and lack of labor regulation. This reading is also reflected by officials in the Ministry of Labour, in the National Union of Road Transport Workers and in the National Labour Congress who do not consider digital taxi driving a formal activity because drivers are neither subject to Nigerian labor laws nor are they formally registered as small businesses. Far from creating quality jobs, digital taxi platforms generate informalized work that relevant government bodies and the majority of drivers do not recognize as a real job.

*Transport licensing and planning*

In addition to a marginal contribution to job creation or economic inclusion, digital taxi platforms were found to contribute little to urban transport and planning needs. By claiming to be technology rather than transport firms, digital taxi companies enhance their competitiveness by avoiding formal licensing and taxation requirements applicable within the taxi industry. According to the General Secretary of a prominent Lagos taxi association, digital taxi companies and drivers avoid a range of taxes that regular taxis have to pay, leading him to exclaim, "Uber are cheating us!". Digital taxi drivers have avoided the annual driver certification, the annual fee for the taxi label, the increment on the Road Worthiness tax for commercial vehicles and the taxi license, all of which add up to NGN 11,000, of which NGN 9,500 involves annual fees. Until late 2020, digital taxi companies avoided the franchise tax that taxi companies with multiple vehicles have to pay to the state. Digital taxi companies lobbied actively for an exemption from the franchise fee and lobbied for a 20 percent reduction when the fee was finally imposed in 2020. A member of Bolt staff explained that digital taxis need the government to provide a more "conducive environment" given their contribution to employment, improved transport planning and alleviating urban traffic congestion, benefits that do not seem to withstand scrutiny (Interview, Lagos, 4 July 2018). Uber is also well known for "actively working with regulators" to avoid being required to comply with tax and licensing laws (Ama Nti Osei 2018).

Yet officials within state and municipal transport bodies feel that digital taxis fall short of adequate contributions to the public good, particularly with regard to revenue, statistics and congestion. With regard to revenue, taxi licenses and fees play an important role in funding improvements in the public transport systems in both Lagos and Abuja (World Bank 2016), both of which have active transport development strategies. By avoiding license fees and taxes, digital taxi platforms withhold a key contribution to the public good. Officials in Lagos also noted that digital platforms do little to improve planning, since digital taxis are "statistically invisible" to planners. The Lagos Metropolitan Area Transport Authority (LAMATA) cannot distinguish digital taxis from private cars owing to the lack of insignia or registration. While digital taxi companies have extensive data on drivers, riders and traffic patterns, they have been unwilling to share their data with government bodies. Digital taxi platforms consider their data "commercial secrets" and have actively resisted demands by both the Lagos State Ministry of Transport and the Federal Capital Territory Transport Secretariat for access to their data and software platforms (Interview, FCT Transport Secretariat, 11 July 2018; Interview, LAMATA, 6 July 2018; Interview, Oga Taxi, 4 July 2018; Ama Nti Osei 2018).

While digital taxis are recognized as having a place in the urban transport ecosystem, local transport authorities in Lagos and Abuja feel that they contribute little to the overall development of urban transport. The urban transport strategy in both cities is based on mass transport to reduce costs and congestion. While digital taxis are cheaper than regular taxis in Lagos and parts of Abuja, mass transport, which is used by the vast majority of the urban population, is less than 25 percent of the cost of a digital taxi ride in both cities. Given prevailing low incomes and the fact that less than 20 percent of Nigerians own smartphones capable of supporting digital taxi apps, digital taxis are viewed as an elite transport solution, not a key source of urban transport. Indeed, officials from LAMATA felt that digital transport platforms were poorly aligned with official transport strategies, stating, "we have completely different agendas" (Interview, Lagos, 6 July 2018). The objective of the Lagos transport strategy is to take cars off the road, while they feel that digital taxis put cars on the road. Efforts to turn idle cars into income generators mean that vehicles that are normally used intermittently now ply the roads all day. In Abuja as well, officials see cheaper mass transport rather than individual taxis as the key to urban transport efficiency. "Everywhere in the world, taxis are for big men. If your bus system is working, what do you need with taxis?" (Interview, Abuja, 11 July 2018).

While the onset of the pandemic highlighted the vulnerability of digital taxi drivers, it also drew attention to the structural tensions between the interests of platforms, drivers and the state. During Nigeria's lockdown from 31 March 2020, Uber and Bolt suspended service for over one month followed by further weeks of curfews, leading to a collapse in drivers' incomes. While platforms introduced limited health measures and experimented with pivots into delivery, no economic support measures were offered to drivers. In fact, amid efforts by Lagos State to tax platforms in August 2020, Uber and Bolt negotiated to shift part of the burden onto drivers, exacerbating the economic pressures on drivers under Covid-19 conditions (Kanife 2020; Omilana 2020a). This and a subsequent change in pricing formulas triggered strikes by digital taxi drivers in early September and October 2020 (Alade 2020; Omilana 2020b). Drivers protested that they were not consulted on these changes by the state or by the platforms, further emphasizing the fiction of calling them independent contractors while imposing conditions that increase their precarity and deprive them of protection (Omilana 2020b). The only gesture of economic support during the pandemic was the inclusion of digital taxi drivers in a one-off relief grant of NGN 30,000 from the federal government—amounting to one month's minimum wage after nine months of severe income disruption (Akande 2020). These events question whether what is most needed from a new social contract is basic social protection, when the very structure of the gig economy strips digital taxi drivers of *labor* protection and political voice (Howson et al. 2020).

## Rethinking the Social Contract

Digital taxi platforms make strong claims about their potential to contribute to the public good by creating modern jobs and improving the convenience and efficiency of urban transport. Evidence from Nigeria shows that they significantly overstate their potential for job creation and decent work, as well as offering a problematic contribution to improving urban transport. In fact, digital taxi jobs are regarded as informal, low-status work by the majority of drivers as well as by labor and transport officials. Worse still, they are displacing better-paying, more stable and sustainable work in the traditional taxi industry and raising questions about the potential for net job creation. Most problematic of all, the competitiveness of digital taxis is less a product of modern technology than of the evasion of labor and licensing regulations, cutting costs by evading contributions to decent livelihoods and state revenue. Demands for a new social contract based on low-level benefits for precarious workers not only ignore their ongoing loss of a wider range of labor rights but also shift the financial burden of social protection from capital to the state. If this creates a twenty-first-century social contract that is fit for purpose, one would do well to ask "whose purpose?".

While some suggest that the gig economy has become the catalyst for a fairer social contract from which all informal and nonstandard workers can benefit, others point out that the novelty of digital technology is providing futuristic cover for the informalization of employment (Ettlinger 2017; World Bank 2018). Clarifying the real purpose of a social contract for the gig economy calls for closer examination of how it redistributes resources and power within society. As Graham et al. (2017: 152) argue in their analysis of digital employment platforms, what is "needed is more detailed empirical inquiry into flows of value . . . and further research about who creates it, who captures it, how flows are being reconfigured and who benefits from those reconfigurations."

To make a start at understanding how value flows are being reconfigured through demands for a new social contract, we return to three issues raised earlier: the role of capital, distributive fairness and regulatory choices. The airbrushing of capital out of many discussions of a twenty-first-century social contract is problematic, since it eliminates a key element of resource distribution from the conversation. Scrutinizing the fairness of the social contract calls for a shift of the narrative away from decrying the "unfairness" of protecting formal workers while excluding informal workers. Attention needs to be shifted to the "unfairness" of allowing corporate employers to further withdraw from the provision of social protection and decent incomes for their workers, while shifting the responsibility for social protection to the state. Closer scrutiny of regulatory choices challenges the notion that the precarity of gig workers is the inevitable product of globalization and technological change. The active dismantling of the social contract under neoliberal market reforms has played a central role in the expansion of precarious work, while the structure of digital platforms facilitates ongoing evasion of labor regulations, while using narratives of innovation, job creation and "fairness" to convince regulators to play along.

Examined from this perspective, the shifts in regulatory arrangements that underpin the gig economy tend to maximize corporate profitability at the expense of workers and the public good. The call for a new social contract seems to be less about a better deal for precarious workers than about legitimizing "an emergent regime of accumulation that encompasses . . . a new capital-labor relation that institutionalizes informal work" (Ettlinger 2017: 69). Yet stabilizing a new regime of accumulation for the gig economy, as Stanford (2017) reminds us, requires consent as well as control. Talk of a new social contract focuses attention on remoralizing rather than redressing precarious work, emphasizing basic social protection and job creation rather than labor rights, social dignity and the accountability of capital to the public interest.

Covid-19 and the accompanying lockdown measures have highlighted the economic and physical vulnerability of gig workers, but the asymmetrical power relations that perpetuate this vulnerability are less clearly revealed (Masiero 2021). Attention has been focused on the need of gig workers for social protection, while ignoring the disempowering structure of platform-based labor relations that strip them of labor protection and often of political voice (Ustek-Spilda et al. 2020). As Masiero (2021) notes, discussions of a digital social contract are often top-down, treating gig workers as third parties rather than signatories in their own right. Worse still, the contract on offer does not seek to transform the conditions of gig workers so much as to stabilize their precarity.

### Toward a more equitable social contract

The quest for a new social contract more genuinely committed to distributive fairness in the twenty-first-century economy calls for greater attention to technological capacities, regulatory clarity and social struggles. There is a need to dispel the notion that digital technology naturally leads to increased precarity of employment. Digital technologies can combine employment creation and efficiency with respect to labor rights and paying taxes. As Graham et al. (2017) point out, algorithms can be formulated to apply rather than bypass local labor laws, and digital platforms can be licensed and taxed in the various countries in which they operate. The key to a viable social contract is not derisory universal social protection but aligning the uses of new technology with respect for workers' rights and meeting tax obligations to the state (Houeland 2018).

The exploitation of "gray areas" in the employment status of gig workers and the sectoral classification of digital employment platforms is central to the regulatory limbo associated with the gig economy. Yet, as evidence from Nigeria reveals, the problem is less a lack of appropriate regulations than mystifying narratives and active lobbying to deter regulators from applying the rules to the gig economy. An EU report (Askitas et al. 2018: 92–93) on the issue contends that what is needed to regulate the gig economy is not new regulation but more effective application of existing regulation committed to stemming the rise of "bogus self-employment" and unfair evasion of sectoral regulations. The main obstacle has less to do with regulatory confusion than reluctance on the part of regulators to constrain innovation and investment even at the cost of decent work and distributive justice (Askitas et al. 2018; Hauben et al. 2020).

While regulators dither, many of these issues are being settled on the ground through social contestation rather than social contracts. Despite their popularity with well-heeled customers, digital taxi firms have had contentious relations with governments and drivers alike. Uber has been banned or partially banned in seven countries, and both Uber and Bolt have been targets of violent attacks by regular taxi drivers, particularly in South Africa and Kenya (Geitung 2017; Houeland 2018; Mohammed 2018). In the global South, digital workers are developing new forms of collective resistance involving social media, digital workers' unions and alliances with established unions (Howson et al. 2020). In Nigeria, a growing number of digital workers are joining WhatsApp and other social media groups, which have been used to mobilize numerous strikes, while new digital workers' unions are emerging and gaining in strength (Alade 2020; Ehiaghe 2018; Omilana 2020a). In Europe, more established unions are also developing mechanisms of organizing and allying with gig workers, providing representation and bringing cases to court. Europe's largest industrial union, IG Metall, connects gig workers with appropriate labor unions, while British, European and South African trade unions have partnered with gig workers to defend workers' rights in court, yielding a growing number of judgments in favor of greater labor rights, rather than just social protection (Askitas et al. 2018; Croft and Venkataramakrishnan 2021; Geitung 2017; Houeland 2018). In response to the landmark decision of the UK Supreme Court on 19 February 2021 that Uber drivers are workers entitled to workers' rights, South Africa and Nigeria are launching class action suits, highlighting the central role of labor unions and the judiciary in determining the shape of any future social contract (Cheng 2021).

But there is no room for complacency. In Nigeria, the growing frustration and resistance of digital taxi drivers send a message not only about the role of a social contract in securing consent but also about the limits of consent. In the face of asymmetric power relations, the persistent ability of digital platforms to evade fiscal and labor obligations, and the intensifying precarity and disaffection among workers, it is important to remember that resistance is not always progressive, particularly where livelihoods are most insecure. Far from offering a solution to poverty and social unrest in contemporary Africa, the gig economy and its derisory new social contract threaten to exacerbate both.

# References

Adecco Group. 2017. "Time to Act: Creating a New Social Contract for Work in the 21st Century." *White Paper*. Zurich: Adecco Group.

Adepoju, P. 2017. "Q&A: Taxify Reveals Plans to Take on Uber in Nigeria by Being More 'Driver Friendly.'" *Ventureburn*, 26 May.

AfDB (African Development Bank). 2017. *Jobs for Youth in Africa: Strategy for Creating 25 Million Jobs and Equipping 50 Million Youth—2016–2025*. Abidjan: African Development Bank.

AfDB/OECD/UNDP. 2012. *African Economic Outlook: Promoting Youth Employment*. Paris: OECD.

AfDB/OECD/UNDP. 2018. *African Economic Outlook 2018*. Paris: OECD.

Akande, Laolu. 2020. "Nigerian Govt Commences Payment of N30,000 Grant to Taxi, Bus, Okada Drivers." *Premium Times*, 6 December.

Alade, Benjamin. 2020. "Riders to Pay More as Bolt, Uber Increase Fares." *The Guardian*, 23 October.

Ama Nti Osei, Oheneba. 2018. "Lola Kassim: 'We Don't Sell Rider Details.'" *The Africa Report*, 5 March.

Askitas, Nikos, Romain Bosc, Willem Pieter de Groen, Werber Eichhorst, Zachary Kilhoffer, Karolien Lenaerts and Nicolas Salez. 2018. *Online Talent Platforms, Labour Market Intermediaries and the Changing World of Work*. Brussels/Bonn: Centre for European Policy Studies/Institute of Labor Economics.

Bellace, Janice R. 2016. "Back to the Future: Freedom of Association, the Right to Strike and National Law." *King's Law Journal*, 27(1): 24–45.

Boucher, David and Paul Kelly. 1994. "The Social Contract and Its Critics." In *The Social Contract from Hobbes to Rawls*, edited by David Boucher and Paul Kelly, 1–34. London: Routledge.

Breman, Jan and Marcel van der Linden. 2014. "Informalizing the Economy: The Return of the Social Question at a Global Level." *Development and Change*, 45(5): 920–940.

Cenfri. 2020. "Livelihood Experiences of Nigeria's E-hailing Workers." *Focus Note*. Bellville, SA: Cenfri.

Cheng, Michelle. 2021. "Uber Drivers in Africa Are Taking Notes from Their Triumphant British Peers." *Quartz Africa*, 18 April.

Connectivity at the BoP Forum. 2017. "Connectivity at the Bottom of the Pyramid: ICT4D and Informal Economic Inclusion in Africa." *Bellagio Centre White Paper*. Bellagio, IT: Bellagio Centre.

Croft, Jane and Siddharth Venkataramakrishnan. 2021. "Uber Loses Landmark UK Battle as Supreme Court Rules Drivers Are Workers." *Financial Times*, 19 February.

Ehiaghe, Gloria. 2018. "Nigeria: Uber, Taxify Drivers Form Union, Raises the Alarm over Ridiculous Charges by Foreign APP Companies." *The Guardian*, 14 June.

Ettlinger, Nancy. 2017. "Open Innovation and Its Discontents." *Geoforum*, 80: 61–71.

Ferguson, James. 2015. *Give a Man a Fish: Reflections on the New Politics of Distribution*. Durham, NC: Duke University Press.

Geitung, Ine. 2017. "Uber Drivers in Cape Town: Working Conditions and Worker Agency in the Sharing Economy." Master's Thesis, University of Oslo, Norway.

Graham, Mark, Isis Hjorth and Vili Lehdonvirta. 2017. "Digital Labour and Development: Impacts of Global Digital Labour Platforms and the Gig Economy on Worker Livelihoods." *Transfer: European Review of Labour and Research*, 23(2): 135–162.

Grunewald, Adam. 2017. *From the Informal Economy to the Gig Economy*. Washington, DC: Pyxera Global.

Hauben, Harald, Karolien Lenaerts and Willem Waeyaert. 2020. "The Platform Economy and Precarious Work." *PE 652.734. Policy Department for Economic, Scientific and Quality of Life Policies*. Brussels: European Parliament.

Heeks, Richard. 2019. "How Many Platform Workers Are There in the Global South?" *ICTs for Development (blog)*, 29 January. https://ict4dblog.wordpress.com/2019/01/29/how-many-platform-workers-are-there-in-the-global-south/.

Hickey, Sam. 2011. "The Politics of Social Protection: What Do We Get From a 'Social Contract' Approach?'" *Canadian Journal of Development Studies/Revue Canadienne d'Études du Développement*, 32(4): 426–438.

Houeland, Camilla. 2018. "What Is Uber up to in Africa?" *Africa Is a Country (blog)*, 9 April. https://africasacountry.com/2018/04/what-is-uber-up-to-in-africa.

Howson, Kelle, Funda Ustek-Spilda, Rafael Grohmann, Nancy Salem, Rodrigo Carelli, Daniel Abs, Julice Salvagni, Mark Graham, Maria Belen Balbornoz, Henry Chavez, Arturo Arriagada and Macarena Bonhomme. 2020. "'Just Because You Don't See Your Boss, Doesn't Mean You Don't Have a Boss': COVID-19 and Gig Worker Strikes across Latin America." *International Union Rights*, 27(3): 20–28.

Hunt, Abigail and Fortunate Machingura. 2016. "A Good Gig? The Rise of On-Demand Domestic Work." *Development Progress Working Paper No. 7*. London: Overseas Development Institute.

ILO (International Labour Organization). 1999. *Decent Work*. International Labour Conference, 87th Session. Geneva: ILO.

ILO (International Labour Organization). 2016. *Non-Standard Employment around the World: Understanding Challenges, Shaping Prospects*. Geneva: ILO.

ILO (International Labour Organization). 2019. *Work for a Brighter Future—Global Commission on the Future of Work*. Geneva: ILO.

Johnston, Hannah and Christopher Land-Kazlauskas. 2018. "Organizing On-Demand Representation, Voice, and Collective Bargaining in the Gig Economy." *ILO Working Papers, Conditions of Work and Employment Series No. 94*. Geneva: International Labour Organization.

Jütting, Johannes and Juan R. de Laiglesia (eds.). 2009. "Is Informal Normal? Towards More and Better Jobs in Developing Countries." *Policy Brief*. Paris: Organisation for Economic Co-operation and Development.

Kanife, Ejike. 2020. "E-Hailing Drivers Union Begin Week-long Boycott of Uber and Bolt Apps in Protest against New Lagos Regulation." *Technext*, 31 August.

Katta, Srujana, Adam Badger, Mark Graham, Kelle Howson, Funda Ustek-Spilda and Alessio Bertolini. 2020. "(Dis)Embeddedness and (De)Commodification: COVID-19, Uber, and the Unravelling Logics of the Gig Economy." *Dialogues in Human Geography*, 10(2): 203–207.

Kazeem, Yomi. 2016. "Uber Has a New Problem in Nigeria—Driver Strikes in Abuja." *Quartz Africa*, 31 October.

Lavietes, Matthew and Michael McCoy. 2020. "Waiting for Work: Pandemic Leaves U.S. Gig Workers Clamoring for Jobs." *Reuters*, 19 October.

Lee, Ching Kwan and Yelizavetta Kofman. 2012. "The Politics of Precarity: Views beyond the United States." *Work and Occupations*, 39(4): 388–408.

Lund, Frances. 2009. "Social Protection, Citizenship and the Employment Relationship." *WIEGO Working Paper No. 10*. Manchester: Women in Informal Employment: Globalizing and Organizing.

Malinga, Sibahle. 2020. "Bolt Eyes Africa, Europe Expansion with R1.9bn Funding." *IT Web*, 26 May.

Masiero, Silvia. 2021. "Digital Platform Workers under COVID-19: A Subaltern Perspective." *Proceedings of the 54th Hawaii International Conference on System Sciences*, 6349–6358.

McKinsey Global Institute. 2018. "Smart Cities: Digital Solutions for a More Livable Future." New York: McKinsey and Company.

Meagher, Kate. 2020. "Illusions of Inclusion: Assessment of the World Development Report 2019 on the Changing Nature of Work." *Development and Change*, 51(2): 667–682.

Meagher, Kate, Laura Mann and Maxim Bolt. 2016. "Introduction: Global Economic Inclusion and African Workers." *The Journal of Development Studies*, 52(4): 471–482.

Mkandawire, Thandika and Charles C. Soludo. 1999. *Our Continent, Our Future: African Perspectives on Structural Adjustment*. Dakar, SE/Ottawa, CA/Asmara, ER: Council for the Development of Social Science Research in Africa, International Development Research Centre and Africa World Press.

Mohammed, Omar. 2018. "How Taxify Plans to Take on Uber in East Africa." *Reuters*, 10 August.

Murphy, James T. and Pádraig Carmody. 2015. *Africa's Information Revolution: Technical Regimes and Production Networks in South Africa and Tanzania*. London: Wiley.

Mustapha, Abdul Raufu and Lindsay Whitfield. 2009. *Turning Points in African Democracy*. Suffolk, UK: James Currey.

Neilson, Brett and Ned Rossiter. 2008. "Precarity as a Political Concept, or, Fordism as Exception." *Theory, Culture & Society*, 25(7–8): 51–72.

Nugent, Paul. 2010. "States and Social Contracts in Africa." *New Left Review*, 63: 35–68.

Omilana, Timileyin. 2020a. "Uber, Bolt Drivers Begin One Week-Strike in Lagos." *The Guardian*, 31 August.

Omilana, Timileyin. 2020b. "Uber, Bolt Drivers in Abuja May Go on Strike over Fare Charges, Conditions." *The Guardian*, 14 September.

Perry, Guillermo E., William F. Maloney, Omar S. Arias, Pablo Fajnzylber, Andrew D. Mason and Jaime Saavedra-Chanduvi. 2007. *Informality: Exit and Exclusion*. Washington, DC: World Bank.

Risher, Howard. 2020. "The Gig Economy and the BLS Surveys." *Government Executive*, 13 February.

Rockefeller Foundation. 2014. *Online Work: A New Frontier for Digital Jobs*. New York: Rockefeller Foundation.

Rogers, Brishen. 2015. "The Social Costs of Uber." *University of Chicago Law Review Online*, 8(1): 85–102.

Scully, Ben. 2016. "Precarity North and South: A Southern Critique of Guy Standing." *Global Labour Journal*, 7(2): 160–173.

Shafik, Nemat. 2018. "A New Social Contract." *Finance and Development*, 55(4): 4–8.

Stanford, Jim. 2017. "The Resurgence of Gig Work: Historical and Theoretical Perspectives." *The Economic and Labour Relations Review*, 28(3): 382–401.

UNRISD (United Nations Research Institute for Social Development). 2016. *Policy Innovations for Transformative Change: Implementing the 2030 Agenda for Sustainable Development*. Geneva: UNRISD.

Ustek-Spilda, Funda, Mark Graham, Alessio Bertolini, Srujana Katta, Fabian Ferrari and Kelle Howson. 2020. *From Social Distancing to Social Solidarity: Gig Economy and the COVID-19*. Paris: OECD Development Matters.

van Doorn, Niels and Julie Yujie Chen. 2021. "Odds Stacked Against Workers: Datafied Gamification on Chinese and American Food Delivery Platforms." *Socio-Economic Review*, 1–23.

Vanguard. 2018. "Uber Monthly Passenger Base in Nigeria Hits 267,000." 15 August.

Weiner, Joann. 2015. "The Hidden Costs of being an Uber driver." *Washington Post*, 20 February.

World Bank. 2016. *Lagos Urban Transport Project. Project Performance Assessment Report No. 103068*. Washington, DC: World Bank.

World Bank. 2018. *World Development Report 2019: The Changing Nature of Work*. Washington, DC: World Bank.

# Chapter 6

## UNDERSTANDING RISKS OF REPRODUCING INEQUALITIES IN THE IMPLEMENTATION OF INCLUSION POLICIES

### BRAZIL, MEXICO AND PERU

Roberto Pires

*Introduction*

Latin America is home to some of the most unequal societies in the world. Despite important advances in poverty reduction in the region in the first decade of the twenty-first century, extreme poverty and inequality rates were on the rise again by the end of the second decade (ECLAC 2019; Neri 2018). The sanitary and economic crises spurred by the Covid-19 pandemic beginning in 2020 have further intensified these trends to levels (and with implications) yet to be fully understood. Despite these recent fluctuations and the urgency imposed by the pandemic's unfolding, when we look back in history, we are forced to recognize social inequality as an enduring feature of Latin American societies. In Brazil, for example, we can see a great deal of stability in income and wealth inequalities when we take into consideration the last 100 years (Souza 2018). Such enduring stability suggests that reproduction processes are underway—that is, consequential (but not always visible) forces acting to maintain social inequality as it is. Closer attention must be paid to these dynamics and their effects.

Dynamics of inequality reproduction operate in multiple spheres of social life. Chief among them are the day-to-day interactions people have with government organizations that provide public goods and services. In modern societies, these interactions abound in one's life trajectory. From birth to death, social construction is mediated by operations of certification, classification and provision of voluntary (e.g., health care, education) and involuntary (e.g., tax, policing) services performed by multiple government agents.

This chapter focuses on the risks of social inequality reproduction engendered by these interactions. More specifically, I center on the provision of public services and goods aimed at expanding socioeconomic inclusion or mitigating the effects of exclusion. I will refer to them generically as "inclusion policies." Considering the context of deep inequality that characterizes many Latin American societies and their governments' limited capacities and resources, our goal is to understand how these inclusion policies are undermined in the implementation process, reinforcing existing social inequalities.

This counterintuitive perspective finds support in classic and contemporary discussions on policy implementation. Since the 1970s, implementation scholars have challenged the idea that laws and political decisions are seamlessly executed by government bureaucracies as planned, arguing that implementation processes inevitably introduce transformations. Implementation processes involve a multiplicity of (organizational and individual) actors whose behaviors and (inter) actions influence not only policy form but also its contents and results (Brodkin 1990; Hill and Hupe 2014; Lipsky 1980; Pressman and Wildavsky 1973). Rather than a set of supposedly neutral administrative acts and procedures, implementation is a space for policy politics (Brodkin 1990), with clear implications in terms of who gets what and how (Nakamura and Smallwood 1980; Thomas and Grindle 1990). As a result, policy outputs cannot be reduced to a mechanical unfolding of formal decisions, rules and structures. Implementation processes create effects other than those formally desired. They are rather hotbeds of unintended effects, including both side effects and perverse effects (Vedung 2013).[1]

In that sense, in addition to looking at the desired effects of public policies, we must also pay close attention to unintended effects on targeted (or adjacent) populations resulting from actual processes of implementation. Unintended effects can be both material and symbolic, and reinforce existing social inequalities by different means. Material effects relate to access and distribution of public services/benefits to different social groups. Implementation dynamics may introduce informal barriers and selectivity, disproportionally harming one segment of the population in comparison with others and blocking distributive justice. In extremely unequal societies, these effects tend to be even more acute, as they contribute to the accumulation of material disadvantages by social groups who already experience some form of material vulnerability (Cárdenas et al. 2010).

Symbolic effects, in turn, refer to how day-to-day interactions with state agents interfere with the way citizens come to define their social positions, identities and sense of value in society (Dubois 1999; Siblot 2006). This understanding of symbolic effects is in line with contemporary debates on intersectionality, as it calls attention to the adverse combination of multiple markers of vulnerability—class, race, gender and so on—and to how they constitute diverse experiences of social exclusion (Crenshaw 1995; Hankivsky and Cormier 2011). While material and symbolic effects can be analytically separated, they often appear strongly linked in living experiences. Together, these unintended effects of implementation processes contribute to the persistence of social inequalities by gradually producing the symbolic differentiation of segments of the public and the accumulation of

---

1. Side effects take place outside the main target of the intervention and can be anticipated or not. Perverse effects, on the other hand, are often not anticipated and hit the target but produce effects contrary to those originally intended by the intervention (Vedung 2013).

material disadvantages of social groups that traditionally experience forms of vulnerability (ECLAC 2016; Lamont 2017).

Understanding these unintended effects of implementation is relevant because it illuminates consequential dynamics that are often neglected or rarely approached in political debates. Attention to these dynamics may help us better understand the role institutions play in the perpetuation of inequalities, through a focus on the micro processes that organize on a day-to-day basis the relationships between the state and disadvantaged or vulnerable groups (Gupta 2012; Lamont et al. 2014). The fact that implementation takes place in the hidden recesses of routine, or in the obscure actions and inactions of public agents, does not mean it should remain immune to public scrutiny. The less it is exposed and discussed, the more likely it will remain as a viable option for governments (and societies) to play the double game of maintaining inclusive legal norms or political discourses while allowing room for "implementation tricks" (Dubois 2010) or "bureaucratic disentitlement" (Lipsky 1984), processes through which social rights retrenchment can be achieved in practice through the ordinary actions of public agents rather than by policy change and legal reform.

In this chapter, I propose an analytical framework for evaluating the ways through which policy implementation processes may contribute to the perpetuation of inequalities. The framework was developed from the analysis of empirical cases in Brazil, Mexico and Peru. By drawing from actual experiences of policy implementation, the framework directs our attention to five different types of mechanisms through which the day-to-day operations of government and the encounters between service workers and users may engender risks of inequality reproduction. It offers a tool for linking policy implementation processes to the material and symbolic effects leading to the perpetuation of social inequalities.

## *Drawing Insights from Experience*

The proposed analytical framework draws from the qualitative analysis of multiple cases of policy implementation and the concrete experiences of policy makers, workers and users. It results from the work of a group of 44 researchers in Latin America, mobilized through a call for papers in the beginning of 2018. The group brought together empirical analysis of 39 cases of policy implementation in the region, in different countries and policy domains (Table 6.1). Each case was subject to (individual or comparative) analysis exploring how implementation dynamics produced unintended effects on their clientele, potentially reinforcing preexisting social inequalities. The case study reports were published as an edited book (Pires 2019). The set of cases provided a database for further analysis and identification of the mechanisms linking policy implementation to inequality reproduction. It is worth noting that the data produced was not designed to be representative of a larger population of public programs or services (it is rather a convenience

**Table 6.1** Variations in the set of cases

| Policy domain | Number of cases | Countries |
|---|:---:|---|
| Social assistance | 8 | Brazil, Mexico |
| Health care | 5 | Brazil |
| Infrastructure | 5 | Brazil, Mexico |
| Justice and public order | 5 | Brazil, Mexico |
| Education | 4 | Brazil, Mexico |
| Rural development | 4 | Brazil |
| Urban services | 3 | Mexico |
| Housing | 2 | Brazil |
| Work and income | 1 | Brazil |
| Culture | 1 | Brazil |
| Water and environment | 1 | Peru |
| Total | 39 | — |

*Source*: Pires (2019).

sample).[2] While the database may not be suitable for estimating generalizable effects, it offers a unique opportunity for developing a qualitative understanding of the mechanisms in a diverse set of cases.

The 39 cases have one characteristic in common: they are public programs or services directed at the poor and other vulnerable segments of the population. Therefore, they allow us to explore the effects of their implementation dynamics (and their related mechanisms) on these social groups under different national contexts and policy domains. We then systematically compared the cases. First, for each of the programs/services we identified their stated objectives, the unintended effects observed by the researchers and the mechanisms that engendered such effects. Second, by focusing on the mechanisms, we further specified their connections to the observed effects and compared across the cases in order to identify the main patterns running across diverse contexts (Table 6.1). By doing so, we were able to identify and analyze recurrent mechanisms that played similar roles in different cases and contexts, which, taken together, give important insights into the risks of inequality reproduction in policy implementation.

## *A Framework for Evaluating the Reproduction of Inequalities in Implementation Processes*

The comparative analysis of the cases revealed a set of mechanisms that emerge during implementation dynamics, leading to material and symbolic effects on the

---

2. Convenience sampling is a type of non-probability sampling that involves the sample being drawn from that part of the population that is close to hand (i.e., within the reach of the network of researchers involved). This type of sampling is most useful for exploratory studies and pilot testing.

targeted population, which contribute to the perpetuation of disadvantage and vulnerability in certain population groups. Figure 6.1 presents the five mechanisms identified through the analytical process described in the preceding section, grouping them in two dimensions of analysis of implementation processes. In this section, I will define and illustrate each of these mechanisms, drawing examples mainly from empirical studies carried out in Brazil.

### Institutional design and governance

Top-down approaches to policy implementation have underscored institutional design as a key dimension in understanding how policy goals, contents and formats get transformed through the course of implementation (Hill and Hupe 2014). Putting in practice legal norms and political decisions frequently requires the involvement and coordination of multiple actors (both government and nongovernment) and resources (financial, administrative, technological, etc.) in institutional arrangements that provide the organizational support for actual service provision (Pires and Gomide 2016). These institutional arrangements constitute the governance framework for implementation processes (Capano et al. 2015). Attention to institutional design and the governance of implementation leads us to two mechanisms and their different ways of reproducing inequalities in the daily operation of public services.

a) Representation, power imbalances and poor coordination

Who is entitled (or not) to participate and have their interests and points of view institutionally represented in implementation arrangements? Given that the distribution of power, resources and roles among the different actors involved is often unequal, what are the implications for the capacity of the different actors to intervene in critical decisions regarding implementation strategies and courses of action? The answers to these questions lead us to a first mechanism engendering risks

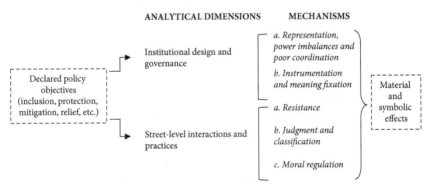

**Figure 6.1** Mechanisms leading to risks of inequality reproduction in policy implementation processes. *Source*: Adapted from Pires (2019).

of exclusion, lack of attention and harm to disadvantaged groups in implementation processes. The implementation phase of the policy process is also an important political arena, in which interested actors seek to participate, influence and control decisions related to operational strategies and actions that ultimately define who gets what and how (Grindle 1980). Therefore, looking at the actors who succeed in taking part in implementation arrangements and those who are left out (or aside), as well as at their levels of connectivity, is an important step in understanding the risks of inequality reproduction in implementation processes.

One illustrative example of this particular mechanism comes from the implementation of employment and professional training policies in Brazil. Mendes (2019) examined the operation of the Conselho Diretor do Fundo de Amparo ao Trabalhador (CODEFAT, Council of the Fund for Workers' Support), a decision-making body composed of representatives of government, workers' unions and business associations responsible for creating and funding professional and technological training programs, as well as regulating the unemployment insurance program, in order to correct distortions and support the development of the Brazilian labor market. Mendes analyzed the proceedings of the meetings and the council's decisions between 1990 and 2016. He discovered that despite statistically visible and persistent gender inequalities operating in the Brazilian labor market over the period (wage gaps, informality, etc.), the topic was rarely approached by CODEFAT (only 12 out of 780 council resolutions). The investigation of the underlying mechanisms revealed, first, that female presence in the council was very low (only 5.9 percent of the councilors, on average). Second, during the course of the meetings, whenever issues associated with gender inequality or the conditions of women in the labor market came up, councilors employed four kinds of discursive tactics to avoid them: not speaking about the topic, postponing, failing to seek additional information or leaving issues in abstract form and not specifying them. Finally, the council neither sought out nor welcomed institutional partnerships with other government bodies responsible for promoting gender equality or programs and services targeting women. As a result, CODEFAT has remained blind to gender issues and the challenges faced by female workers. The combination of insufficient female representation in the council responsible for the design and funding of important labor market interventions, unequal distribution of resources and power among the different actors (male and female councilors) and the absence of institutional partnerships with gender-sensitive organizations in the external environment reinforced barriers to the inclusion of gender issues in CODEFAT's agenda.

In other cases, I observed that different stakeholders and their points of view were formally represented in implementation arrangements. The so-called intersectoral or transversal strategies are characterized precisely by bringing together different types of government and nongovernment actors in order to face complex problems. In these situations, we may see advances in terms of the representation of social groups or different areas of government. Nevertheless, lack of adequate coordination among these diverse actors may also lead to risks of inequality reproduction in implementation processes.

The Fica Vivo! program, operating in the state of Minas Gerais (Brazil) since 2006, which aims to reduce crime rates among youth in communities marked by violence, offers such an example. According to Jesus (2019), the program's institutional arrangement was based on partnerships between the police, the social service department and civil society organizations (such as neighborhood associations and nongovernmental organizations) aiming to combine social development actions (i.e., professional training, cultural activities and social services and benefits) with strategic policing and criminal justice interventions. The discourse of the integrated approach was key in increasing the budget allocations to criminality prevention, when compared with previous attempts in the area. However, as implementation actions unfolded, power imbalances and coordination problems led to a greater appropriation of the funds by police interventions and, consequently, to the underdevelopment of the social component. In the end, such disarticulation produced a public intervention that disproportionally emphasized policing activities in the territories inhabited by poor—and mostly Black—families. Their overexposure to state surveillance contributed not only to increasing tensions and levels of incarceration of this specific group but also to the symbolic reinforcement of stereotypical associations between poverty, race and violence.

Yet another example of the risks associated with poor institutional coordination is provided by Sandim and Assis (2019) in their analysis of the Programa de Assistência Integral a Famílias (PAIF, Program for Integral Assistance to Families), a component of the Sistema Único de Assistência Social (SUAS, National Social Assistance System) in Brazil. Here again PAIF's institutional arrangement was based on the coordination of a network of services involving health care units, the justice department, energy and water provision companies, and kindergarten facilities, among others. However, the investigation of the actual implementation of the program in two municipalities (Belo Horizonte and São Paulo) indicated that the coordination of actions among the different services in the network failed rather frequently. Communication was poor, procedures were not sufficiently aligned and actual collaboration was incipient. These failures tended to affect the poorest families most strongly because the costs of "repairing" the problems of institutional coordination were completely transferred to them: the transportation costs, delays and longer waiting times to access benefits, as well as the burden of repeatedly providing documentation and proof of their precarious life conditions each time they accessed the supposedly networked services. In situations like this, the very search for needed public support can become part of a process in which conditions of vulnerability (materially and symbolically) deteriorate (Herd and Moynihan 2019).

## b) Instrumentation and meaning fixation

In addition to interest representation, power imbalances and poor coordination, another important aspect in the analysis of institutional arrangements for policy implementation is how relationships among the multiple actors involved become stabilized and are made routine through the adoption or development of instruments. Instruments are used by actors to formalize and standardize operations and procedures as well as relationships between different actors involved in the implementation of a service (Le Galès 2010). Examples include information systems, protocols, standard operating procedures, indicators and registration sheets, among others, which establish a routine for exchanges among government organizations, as well as between them and the users of public services. According to Lascoumes and Le Galès (2007), instruments are not only technical but also social devices, because they carry with them social representations about the actors, and they contribute to the convergence of the meanings that actors attribute to their interactions. Consequently, instruments embody preconceptions and values and, therefore, are not neutral. They may empower or disempower, they unevenly distribute responsibilities and benefits, and they make things easier and more accessible for some, while more difficult or out of reach for others.

As instruments take part in arrangements for policy implementation, what visions, values and preconceptions about the users of a service or program become fixed? What are the implications of these instruments for the users? By looking at the instruments that organize relationships among the multiple actors involved in the implementation effort, we gain insight into how different social groups may be treated differently through the operation of apparently neutral devices.

One of the clearest examples of this type of mechanism can be found in the implementation of the Programa Bolsa Família (PBF, Bolsa Familia Program). This internationally renowned conditional cash transfer program in Brazil aims at alleviating extreme poverty and interrupting the intergenerational cycle of poverty by requiring the children of impoverished families to regularly attend school and utilize preventative health care services. PBF's standard operating procedure is transferring the cash directly to the mother (rather than the father), because they are perceived as more likely to use the money to meet their children's needs (i.e., food, hygiene and school supplies). As a result, for many poor women, the cash transfer is their first and only independent source of revenue, contributing to their empowerment in the management of the household. But, as Marins (2019) and Melo and Marques (2019) argue, PBF's standard operating procedure also ends up reinforcing expectations upon the female beneficiaries as the sole responsible party in the care of children, reproducing traditional gender stereotypes and the burden of care that comes with it. This has had clear impacts on the life chances of women by amplifying their disadvantages and reducing their future opportunities in the formal job market, owing to both time restrictions and their own and others' perceptions about their roles.

Another example in a different policy domain regards the selection procedure for accessing public university-level education. Goellner (2019) compared three different admission processes employed by the University of Brasília analyzing data from the years 2012–2016. The first and oldest method is a test of formal knowledge administered at the completion of secondary school (*vestibular*). The second, named Programa de Avaliação Seriada (PAS, Serial Evaluation Program), is also based on secondary school formal knowledge, but it is administered at the end of each of the three years of secondary school. The third and most recent method, Exame Nacional do Ensino Médio-Sistema de Seleção Unificada (Enem-SISU, National

Exam of Secondary Education-Unified Admission System), focuses on the interface of contents, rather than their separation by disciplines, and takes place twice every year. While the first two are administered by the University of Brasília, the third is a national-level standardized test, administered by the Ministry of Education and valid for all federal universities in the country. In sum, the selection procedures differ in terms of their form, content and regulation. Statistical analysis confirmed that the three methods selected significantly different groups of new entrants. While the first two tended to favor the selection of white students from families with higher incomes and with previous experiences in private schools (which, on average, provide higher quality secondary education and preparatory classes for university admissions), the third selection procedure opened greater space for the selection of Black students from lower-income families who had only attended public schools. As this case illustrates, depending on the instruments used to provide access to public universities, additional hurdles may be imposed on the disadvantaged while already established groups may be favored, perpetuating existing inequalities.

## Street-level interactions and practices

Scholarly debates on policy implementation have long asserted the analytical gains derived from a bottom-up perspective, which brings emphasis to the role of implementation agents, their beliefs, behaviors and day-to-day practices and interactions with service users (Hill and Hupe 2014). According to this perspective, we cannot fully understand the risks engendered by implementation processes for the reproduction of inequalities by looking only at institutional designs. The concept of "street-level bureaucracy" (Hupe et al. 2015; Lipsky 1980) sought precisely to focus our attention on the implications of the work performed by implementation agents at the front lines of public service delivery for the objectives of public policies and for the beneficiaries of these policies. Given the conditions under which these frontline agents often perform their jobs—complex rules, shortage of resources, excessive demands, away from superiors' oversight and in face-to-face interactions with users—they inevitably enjoy some level of discretion in the execution of their ordinary tasks. The use of discretion by these agents in turn creates opportunities for creative adjustments, through the introduction of elements and references alien to the formal program or service rules and prescriptions. These adjustments of rules and prescriptions tend to be motivated by implementation agents' desires to gain control over their routines and workloads, as well as by moral judgments based on social values and preconceptions shared by them (and sometimes also by the users). These discretionary accommodations can lead not only to innovations or solutions to emerging problems but also to undesired consequences for beneficiaries (Dubois 1999, 2010). In what follows, we look into the potentially negative consequences of discretional behavior by administrative agents and explore three different kinds of mechanisms (as previewed in Figure 6.1), linking the behaviors and practices of implementation agents to material and symbolic effects associated with the perpetuation of social inequalities.

a) Resistance

The examination of the empirical cases revealed that one of the mechanisms associated with the use of discretion by street-level workers is resistance to formal norms, policy prescriptions and guidelines, and superiors' decisions. In some circumstances, frontline workers may decide to simply ignore or diverge from these institutional mandates. When the institutional rules point toward procedures for inclusion, expansion of access or focalization of vulnerable groups, the resistance of implementation agents to follow through may result in lack of attention, invisibility or inadequate support for those in need.

The case studied by Milanezi and Silva (2019) provides an illustrative example. They examined the implementation of the Política Nacional de Saúde Integral da População Negra (PNSIPN, National Program for Integral Health Care of the Black Population) in local health care centers in the city of Rio de Janeiro. The program was aimed at improving the health of the Black population, in response to statistical evidence demonstrating the disparities in health conditions between Blacks and whites in Brazil. PNSIPN emphasized special attention to that segment of the population and prescribed the local coordination of health care equipment and services for these communities. The research revealed a form of resistance that operated through silence. Local health care professionals rarely talked about the PNSIPN, it was never an issue at their regular team meetings and measures to transform program proposals into formal or informal protocols for practice were not in place. Aiming to understand the motivations behind the silence, the authors found that local health care professionals did not agree with the provision of differential treatment for Black people. They understood this as racism and believed they should deny racial differences in order to provide universal access to service users. They resisted the national program guidelines and formal rules because they did not have the same vision of the problem as policy makers. Meanwhile, a segment of the population needing special attention and treatment remained invisible and not adequately served.

Another example in which mechanisms of resistance emerged in implementation processes and led to unfavorable results for vulnerable segments of the population was the case of the Política Nacional de Assistência Social (PNAS, National Program for Social Assistance) in Brazil (Jaccoud and Abreu 2019). The program was created in 2004 and defined social services and benefits as social rights and government responsibilities. In 2005, a national system for social services was put in place, with a clear division of roles between the federal, state and municipal governments. In 2016, there were a total of 10,000 public facilities and 240,000 social workers providing services at the local level. Jaccoud and Abreu (2019) ran a national survey with the goal of understanding the perceptions of implementation agents in terms of how they conceived of the national policy, their work and the beneficiaries they were meant to serve. The findings indicated significant divergence in these understandings. While some professionals adhered to the formal prescriptions of the program (i.e., a rights-based perspective), others systematically depicted users as "lazy," "opportunistic" and to be blamed for their position in life. For the latter, services and benefits were understood as a gift or favor, rather than a government responsibility to care for those in need. So, in this case, resistance to formal policy, guidelines and rules appeared in the form of divergent interpretations by the workers in charge of implementing policy goals and procedures. In both this and the previous example, the resistance of local implementation agents contributed to weakening the programs' formal objectives of inclusion in terms of providing for the specific needs of vulnerable groups.

### b) Judgment and classification

A second type of mechanism that plays out during street-level encounters between service workers and users is classification. The use of discretion by implementation agents brings up uncertainties and dilemmas about how to proceed in each situation. In reaction, frontline workers develop practical strategies for reducing complexities and uncertainties over time. Chief among these strategies are informal classification systems that allow them to quickly differentiate users and respond accordingly (i.e., deliver service, deny service, demand more documentation). These classification systems often embody preconceptions about the users and mobilize collectively shared stereotypes, which allow implementation agents to judge, in each situation they face, which users "truly" deserve these services (Maynard-Moody and Musheno 2003, 2012). If this practice of classifying the public becomes necessary for making street-level implementation work feasible (Lipsky 1980), it is not without consequences to service users. The practical solutions to the challenges faced by the agents—based on their perceptions, values and representations of the users—often lead to institutional discrimination, lack of attention and selective mistreatment toward vulnerable groups of the population.

Penna's (2019) study of rural development and agrarian reform services in the north of Brazil provides an illustrative example of this mechanism. The ethnography focused on the ordinary interactions between agrarian reform agents and settlers of new colonization projects. Special attention was given to these agents' efforts to adapt complex and demanding national legislation to the local situations. Agrarian reform agents are responsible for validating the regular occupation of lots, a key step for granting settlers access to the benefits of land reform programs. When deciding which lots or families were to be considered part of the program or be deemed an irregular occupant and forced off the lot, agrarian reform agents mobilized additional informal tactics beyond the verification of the family's presence on the lot. They examined their hands and skin to determine whether the family was engaged in agricultural work. They introduced new criteria, such as whether or not the family had a stove and the type of food they consumed (whether it was locally produced or not). While these informal classification schemes proved useful and expedient for agents, helping them to assess the "client's profile," they also led to the exclusion of families that did not meet the agents' expectations of a "good client," even though these families still met the formal program criteria and depended on the program for a living.

I observed the same type of mechanism operating in the case of a public secondary school in Rio de Janeiro that implemented a special class focused on students with educational delays aimed at correcting age-grade deficits. Oliveira and Carvalho (2019) focused their analysis on the decisions principals and teachers took in selecting which students to place in these special classes. They found out that beyond the formal policy criterion (i.e., age-grade deficit of at least two years) other informal criteria were applied in the judgment and classification of students by these implementation agents. Principals and teachers cultivated a narrative about the "ideal profile" for students in these special classes, differentiating those whose educational delay derived from their learning difficulties (cognitive aspect) from those whose delay was related to behavior. Such differentiation was then associated with two main types of responses by school staff: an extraordinary service for students they classified as "deserving," who were placed in the special classes, and an inferior service for students they classified as "undeserving," who remained in regular classes facing educational delays. Principals and teachers would frequently justify their practices in terms of "saving those who can be saved." Consequently, students whose educational delay was identified as related to poor discipline, disinterest or lack of "good will" were readily stigmatized and dismissed from any special kind of support. The informal classification practices performed by principals and teachers not only helped them deal with their difficult working conditions but also contributed to leaving behind a critically disadvantaged group.

c) Moral regulation

The third type of mechanism creating risks of inequality reproduction in the course of street-level implementation relates to the moral regulation of the conduct of users/beneficiaries. While the two previously described mechanisms—resistance and classification—tend to occur when making decisions about access to public services or goods, moral regulation is more likely to occur during service interactions once a person has already become a user or beneficiary. This mechanism highlights the fact that being a user of a public program entails consequences for the users, in particular social stigma, along with the service or benefit provided. The moral regulation of users' conduct can be exercised not only by implementation agents but also by other users and their local communities. Such a practice is associated with symbolic effects, as service interactions may interfere with the users' sense of social place and value (Dubois 1999; Siblot 2006).

Oliveira and do Carmo Peixoto's (2019) analysis of Programa Oportunidades, the well-known conditional cash transfer in Mexico, provides a clear example of how the mechanism of moral regulation plays out. The authors focused on the implementation dynamics involved in the monitoring of the program's educational component—mandated school attendance—and on the interactions between service workers and beneficiaries. Many elementary schools in Mexico have long suffered from underfunding. As a response, school managers have relied on spontaneous monthly donations from parents. In this scenario, those mothers receiving grants from Oportunidades became a target of the collection effort. Since beneficiaries receive a regular stipend from the government, school principals and teachers felt they had a moral obligation to contribute. In some cases, school managers even called upon Oportunidades staff to come to the school to lecture and put pressure on the mothers. School managers felt that because these benefits were coming from the government, they had the right to request donations and other services to the school, such as facility maintenance. If they refused, they would refer to these mothers as opportunistic and uncommitted to the school and to caring for their children. None of these criteria were formal requirements of the program, and their informal introduction by the school staff ended up increasing the burden on poor mothers, in addition to imposing on them a sense of moral debt to the government and their officials.

Eiró (2019) studied the local implementation of the PBF in Brazil and discovered that the same type of mechanism was at play as in the Mexican case. The social workers involved in monitoring beneficiaries were going beyond their formally prescribed roles and performing domicile visits in order to assess how the mothers were spending the money provided by the government. The ethnographic research revealed that a moral hierarchy of spending oriented these assessments. PBF workers approved when the mothers spent the money on their children (food, school supplies, clothing, etc.) but disapproved of other expenses they considered "frivolous," such as new appliances, a cell phone or a motorcycle. PBF workers perceived the latter as indicative of the family's lack of need, which signaled to them that the benefit should be reallocated to other families. As developed by Eiró (2019), these daily interactions reinforced the internalization of social representations of poverty by the poor. In order to maintain the needed benefit, beneficiaries had to conform to social expectations about what it means to be poor, reproducing a subordinate social position.

Finally, in some cases, moral regulation played out among beneficiaries and between beneficiaries and their local communities. Also studying the Bolsa Família case, Marins (2019) explored the implications of being a program beneficiary for the women themselves. The research revealed attempts by these mothers to hide their status at their children's school—for example, because they felt ashamed of receiving a benefit or being considered by the government as "extremely poor" (a formal condition to access the benefit). In relation to their neighbors, these beneficiaries also felt constantly judged in their spending habits. Furthermore, being a beneficiary can be understood as "being in debt with the government"—rather than exercising a right or citizenry—as well as open space for moral regulation by others. By reflecting on a similar situation observed in France, Dubois (2015: 2) asserted that "the precarisation of working-class individuals and the heightened competition for jobs, housing and welfare benefits among them have been conducive to renewed forms of social and symbolic separation (Lamont 2000) between those who work and those who do not work, and, among them, those who 'deserve' support and behave properly and those who do not."

## Final Considerations

For many countries in Latin America, fighting extreme social inequalities remains a fundamental challenge, especially given its long-term persistence. Despite important advances in the first decade of the twenty-first century, since 2015 there have been clear signs of backsliding, especially owing to the increase of extreme poverty in the region (ECLAC 2019). In 2020, the sanitary and economic crises provoked by the Covid-19 pandemic have intensified the tendency toward impoverishment observed in previous years and further contributed to amplifying social inequalities, as opportunities for absorbing the burdens of social isolation and loss of income were very unequally distributed across the rich and the poor. This situation will certainly demand new government actions in the following years in terms of public services provision, relief programs and protections against social exclusion and extreme vulnerability.

Considering present and future needs for inclusion policies and the capacity and resource limitations that characterize governments in developing countries, I proposed an analytical framework aimed at producing applicable knowledge for reinforcing the inclusion of and adequate attention to disadvantaged and vulnerable groups. The framework starts from the recognition that the implementation of policies formally and explicitly aimed at fighting social inequalities may also reinforce it, through day-to-day operations of institutions and ordinary interactions between state agents and the public. Based on the examination of concrete cases of policy implementation in Brazil, Mexico and Peru (a case that was not specifically discussed in this chapter), we identified an array of mechanisms linking implementation dynamics to the material and symbolic effects that reinforce existing inequalities.

I argue that the challenge of making inclusion policies more effective requires governments and their public policy managers and professionals to develop greater awareness and gain a better understanding of the risks of inequality reproduction in implementation processes. Being able to recognize these risks and identify the mechanisms through which they operate is a crucial step in preventing unintended effects from watering down governments' efforts at promoting inclusion.

Developing this type of commitment toward effective inclusion requires continuous efforts in terms of monitoring and evaluating public policy implementation. I recommend these efforts should take risks of inequality reproduction more seriously. The analytical framework presented (Figure 6.1) can be used for such purposes as a tool for guiding preventative assessments (*ex ante*) or evaluations (*ex post*) of public programs/services and their implementation strategies. The framework calls attention to how issues of representation, power imbalances, and lack of coordination, instruments and resources can be analyzed when we look at the institutional design of implementation processes. Moreover, it brings to light the actual behavior and practices of frontline workers such as resistance toward policy objectives, discrimination and moral judgment of the people they serve. The framework helps us move beyond the usual focus on the intended effects of public policies by calling attention to the consequential but often neglected dynamics through which inequalities get reproduced in the day-to-day operations of governments and bureaucracies.

## References

Brodkin, Evelyn. 1990. "Implementation as Policy Politics." In *Implementation and Policy Process: Opening Up the Black Box*, edited by Dennis Palumbo and Donald Calista, 107–118. Westport, CT: Greenwood.

Capano, Giliberto, Michael Howlett and M. Ramesh. 2015. "Re-thinking Governance in Public Policy: Dynamics, Strategy and Capacities." In *Varieties of Governance*, edited by Giliberto Capano, Michael Howlett and M. Ramesh, 3–24. London: Palgrave Macmillan.

Cardenas, Juan-Camilo, Natalia Candelo, Alejandro Gaviria, Sandra Polanía and Rajiv Sethi. 2010. "Discriminación en la Prestación de Servicios Sociales para los Pobres: Un Studio Experimental de Campo." In *Discrimination in Latin America: An Economic Perspective*, edited by Hugo Nopo, Alberto Chong and Andrea Moro, 41–106. Washington, DC: Inter-American Development Bank and the World Bank.

Crenshaw, Kimberlé. 1995. "Mapping the Margins: Intersectionality, Identity Politics, and Violence against Women of Color." *Stanford Law Review*, 43(6): 1241–1299.

Dubois, Vincent. 1999. *La Vie au Guichet: Relation Administrative et Traitement de la Misère*. Paris: Economica (Collection Études Politiques).

Dubois, Vincent. 2010. "Politiques au Guichet, Politiques du Guichet." In *Politiques Publiques: Des Politiques Pour Changer la Société?*, edited by Olivier Borraz and Vincent Guiraudon, 265–285. Paris: Presses de Sciences-Po.

Dubois, Vincent. 2015. "What Do Public Policies Do to Their Publics?" Keynote Speech made at the 10th International Conference on Interpretive Policy Analysis, Lille, France, 8 July.

ECLAC (Economic Commission for Latin America and the Caribbean). 2016. *La Matriz de la Desigualdad Social en América Latina*. Santiago: ECLAC.

ECLAC (Economic Commission for Latin America and the Caribbean). 2019. *Panorama Social de América Latina 2018*. Santiago: ECLAC.

Eiró, Flávio. 2019. "A 'Boa Implementação' do Programa Bolsa Família: A Interação Entre Assistentes Sociais e Beneficiárias para Além das Regras Burocráticas." In *Implementando Desigualdades: Reprodução de Desigualdades na Implementação de Políticas Públicas*, edited by Roberto Pires, 617–636. Rio de Janeiro: Instituto de Pesquisa Econômica Aplicada.

Goellner, Isabella. 2019. "Estratificação Universitária Através de Dispositivos de Seleção: O Caso da Universidade de Brasília." In *Implementando Desigualdades: Reprodução de Desigualdades na Implementação de Políticas Públicas*, edited by Roberto Pires, 349–374. Rio de Janeiro: Instituto de Pesquisa Econômica Aplicada.

Grindle, Marilee. 1980. *Politics and Policy Implementation in the Third World*. Princeton, NJ: Princeton University Press.

Gupta, Akhil. 2012. *Red Tape: Bureaucracy, Structural Violence, and Poverty in India*. Durham, NC: Duke University Press.

Hankivsky, Olena and Renee Cormier. 2011. "Intersectionality and Public Policy: Some Lessons from Existing Models." *Political Research Quarterly*, 64(1): 217–229.

Herd, Pamela and Donald Moynihan. 2019. *Administrative Burden: Policymaking by Other Means*. New York: Russell Sage Foundation.

Hill, Michael and Peter Hupe. 2014. *Implementing Public Policy: An Introduction to the Study of Operational Governance*. London: Sage.

Hupe, Peter, Michael Hill and Aurelien Buffat. 2015. *Understanding Street-Level Bureaucracy*. Bristol: University of Bristol.

Jaccoud, Luciana and Maria Cristina Abreu. 2019. "Entre o Direito e a Culpabilização das Famílias: o que Pensam os Trabalhadores do SUAS sobre as Ofertas e os Beneficiários." In *Implementando Desigualdades: Reprodução de Desigualdades na Implementação de Políticas Públicas*, edited by Roberto Pires, 485–504. Rio de Janeiro: Instituto de Pesquisa Econômica Aplicada.

Jesus, Andrea. 2019. "A Política de Prevenção à Criminalidade Como Perpetuação do Racismo de Estado." In *Implementando Desigualdades: Reprodução de Desigualdades na Implementação de Políticas Públicas*, edited by Roberto Pires, 267–282. Rio de Janeiro: Instituto de Pesquisa Econômica Aplicada.

Lamont, Michèlle. 2000. *The Dignity of Working Men: Morality and the Boundaries of Race, Class, and Immigration*. New York: Russell Sage Foundation.

Lamont, Michèlle. 2017. "Prisms of Inequality: Moral Boundaries, Exclusion, and Academic Evaluation." In *Praemium Erasmianum Essay 2017*, 9–48. Amsterdam: Praemium Erasmianum Foundation.

Lamont, Michèlle, Stephan Beljean and Matthew Clair. 2014. "What Is Missing? Cultural Processes and Causal Pathways to Inequality." *Socio-Economic Review*, 12: 573–608.

Lascoumes, Pierre and Patrick Le Galès. 2007. "Introduction: Understanding Public Policy Through Its Instruments: From the Nature of Instruments to the Sociology of Public Policy Instrumentation." *Governance*, 20(1): 1–21.

Le Galès, Patrick. 2010. "Policy Instruments and Governance." In *The SAGE Handbook of Governance*, edited by Mark Bevir, 235–253. London: SAGE Publications.

Lipsky, Michael. 1980. *Street Level Bureaucracy: Dilemmas of the Individual in Public Services*. New York: Russell Sage Foundation.

Lipsky, Michael. 1984. "Bureaucratic Disentitlement in Social Welfare Programs." *Social Service Review*, 58(1): 3–27.

Marins, Mani. 2019. "Estigma e Repercussões do Status de Beneficiária." In *Implementando Desigualdades: Reprodução de Desigualdades na Implementação de Políticas Públicas*, edited by Roberto Pires, 657–678. Rio de Janeiro: Instituto de Pesquisa Econômica Aplicada.

Maynard-Moody, Steven and Michael Musheno. 2003. *Cops, Teachers, Counselors: Narratives of Street-Level Judgment*. Ann Arbor: University of Michigan Press.

Maynard-Moody, Steven and Michael Musheno. 2012. "Social Equities and Inequities in Practice: Street-Level Workers as Agents and Pragmatists." *Public Administration Review*, 71(1): 16–23.

Melo, Janine and Danusa Marques. 2019. "Dos Estereótipos à Cidadania: Sobre Mulheres, Estado e Políticas Públicas." In *Implementando Desigualdades: Reprodução de Desigualdades na Implementação de Políticas Públicas*, edited by Roberto Pires, 375–402. Rio de Janeiro: Instituto de Pesquisa Econômica Aplicada.

Mendes, Cassio. 2019. "A Sub-Representação Feminina no Codefat: Táticas de Acomodação e Barreiras Sociais e Institucionais." In *Implementando Desigualdades: Reprodução de Desigualdades na Implementação de Políticas Públicas*, edited by Roberto Pires, 283–302. Rio de Janeiro: Instituto de Pesquisa Econômica Aplicada.

Milanezi, Jaciane and Graziella Silva. 2019. "Silêncio—Reagindo à Saúde da População Negra em Burocracias do SUS." In *Implementando Desigualdades: Reprodução de Desigualdades na Implementação de Políticas Públicas*, edited by Roberto Pires, 441–462. Rio de Janeiro: Instituto de Pesquisa Econômica Aplicada.

Nakamura, Robert and Frank Smallwood. 1980. *The Politics of Policy Implementation*. New York: Saint Martin's Press.

Neri, Marcelo. 2018. "Sumário-Executivo: Qual Foi o Impacto da Crise sobre Pobreza e Distribuição de Renda?" *FGV Social*, 10 September.

Oliveira, Marina and Cynthia Carvalho. 2019. "Enfrentando o Fracasso Escolar No Nível Local: A Atuação Discricionária de Professores e Diretores Escolares na Implementação de uma Política Educacional." In *Implementando Desigualdades:*

*Reprodução de Desigualdades na Implementação de Políticas Públicas*, edited by Roberto Pires, 549–570. Rio de Janeiro: Instituto de Pesquisa Econômica Aplicada.

Oliveira, Breyner and Peixoto Maria do Carmo. 2019. "Trazendo à Tona Aspectos Invisíveis No Processo de Implementação de Políticas Públicas: Uma Análise a Partir do Programa Oportunidades." In *Implementando Desigualdades: Reprodução de Desigualdades na Implementação de Políticas Públicas*, edited by Roberto Pires, 637–656. Rio de Janeiro: Instituto de Pesquisa Econômica Aplicada.

Penna, Camila. 2019. "Parceria e Construção do 'Perfil de Cliente da Reforma Agrária' Como Estratégias para a Implementação de Políticas Públicas Pelo INCRA." In *Implementando Desigualdades: Reprodução de Desigualdades na Implementação de Políticas Públicas*, edited by Roberto Pires, 595–616. Rio de Janeiro: Instituto de Pesquisa Econômica Aplicada.

Pires, Roberto. 2019. "Introdução." In *Implementando Desigualdades: Reprodução de Desigualdades na Implementação de Políticas Públicas*, edited by Roberto Pires, 13–52. Rio de Janeiro: Ipea.

Pires, Roberto and Alexandre Gomide. 2016. "Governança e Capacidades Estatais: Uma Análise Comparativa de Programas Federais." *Revista de Sociologia e Política*, 24(58): 121–143.

Pressman, Jeffrey and Aaron Wildavsky. 1973. *Implementation: How Great Expectations in Washington Are Dashed in Oakland; Or, Why It's Amazing that Federal Programs Work at All, This Being a Saga of the Economic Development Administration as Told by Two Sympathetic Observers Who Seek to Build Morals on a Foundation of Ruined Hopes.* California: University of California Press.

Sandim, Tatiana and Marcos Assis. 2019. "O Arranjo Institucional de Implementação do PAIF e seus Potenciais Efeitos No Cotidiano de Operação do Serviço: Introduzindo Questões para o Debate." In *Implementando Desigualdades: Reprodução de Desigualdades na Implementação de Políticas Públicas*, edited by Roberto Pires, 201–221. Rio de Janeiro: Instituto de Pesquisa Econômica Aplicada.

Siblot, Yasmine. 2006. *Faire Valoir ses Droits au Quotidien: Les Services Publics dans les Quartier Populaire.* Paris: Presses de Sciences-Po.

Souza, Pedro. 2018. *Uma História de Desigualdade: a Concentração de Renda Entre os Ricos no Brasil, 1926–2013.* São Paulo: Hucitec.

Thomas, John and Marilee Grindle. 1990. "After the Decision: Implementing Policy Reforms in Developing Countries." *World Development*, 18(8): 1163–1181.

Vedung, Evert. 2013. "Side Effects, Perverse Effects and Other Strange Effects of Public Interventions". In *Capturing Effects of Projects and Programmes*, edited by Lennart Svensson, Göran Brulin, Sven Jansson and Karin Sjöberg, 35–62. Lund: Studentlitteratur.

## Chapter 7

# CITY-TO-CITY COOPERATION AND THE PROMISE OF A DEMOCRATIC "RIGHT TO THE CITY"

## EXPERIENCES FROM BRAZIL AND MOZAMBIQUE

Fritz Nganje

### *Introduction*

The challenges associated with rising urbanization in Africa, and elsewhere in the developing world, have brought renewed attention to the way cities and other urban areas are governed. In particular, against the backdrop of the neoliberal restructuring of global capitalism and its adverse impacts on urban politics and development, there have been growing concerns about the erosion of democracy in cities, with many academics and social activists calling for new forms of urban governance that allow urban residents to reclaim control over the decisions that shape the city. It is in this context that the idea of the "right to the city," coined in the 1960s by French philosopher and sociologist Henri Lefebvre (1968), has been resuscitated and given prominence in the works of academics and social activists. Initially introduced by Lefebvre to challenge the exclusion and disempowerment inherent in functionalist urban planning, the right to the city is invoked today as a democratic response to the urban manifestations of neoliberal globalization.

Since the late 1960s, the notion of the right to the city has not only inspired social movement struggles in cities across the world but also gained traction with UN agencies that promote inclusive urban governance such as UN-Habitat and the UN Educational, Scientific and Cultural Organization (UNESCO). However, it is in Brazil that the idea has taken on concrete institutional form with the adoption in 2001 of the City Statute, which enjoins federal, state and local governments to promote social justice and the democratic management of the country's cities. As detailed in subsequent sections of this chapter, the implementation of this legislation has produced mixed results. However, against the backdrop of the contemporary discourse on South–South cooperation, many Brazilian cities have been at the forefront of efforts to transform urban governance processes in other developing countries, notably in Africa, based on their own experiences with institutionalizing and implementing the idea of a democratic right to the city.

This chapter analyzes the contribution of Brazilian cities to efforts aimed at institutionalizing and implementing the right to the city and enhancing democratic local governance in Mozambique through city-to-city cooperation. It departs from the premise that city-to-city cooperation has the potential to improve urban governance and development by exposing local authorities and communities to useful experiences, best practices and innovative ideas. However, I argue that the ability of city-to-city cooperation to enhance urban democracy and inclusive development in a manner that gives expression to the idea of the right to the city has been undermined by its predominantly technocratic and depoliticized approach. This has enabled the urban elite to thwart the transformative potential of city-to-city cooperation by using their position as gatekeepers of the institutional landscape of cities to determine which foreign ideas are localized and how.

The argument is developed in five sections. I start by reviewing the neoliberal dynamics that breed urban inequality and exclusion, and which have given rise to advocacy for the right to the city. I then examine the Brazilian experience in implementing the right to the city, before discussing attempts to export this experience to Mozambique through city-to-city cooperation. The fourth part is dedicated to a critique of city-to-city cooperation as a tool for promoting inclusive development. I conclude the chapter by making the case for repoliticizing city-to-city cooperation in the global South in order to unlock its transformative capacity.

## Neoliberal Urbanism, Disenfranchisement and the Right to the City

Cities around the world find themselves at the coalface of the current restructuring of global capitalism. Not only do they constitute the strategic nodes of an increasingly networked global economy, but as scholars such as Simon Curtis (2011) and Saskia Sassen (2005) have observed, they have also become sites where many of the contradictory processes of neoliberal globalization assume concrete and localized forms. More importantly, the prominence of cities in the current phase of global capitalism has been accompanied by far-reaching changes in the way these urban areas are governed, with significant implications for democracy and enfranchisement in cities. Mark Purcell (2002) has identified three ways in which governance is being reconfigured in deference to the dictates of neoliberal capitalism. First, governance is being rescaled to allow new supranational institutions and subnational governments to assume more powers and responsibilities alongside nation-states. Second, as cities have become relatively autonomous entities that are connected more to the global economy than their national economies, the policy orientation of city governments has also shifted from demand-oriented redistribution toward promoting the economic competitiveness of their localities. Third, in a bid to enhance their competitiveness in a global economy, cities have embraced a corporate governance ethos that prioritizes efficiency over all other considerations, and many have resorted to outsourcing some of their functions and powers to quasi-state and non-state entities that are "not directly accountable to the local electorate and conventional democratic control" (Purcell 2002: 101). Thus, out of all these changes have emerged new forms of urban governance that are largely undemocratic and "exclude local inhabitants from the decisions that shape their cities" (Purcell 2002: 100–101). For example, Sophie Didier and her colleagues show how neoliberal-inspired city improvement district models implemented in South African cities such as Cape Town and Johannesburg have contributed to reinforcing apartheid-era socio-spatial inequalities, thanks to "their profit-oriented conception of redevelopment through the creation of commodified spaces of elite consumption, the intensified surveillance of public spaces and collateral exclusionary processes" (Didier et al. 2013: 121).

In response to the neoliberal disenfranchisement of a large segment of the contemporary urban population, many scholars and social activists have invoked Henri Lefebvre's notion of the right to the city to advocate for more inclusive forms of urban existence and greater democratic governance in the city. The right to the city was originally advocated by Lefebvre as a critique of modernist conceptions of the city as a technical object that must be planned and built by technocrats with objectivity and scientific accuracy. Lefebvre argued that "the city was not a backdrop but a space produced ideologically and politically, and a medium for strategies and struggles" (Morange and Spire 2015: 1). In this regard, he criticized the functionalist approach to urban planning, which while pursuing the ideal of an orderly and efficient city was accompanied by the eviction of the working classes from the inner city and the stifling of the autonomous social practices, such as the production of graffiti and street art, through which city-dwellers took part in the production of urban space (Morange and Spire 2015). The Lefebvrian right to the city is, therefore, a call for the radical transformation of "the power relations that underlie the production of urban space, fundamentally shifting control away from capital and the state and toward urban inhabitants" (Purcell 2002: 101–102).

Somewhat different from its original and radical conception, the right to the city is deployed today mainly as a progressive response to the urban manifestations of neoliberal capitalism, which, as pointed out earlier, has brought about the democratic disenfranchisement of urban residents, excluding the vast majority of the urban population from the making of decisions that shape the city. It advocates for enhanced urban democracy to redress traditional and elitist forms of urban governance, which create cities that prioritize the interests of business and the wealthy class while generating urban poverty, socio-spatial exclusion, gentrification and environmental degradation (Attoh 2011; Morange and Spire 2015). Thus, in its current iteration, the right to the city embodies a fundamental challenge and an attempt to undo the modern politico-legal framework that, in the urban context, purports to represent the interests and aspirations of all city-dwellers, but in reality it only reinforces and reproduces the privileges of a few. It is a call for a shift from procedural democracy with its emphasis on electoral politics to substantive democracy that opens up possibilities for socioeconomic and cultural justice in the city (see Purcell 2008). It is for this reason that Melissa Lamarca (2009) has cautioned against depoliticizing the right to the city movement, questioning whether "a concept based in fundamentally changing current social, political and economic relations in the city [can] actually become part of existing institutions such as municipalities and UN agencies."

However, some scholars have cautioned against embracing the notion of the right to the city as a panacea to the problem of neoliberal disenfranchisement in the city. In particular, attention has been drawn to the challenge of putting into practice the right to the city given the contradictions and tensions inherent in the idea. For example, Kafui Attoh (2011) has argued that because rights are understood differently by different groups in society, instituting the right to the city—say by emphasizing second-generation rights intended to combat socioeconomic injustices such as the right to shelter—may come at the expense of other equally important rights, notably classical first-generation rights that seek to protect the liberties and privileges of citizens such as the right to private ownership of property. This is bound to generate political conflict, which may only be resolved through negotiations and trade-offs. Purcell (2002) makes a similar case, arguing that rather than offer a precise and more progressive alternative to neoliberal urbanism and its undemocratic structures, Lefebvre's right to the city only opens up the possibilities of a new "urban politics of the inhabitant," the outcomes of which cannot be known a priori. As a catalyst for a new political struggle, the right to the city may give rise to either greater urban democracy or new forms of political domination.

### Implementing the Right to the City: The Brazilian Experiment

Brazil presents a unique case where the idea of the right to the city has been translated into binding legislation and could therefore be seen as a sociopolitical laboratory that holds significant insights into the practical challenges associated with the implementation of the right to the city. Brazil went through a process of rapid urbanization in the 1900s, becoming one of the most urbanized developing countries by the end of the twentieth century. In 2015, 85.7 percent of Brazil's total population of just under 208 million people was living in urban areas. In the words of Leonardo Avritzer (2010: 153), during this period "Brazilian cities grew in an unfair, disorderly and illegal way." With the exclusion of the poor from urban planning and development processes in major Brazilian cities such as São Paulo, Belo Horizonte and Porto Alegre, the illegal occupation of state land by the homeless and the proliferation of slums—the so-called favelas—became two key features of urbanization in the Brazilian context. These conditions would subsequently give rise to social movements of mainly neighborhood associations and favela residents, which advocated for access to better housing and the legalization of occupied state land (Avritzer 2010; Friendly 2013).

However, it was Brazil's transition from military dictatorship to democracy in the 1980s that inspired the emergence of a national urban reform movement, which was at the forefront of efforts to legalize and institutionalize the right to the city. The Movimento Nacional de Reforma Urbana (MNRU, National Movement for Urban Reform), today the Fórum Nacional para Reforma Urbana

(FNRU, National Forum for Urban Reform), was established in 1982 as a coalition of diverse social actors, including popular movements, neighborhood associations, nongovernmental organizations, professional groups and trade unions. Its activism during Brazil's constitution-making process, from 1987 to 1988, succeeded in enshrining the fundamental principles of the right to the city in the 1988 Constitution (Friendly 2013; Avritzer 2010). Articles 182 and 183 of the constitution recognize the social function of urban property and make provisions for the legalization of the occupation of urban land by the homeless poor (Government of Brazil 1988). Against the backdrop of a protracted legislative process characterized by lobbying, political horse-trading and even legal battles, the constitutional principles on urban reform policy were elaborated in a federal law, the Statute of the City, which was adopted in the Brazilian Congress in 2001.

As a legal embodiment of the right to the city principle, the Statute of the City enjoins and enhances the capacity of Brazil's federal, state and local governments to promote the social function of cities and urban property, as well as the democratic management of cities, with a view to realizing the collective interests of all urban inhabitants. Among the innovative instruments designed to foster social justice in the production and use of urban space, the statute empowers local governments to progressively raise taxes on undeveloped urban land belonging to private property developers and even expropriate unused urban buildings. These, and a related tool that authorizes local administrations to raise revenue for social projects by taxing certain categories of private property development, are intended to discourage land and real estate speculation while redistributing the costs and benefits of urban development. Additionally, the Statute of the City makes provisions for city governments to protect poor communities from being evicted from urban land they occupy, formalize favelas and legalize, under certain conditions, the occupation of urban land by the poor. With regard to the democratic management of cities, the statute mandates the effective participation of urban residents and their associations in all significant decision-making processes of city governments and institutes a set of mechanisms through which this should be realized. These include participation in the formulation of compulsory master plans for cities with a population of 200,000 inhabitants or more, public hearings, municipal conferences and participatory budgeting (Friendly 2013).

The implementation of the principles and provisions contained in Brazil's constitution and Statute of the City has produced mixed results. On the one hand, this new legal order has allowed some Brazilian cities to experiment with progressive strategies for democratizing urban governance and development, such as the innovative participatory budgeting process pioneered by Porto Alegre in the 1990s, resulting in improved access to housing and other social services for the urban poor (Avritzer 2010; Friendly 2013). In such cities, exemplified by Porto Alegre, the dominance of left-wing political parties and a strong tradition of grassroots social activism have been key contributing factors to the relatively successful implementation of the democratic ideals embodied in the constitution and City Statute. Generally, the legalization and institutionalization of the right to the city in Brazil owes much to the strong activism and resilience of local and national civil society, as well as the improved political fortunes of the Partido dos Trabalhadores (PT, Workers' Party), which took over the reins of the federal government in 2003. Not only did PT parliamentarians serve as allies of the MNRU in the Brazilian Congress, but once in power, President Luiz Inácio Lula da Silva (commonly known as Lula) established a Ministry of Cities, with a mandate to assist municipalities to implement the provisions of the Statute of the City (Avritzer 2010). On the other hand, against the backdrop of Brazil's neoliberal turn in the 1990s, the urban reform initiatives inspired by the right to the city have faced significant resistance and backlash from conservative segments of society, to the extent that "important local elections have been lost, ground-breaking programs have been discontinued, forced eviction has taken place in some cases, and bills of law altering the City Statute have been proposed" (Fernandes 2007: 218; Lamarca 2011). In cities such as São Paulo and Salvador, where property interests are well organized and conservative and right-wing political parties have had a strong hold on local government, efforts to implement the statute have been particularly fraught with tensions and conflict between progressive and conservative forces (Avritzer 2010).

Notwithstanding these setbacks, Brazil's experimentation with the idea of the right to the city has attracted significant international attention, as it is seen to provide a useful model of democratic urban planning and management. Not surprisingly, against the backdrop of Lula's foreign policy commitment to promote South–South solidarity, there emerged a number of initiatives to leverage the Brazilian experience—through city-to-city cooperation—to inspire democratic governance and inclusive development in other cities across the developing world. We will now proceed to analyze the dynamics of these learning initiatives and explore their potential to institutionalize the right to the city, drawing on the case of cooperation between Brazilian cities and their Mozambican counterparts.

## City-to-City Cooperation and the Right to the City: Exporting the Brazilian Experience to Mozambique

Brazil's attempts at urban reform coincided with a period of renewed belief in the benefits of South–South cooperation, which in the twenty-first century has evolved to include exchanges between an array of sub-state and non-state actors, including city and other local governments. City-to-city development cooperation in this context, therefore, embodies the key principles and features of South–South cooperation, including the primacy of autonomous local development, noninterference in the domestic affairs of other states and a strong statist approach to cooperation (see, e.g., UCLG 2017).

Partnerships between Brazilian and Mozambican cities for enhancing the democratic rights of urban residents have been driven by four key factors. The first driver is the aspiration of Brazilian cities for global recognition and influence. Major Brazilian cities such as São Paulo, Rio de Janeiro, Belo Horizonte and Porto Alegre have used place-branding strategies to project a positive image of and position themselves favorably in a global economy that is also increasingly being organized around the productivity of cities and other urban areas. These cities have taken an interest in sharing their innovative urban policies and practices with their counterparts in Mozambique and the rest of the developing world, as a way of building a positive global reputation and developing networks of influence. City-to-city cooperation in this context has also afforded Brazilian cities, especially those governed by anti-neoliberal parties such as the left-wing PT, the opportunity to legitimize their pioneering urban policies and build a transnational network that is capable of influencing global policy discourses in favor of pro-poor and pro-democracy approaches to urban governance and development (Nganje 2016).

A second driver of cooperation between Brazilian and Mozambican cities was Brazil's foreign policy during the presidency of Lula da Silva from 2003 to 2011. With its focus on strengthening South–South cooperation as a strategy to project Brazil's influence globally and challenge the neoliberal hegemony of the West, Lula's foreign policy created sufficient space for city governments—especially those governed by the PT—to assume a proactive role in international relations. Salomon argues that during this time the attitude of the federal government toward the international activities of Brazilian states and cities shifted from mere acceptance to actually incorporating them into its own foreign policy strategies, especially in the domain of development cooperation (Salomon 2011: 60–61). Against the backdrop of the central role played by the PT in championing Brazil's pro-poor and pro-democracy urban reform process, Lula's administration actively encouraged Brazilian cities to disseminate their experience in institutionalizing the right to city to Africa and other developing countries.

To this end, Brazil partnered with the French government in 2011 to establish a program on trilateral city-to-city cooperation, which allowed French and Brazilian cities to jointly provide technical assistance to their counterparts in Haiti and Africa. Among the projects that have been supported under this framework is the trilateral cooperation initiative involving the Brazilian city of Guarulhos, its French counterpart of Seine-Saint-Denis, and the Mozambican cities of Maputo and Matola (Leite et al. 2014). This project built on existing sister-city partnerships between Maputo and Guarulhos on the one hand and Matola and Seine-Saint-Denis on the other hand, and provided resources and institutional support, which enabled the Mozambican cities to learn from the experience of their Brazilian and French counterparts in sustainable and inclusive urban waste management.[1] In February 2012, the Brazilian government launched another program on decentralized South–South technical cooperation, through which the country's state and municipal governments received financial and technical support from Brazil's development cooperation agency to share successful public policies with their counterparts in other developing countries. Under this program, the Brazilian city of Vitória shared its participatory urban planning techniques and

---

1. Personal conversations with an official in the international relations directorate of the Maputo City Council, October 2014 and April 2015.

its agricultural development technologies with the city of Xai-Xai in Mozambique (Leite et al. 2014).

The third driver of cooperation between Brazilian and Mozambican cities is related to the role of Western donors, multilateral development organizations and city networks. Organizations such as the World Bank, the United Nations Development Programme (UNDP), the International Labour Organization (ILO), UN-Habitat and Cities Alliance played a major role in supporting Brazil's progressive urban reform process in the 1990s and early 2000s. Not surprisingly, these organizations have championed initiatives intended to transfer lessons and best practices from this experience to other developing countries, including through South–South knowledge exchanges between cities. Notable examples of cooperation between Brazilian and Mozambican cities promoted by international organizations include an initiative undertaken under the auspices of the ILO's Decent Work Agenda. This project created a framework for the Brazilian cities of Porto Alegre and Belo Horizonte, as well as Durban in South Africa, to share their experiences and insights into managing informal inner-city trading with Maputo and other Mozambican cities. Another example of a city-to-city cooperation initiative sponsored by an international organization is the technical exchange program between Maputo and the Brazilian state of Paraná and its associated cities. Supported by the World Bank, this initiative sought to improve the Mozambican capital city's capacity to collect property taxes and raise revenue for the enhanced delivery of municipal services (Nganje 2016).

A fourth major driver of cooperation between Brazilian and Mozambican cities has been their active membership in United Cities and Local Governments (UCLG), a global network of local and regional governments. Since 2005, the network has encouraged and supported learning exchanges and mentorship between cities in Mozambique and Brazil as part of a decentralized cooperation program that seeks to leverage the benefits of South–South cooperation to enhance urban management policies and practices in the developing world. The first phase of this program, named City Future project, was funded by the Norwegian government and Cities Alliance, and brought together eight cities from Mozambique and six from Brazil into a loose collaborative framework that allowed the latter to share their experiences and best practices on urban management and development with their Mozambican counterparts (UCLG 2013, 2014). The second phase of the program was launched in January 2013 and ended in June 2015. Building on the initial City Future project, this phase of the program adopted a rather ambitious goal of democratizing the participating cities in line with the concept of a right to the city. In the words of the UCLG, "the project's aim was to improve the management of local development in terms of effective governance, sustainability and participation to extend the population's right to the city" (UCLG 2015). As Table 7.1 suggests, the areas chosen for this city-to-city cooperation mirrored the democratic imperative at the heart of the project.

According to a post-project report produced by the UCLG, the exchanges between Brazilian cities and their Mozambican counterparts "effectively fulfilled the [promise] of contributing to the strengthening of municipal capacities"

**Table 7.1** UCLG's Brazil–Mozambique city-to-city partnerships to democratize the city

| Brazilian city | Mozambican partner | Area of cooperation |
|---|---|---|
| Canoas | Matola | Participatory budgeting |
| Belo Horizonte | Maputo | Management of informal settlements |
| Porto Alegre | Inhambane | Participatory budgeting, urban management |
| Guarulhos | Dondo | Participatory budgeting and social participation |
| Guarulhos | Nampula | Urban planning and inclusive cadastral system |
| Vitória | Xai-Xai | Urban planning |
| Maringa | Lichinga and Manhica | Inclusive cadaster |

*Source*: Author's construction based on UCLG (2015).

(UCLG 2015: 63). In particular, the report underscored the contribution of the project in empowering Mozambican city officials with the knowledge and capacity to use inclusive cadasters to improve the use and management of urban land, develop urban plans through participatory processes, and design and implement effective participatory budgeting mechanisms. More importantly, the report argued that by adopting a methodology that involved both technical experts and the political leadership of cities, the city-to-city exchanges "allowed local leaders to follow innovative routes and make direct commitments to their citizens" in terms of governing and developing the cities through democratic, participatory and inclusive processes. The only challenge that was foreseen in securing the gains in democratic local governance and inclusive urban planning resulting from city partnerships was the sustainability of learning exchanges once the resources and institutional support associated with the project were withdrawn (UCLG 2015).

However, I argue in the next section that there are more fundamental obstacles to institutionalizing the democratic right to the city through city-to-city exchanges than the uncertainty of financial resources or institutional commitment from donors to sustain cooperation between participating cities. The major weakness of city-to-city cooperation as a tool for delivering on the promise of enhanced local democracy and inclusive processes of urban development is the inability of the mechanism to influence power relations in Mozambican cities in favor of marginalized poor urban residents. City-to-city cooperation in this context has generally assumed a rather technocratic and depoliticized approach to urban reform, which fails to take into account the politically contested nature of the process that took place to institutionalize the right to the city in Brazil.

## The Limits of City-to-City Cooperation as a Tool for Democratic Urban Reform

The introduction of democratic statutory local government in Mozambique in the 1990s was championed by Western donors and development agencies as a tool to foster both democratization and socioeconomic development, especially in urban areas such as Maputo, which were struggling to cope with a population explosion amid an economic crisis (Ginisty and Vivet 2012). Prior to this period, a centralized state directed the political and administrative affairs of the country's urban areas. However, the creation of, and the devolution of power to, democratic local authorities has for the most part failed to engender inclusive development and participatory governance in Mozambique's rapidly urbanizing cities. As the capital and largest city of Mozambique, Maputo embodies most of the challenges that have undermined Mozambique's experimentation with democratic local governance. In addition to the weak financial and technical capacity of the municipal government, the city's embrace of neoliberal economic policies has privileged urban management practices that have benefited mainly the economic and political elites. The majority of the urban population has been excluded from formal housing and land use and remained without access to basic social services in the city (Jenkins 2000). Moreover, as Ginisty and Vivet (2012) have argued, the decentralized structure of governance that was designed to promote participatory local democracy and give urban residents a voice in the management of the city has largely been reduced to a tool for entrenching the hegemony of the ruling Frelimo party, and its system of patronage and corruption in Maputo. Even after the introduction of decentralized local governance, party structures continued to be fused with local government structures, allowing Frelimo officials to stifle democracy at this level of governance (see Maschietto 2016).

It is in this context that the Maputo City Council, under the political leadership of a relatively progressive mayor, Eneas Comiche (2003–2008), and encouraged by Western donors and city networks such as the UCLG and Cities Alliance, turned to Brazil for lessons and ideas on alternative and more inclusive forms of urban management and development. Maputo previously had sister-city partnerships or had engaged in technical cooperation with a number of metropolitan and intermediary cities from Brazil, including Rio de Janeiro, Guarulhos, Porto Alegre and Belo Horizonte. It also had a partnership on technical cooperation with the Brazilian federated state of Paraná. As was the case with other Mozambican cities, Maputo's "look south" policy in its city-to-city cooperation was motivated by a desire to replicate Brazil's urban reform experiment in the Mozambican capital city, with the promise of extending the democratic right of the city's marginalized poor population, defined in this context mainly in terms of socioeconomic inclusion.

Turning this noble vision into an urban reality, however, has proven to be a challenge for Maputo city officials and their international sponsors, owing primarily to sociopolitical differences in the Brazilian and Mozambican contexts, and the failure of the design of city-to-city cooperation mechanisms to reflect these disparities. As detailed earlier in this chapter, the institution of the right to the city as a legal principle in Brazil, and its relatively successful implementation in a number of Brazilian cities, resulted from the convergence of favorable sociopolitical dynamics, most notably Brazil's strong culture of grassroots social activism and the influence of the PT in Brazilian politics at the time. The combined strength of these two forces not only contributed to diluting the traditional liberal politico-legal order that had for centuries bred marginalization and poverty in Brazilian cities but also provided a formidable bulwark against the onslaught of neoliberal and conservative constituencies aiming to reverse the gains in democratic urban reform.

The Mozambican context lacks both of these key determining factors for democratic urban reform. Although cities such as Maputo have seen the emergence of grassroots associations of marginalized and poor urban residents, these remain weak and have been unable to effectively defend and promote their respective interests, let alone constitute the nucleus of a broad urban reform movement. What is more, with the advent of political and economic liberalization in Mozambique, the ruling Frelimo party, which has also governed the city of Maputo since 1998, has been reduced to a vehicle for protecting the interests of the elite through a system of clientelism and corruption (Sumich 2008). In such a society where political and economic power is wielded by a highly conservative and elitist class, and the mobilizing ability of civil society remains weak, the contribution of city-to-city cooperation to institutionalizing a transformative urban agenda has been limited. As gatekeepers of the institutional landscape of the city, the local elite have determined which ideas and best practices derived from city-to-city cooperation are localized and how this is carried out. Needless to say, ideas and practices that are perceived to threaten the power and interests of the elite have been fiercely resisted.

The ability of Maputo's political and economic elite to undermine the transformative agenda of city-to-city cooperation is reinforced by the rather depoliticized nature of the process through which lessons and tools from Brazil's democratic urban reform experience have been transferred to the Mozambican context. City-to-city cooperation between Maputo and its Brazilian counterparts has been a predominantly technocratic exercise, which focuses on broadening the knowledge, awareness and expertise of municipal officials, without challenging the political dynamics that reproduce poverty, inequality and exclusion in the city. Admittedly, Maputo's knowledge exchange and capacity-building initiatives have had the backing of the city's top leadership and in some instances have actually been championed by reform-minded mayors. However, without incorporating an element that seeks to empower marginalized urban communities and groups to better mobilize and challenge existing power relations as was the case in Brazil, city-to-city cooperation has achieved little more than improving the technical and administrative capacity of the city government. The goal of democratizing the city and broadening the right of all residents to produce and use urban space has largely remained a pipe dream. In what follows, I draw on three examples of Maputo's city-to-city cooperation with its Brazilian partners to illustrate this argument.

*Promoting the right to trade in the inner city*

In 2012, the UCLG and the ILO initiated a city-to-city cooperation project involving the city of Maputo, the Brazilian cities of Belo Horizonte and Porto Alegre, and the South African city of Durban. As Kamete and Lindell (2010) documented, Maputo has since the 1980s struggled to reconcile the aspirations of the local elite to create and project a modern city image with the rapidly increasing informal trading activities of the urban poor. The initiative thus aimed to assist Maputo to develop a more inclusive approach to managing the use of its inner-city space by drawing on the experiences of the two Brazilian cities and their South African counterpart. These three cities have earned a reputation for experimenting with urban planning policies and practices that recognize and seek to protect the right of street vendors to use the inner-city space as a source of livelihood. As a number of scholars have observed, even in the context of relatively progressive urban management policies, upholding the right to the city of street vendors in Belo Horizonte, Porto Alegre and Durban has been a constant struggle. These efforts have pitted informal traders against private property interests and conservative elements of society (see, e.g., Carrieri and Murta 2011; Itikawa et al. 2014; Salej 2010; Skinner 2009).

The Maputo mentoring and learning exercise made use of collaborative exchanges and reflective workshops, including site visits to informal markets in the Maputo city center, to explore ways in which the experiences of participating Brazilian and South African cities in promoting the inclusive use of the inner-city space could be adapted to the local context in Maputo. A key outcome of the exercise was a change in attitude on the part of municipal officials in Maputo, who came to acknowledge the right of street vendors to use the inner-city space for their livelihood. Among other changes, this required the city to reconsider and possibly end its practice of arbitrarily evicting street vendors from the city center and relocating them to sections of the city that were not economically viable, thereby compromising the livelihoods of informal traders. It also put an obligation on the authorities to consult and collaborate with street vendors and other stakeholders in making decisions on the use of the inner-city space (UCLG 2012).

Implementing these best practices, however, proved to be difficult in the context of Maputo where, as Kamete and Lindell (2010) note, the local political and economic elite are traditionally opposed to the idea of street vending in the city center, and the approach of local authorities has been to restrict these activities. The tension between the right to city space and welfare of street vendors, and the interests of the local elite, has determined the extent to which the progressive ideas emanating from the city-to-city learning exchange have influenced Maputo's attitude toward street vendors.[2] In the context of the weak mobilizing power of street vendors, the preferences and interests of the local elite have generally trumped the right of the former to use the inner-city space to secure their livelihood. A draft municipal policy proposed by city officials and which would have institutionalized the lessons and best practices derived from the city-to-city exchange was rejected by the Maputo Municipal Assembly.[3]

2. Personal conversation with officials of the Maputo City Council, Maputo, 7 October 2014.

3. Personal conversation with officials of the Maputo City Council, Maputo, 7 October 2014.

*The struggle to institute participatory budgeting in Maputo*

The political dynamics around early attempts to implement the idea of participatory budgeting in Maputo also illustrate the limitations of city-to-city cooperation as a mechanism for institutionalizing the democratic right to the city. In 2003, the then mayor of Maputo, Eneas Comiche, launched a process of introducing participatory budgeting to the city's planning processes based on the experience of Porto Alegre in Brazil. In addition to deploying two municipal employees to intern in Porto Alegre, Comiche himself visited the Brazilian city to personally appreciate its participatory budgeting processes (Nylen 2014). Moreover, at the invitation of the mayor of Porto Alegre, a group of technical experts from Maputo visited Porto Alegre in 2006 to learn more about participatory budgeting processes (Carolini 2015).

Following these city-to-city exchanges, and with the support of the World Bank Institute, UN-Habitat and Cities Alliance, Maputo adopted a model of participatory budgeting that gave expression to the idea that all urban residents have a right to actively participate in the management of their city. The Brazilian-inspired model of participatory budgeting allowed residents in Maputo's 63 neighborhoods and seven districts to deliberate and identify priority public works projects that the city council would invest in. Approximately 15 percent of the city's investment budget was dedicated to projects emanating from this process (Nylen 2014).

However, in the absence of a dedicated grassroots civil society movement and a governing party committed to participatory local democracy, as was the case in Porto Alegre, Maputo's experimentation with the Brazilian model of participatory budgeting struggled to take root in the city. On the one hand, antireform elements within the ruling Frelimo party adamantly opposed any process that would challenge the entrenched system of patronage through which the city was managed. On the other hand, because of the conflation of Frelimo and local government structures in Maputo, participatory budgeting turned out to be "an instrument of partisan mobilization or manipulation rather than empowerment or oversight" (Nylen 2014: 18). In the end, the Brazilian model of participatory budgeting, infused with the radical democratic idea of a right to the city, was abandoned in favor of a so-called community development version of participatory budgeting—which was championed by the World Bank. Although designed to weaken the influence of the party-state officials and enhance citizen participation, this model of participatory budgeting was considerably scaled down in terms of both budgetary allocation for projects and the scope of participation (Nylen 2014).

*Securing the right of* catadores *to earn a living from city waste*

Maputo's technical cooperation with the Brazilian city of Guarulhos on solid waste management also highlights the difficulty in promoting democratic urban reform through a predominantly technocratic approach to city-to-city cooperation. Guarulhos, like many other Brazilian cities, is reputed for its integrated and participative approach to solid waste management, which hinges on collaboration between the municipality and waste recycling cooperatives. More importantly, consistent with the right to the city principle, Guarulhos' approach to solid waste management recognizes and actively promotes waste picking as a source of livelihood for the urban poor. Since 2011, and with partial support from the decentralized cooperation program sponsored by the Brazilian and French governments, Maputo and Guarulhos have engaged in a series of technical exchanges with the aim of giving the Mozambican city the opportunity to learn from Guarulhos' experience in integrating *catadores* (waste pickers) into the city's solid waste management system.

However, efforts to transform Maputo's solid waste management system into an inclusive and participatory enterprise that secures the livelihood of *catadores* have largely been stymied by the fact that the latter are marginalized in Mozambican society. According to officials directly involved in the technical exchange with Guarulhos, part of the challenge in localizing the Brazilian model of waste management in Maputo lies in the enduring negative attitude of local communities and authorities toward *catadores* and their activities. *Catadores* are generally stigmatized as criminals, outcasts or failures, and although the municipality's attitude toward them is believed to have improved over the years as a result of the exposure to Brazil's urban reform experience, there is still significant resistance to their official recognition and incorporation into Maputo's solid waste management system (Allen and Jossias 2011).[4]

As Allen and Jossias (2011: 11–12) have correctly argued, the continued marginalization of *catadores* in Maputo is reinforced by the fact that this constituency is not fully conscious of its potential, and that it has had limited exposure to the experiences of their peers in other countries, including, for example, "the achievements of the *catadores* in Brazil in obtaining legal recognition and rights and self-respect." This perspective brings into sharp relief the shortcomings inherent in promoting democratic urban reform through a predominantly technocratic approach to city-to-city cooperation. Arguably, a more holistic approach to the cooperation between Maputo and Guarulhos— which, in addition to exchanges between municipal officials and technicians, also made provision for networking between *catadores* and other civil society actors from both cities—would have a much greater impact on the transformation of solid waste management practices in Maputo by empowering *catadores* to assert their right to earn a living from the city's landfills.

### Conclusion: Bringing Back Politics to City-to-City Cooperation

The combination of rapid urbanization and neoliberal capitalism has turned modern cities into new sites of political contestation, as different constituencies

---

4. Information in this section was obtained partly from personal conversation with officials of the Maputo City Council, October 2014, April 2015 and January 2016.

in the city assert their right to produce and use urban space in pursuit of diverse interests and aspirations. In the developing world, Brazil stands out as a country where a radical democratic constituency, inspired by Henri Lefebvre's idea of a right to the city, was able to secure some degree of urban reforms in favor of impoverished and disenfranchised city residents. Despite the increasingly fragile nature of Brazil's experiment on democratic urban reform, it has inspired similar efforts in Africa and other developing countries. In this chapter, I have used the example of partnerships between Brazilian and Mozambican cities to critique attempts to democratize urban governance and development through city-to-city cooperation. I have argued that a narrow and technocratic approach to city-to-city cooperation is incapable of inducing the kind of democratic reform that the right to the city demands. As was the case in Brazil, this requires significant redistribution of power in the local political society. Without aiming to transform urban power relations, city-to-city cooperation can at best improve the capacity of local authorities to plan and deliver social services in an inclusive and efficient manner. At worst, it can serve to reinforce the disenfranchisement of marginalized urban communities.

What is required therefore is a reconception of city-to-city partnerships, not as neutral technical exchanges but as inherently political tools that can either reinforce unequal power relations in cities or be fashioned into catalysts for inclusive urban transformation. Against the backdrop of the discourse to undo the inequalities that have become pervasive in urban spaces, the challenge then is to design these partnerships in a manner that is sensitive to their implications for the distribution of power among stakeholders in the city. One way to do it is to democratize this aspect of urban governance by incorporating exchanges between a cross section of relevant stakeholders into the design of city-to-city partnerships. This would ensure that key social groups with a stake in a particular urban issue are actively involved in the transnational linkages that shape the governance of this issue. The implications of such an inclusive design for the fight against inequality and exclusion in the city are twofold. First, by broadening the actors involved in city-to-city cooperation and embedding these exchanges in the social dynamics in the city, these exchanges are transformed into a site for renegotiating power relations in the city rather than just reinforcing them. Second, an inclusive approach to city-to-city cooperation would afford marginalized urban groups the opportunity to network with, and draw inspiration from, their peers in other countries, with the potential for effective social activism.

Furthermore, the analysis of Maputo's experience with the right to the city underscores the difficulty in implementing this principle given the contested nature of rights and the strong vested interests in the existing politico-legal order. This makes a sustained, broad-based national movement critical for making any gains in democratizing the city. Finally, the Mozambican case analyzed here reinforces the limitations associated with the predominant statist approach to South–South cooperation. It is therefore prudent for organizations such as the UCLG, ILO and UNDP interested in tapping into the developmental potential of South–South cooperation to conceive of and design their projects in a manner that gives agency to critical non-state actors.

## References

Allen, Charlotte and Elísio Jossias. 2011. "Mapping of the Policy Context and Catadores Organizations in Maputo, Mozambique." *WEIGO Organizing Brief No. 6*. Manchester: Women in Informal Employment: Globalizing and Organizing.

Attoh, Kafui A. 2011. "What Kind of Right Is the Right to the City?" *Progress in Human Geography*, 35(5):669–685.

Avritzer, Leonardo. 2010. "Democratising Urban Policy in Brazil: Participation and the Right to the City." In *Citizen Action and National Policy Reform: Making Change Happen*, edited by John Gaventa and Rosemary McGee, 153–173. London and New York: Zed Books.

Carolini, Gabriella. 2015. "Valuing Possibility: South–South Co-operation and Participatory Budgeting in Maputo." In *Urban Planning in Sub-Saharan Africa: Colonial and Post-Colonial Planning Cultures*, edited by Carlos N. Silva, 285–300. New York: Routledge.

Carrieri, Alexandre and Ivana Murta. 2011. "Cleaning Up the City: A Study on the Removal of Street Vendors from Downtown Belo Horizonte, Brazil." *Canadian Journal of Administrative Science*, 28(2): 217–225.

Curtis, Simon. 2011. "Global Cities and the Transformation of the International System." *Review of International Studies*, 37(4): 1923–1947.

Didier, Sophie, Marianne Morange and Elisabeth Peyroux. 2013. "The Adaptative Nature of Neoliberalism at the Local Scale: Fifteen Years of City Improvement Districts in Cape Town and Johannesburg." *Antipode: A Radical Journal of Geography*, 45(1): 121–139.

Fernandes, Edésio. 2007. "Constructing the 'Right to the City' in Brazil." *Social and Legal Studies*, 16(2): 201–219.

Friendly, Abigail. 2013. "The Right to the City: Theory and Practice in Brazil." *Planning Theory & Practice*, 14(2): 158–179.

Ginisty, Karine and Jeanne Vivet. 2012. "Frelimo Territoriality in Town: The Example of Maputo." *L'Espace Politique*, 18(3).

Government of Brazil. 1988. *Constitution of the Federative Republic of Brazil 1988*. Brasília: Government of Brazil.

Itikawa, Luciana, Andre Alcantara, Geilson Sampaio, Luiz Kohara, Carolina Ferro and Francisco Comarú. 2014. *Street Vendors and the Right to the City*. São Paulo: Gaspar Garcia Center for Human Rights.

Jenkins, Paul. 2000. "Urban Management, Urban Poverty and Urban Governance: Planning and Land Management in Maputo." *Environment & Urbanisation*, 12(1): 137–152.

Kamete, Amin Y. and Ilda Lindell. 2010. "The Politics of 'Non-Planning' Interventions in African Cities: Unravelling the International and Local Dimensions in Harare and Maputo." *Journal of Southern African Studies*, 36(4): 889–912.

Lamarca, Melissa Garcia. 2009. "The Right to the City: Reflections on Theory and Practice." *Polis*, 11 November.

Lamarca, Melissa Garcia. 2011. "Right to the City in Brazil." *Polis*, 14 October.

Lefebvre, Henri. 1968. *Le Droit de la Ville*. Paris: Anthropos.

Leite, Iara C., Melissa Pomeroy, Laura T. Waisbich, and Bianca Suyama. 2014. "Brazil's Engagement in International Development Cooperation: The State of the Debate." *Institute of Development Studies, Evidence Report No. 59*. Sussex: IDS.

Maschietto, Roberta Holanda. 2016. "Decentralisation and Local Governance in Mozambique: The Challenges of Promoting Bottom-up Dynamics from the Top Down." *Conflict, Security & Development*, 16(2): 103–123.

Morange, Marianne and Amandine Spire. 2015. "A Right to the City in the Global South?" *Metropolitics*, 7 April.

Nganje, Fritz. 2016. "Brazilian Cities in Mozambique: South-South Development Cooperation or the Projection of Soft Power?" *Journal of Southern African Studies*, 42(4): 659–674.

Nylen, William R. 2014. *Participatory Budgeting in a Competitive-Authoritarian Regime: A Case Study (Maputo, Mozambique)*. Maputo: Instituto de Estudos Sociaise Económicos.

Purcell, Mark. 2002. "Excavating Lefebvre: The Right to the City and Its Urban Politics of the Inhabitant." *GeoJournal*, 58(2–3): 99–108.

Purcell, Mark. 2008. *Recapturing Democracy: Neoliberalization and the Struggle for Alternative Urban Futures*. New York: Routledge.

Salej, Ana P. 2010. "Informal Economy Budget Analysis in Brazil and Belo Horizonte." *WIEGO Working Paper No. 15*. Manchester: Women in Informal Employment: Globalizing and Organizing.

Salomon, Monica. 2011. "Paradiplomacy in the Developing World: The Case of Brazil." In *Cities and Global Governance: New Sites for International Relations*, edited by Mark Amen, Noah J. Toly, Patricia L. McCarney and Klaus Segbers, 45–68. Burlington: Ashgate.

Sassen, Saskia. 2005. "The Global City: Introducing a Concept." *Brown Journal of World Affairs*, 11(2): 27–43.

Skinner, Caroline. 2009. "Challenging City Imaginaries: Street Traders Struggles in Warwick Junction." *Agenda: Empowering Women for Equity*, 23(81): 101–109.

Sumich, Jason. 2008. "Politics after the Time of Hunger in Mozambique: A Critique of Neo-Patrimonial Interpretation of African Elites." *Journal of Southern African Studies*, 34(1): 111–125.

UCLG (United Cities and Local Governments). 2012. "Peer Learning in Maputo City, Mozambique: 'Hygiene, Health and Markets.'" *PLN-3*. Barcelona: UCLG.

UCLG (United Cities and Local Governments). 2013. *Decentralised Cooperation between Mozambique and Brazil Advances through Technical Exchange*. Barcelona: UCLG.

UCLG (United Cities and Local Governments). 2014. *Decentralised Cooperation in the South: An Effective Tool to Promote Development*. Barcelona: UCLG.

UCLG (United Cities and Local Governments). 2015. *Decentralised Cooperation to Democratise Cities: Pro Project to Improve the Institutional Capacities of Local Authorities in Brazil and Mozambique as Actors of Decentralised Cooperation*. Barcelona: UCLG.

UCLG (United Cities and Local Governments). 2017. *UCLG Shares City-to-City Dimensions of South-South Cooperation at the ILO Academy on Social and Solidarity Economy*. Barcelona: UCLG.

**Part III**

ELITE IDEOLOGY AND PERCEPTIONS OF INEQUALITY: IMPLICATIONS FOR REDISTRIBUTION AND SOCIAL COHESION

# Chapter 8

## ELITES, IDEAS AND THE POLITICS OF INCLUSIVE DEVELOPMENT

Tom Lavers[1]

### Introduction

Under what circumstances do political elites take action to address forms of inequality and what motivates their decision to do so? This chapter argues that ideas are a key factor shaping the structures that produce inequality—from intra-elite power relations to institutions—and that ideational change can play an important role in tackling inequality, including by shaping patterns of accumulation, redistribution and recognition.

Ideas—along with material interests, institutions and psychology—are one of the four main modes of explanation in political analysis (Parsons 2007). While materialist and institutionalist approaches have dominated political science, those who would deny the causal role of ideas in the social world face something of an uphill battle. As Mehta (2011) argues, if ideas were not influential, then the entire professions of marketing, advocacy and political spin doctors would be obsolete. Likewise,

> Asserting that ideas do not matter would mean that shifting ideals about science, religion, democracy, slavery, colonization, gender, race, and homosexuality, to pick just a few salient examples, either have not appreciably affected how people act or were themselves the product of technological, economic, or other material forces. (Mehta 2011: 24)

The challenge therefore is not really to prove that ideas are important but to show how ideas can be analyzed and to demonstrate how this adds value. This chapter makes a modest contribution to this debate by assessing how an analytical focus on ideas might be integrated into recent work in the politics of development and

1. This chapter was written as part of the Effective States and Inclusive Development (ESID) Research Centre based at the University of Manchester. This document is an output from a project funded by UK Aid from the UK government for the benefit of developing countries. However, the views expressed and information contained in it are not necessarily those of, or endorsed by, the UK government, which can accept no responsibility for such views or information or for any reliance placed on them.

how this deepens our understanding of the ways in which politics shapes patterns of resource distribution and in/equality.

To do so, the chapter focuses on the political settlements framework that has attracted a great deal of attention in development studies in recent years. Khan (2010) defines a political settlement as a compatible balance between the holding power of different elite and nonelite factions, and the distribution of resources resulting from formal and informal institutions. Holding power, meanwhile, is defined as "the capability of an individual or group to engage and survive in conflicts" and is a product of diverse factors including economic resources, organizational capacity and the ability to absorb costs (Khan 2010: 6). A common theme of this political settlements literature has been to distinguish between dominant political settlements, where the ruling coalition has centralized power and faces little in the way of political opposition, and competitive ones, where powerful challengers threaten the ruling coalition's hold on power, whether through electoral or non-electoral means. While this literature has made many positive contributions to understandings of the politics of development, ideas are relatively neglected in the framework. The focus of this chapter is to rethink the political settlements framework with a view to incorporating a focus on ideas, going beyond the usual focus on ideas as a means to "mop up some unexplained variance in a particular outcome of interest" (Blyth 2011: 84).

The next section examines different theoretical approaches to the analysis of ideas and highlights how these theories necessitate a rethink of the political settlements framework. This adapted political settlements framework is then used to synthesize the results of three recent research projects examining the politics of natural resources, social protection and gender. This analysis highlights the importance of ideas—from the global spread of policy-specific ideas to broader ideas that underpin national political settlements—in shaping patterns of inequality and contributing to progressive change.

## Conceptualizing Ideas, Elites and Politics

Recent work examining how politics shapes patterns of accumulation and distribution has been influential in highlighting the need to move beyond a narrow focus on institutions to understand how power relations shape the functioning of formal and informal institutions that distribute resources within society (Acemoglu and Robinson 2012; Khan 2010; North et al. 2009). Though distinct in many ways, these works have a common focus on intra-elite power relations that shape the formal and informal institutions that govern society. This is not to say—as some critics suggest—that the sole analytical focus is on elite politics, since the mobilization of nonelites as well as the distribution of power within society as a whole remains a central part of these theories. Rather, a focus on elites is justified in terms of these actors' disproportionate influence on the political system. Following Di John and Putzel (2009), elites principally comprise the main capitalists in agriculture, manufacturing and services; traditional chiefs, landlords and regional political leaders; traditional and religious leaders; and political party leaders.

Khan's (2010) political settlements framework and North, Wallis and Weingast's (2009) access orders framework were conceived as responses to new institutional economics and the limitations that result from focusing exclusively on how institutions shape human behavior. Retaining the materialist underpinnings of new institutional economics, however, they pay relatively little attention to ideas. Khan (2010) does highlight the potential use of ideas by elites to mobilize political support as a means of achieving their predefined interests but does not acknowledge the potential for ideas to shape those interests. North, Wallis and Weingast (2009), meanwhile, acknowledge that beliefs are one constitutive element of the access orders that are the focus of their work. Nonetheless, the main analytical use of beliefs in their work is to show that particular beliefs can support or hinder institutional enforcement—a usage that fits well in the category of mopping up unexplained variance, noted earlier.

While these various approaches to studying the politics of development have made significant contributions, there are also clearly gaps. Ultimately, the political settlements framework provides an explanation for some constraints faced by political elites but offers little insight as to why particular policies are chosen over other plausible alternatives (Sen 2012). The proposition analyzed in this chapter is that a focus on ideas can not only fill this gap regarding policy choices but also deepen our understanding of how political settlements are negotiated, maintained and contested.

Anyone attempting to take the analysis of ideas seriously will quickly find themselves in tension with the rational choice assumptions that underpin the political settlements framework. Rational choice theories adopt simplifying assumptions that render social actors predictable and thereby enable a social science modeled on the natural sciences. These assumptions are that actors act rationally in pursuit of their own self-interest and that these interests can be derived from the material context within which they operate (Hay 2011). Individual agency is effectively assumed away, with the result that actors' behavior becomes a logical consequence of their environment and therefore predictable. While these assumptions might be justified as a means to constructing parsimonious theories, they are evidently a major simplification.

Recent work on discursive, ideational or constructivist institutionalism (Blyth 2002, 2011; Hay 2011; Schmidt 2008) offers an alternative approach. From this constructivist perspective, there is no such thing as material interests; rather interests are only ever perceived interests that are based on an individual's subjective interpretation of material reality based on a set of causal beliefs (Hay 2011; Schmidt 2011). One of the logical implications of this constructivist approach is to give a central role in analysis to agency, since an analytical focus on ideas cannot be separated from the actors that formulate and promote ideas and whose perceptions are, in turn, shaped by them (Campbell 2004). This constructivist standpoint and the emphasis on individual agency undermine the possibility of a political science modeled on the natural sciences. To many, therefore, this discursive institutionalism "risks appearing highly voluntaristic unless the structural constraints derived from the three new institutionalisms are included" (Schmidt 2011: 60).

## Ideas, ideational stability and change

A common critique of ideational analysis has been that ideas are vague concepts and, as such, are not amenable to analytical usage. It is therefore essential that any attempt to take ideas seriously within the politics of development must clearly differentiate between the many different types of ideas. Several theorists have proposed typologies of ideas, particularly focusing on the level of generality.

To take an influential example, Kingdon (1984) proposes three main levels of ideas: policy ideas that offer potential solutions to predefined problems; problem definitions that define how a particular social issue should be understood, in the process limiting the scope for potential policy ideas; and public philosophies and the zeitgeist. Here, public philosophies "are broader ideas that cut across substantive areas," in particular "how to understand the purpose of government or public policy in light of a certain set of assumptions about the society and the market" (Mehta 2011: 27). Meanwhile, the zeitgeist is "a set of assumptions that are widely shared [within society] and not open to criticism in a particular historical moment" (Mehta 2011: 27). Though differing in terminology, Hall (1993), Sabatier (1988) and Schmidt (2008) propose largely compatible typologies that highlight the scope or breadth of different types of ideas.

Just as institutions are "sticky," so ideas tend to be path dependent (Hall 1993; Cox 2001; Blyth 2002). However, there is likely to be considerable difference in the degree of path dependence between different levels of ideas. While lower-level ideas—such as policy ideas—may be relatively amenable to change over a short period of time, changes to philosophies or paradigmatic ideas are akin to religious conversions and are only likely to occur infrequently. Research has frequently identified shocks and uncertainty as key drivers of ideational change (Blyth 2002). Outside periods of crisis, ideas—particularly paradigmatic ideas—are likely to be relatively stable, leading to stability also in actors' perceived interests. However, during episodes of extreme uncertainty—for example, during economic crises in which dominant theory fails to provide an explanation of current events—actors are unsure not just about how to achieve their perceived interests but also about what their interests actually are (Blyth 2002). It is during these periods of extreme uncertainty that paradigmatic ideas are open to revision and actors seek out alternative paradigms that can provide a guide.

## Integrating ideas into an extended political settlements framework

The University of Manchester's Effective States and Inclusive Development (ESID) Research Centre sought to test the explanatory power of political settlements across a range of sectors and, in doing so, has extended Khan's (2010) political settlements framework in three main areas (Hickey 2013). First, ESID's framework complements the concept of the political settlement itself, with an analytical focus on particular policy domains, examining the ways in which the political settlement influences different sectors. Second, ESID's work emphasizes the interaction between political settlements—which focus attention almost exclusively on domestic politics—and transnational processes. Third, and most important for this chapter, ESID seeks to expand beyond the interests-based focus of the political settlements framework to include a focus on ideas.

Ideas are inherently intertwined with the interests and institutions that are the key elements of the political settlements framework. In this section, I outline the key elements of an ideational approach to political settlements analysis. In doing so, the framework necessarily broadens the conception of power from the focus on holding power in Khan's work—the ability of actors and groups to survive in conflict—to incorporate forms of ideational power (Carstensen and Schmidt 2016; Parsons 2016). Ideational power is the capacity of actors to shape the beliefs and actions of others, by using ideas as tools of persuasion; imposing preferred ideas and limiting space for alternatives; and shaping structures and institutions that, in turn, influence the behavior of other actors (Carstensen and Schmidt 2016). As with other forms of power, elites by definition have disproportionate control of—though far from a monopoly on—this ideational power.

Within the political settlement itself, the formal and informal institutions that are subject to negotiation and contestation between contending factions "are built on ideational foundations" (Hay 2011: 69). Ideas provide the blueprints for these institutions (Schmidt 2008), and they also continue to exert an independent influence on their development and enforcement (Hay 2011). In this sense, a political settlement is defined not just by a set of institutions that deliver an acceptable distribution of resources but by shared ideas between factions that form a constitutive component of the political settlement itself. In turn, the forging of political settlements is also a discursive process used to secure the support of contending factions and shape perceptions of the legitimacy of the political settlement. As such, ideas can play important roles as "coalition magnets," providing a shared sense of meaning and purpose to groups that would otherwise have distinct interests (Béland and Cox 2016). Of particular relevance to the stability and dynamics of political settlements as a whole are likely to be the broadest level of ideas, including public philosophies and paradigmatic ideas that provide an overarching road map or "a relatively coherent set of assumptions about the functioning of economic, social and political institutions" (Béland 2005: 8). Indeed, research has frequently noted that a key virtue of ideas that act as coalition magnets can be their ambiguity (Béland and Cox 2016) or "multi-vocality" (Parsons 2016: 456), which allows groups with otherwise diverse interests to see value in the same idea.

In addition, the interests of the contending factions within a political settlement are not material interests but perceived interests that are the product of ideational influence (Hay 2011). While these perceived interests may be relatively stable for considerable periods—and therefore may appear to approximate the assumptions of material interests—they are open to change and critical re-evaluation during periods of extreme uncertainty (Blyth 2002). Furthermore, not only do ideas shape interests, but ideas can also be actively used by actors to achieve their perceived interests: for example, with political elites securing the support or acquiescence of lower-level factions through appeals to ideas such as nationalism, development, social justice or religion (Blyth 2002; Khan 2010; Schmidt 2008).

Ideas are likely to be just as influential at the level of the policy domain. Here Sabatier's (1988) advocacy coalition framework provides some useful insights. Advocacy or policy coalitions operate within a particular policy domain and comprise a network of individuals and groups that "share a set of normative and causal beliefs" and "engage in a nontrivial degree of coordinated activity over time" (Sabatier and Jenkins-Smith 1999: 120). Sabatier and Jenkins-Smith (1999: 122) hypothesize that it is what they call "policy core" ideas—roughly equivalent to problem definitions, as defined earlier—that provide "the fundamental glue of coalitions" within a particular policy domain, just as paradigmatic ideas have the potential to play a similar role in national-level political settlements. Figure 8.1 summarizes these insights and proposes an adapted version of the political settlements framework.

## Insights into the Role of Ideas: Research Findings

This section synthesizes the results of three ESID projects and situates them with respect to this adapted political settlements framework and their implications for tackling inequality. These projects examine the political drivers of institutional change in mineral and hydrocarbon extraction in Bolivia, Ghana, Peru and Zambia (Bebbington et al. 2018); the politics of the adoption and expansion of social protection in Ethiopia, Kenya, Rwanda, Uganda and Zambia (Hickey et al. 2019); and the politics of domestic violence legislation in Bangladesh, Ghana, Rwanda and Uganda (Nazneen et al. 2019). The discussion is structured around the three components of the framework in which ideas play a major role, namely the political settlement, the transnational sphere and the policy domain.

### Ideas within the political settlement

The causal role of ideas in negotiating and sustaining a political settlement is perhaps most clearly apparent in dominant party settings where power is highly centralized and the ruling coalition faces little organized opposition. In Ethiopia and Rwanda, a set of paradigmatic ideas are widely shared and uncontested within the ruling elite and, arguably, form part of the basis of the political settlements themselves.[2] In both cases, these paradigmatic ideas concern the need for rapid socioeconomic

2. The dramatic events that have occurred in Ethiopia since 2018, though not covered here, involve questioning many of these core paradigmatic ideas and have contributed to considerable uncertainty and instability.

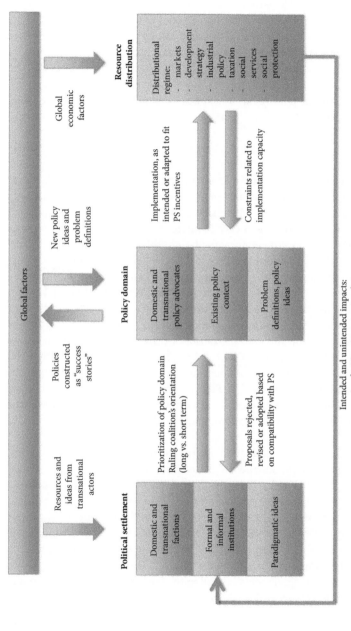

**Figure 8.1** Adapted political settlements framework. *Source: Revised based on an earlier version in Lavers and Hickey (2016).*

development as a means of ensuring peace and stability. By implication in Rwanda and explicitly in Ethiopia, rapid development is also considered to be a means of ensuring the political legitimacy of the ruling coalition. In each case, some degree of upheaval was necessary to achieve this ideational coherence within the ruling coalition. In Rwanda, this occurred through a series of defections and expulsions from the ruling coalition in the early 2000s, including the departure of the prime minister, president and speaker of the national assembly. This realignment of elites took place alongside a series of debates on the future of the country and the national development strategy. In Ethiopia, the key event was a split in the ruling party in 2001, which was followed by an explicit attempt by Prime Minister Meles Zenawi to make developmentalism "a hegemonic project in the Gramscian sense" (Zenawi 2012: 167).

In Bolivia, Ghana, Peru and Zambia, bargaining over natural resource rents is a central feature of the political settlement. As such, competing ideas regarding the management of natural resources and, in particular, normative justifications for different revenue-sharing arrangements between national, transnational and subnational groups are key influences on elite bargains and institutional design. One of the most prominent paradigmatic ideas has been that of resource nationalism, which justifies the management and utilization of natural resources for the benefit of the nation and the people, in direct response to transnational influences of colonialism and postcolonialism (discussed in the following section). Ideas of resource nationalism have clearly influenced institutional design and thereby the political settlement itself through, for example, the inclusion of provisions in national constitutions stipulating that the state is the owner of sub-soil mineral resources and the nationalization of extractive industries. Resource nationalism has been influential in all the four cases but has particularly been employed by elites during periods of dominant party rule in Kaunda's Zambia in the late 1960s and early 1970s and in Peru under the nationalist revolutionary government of 1969–1974. More recently, resource nationalism was a key element of the Movimiento al Socialismo that brought Evo Morales to power in Bolivia in 2006.

Ideas have also been influential in the contestation over revenue-sharing between national and subnational elites. Discourses of national unity have been deployed by the Bolivian and Ghanaian governments in an attempt to counter subnational claims and secure a greater proportion of the rents for the national government. In contrast, there are examples in Peru and Bolivia where Indigenous groups and their leaders in new areas of resource extraction have contested this focus on national unity with competing ideas on Indigenous rights and the need to overcome histories of marginalization and exclusion. These ideational battles are the basis of institutional agreements regarding the bargains over natural resource rents and, indeed, the terms under which excluded factions are brought into the ruling coalition.

Ideas relating to the governance of natural resources are a major influence on rent allocation and therefore the political settlement itself. In contrast, the findings from the projects on social protection and gender suggest that paradigmatic ideas on either issue had yet to become central features of political settlements, reflecting the comparatively marginal status of these policy domains in elite politics. A partial exception here is Rwanda, where the particular history of extreme conflict and gender-based violence has resulted in a strong commitment within the executive to paradigmatic ideas on gender equality. Gender equality has been supported and promoted by the president—by far the most powerful actor in the dominant coalition—resulting in legislation on quotas for female MPs, co-ownership of land and domestic violence legislation. Even here, though, while gender equality does appear to enjoy widespread support within the ruling coalition, it is unclear whether ideas on gender equality constitute an integral feature of the political settlement in the sense that a loss of consensus would threaten the legitimacy or stability of the settlement itself. As such, there is a difference between gender equality and the dominant narrative on the need to transcend ethnicity and promote national unity, which is very much an integral feature of the current Rwandan political settlement.

In both Ethiopia and Rwanda, while specific ideas on social protection do not form an integral part of the political settlement, core paradigmatic ideas regarding the need for rapid and broad-based socioeconomic development did provide part of the justification for the adoption and expansion of social protection programs. In each country, these paradigmatic ideas were a central reference point for all government policies and exerted a strong influence on the types of policies that are deemed acceptable. Furthermore, commitment to social protection in Ethiopia and Rwanda can be traced to distributional crises that were perceived by ruling elites as threats to the stability and legitimacy of the ruling coalition itself. While ideas on social protection may not yet be an integral feature of the political settlement, social protection has nonetheless been used to reinforce or protect the settlement.

The case studies highlight something of a difference in the types of ideas that underpin different types of political settlement. The paradigmatic ideas underpinning the dominant coalitions in Ethiopia and Rwanda are primarily programmatic in nature. Here a shared commitment to rapid development and an interventionist role for the state in directing this development are central to each political settlement. For the most part, in the competitive settlements politics tends to be based on personality, ethnicity or region, rather than strong programmatic commitments. Here, as Levitsky and Way (2010: 5) have argued, regular elections have become embedded and "widely viewed as the primary means of gaining power," even if there is an extremely unequal playing field between incumbents and opposition. To paraphrase Linz and Stepan (1996) slightly, while elections may not be the "only game in town," they are at least one of the important ones. As such, the idea of electoral competition is one of the defining features of competitive settlements, whereby elections are seen as a viable means of cycling competing coalitions of elite factions in and out of power, providing a degree of stability within the political settlement (Khan 2010).

### The influence of transnational ideas

Transnational ideas have helped shape political settlements in all the country cases. The global norm of electoral competition has resulted in multiparty elections in all the cases, albeit that the degree to which competition is meaningful varies sharply between, for example, highly competitive Ghana and Zambia to dominant party regimes in Bangladesh, Ethiopia and Rwanda. Meanwhile, the ruling coalition in Ethiopia has explicitly sought to emulate developmental states in East Asia, adopting "developmentalism" as a central focus of the political settlement.

Moreover, transnational ideas have been an important influence on all the policy domains and all the country cases covered by the research. Over the last 15 years, a range of international organizations, bilateral donors and international nongovernmental organizations (NGOs) have sought to promote competing models of social protection. The result of these ideational battles has been a growing body of transnational norms, standards and forums on social protection, including the ILO's Recommendation on National Social Protection Floors (ILO 2012), the Sustainable Development Goals and the African Union Social Policy Framework (African Union 2008). These transnational ideas enter national-level policy making through diverse mechanisms, primarily where particular bilateral donors or international organizations pursue direct advocacy, the provision of resources to finance social protection, technical assistance and training workshops, and paid study tours for government officials to see favored programs in other countries. These activities thereby incorporate an epistemic community (Haas 2000; Stone 2008) of academics, think tanks and consultants involved in the generation of evidence and dissemination of ideas about social protection. Just as Deacon (2013) has identified a global "War of Position" between a narrow antipoverty focus at the World Bank and a broader lifecycle approach to social protection among many UN agencies, a similar battle often plays out within countries, with different agencies promoting distinct approaches to social protection to national governments through competing training programs, favored foreign policy models and networks of aligned consultants. Global agreements—from the 1993 UN Declaration on the Elimination of Violence Against Women (UN 1993) onwards—and evolving transnational norms have also been an important influence on the adoption of domestic violence legislation in all the four countries studied. Nonetheless, the pace of the passage of legislation and the extent to which laws were actually enforced are instead shaped primarily by domestic political factors, not transnational influence.

Transnational ideas have also proven to be important influences on the governance of natural resources in all the case studies. In all four cases—but especially Bolivia and Zambia—the management of extractive industries is tied up with narratives of colonialism and truncated postcolonial transitions, with the result that politicians have sought to frame natural resource governance as a means of asserting sovereignty and limiting dependence. Furthermore, while episodes of nationalization and privatization of extractive industries have clearly been linked to national political processes, they have also been influenced by shifts in the dominant economic paradigm at the global level. This is particularly the case with the shift from state-led development to liberalization in the 1980s and 1990s with a particular focus on the privatization of mining, not least thanks to World Bank advocacy. The strong role of transnational capital in extractive industries that resulted from this wave of privatization has meant that natural resource governance is also increasingly influenced by transnational problem definitions and policy ideas. For example, corporate social responsibility has been promoted across the case studies as a policy response to the negative social and environmental effects of mining and one that is consistent with the dominant neoliberal paradigm. This transnational idea, nonetheless, is implemented very differently in different settings depending on its intersection with national political dynamics.

Finally, the research provides valuable insights into the processes through which policy ideas are transferred from one country to another. There is evidence that regional frontrunners in domestic violence legislation influenced legislation in case study countries, with India and Malaysia proving influential in Bangladesh, and South Africa serving as a reference point in Ghana, Rwanda and Uganda. There is also some indication that Bolivia's resource nationalism may have influenced other developing countries in terms of natural resource governance. Finally, foreign policy models have provided an important source of transnational ideas in social protection policy making. Brazil's Bolsa Família, Mexico's Progresa and India's National Rural Employment Guarantee Act were initially constructed by the likes of the World Bank as global policy models. Moreover, within Africa, early programs such as Ethiopia's Productive Safety Net Program (PSNP) and Zambia's Kalomo social cash transfer pilot were constructed by influential donors and, to some degree, governments, as success stories that could be replicated in other countries. Elements of the PSNP model were subsequently taken up by Rwanda and Tanzania, while Kalomo influenced program design in Kenya and Uganda, among others.

*Ideas within the policy coalition*

Policy coalitions and the discursive strategies that they employ to secure support for their policy agendas have been particularly influential in the domains of social protection and gender. The relevance of policy coalitions to the natural resources sector is less clear, however. Given how central ideas and agreements over natural resource governance are to the political settlement itself, it is frequently hard to distinguish a policy domain that is distinct from the political settlement. This may reflect Khan's (2010) distinction between the negotiation and contestation that occurs in the formation of the political settlement itself (natural resources) and that which occurs within the context of an existing political settlement (social protection and gender).

In Kenya, Uganda and Zambia social protection policy coalitions closely resemble Sabatier's advocacy coalitions. While these were undoubtedly donor initiated and led in each country, they also comprised politicians, bureaucrats and some civil society representatives. Moreover, they appear to have been held together by some common set of problem definitions and policy ideas. In each case, a key influence was what some respondents described as an almost "messianic" belief on the part of the UK Department for International Development (DFID) headquarters regarding the potential of cash transfers. In an attempt to broaden participation and secure the support of key decision makers within government, however, these policy coalitions have frequently adapted their preferred policies and the framing used to justify them.

There are several examples in which incompatibility between ideas and framings acted as a barrier to policy adoption, while shifting the problem framing was vital to securing some degree of elite commitment to social protection. In all the countries, concerns about the dangers of welfare dependency are extremely influential. This idea is sufficiently widespread that it can be seen as part of the zeitgeist and is linked to particular problem definitions whereby poor people are considered to be poor, in part, because they are lazy. In Uganda, the conscious switch by the DFID-led policy coalition from defining the problem as one of poverty to one of vulnerability was vital to circumvent government concerns about dependency and secure approval for a pilot program.

Likewise, policy coalitions promoting domestic violence legislation have adapted their discursive framing as part of their strategies for securing political support. Legislation on domestic violence has been seen by many as an encroachment on patriarchal social norms and has, therefore, been resisted, for example by conservative-religious groups. As such, policy coalitions in Ghana and Uganda identified key actors and groups that they needed to win over and adapted their discursive strategy as a means of doing so, watering down their approach as a result. Policy coalitions have also sought to fit problem frames to dominant social norms in order to expand their coalition and circumvent powerful potential opponents. Examples include a focus on the role of men as protectors in Rwanda, the need to support family values and stability in Bangladesh and the need to protect men as well as women, rather than focusing on women's rights alone, in Ghana and Uganda. Furthermore, in some cases domestic policy advocates sought to downplay the influence of transnational ideas to avoid the problematic perception that domestic violence legislation was a Western agenda. While these discursive strategies have helped to secure support for legislation, they have proven to be insufficient to create commitment to implementation in Bangladesh, Ghana and Uganda.

Policy coalitions appear to play very different roles in dominant coalitions compared with other types of political settlement, with important implications for the influence of ideas. In Ethiopia and Rwanda, governments place a strong emphasis on maintaining a unified front to the outside world, whatever internal debates may be taking place within the ruling coalition. In these circumstances there is no space for government officials to join donor-led policy coalitions advocating for change. For example, the policy coalition advocating a safety net in Ethiopia in the early 2000s initially exclusively comprised actors external to the ruling coalition, namely development partners and international NGOs. It is only once key elites within the ruling coalition have accepted that a problem exists and that a policy response is required that a policy coalition can work with government officials. At this point, elite approval creates the space for government officials, development partners and, sometimes, NGOs to work together and design policy interventions. In Ethiopia and Rwanda, social protection only secured this elite approval following perceived existential crises that threatened the ruling coalition. Paradigmatic ideas proved highly influential in these cases by shaping the design of social protection programs in favor of productive economic contributions, as well as protecting the poor and vulnerable.

However, these working groups fall short of the advocacy coalitions as defined by Sabatier (1988). In particular, the participants in these working groups do not necessarily share any paradigmatic ideas or problem definitions but frequently see quite different advantages to the promotion of a particular shared policy model. This highlights the potential compatibility of any one policy model with multiple problem definitions and paradigmatic ideas. For example, while donors framed the programs in Ethiopia and Rwanda (the PSNP and Vision 2020 Umurenge respectively) as examples of social protection, the governments in each case were, at best, ambivalent about the term "social protection," instead viewing these policies as part of integrated rural development strategies that had a much broader range of objectives, including infrastructure development, environmental protection and villagization.

A somewhat similar pattern is evident in the passage of domestic violence legislation in Rwanda. Here there was no clear policy coalition advocating for change. Instead, strong presidential support had already legitimized gender equality as a policy agenda and framed the debate in terms of rights, leading to the adoption of potentially contentious legislation on the co-ownership of land and laws on rape and sexual violence. This policy legacy smoothed the way for the passage of domestic violence legislation when it was proposed by women MPs.

Overall, the clear implication of this analysis of the policy domain is that while policy coalitions have the potential to contribute to progressive change, addressing entrenched forms of inequality—whether related to income or gender—their ability to do so is necessarily shaped by the dominant paradigmatic ideas within the political settlement. Where these paradigmatic ideas are in tension with advocated policies that aim to tackle inequality, proponents are likely to be frustrated and limited to more modest, incremental efforts. However, rare but significant change in paradigmatic ideas is often essential, opening up space for new and more substantive policy ideas for progressive change.

## Conclusions

Efforts to tackle entrenched forms of inequality—whether related to patterns of accumulation, redistribution of resources or recognition—inevitably confront the political dynamics that produce these patterns of inequality in the first place. Much research to date has tended to focus on the role played by material interests, power relations and institutions in shaping these inequalities. This chapter aims to make a modest contribution by highlighting the importance of ideas as both a key source of inequality—with ideas underpinning existing power relations and institutions—and a potential source of change.

The foregoing discussion has shown that ideas are central features of every aspect of the adapted political settlements framework and not just a useful add-on that helps fill in the gaps of a primarily interests-based framework. Ideas provide blueprints for institutions, constitute individuals' perceptions of what their interests are and how they might best be achieved, and provide the shared understanding between factions on which political settlements are based. Ideas are also a key factor at the level of the policy domain where proposals for progressive change originate. Shared ideas—frequently problem definitions or policy ideas—are the glue that binds together diverse actors and provides the motivation to coordinate their activities. Within this policy domain, policy coalitions promoting particular problem definitions and policy ideas are constrained or influenced by the degree to which these ideas fit with dominant paradigmatic ideas that underpin the political settlement, but ideational contestation within these policy domains rarely challenges the political settlement itself.

These findings suggest a number of important implications for policy makers and policy advocates looking to tackle inequalities. A solid understanding of the politics of the policy domain and how these relate to the political settlement is essential to enable advocates of policy change to adapt their advocacy strategies to the ideational commitments and perceived interests of key decision makers. One plausible response to this analysis may be to adapt policy proposals, with advocates advocating "second-best" policies that are more politically feasible than their preferred option. However, there are also instances in which adapting the framing of policies in particular ways can be sufficient to secure support for favored approaches without any real change in policy content.

Vitally, the dominant form of ideas to which policy proposals must fit is likely to vary by the type of political settlement. Where a dominant coalition is committed to particular programmatic, paradigmatic ideas, these are likely to exert a strong influence on policy. These paradigmatic ideas are likely to be resistant to change in the short run at least. Policy advocacy will need to take this into account and adapt policy design and problem framings for consistency with these paradigmatic ideas. In competitive settings ruling coalitions are less likely to have strong programmatic commitments, but advocates of policy change will still need to adapt framings to social norms. In all settings, meanwhile, periods of instability are likely to offer windows of opportunity for ideational change. Indeed, rare periods of extreme uncertainty may provide opportunities for transformation of paradigmatic ideas, beyond the more limited potential for ideational influence that occurs during business as usual.

Regarding crisis and uncertainty, of particular relevance at the time of writing is the global crisis that is the ongoing Covid-19 pandemic. The pandemic and the lockdowns resorted to in many countries as a means of limiting the spread of the virus have already challenged existing approaches to social protection that have tended to be based on narrow poverty targeting. As a result of the pandemic and economic disruption, many of those in need of support are not only among the poorest that have previously been prioritized by such programs but also include workers in the informal sector who are unable to work or laid-off formal sector employees. Initial responses by many governments have been to extend coverage through existing or new programs on a temporary basis (Gentilini et al. 2020). Time will tell whether in the long run this will contribute to a reassessment of the previous dominant focus of global social protection on poverty to broader concerns with inequality.

## References

Acemoglu, Daron and James A. Robinson. 2012. *Why Nations Fail: The Origins of Power, Prosperity and Poverty*. London: Profile Books.

African Union. 2008. *Social Policy Framework for Africa*. Addis Ababa: African Union.

Bebbington, Anthony, Abdul-Gafaru Abdulai, Denise Humphreys Bebbington, Marja Hinfelaar and Cynthia Sanborn. 2018. *Governing Extractive Industries: Politics, Histories, Ideas*. Oxford: Oxford University Press.

Béland, Daniel. 2005. "Ideas and Social Policy: An Institutionalist Perspective." *Social Policy & Administration*, 39(1): 1–18.

Béland, Daniel and Robert H. Cox. 2016. "Ideas as Coalition Magnets: Coalition Building, Policy Entrepreneurs, and Power Relations." *Journal of European Public Policy*, 23(3): 428–445.

Blyth, Mark. 2002. *Great Transformations: Economic Ideas and Institutional Change in the Twentieth Century*. Cambridge: Cambridge University Press.

Blyth, Mark. 2011. "Ideas, Uncertainty and Evolution." In *Ideas and Politics in Social Science Research*, edited by Daniel Béland and Robert H. Cox, 83–101. Oxford: Oxford University Press.

Campbell, John L. 2004. *Institutional Change and Globalization*. Princeton, NJ: Princeton University Press.

Carstensen, Martin B. and Vivien A. Schmidt. 2016. "Power Through, Over and in Ideas: Conceptualizing Ideational Power in Discursive Institutionalism." *Journal of European Public Policy*, 23(3): 318–337.

Cox, Robert H. 2001. "The Social Construction of an Imperative: Why Welfare Reform Happened in Denmark and the Netherlands But Not in Germany." *World Politics*, 53(03): 463–498.

Deacon, Bob. 2013. *Global Social Policy in the Making*. Bristol: Policy Press.

Di John, Jonathan and James Putzel. 2009. "Political Settlements." *GSDRC Issues Paper*.

Gentilini, Ugo, Mohamed Almenfi, Ian Orton and Pamela Dale. 2020. *Social Protection and Jobs Responses to COVID-19: A Real-Time Review of Country Measures*. Washington, DC: International Labour Organization, UNICEF, World Bank.

Haas, Peter M. 2000. "International Institutions and Social Learning in the Management of Global Environmental Risks." *Policy Studies Journal*, 28(3): 558–575.

Hall, Peter A. 1993. "Policy Paradigms, Social Learning, and the State: The Case of Economic Policymaking in Britain." *Comparative Politics*, 25(3): 275–296.

Hay, Colin. 2011. "Ideas and the Construction of Interests." In *Ideas and Politics in Social Science Research*, edited by Daniel Béland and Robert H. Cox, 65–82. Oxford: Oxford University Press.

Hickey, Sam. 2013. "Thinking about the Politics of Inclusive Development: Towards a Relational Approach." *ESID Working Paper No. 1*. Manchester: University of Manchester.

Hickey, Sam, Tom Lavers, Miguel Niño-Zarazúa, and Jeremy Seekings (eds.). 2019. *The Politics of Social Protection in Eastern and Southern Africa*. Oxford: Oxford University Press.

ILO (International Labour Organization). 2012. *Social Protection Floors Recommendation 202*. Geneva: ILO.

Khan, Mushtaq. 2010. *Political Settlements and the Governance of Growth-Enhancing Institutions*. Unpublished working paper. London: School of Oriental and African Studies.

Kingdon, John W. 1984. *Agendas, Alternatives and Public Policies*. New York: Longman.

Lavers, Tom and Sam Hickey. 2016. "Conceptualising the Politics of Social Protection Expansion in Low Income Countries: The Intersection of Transnational Ideas and Domestic Politics." *International Journal of Social Welfare*, 25(4): 388–398.

Levitsky, Steven and Lucan A. Way. 2010. *Competitive Authoritarianism: Hybrid Regimes after the Cold War*. Cambridge: Cambridge University Press.

Linz, Juan J. and Alfred C. Stepan. 1996. *Problems of Democratic Transition and Consolidation: Southern Europe, South America, and Post-Communist Europe*. Baltimore, MD and London: Johns Hopkins University Press.

Mehta, Jal. 2011. "The Varied Roles of Ideas in Politics: From 'Whether' to 'How.'" In *Ideas and Politics in Social Science Research*, edited by Daniel Béland and Robert H. Cox, 23–46. Oxford: Oxford University Press.

Nazneen, Sohela, Sam Hickey and Eleni Sifaki (eds.). 2019. *Negotiating Gender Equity in the Global South: The Politics of Domestic Violence Policy*. London: Routledge.

North, Douglass C., John J. Wallis and Barry R. Weingast. 2009. *Violence and Social Orders: A Conceptual Framework for Interpreting Recorded Human History*. Cambridge: Cambridge University Press.

Parsons, Craig. 2007. *How to Map Arguments in Political Science*. Oxford: Oxford University Press.

Parsons, Craig. 2016. "Ideas and Power: Four Intersections and How to Show Them." *Journal of European Public Policy*, 23(3): 446–463.

Sabatier, Paul A. 1988. "An Advocacy Coalition Framework of Policy Change and the Role of Policy-Oriented Learning Therein." *Policy Sciences*, 21(2–3): 129–168.

Sabatier, Paul A. and Hank C. Jenkins-Smith. 1999. "The Advocacy Coalition Framework: An Assessment." In *Theories of the Policy Process*, edited by Paul A. Sabatier, 117–166. Boulder, CO: Westview Press.

Schmidt, Vivien A. 2008. "Discursive Institutionalism: The Explanatory Power of Ideas and Discourse." *Annual Review of Political Science*, 11(1): 303–326.

Schmidt, Vivien A. 2011. "Reconciling Ideas and Institutions through Discursive Institutionalism." In *Ideas and Politics in Social Science Research*, edited by Daniel Béland and Robert H. Cox, 47–64. Oxford: Oxford University Press.

Sen, Kunal, 2012. "The Political Dynamics of Economic Growth." *ESID Working Paper No. 5*. Manchester: University of Manchester.

Stone, Diane. 2008. "Global Public Policy, Transnational Policy Communities, and Their Networks." *Policy Studies Journal*, 36(1): 19–38.

UN (United Nations). 1993. "Declaration on the Elimination of Violence against Women." *Resolution 48/104*. New York: UN.

Zenawi, Meles. 2012. "States and Markets: Neoliberal Limitations and the Case for a Developmental State." In *Good Growth and Governance in Africa: Rethinking Development Strategies*, edited by Akbar Noman, Kwesi Botchwey, Howard Stein and Joseph E. Stiglitz, 140–174. Oxford: Oxford University Press.

# Chapter 9

## WHO ARE THE ELITE, WHAT DO THEY THINK ABOUT INEQUALITY AND WHY DOES IT MATTER?

### LESSONS FROM BRAZIL AND SOUTH AFRICA

Graziella Moraes Silva, Matias López, Elisa Reis and Chana Teeger

### *Introduction*

The role of elites in the growth and reproduction of inequalities has received considerable attention in recent years (Cousin et al. 2018; Khan 2012). Many studies have highlighted how elites concentrate economic resources (Milanovic 2016; Piketty 2015) that allow them to have disproportional political influence (Gilens 2012; Higley and Moore 1981; Page et al. 2013). Researchers have also focused on diverse mechanisms elites use to maintain their power, for example, elite schools and occupations, resulting in the reproduction of socioeconomic inequalities (Khan 2010; Rivera 2016). Finally, a growing number of researchers have also focused on how elites understand and justify inequalities (Reis and Moore 2005; Sherman 2018). When we compare the operationalization of the concept "elite" in these studies, however, it becomes clear that it is inconsistent, ranging from class-based approaches (e.g., the upper class and super-rich) to position-based ones (e.g., political elites and technocrats), sometimes moving between the two interchangeably. Elite sectors and heterogeneity within elite groups are rarely discussed. In addition, researchers often assume that elites will always oppose redistribution unless under threat.

If, by definition, elites concentrate power and resources, it follows that the design and implementation of redistributive policies depend largely on elite preferences. Understanding such preferences is thus key for unpacking how inequality is reproduced or can be transformed. In this chapter, we explore elites' redistribution preferences by presenting the results of a survey of perceptions of inequality that was administered to random samples of economic, political and civil servant elites in Brazil and South Africa. These two countries transitioned to democracy in the late 1980s and early 1990s, instantly becoming the largest, but also most unequal, democracies in their respective regions. Our aim is to describe how elites in the two countries understand the causes and consequences of inequality, as well as which types of redistributive policies they support or reject.

In the following section, we discuss our definition of "elites" and how we think about their relationship to inequality. Next, we present our cases and outline our data and methods. Moving to the results, we explore the views of South African and Brazilian elites on the relationship between economic growth, redistribution and inequality, as well as their preferred solutions to address these issues. We found that elites across sectors in both countries believed that inequality led to conflict and political patronage and viewed a reduction in inequality as desirable. However, the solutions they proposed varied by country and sector. We review these differences, focusing on variation in elites' views regarding the role of the state versus the market. We conclude the chapter by exploring possible avenues for further comparative research on the links between elites and inequality.

## Defining Elites and Their Relationship to Inequality

Since 2010, increases in inequality in the most developed countries and new methodological tools available to study inequality among those at the top of the social stratification system have turned elites into a prominent research topic. Studies have focused on measurements of inequality at the top (Milanovic 2016; Piketty 2015) and mechanisms of elite reproduction using either classical stratification measures such as years of education and income (Falcon and Bataille 2018) or Bourdieusian concepts of cultural capital, habitus and fields that emphasize taste and networks (Friedman and Reeves 2020; Khan 2010).

This literature has contributed to making the world of elites visible. However, despite the increase in scholarship, considerable conceptual vagueness remains about how elites, and their relationship to inequality, are understood. First, studies tend to define elites either narrowly (e.g., the super-rich, corporate board members) or loosely (e.g., upper middle class, college-degree holders), often confounding the concept of elites with that of class (e.g., Khan 2010; Sherman 2018). Second, elites are generally perceived to be either selfishly interested in maintaining their positions or unaware of their own privilege and role in social exclusion (e.g., Paugam et al. 2017; Wedel 2009). Third, scholars often assume that elites always benefit from inequality and will only be supportive of redistributive agendas under duress (e.g., Acemoglu and Robinson 2005; Boix 2003). Finally, elites are often perceived as homogeneous; national and sector differences are usually ignored or underplayed.

Although important, focusing on socioeconomic status, wealth and privilege neglects the role elites play in shaping and defining institutional and political mechanisms that create and reproduce material inequalities. The implicit assumption that elites will always benefit from inequality ignores the fact that—unless due to exogenous shocks such as war or epidemics—redistribution necessarily follows some kind of elite action, engagement or tacit approval (de Swaan 1988; Reis and Moore 2005). Finally, the assumption of homogeneity ignores the likelihood that political and material incentives are distributed differently across contexts and elite sectors.

Since our interest is in how elites might shape the transformation or reproduction of inequalities, we rely on a positional definition of elites. We focus on those who occupy decision-making positions in different branches of government and in the corporate sector. In analyzing the preferences of individuals holding these positions, we are particularly attentive to (1) the heterogeneity of these preferences, especially across nations and elite sectors; and (2) a comprehensive understanding of these preferences that goes beyond crude assumptions of rational choice approaches as well as the equally narrow view offered by the political culture literature, as we discuss in the following section.

## Understanding Elite Attitudes toward Equality and Redistribution

Our interest in elite attitudes toward inequality was inspired by research conducted by Verba and his coauthors (Verba and Orren 1985, Verba et al. 1987), who showed how national leaders understand equality in different ways and have different preferences regarding ideal levels of economic and political equality. Elites in these studies did care about equality, but their understanding of what equality meant varied by country and sector. Some valued *equality of opportunity*, while others highlighted *equality in outcomes*. In addition, there was variation in the importance placed on *economic equality* (i.e., distribution of economic resources) versus *political equality* (i.e., distribution of power). According to Verba and colleagues, elites' redistribution preferences are shaped by the values they hold about what equality should be.

The notion of values as shaping "individual economic and political behavior" (Verba and Orren 1985: 2) is based on a rigid understanding of political culture as static and resistant to change (Somers 1995). Although proposing that attitudes do not simply reflect interests inherent in one's social position, researchers working in the political values tradition often replace a socioeconomic determinism with a cultural one. In addition, when studies focus on whether or not people know or care about equality, they fail to examine the conditions under which they would be willing to support redistribution (McCall 2013).

More recent studies on elite perceptions of inequalities have addressed the negative consequences of inequalities for elites themselves—how inequality also creates problems for elites such as urban violence (Rueda and Stegmueller 2016) or revolutionary threats (Boix 2003). Others have studied the ways in which elites justify their high income (Hecht 2017) and luxurious consumption patterns (Sherman 2018). Unlike the work of Verba and colleagues, much of this more current research relies on an income-based definition of elites that tends to equate elites and the rich while largely sidestepping the diversity of perceptions across different elite sectors and backgrounds. Our study draws on the comparative and institutional perspectives advanced by Verba and colleagues, by focusing on elite sectors across countries. At the same time, we move beyond their approach by examining in more detail elite preferences toward specific redistribution policies.

*Elite sectors*

In contrast to income or wealth-based definitions, we adopt a positional definition of elites as those individuals capable of influencing political outcomes substantially and regularly (Higley and Burton 2006; Hoffman-Lange 2007). This definition can be traced back to the classical elite theories of Pareto, Michels, Mosca and Weber, as it focuses on power rather than on wealth. As such, this conceptualization of elites also resembles the concept of the "power elite," namely those who occupy dominant positions in central military, economic and political institutions (Mills 1956). Writing in the 1950s, Mills argues that the interwoven and often shared interests of elites shaped the fate of the United States. More recent studies (Gilens 2012; Page et al. 2013) have examined how the interlocking interests of economic and political elites threaten democracy and fuel growing inequality.

Although we agree with Mills's idea that people occupying power positions in dominant institutions do have power to shape politics and policies, we question whether elites' interests will always converge. We agree with Higley and Burton (2006) and Page et al. (2013) that the cohesion (or divergence) of elites is an empirical question. Diversity within elites can come from a number of sources. Individual identification and background (e.g., religion, family's socioeconomic status, gender, sexuality, ethnicity, race) and institutional characteristics (e.g., occupations, elite sectors) may influence how people interpret reality and make decisions. Such diversities have largely been underemphasized in the elite literature, a point also raised in recent reviews (Cousin et al. 2018; Khan 2010; Savage and Williams 2008).

In this chapter, we analyze similarities and differences in preferences about equality and redistribution across elite sectors, taking elite institutional belonging as a potential source of divergence. Even if we acknowledge that there are other sources of power, we believe institutions are still a pivotal locus of influence. On issues of inequality in particular, redistribution decisions have to pass through institutional approval, policy design and implementation. In addition, although elites may in many cases have common markers of distinction and dominance, such as education from elite schools, the different elite positions that they occupy may shape contrasting views and policy preferences. In other words, positions not only enable decision-making authority but constrain the information elites may have access to or the returns that they anticipate in terms of their own power.

We focus on business leaders, elected officials at the national level and top-tier civil servants. These represent the main actors proposing, implementing and potentially funding public policies. Elected officials have an obvious influence on policy; it is in their hands to put forward legislation and budgets. Their attitudes toward redistribution are expected to be shaped by the preferences of voters in the middle of the income distribution, or "median voters," as they are key for politicians' prospects of re-election (Meltzer and Richard 1981). Increasingly, however, authors have found that campaign financing and lobby interests, as well as other macroeconomic constraints, play an important role in shaping the priority given to redistributive policies (Campello 2014). Top-tier civil servants also hold significant power in terms of policy design and agenda setting (Aberbach et al. 1981). The influence of economic elites on policy-making and agenda-setting processes is well documented (Gilens and Page 2014). It flows through campaign financing and lobbying as well as participation (or lack thereof) in public–private partnerships as well as through the growing influence of global philanthropy.

On top of these sectoral differences, elite research tends to focus on individual countries, limiting our ability to understand how preferences toward redistribution are shaped by national contexts. Cross-national differences, when they have been examined and documented, have largely been understood as the result of distinct values or political cultures. Our study, which focuses on variation between and within countries, offers a broader view by considering how redistribution preferences might be shaped by domestic political disputes, in particular about the role of the state, still perceived as the main actor responsible for redistribution.

### Elites in extremely unequal societies: Brazil and South Africa

With rare exception (e.g., Paugam et al. 2017; Reis and Moore 2005), studies on elite attitudes toward inequalities have focused on the global North. And while globalization has made the world feel smaller and transnational processes increasingly shape trends in inequality, domestic politics and policies are still central to shaping redistribution outcomes.

Brazil and South Africa are middle-income countries with histories of European colonization and racialization that have left strong marks on current patterns of inequality (Marx 1998). In both countries, democratization brought to power political elites committed to political projects of equality. Economic elites supported (or at least tolerated) these projects not only out of goodwill or ideological agreement but also out of the acknowledgment that severe levels of inequality had negative consequences for their own well-being and could potentially jeopardize economic growth—for example, by creating the conditions for urban violence (Reis and Moore 2005). Nevertheless, more than two decades after democratization, Brazil and South Africa continue to display extreme levels of inequality, as measured by the Gini coefficient. Figure 9.1 presents the Gini coefficient by year in both countries. In South Africa, inequality has remained fairly stable at alarmingly high rates. The data from Brazil point to extreme levels of inequality that declined slightly in the first decade of the twenty-first century but are on an upward trend again.

Why has this apparent political commitment failed to achieve and sustain redistributive outcomes? Current explanations of the shortcomings of redistribution in the global South range from commodities cycles and macroeconomic policies (Campello 2014; Carbonnier et al. 2017) to the effects of neoliberalism and globalization (Bond 1998; Marais 2013; Souza 2017), as well as formal roadblocks to redistribution placed by elites themselves (Albertus and Menaldo 2018; Seekings and Nattrass 2015). The importance of these macroeconomic and institutional constraints is undeniable, but the effects of such constraints depend greatly on how elites interpret and react to them. Scholars of

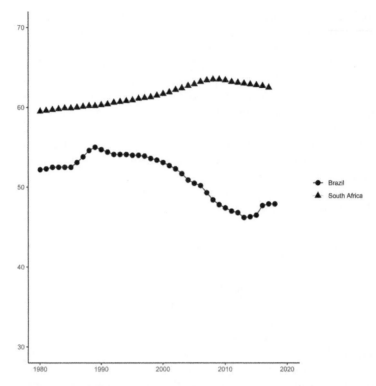

**Figure 9.1** Gini coefficient by year in Brazil and South Africa (after transfers). *Source*: Authors' elaboration based on Solt (2020).

inequality tend to assume that elites' preferences are irrelevant or that elites will always prefer more inequality. In this chapter, we interrogate this assumption by exploring how elites themselves understand inequality and redistribution. We focus on convergences and divergences across the two countries as well as across elite sectors within them.

## Data and Methods

Between 2013 and early 2015, we fielded 362 questionnaires to randomly sampled political, civil servant and business elites in Brazil and South Africa. We interviewed at least 60 respondents per sector in each country.[1] Following a strategy similar to

1. In South Africa, the number of political elites was 63 and the number of business elites was 61. This was because of an error made by the surveying company, which continued to conduct interviews after the quota was filled. Since all interviewees were selected randomly, we decided to allow the extra cases in the data set.

Reis (2000), which relates to Hoffman-Lange's (2007) position method, elites were sampled based on their institutional positions.

For the Brazilian survey, we sampled elites in three groups: (1) elected officials at the federal level from each of Brazil's four main parties (Partido Movimento Democratico Brasileiro [PMDB, Brazilian Democratic Movement], Partido dos Trabalhadores [PT, Workers' Party], Partido Social Democrata Brasileiro [PSDB, Brazilian Social Democracy Party] and Partido Social Democrata [PSD, Social Democratic Party]),[2] (2) top-tier civil servants within the federal government and (3) businesspeople (chief executive officers [CEOs], chief financial officers [CFOs] or chairpersons of boards of the country's top 300 companies).[3] Civil servants were sampled from among those holding top positions in the civil service at the federal level.

In South Africa, we sampled members of the National Assembly from the ruling African National Congress (ANC) and the official opposition party, the Democratic Alliance (DA). We sampled in proportion to each party's representation in the National Assembly at the time, such that two-thirds of our respondents were from the ANC and one-third from the DA. In constructing our sample of civil servants, we strategically chose 20 government departments and randomly sampled top-tier civil servants within them (director generals, deputy director generals, chief operating officers and chief directors). To construct our sample of business elites, we triangulated a list of the top 300 companies (by market capitalization) listed on the Johannesburg Stock Exchange with the "Africa Report Top 500 Companies in Africa" (which was identified as a widely used list by a senior contact at the Competitions Commission). We randomly sampled companies from this list, allowing respondents from the following positions: CEO, CFO and Chairperson of the Board.

The questions were drawn mostly from a previous survey conducted with Brazilian elites (Reis 2000), from items in larger surveys that tapped perceptions about inequality and poverty among a broader population (World Value Survey Program, n.d.; ISSP 2010) and from a survey conducted by the Interdisciplinary Research Network on Inequality (NIED) on the relationship between civil society and the state. We also added new questions, in particular regarding conditional and unconditional social grants in South Africa, and Bolsa Familia, a conditional cash transfer program for poor families in Brazil.[4]

---

2. By "main parties" we refer to those with the largest share of seats in Congress.

3. The list of the top 300 companies comes from a business publication in Brazil, *Revista Exame*, which is a publication widely used in the corporate world, similar to *Forbes*.

4. In South Africa we also included questions about the role of social policies such as Black Economic Empowerment, a program aimed at redressing injustices from the apartheid era by fostering the ownership, management and control of South Africa's financial and economic resources to the majority of its citizens—that is, those historically categorized as Black South African.

Our overall response rate was 32.3 percent for Brazil and 41 percent for South Africa. These response rates are comparable with those of other elite surveys, including those that do not rely on random samples (e.g., Best et al. 2012). Table 9.1 presents a breakdown of response rate by country and sector. The surveys were administered as face-to-face interviews, except for a handful that were conducted over the phone. In the remainder of this chapter, we present the descriptive statistics from this survey and discuss several possible implications for the future of redistribution in the two countries.

## Results

### Elites in Brazil and South Africa

Unsurprisingly, the Brazilian and South African elites we interviewed had education levels higher than average in the general population. Table 9.2 presents the educational background of the interviewees by country and sector. The majority (96.1 percent in Brazil and 77.7 percent in South Africa) held a university diploma, compared with less than 15 percent of adults in the broader population of both countries, according to 2010 and 2011 census data for each country. In both countries, the overwhelming majority of interviewees were men (89 percent in Brazil and 77 percent in South Africa), with the exception of South African politicians, 38 percent of whom were women. In South Africa, whites, who make up only 9 percent of the population (StatsSA 2011), were overrepresented across the three elite sectors. This is particularly striking in the case of business elites, 70 percent of whom identified as white. Brazilian elites were even more racially homogeneous, with over 80 percent identifying as white in a country in which 51 percent of the population (IBGE 2010) identifies as Black or mixed race.

That said, there are interesting differences across elite sectors. Political elites constitute the most heterogeneous sector in both countries, albeit more so in South Africa, where under half the interviewees possessed a university degree. Heterogeneity also seems to characterize (though to a lesser extent) the South African civil service sector. Business elites appear to be the most homogeneous sector (i.e., largely white, male and having more years of formal schooling) in both countries, even though most interviewees in this sector were first-generation college graduates.

The Brazilian and South African elites in our survey were largely aware of their status as elites. When asked if they consider themselves to be part of the elite, the great majority of interviewees—82 percent in Brazil and 66 percent in

**Table 9.1** Response rate by country and sector

|  | Elected officials | Civil servants | Businesspeople |
|---|---|---|---|
| Brazil | 30% | 51% | 25% |
| South Africa | 65% | 35% | 32% |

*Source*: Survey—Elites and Perceptions of Inequality (NIED/UFRJ 2014).

**Table 9.2** Background characteristics of interviewees by country and sector

| | Brazil | | | | South Africa | | | |
|---|---|---|---|---|---|---|---|---|
| | Politicians | Civil servants | Business | Total | Politicians | Civil servants | Business | Total |
| University degree or higher | 93.3% | 100.0% | 95.0% | 96.1% | 40.8% | 96.7% | 86.9% | 77.7% |
| Father w/ secondary or higher | 51.7% | 67.8% | 65.0% | 61.6% | 31.7% | 53.3% | 68.9% | 51.1% |
| Father w/ university or higher | 25.9% | 50.8% | 45.0% | 40.6% | 9.5% | 23.2% | 31.1% | 21.2% |
| Mother w/ secondary or higher | 41.7% | 61.7% | 66.7% | 56.7% | 30.2% | 51.7% | 70.5% | 50.5% |
| Mother w/ university or higher | 15.0% | 26.7% | 35.0% | 25.6% | 1.6% | 11.7% | 14.8% | 9.2% |
| Identify as white | 68.3% | 75.0% | 96.7% | 80.0% | 19.0% | 20.0% | 70.5% | 36.4% |
| % male | 91.7% | 78.3% | 98.3% | 89.4% | 62% | 73% | 95% | 77% |
| Total (N) | 60 | 60 | 60 | 180 | 63 | 60 | 61 | 184 |

*Source:* Survey—Elites and Perceptions of Inequality (NIED/UFRJ 2014).

South Africa—answered affirmatively. Agreement was much more common among businesspeople (BR: 90 percent; SA: 84 percent) than among politicians (BR: 71 percent; SA: 41 percent). The latter explained that they did not consider themselves to be members of the elite because they came from working class or rural backgrounds. Nevertheless, elites were not unanimous that their elite status was due to their earnings. While income was cited as the main reason for elite identification among business (BR: 35 percent; SA: 49 percent) and civil servant respondents (BR: 34 percent and SA: 30 percent), power was also mentioned by a significant minority (BR: 28 percent for business and 22 percent for civil servants; SA: 21 percent for business and 30 percent for civil servants). In contrast, power (rather than income) was cited as the main factor determining elite membership by politicians in both countries. This was much more pronounced in Brazil than in South Africa (BR: 53 percent; SA: 27 percent). In fact, political elites in South Africa were the only group who largely rejected an "elite" identity (54 percent did not identify as elites). When asked to explain the reason that they did not identify as elites, South African politicians did not point to their lack of income or power (the options presented to them in the questionnaire). Instead, they chose the "other" option and explained that they did not see themselves as elites because of the role they played in the anti-apartheid struggle or working-class movements.

### Seeing inequality from the top

Research has shown that elites' acknowledgment of negative consequences of poverty and inequality for themselves—what the literature often calls negative externalities—are key variables explaining their preferred redistribution strategies. For example, Rueda and Stegmueller (2016) found that elites (defined as the rich) are more likely to support redistribution when they understand inequality to be the cause of criminal violence (2016). López et al. (2020) similarly show that perception of the poor as easily susceptible to political patronage can lead to cleavages among the elite that hinder the type of coordinated action needed to address inequality from the top.

Elites in Brazil and South Africa viewed inequality as a problem (BR: 98.3 percent; SA: 99.5 percent), as indeed has been documented in previous studies (Kalati and Manor 2005; Reis 2000). Most interviewees in both countries, however, believed that inequality was lower than it was 20 years prior. As seen in Figure 9.1, this perceived reduction in inequality is more accurate in Brazil than in South Africa. Figure 9.2 presents participants' answers to a question asking them to identify the main consequences of poverty and inequality. Responses are presented by country and sector (with the boxes showing the frequency at which each item was mentioned and the lines representing confidence intervals for the larger population from which the sample draws). The results of Figure 9.2 echo previous studies: crime and violence were the most cited consequences of poverty and inequality in both countries (even if political elites in South Africa mentioned these to a much smaller degree than political elites in Brazil and other elite sectors in both countries), with political patronage taking a close

**Brazil**

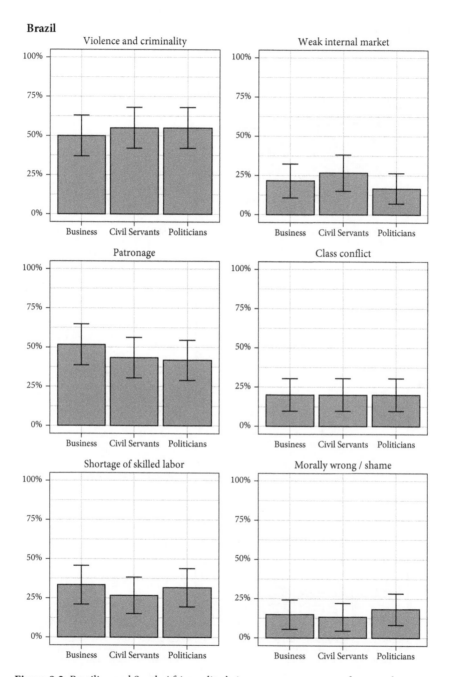

**Figure 9.2** Brazilian and South African elites' views on consequences of poverty by sector. *Source*: Survey—Elites and Perceptions of Inequality (NIED/UFRJ 2014). Confidence intervals at 95 percent confidence.

**South Africa**

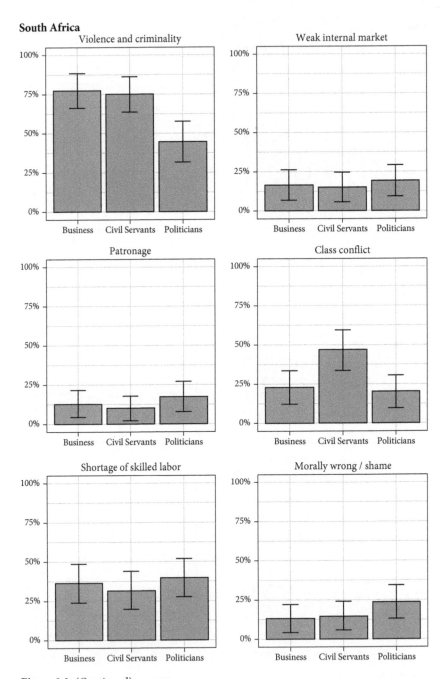

**Figure 9.2** (Continued).

second in Brazil. These findings indicate that many elites see the poor as a threat owing to violence (i.e., potential criminals) or politics (i.e., easily manipulated voters), suggesting that elites draw strong symbolic boundaries (or conceptual distinctions) against the poor—viewing them as categorically different from themselves (see also Moraes Silva and López 2015).

The elites in our study also acknowledged the economic consequences of inequality. In South Africa, the second most frequently cited consequence of inequality was the lack of a skilled labor force. A weak domestic consumer market was also mentioned by a sizable minority of respondents in each country, suggesting that inequality is often perceived as a drawback for business. Interestingly, civil servants in South Africa saw class conflict as the second most important consequence of poverty and inequality, a point rarely mentioned by the other groups. Overall, participants' views indicate a more instrumental, rather than moral, perception of the wasted economic potential of the poor.

Despite recognizing inequality as a problem that leads to a variety of negative consequences, most interviewees chose economic growth over redistribution when asked directly which of the two should be prioritized by the government. South African elites were fairly consistent across sectors in privileging economic growth. In contrast, Brazilian elites displayed more variation across sectors. There, business elites expressed views similar to those of their South African counterparts, with over 80 percent choosing economic growth over redistribution. Brazilian politicians and civil servants were more split, with just under half choosing redistribution over economic growth.

When asked more generally about the goals for the country in the medium term, the most frequent response was to "Prioritize continued economic growth," followed by "Eradicate poverty and decrease inequality." "Reduce the state interference in economy" was third in Brazil, largely driven by the preferences of Brazilian business elites. In South Africa, "Encourage greater citizen participation in political decisions" was mentioned by nearly 40 percent of political elites.[5] Figure 9.3 presents these results. In short, these findings show that significant percentages of Brazilian and South African elites—particularly in the business sector—seem to have adopted a version of trickle-down economics. While they agreed that inequality was a problem, they seemed to suggest that economic growth may be a sufficient condition (or at least a necessary one) to address poverty and inequality.

5. The other options were "Maintain the order in the country" (BR 1.1 percent, SA 2.2 percent), "Integrate with the world market" (BR 6.1 percent, SA 1.6 percent), "Build stronger relationships with countries of the region" (BR 0 percent, SA 1.6 percent) and "Protect the environment" (BR: 0 percent, SA 0.5 percent). It is worth noting the lack of relevance of environmental issues in both countries.

**Brazil**

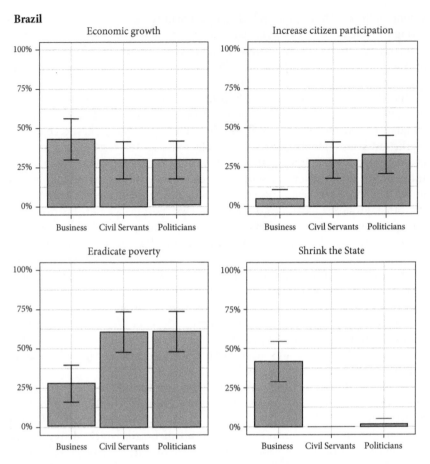

**Figure 9.3** Two most important goals of the country for elites in Brazil and South Africa. *Source*: Survey—Elites and Perceptions of Inequality (NIED/UFRJ 2014). Confidence intervals at 95 percent confidence.

Yet most did view redistributive policies as necessary, even if some downplayed them in relation to economic growth. When asked directly, a majority of respondents in both countries agreed that "redistribution policies are necessary" rather than "should be avoided." The lower support for redistributive policies in South Africa than in Brazil was driven by South African business elites who were more divided on this issue than elites in other sectors. This raises more specific questions about elites' views on how redistribution should be done and what policies they would be willing to support.

**South Africa**

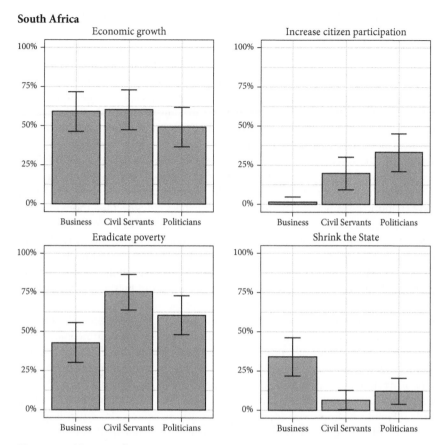

Figure 9.3 (Continued).

*How to Solve Inequality: Redistributive Policies and the Role of the State*

In both countries, and across all sectors, elites identified the government as the actor most responsible for combating poverty and inequality.[6] They

6. In Brazil, 26.7 percent of business elites pointed to "organized civil society," making it the second most frequently cited responsible actor. In contrast, in South Africa, "people like you" came in second place, mentioned by 18.3 percent of civil servants and 11.5 percent of business elites.

also agreed that more government investment in public services, such as infrastructure and health, was necessary. But when it came to identifying more specific interventions, elite preferences were more divided. Business elites in both countries were much more likely than elites in other sectors to support economic deregulation. We asked participants to indicate what they believed to be the two most important initiatives for reducing inequality. As shown in Figure 9.4, over half of businesspeople in each country chose economic deregulation, as compared with less than 25 percent of politicians. This does not mean that business elites were unitarily committed to a neoliberal agenda. On the contrary, many also identified more efficient public social services as a key initiative for the reduction of inequality. This was more pronounced for Brazilian business elites, who identified more efficient public services more frequently than they did economic deregulation. South African business elites seemed more likely to favor a free market, with over 50 percent identifying this as the most important initiative to reduce inequality and less than 40 percent identifying more efficient public social services. Once again, attention to elite differentiation highlights cross-national and sectoral differences in elite beliefs and preferences—here, in terms of their views on the role of the state (versus the market) in addressing economic inequalities.

Social policies, and tax policies that could fund them, were generally not the most popular options chosen by elites to deal with poverty and inequality. For example, in both countries a minority of economic and political elites supported more progressive taxes, or wealth taxes. Brazilian civil servants were more supportive, but also focused on policies rather than taxing. When it comes to land reform, support was even weaker, with the exception of political elites in South Africa. Finally, having more social programs was an option chosen by less than one-third of Brazilian respondents and less than one-fourth of South African respondents.

At the same time, it is important to note that elites may be further differentiated within sectors. One area in which this is likely to occur is among political elites who are divided along party lines. To test this assumption, we divided political elites, distinguishing members of the ruling PT and ANC administrations from other elites. Figure 9.5 presents the results of logistic regressions estimating the probability of elites' support for each of the policies already presented in Figure 9.4 but distinguishing elites in the ruling party from other political elites and comparing them with civil servants with no party affiliation.

The models show that income taxes and economic deregulation are policies that divide elites in Brazil and South Africa. However, this does not reflect a strong support for more taxation from PT and ANC incumbents, who have a predicted probability of mentioning income taxes as a solution to inequality of about 20 percent and a predicted probability of just 14 percent of mentioning wealth taxes. Such likelihood is only high in face of the predicted probabilities of business elites, which are 7 percent in Brazil and 12 percent in South Africa regarding income taxes, and 7 percent for wealth taxes in both countries.

**Brazil**

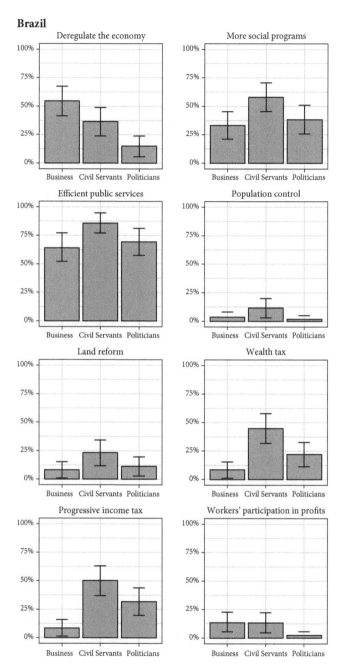

**Figure 9.4** Elites' views on the two most important initiatives for reducing inequality, by country and sector. *Source*: Survey—Elites and Perceptions of Inequality (NIED/UFRJ 2014). Confidence intervals at 95 percent confidence.

**South Africa**

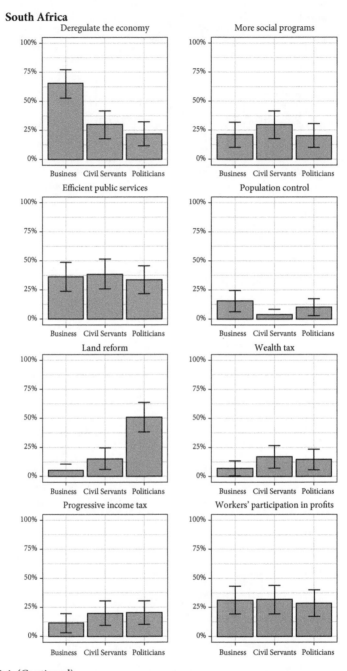

**Figure 9.4** (Continued)

**Brazil**

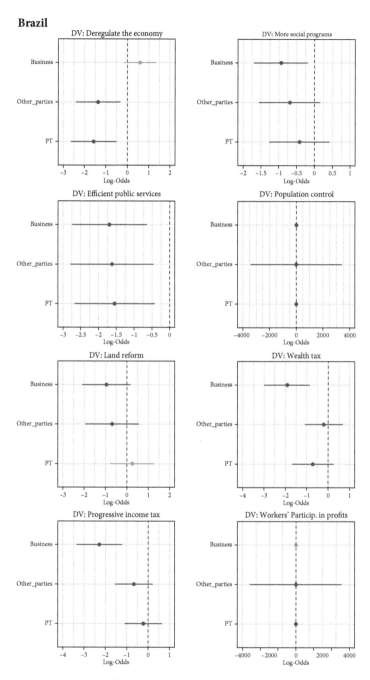

**Figure 9.5** Logistic models for the probability of supporting policies. *Source*: Survey—Elites and Perceptions of Inequality (NIED/UFRJ 2014). Confidence intervals at 95 percent confidence.

## South Africa

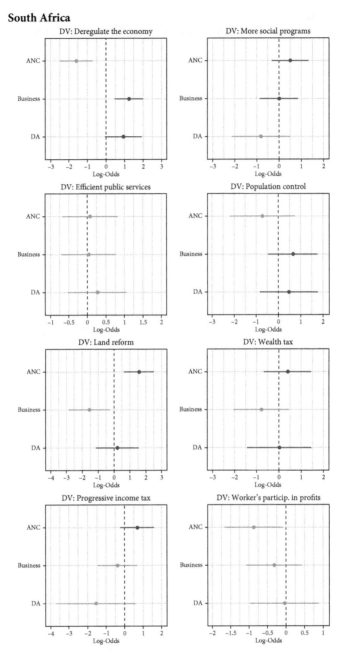

**Figure 9.5** (Continued).

Nearly 50 percent of all PT leaders and 40 percent of ANC leaders are predicted to mention more public services as one of the most important policies to reduce inequality, and 35 percent and 30 percent would name more social programs as predicted by logistic models. PT and ANC leaders also stand out for their support of land reform, with up to 30 percent and 50 percent predicted probability of naming it as one of the two main policies to address inequality, respectively. Leaders of the DA, on the other hand, stand out for their low predicted mention of social programs (13 percent predicted probability) and taxes (5 percent predicted probability of mentioning income taxes and 12 percent of mentioning wealth taxes), as well as a high predicted mention of deregulation (55 percent predicted probability). The latter places the preferences of DA in close proximity to the views of business elites, which was not true for Brazilian center-right parties, according to the models. Future research should further explore within-sector elite differentiation in redistribution preferences.

## Taking Stock and Moving Forward

In this chapter, we have highlighted two important dimensions missing from recent work in the field of elite studies. First, we argued for the importance of considering the differences across elite sectors to better understand how the trade-offs of redistribution are perceived among decision makers. Second, we emphasized cross-national differences in elites' perceptions of the causes and consequences of inequality, as well as in their preferences for redistribution policies. Although we acknowledge that those perceptions are not static values and that decisions about redistribution are not made in a vacuum, we argue that the effects of macroeconomic and institutional constraints depend greatly on how elites interpret and react to them. Overall, we emphasize the need for greater attention to elite preferences and more conceptual and methodological precision on how we define and study elites and their relationship to inequality in order to better understand how redistribution decisions are made and justified. This also has the potential to allow us to better see how they can be challenged.

The data we presented in this chapter show that elites in Brazil and South Africa perceive inequality as a problem—even if they think it is less of a problem than it has been in the past. The fact that these two countries have experienced democratic transitions that brought to power political elites with a redistributive agenda may explain such a positive perspective on inequalities (even if, in the case of South Africa at least, the Gini coefficient suggests that inequality has gotten worse in the last two decades). It is also relevant that the two surveys were conducted after a sustained period of economic growth, which may have increased perceptions of prosperity, even if it did not necessarily reduce inequality. Our findings show that Brazilian and South African elites vary in how they think inequality ranks in relation to other social problems as well as in how they think it should be addressed. Our data broadly suggest that elites' perceptions and preferences are much more heterogeneous than usually assumed. This probably has to do with our conceptualization of elites. Moving beyond a unitary focus on economic elites, our study also includes political and civil servant elites who—like economic elites—hold important decision-making positions in relation to redistribution. Indeed, as compared with political and civil servant elites, business elites' preferences seem more homogeneous, with respondents in this sector choosing economically liberal options much more consistently than elites in other sectors. Still, our data show that this varies across countries, with South African business elites less in favor of state intervention in the economy than their Brazilian counterparts.

In both countries, political elites often expressed views that diverged from those of business elites. This raises important questions about how this distance plays out in actual legislative power. Are political elites in Brazil and South Africa able to maintain independence, or are they limited by institutional or funding hurdles (see Gilens 2012)? Further, our findings raise questions about the relationship between civil servants and elected officials. In Brazil, civil service elites tended to express views most in line with those of political elites. However, in South Africa, their views were, surprisingly, more closely aligned with business elites. What explains these convergences? And what implications might these have for the power of civil service elites to influence policy (see also Aberbach et al. 1981)?

Moving forward, as data on elites become available, we encourage researchers to address these questions by focusing on both similarities and differences across elite sectors and national contexts. Survey studies, such as the one presented in this chapter, offer opportunities to see trends and unpack associations between elite perceptions of inequality and their policy-related preferences. In-depth interviews with elites that more deeply explore the content and contours of these perceptions and preferences would be a welcome addition to our knowledge of how inequality is reproduced—and how it might be reduced. More broadly, the focus on perceptions of redistribution highlights the importance of elite assumptions when making policy decisions about how to address inequality. In the global context of growing concentration of economic and political resources, understanding elite interpretations (and misinterpretations) about redistribution may be a condition to reframe the inequality debate in a more constructive direction.

## References

Aberbach, Joel D., Robert D. Putnam and Bert A. Rockman. 1981. *Bureaucrats and Politicians in Western Democracies.* Cambridge, MA: Harvard University Press.

Acemoglu, Daron and James A. Robinson. 2005. *Economic Origins of Dictatorship and Democracy.* Cambridge: Cambridge University Press.

Albertus, Michael and Victor Menaldo. 2018. *Authoritarianism and the Elite Origins of Democracy.* Cambridge: Cambridge University Press.

Best, Heinrich, György Lengyel and Luca Verzichelli. 2012. *The Europe of Elites: A Study into the Europeanness of Europe's Political and Economic Elites.* Oxford: Oxford University Press.

Boix, Charles. 2003. *Democracy and Redistribution.* Cambridge: Cambridge University Press.

Bond, Patrick. 1998. *Elite Transition: Globalisation and the Rise of Economic Fundamentalism in South Africa*. New York: Pluto Press.

Campello, Daniela. 2014. "The Politics of Financial Booms and Crises: Evidence from Latin America." *Comparative Political Studies*, 47(2): 260–286.

Carbonnier, Gilles, Humberto Campodonico and Sergio Tezanos Vázquez (eds.). 2017. "Alternative Pathways to Sustainable Development: Lessons from Latin America." Foreword. International Development Policy, series no. 9. Geneva, Boston: Graduate Institute Publications, Brill-Nijhoff.

Cousin, Bruno, Shamus Khan and Ashley Mears. 2018. "Theoretical and Methodological Pathways for Research on Elites." *Socio-Economic Review*, 16(2): 225–249.

de Swaan, Abram. 1988. *In Care of the State: Health Care, Education, and Welfare in Europe and the USA in the Modern Era*. Oxford: Oxford University Press.

Falcon, Julie and Pierre Bataille. 2018. "Equalization or Reproduction? Long-Term Trends in the Intergenerational Transmission of Advantages in Higher Education in France." *European Sociological Review*, 34(4): 335–347.

Friedman, Sam and Aaron Reeves. 2020. "From Aristocratic to Ordinary: Shifting Modes of Elite Distinction." *American Sociological Review*, 85(2): 323–350.

Gilens, Martin. 2012. *Affluence and Influence: Economic Inequality and Political Power in America*. Princeton: Princeton University Press.

Gilens, Martin and Benjamin I. Page. 2014. "Testing Theories of American Politics: Elites, Interest Groups, and Average Citizens." *Perspectives on Politics*, 12(3): 564–581.

Hecht, Katharina. 2017. "A Relational Analysis of Top Incomes and Wealth: Economic Evaluation, Relative (Dis)Advantage and the Service to Capital." *LSE International Inequalities Institute Working Paper No. 11*. London: London School of Economics.

Higley, John and Michael Burton. 2006. *Elite Foundations of Liberal Democracy*. Lanham, MA: Rowman & Littlefield Publishers.

Higley, John and Gwen Moore. 1981. "Elite Integration in the United States and Australia." *American Political Science Review*, 75(3): 581–597.

Hoffman-Lange, Ursula. 2007. "Methods of Elite Research." In *The Oxford Handbook of Political Behavior*, edited by Russell J. Dalton and Hans-Dieter Klingemann, 910–928. New York: Oxford University Press.

IBGE (Instituto Brasileiro de Geografia e Estatística). 2010. "Censo 2010." Brasília: IBGE. Accessed on 1 February 2021. https://censo2010.ibge.gov.br/.

ISSP (International Social Survey Program). 2010. "Censo 2010." Mannheim, DE: ISSP. Accessed 1 February 2021. http://w.issp.org/about-issp/.

Kalati, Noushin and James Manor. 2005. "Elite Perceptions of Poverty and Poor People in South Africa." In *Elite Perceptions of Poverty and Inequality*, edited by Elisa Reis and Mick Moore, 156–180. London: Zed Books.

Khan, Shamus R. 2010. *Privilege: The Making of an Adolescent Elite at St. Paul's School*. Princeton: Princeton University Press.

Khan, Shamus R. 2012. "The Sociology of Elites." *Annual Review of Sociology*, 38: 361–377.

López, Matias, Graziella Moraes Silva, Chana Teeger and Pedro Marques. 2020. "Economic and Cultural Determinants of Elite Attitudes toward Redistribution." *Socio-Economic Review*, 1–26.

Marais, Hein. 2013. *South Africa Pushed to the Limit: The Political Economy of Change*. London: Zed Books.

Marx, Anthony W. 1998. *Making Race and Nation: A Comparison of South Africa, the United States, and Brazil*. Cambridge: Cambridge University Press.

McCall, Leslie. 2013. *The Undeserving Rich: American Beliefs about Inequality, Opportunity, and Redistribution*. Cambridge: Cambridge University Press.

Meltzer, Allan H. and Scott F. Richard. 1981. "A Rational Theory of the Size of Government." *Journal of Political Economy*, 89(5): 914–927.

Milanovic, Branko. 2016. *Global Inequality*. Cambridge, MA: Harvard University Press.

Mills, C. Wright. 1956. *Power Elite*. New York: Oxford University Press.

Moraes Silva, Graziella and Matias López. 2015. "'Brazilian People' in the Eyes of Elites: Repertoires and Symbolic Boundaries of Inequality." *Sociologia & Antropologia*, 5(1): 157–182.

NIED/UFRJ (Nucleo Interdiciplinar de Estudos sobre Desigualdade/Universidade Federal do Rio de Janeiro). 2014. "Survey—Elites and Perceptions of Inequality." Rio de Janeiro: NIED/UFRJ. Accessed 1 February 2021. http://www.niedifcs.net/.

Page, Benjamin I., Larry M. Bartels and Jason Seawright. 2013. "Democracy and the Policy Preferences of Wealthy Americans." *Perspectives on Politics*, 11(1): 51–73.

Paugam, Serge, Bruno Cousin, Camila Giorgetti and Jules Naudet. 2017. *Ce que les Riches Pensent des Pauvres*. Paris: Le Seuil.

Piketty, Thomas. 2015. "About Capital in the Twenty-First Century." *American Economic Review*, 105(5): 48–53.

Reis, Elisa P. 2000. "Percepções da Elite sobre Pobreza e Desigualdade." *Revista Brasileira de Ciências Sociais*, 15(42): 143–152.

Reis, Elisa P. and Mick Moore. 2005. *Elite Perceptions of Poverty and Inequality*. London: Zed Books.

Rivera, Lauren A. 2016. *Pedigree: How Elite Students Get Elite Jobs*. Princeton: Princeton University Press.

Rueda, David and Daniel Stegmueller. 2016. "The Externalities of Inequality: Fear of Crime and Preferences for Redistribution in Western Europe." *American Journal of Political Science*, 60(2): 472–489.

Savage, Michael and Karel Williams (eds.). 2008. *Remembering Elites*. London: Wiley-Blackwell.

Seekings, Jeremy and Nicoli Nattrass. 2015. *Policy, Politics and Poverty in South Africa*. London: Springer.

Sherman, Rachel. 2018. "'A Very Expensive Ordinary Life': Consumption, Symbolic Boundaries and Moral Legitimacy among New York Elites." *Socio-Economic Review*, 16(2): 411–433.

Solt, Frederick. 2020. "Measuring Income Inequality across Countries and over Time: The Standardized World Income Inequality Database." *Social Science Quarterly*, 101(3): 1183–1199.

Somers, Margaret R. 1995. "What's Political or Cultural about Political Culture and the Public Sphere? Toward an Historical Sociology of Concept Formation." *Sociological Theory*, 13(2): 113–144.

Souza, Jessé. 2017. *A Elite do Atraso*. São Paulo: LeYa.

StatsSA (Statistics South Africa). 2011. "South African Census 2011." Accessed 1 February 2021. http://www.statssa.gov.za/?page_id=3839.

Verba, Sidney, Steven Kelman, Gary R., Orren, Ichiro Miyake, Joji Watanuki, Ikuo Kabashima and G. Donald Feree Jr. 1987. *Elites and the Idea of Equality: A Comparison of Japan, Sweden, and the United States*. Cambridge, MA: Harvard University Press.

Verba, Sidney and Gary R. Orren. 1985. *Equality in America: The View from the Top*. Cambridge, MA: Harvard University Press.

Wedel, Janine R. 2009. *Shadow Elite: How the World's New Power Brokers Undermine Democracy, Government, and the Free Market*. New York: Basic Books.

World Value Survey Program. n.d. "World Value Survey." Accessed 1 February 2021. http://www.worldvaluessurvey.org/wvs.jsp.

# Chapter 10

## ELITE IDEOLOGY, PUBLIC OPINION AND THE PERSISTENCE OF POVERTY AND INEQUALITY IN EAST AND SOUTHERN AFRICA

Jeremy Seekings

*Inequality, Poverty and Public Policy*

Africa stands out for its weak performance in terms of poverty reduction. Taking into account uneven and missing data, the best estimates suggest that in 1990 about 57 percent of Africa's population lived below the standard international extreme poverty line. By 2015 this poverty rate had fallen only to about 41 percent. Moreover, over the same period, the absolute number of people in extreme poverty in Africa rose, because the population was growing faster than the poverty rate was falling (Beegle et al. 2016; UN 2015). This was a period of strong global economic growth, raising per capita GDP across much of Africa—and at the same time increasing inequality. Africa's poverty rate remained stubbornly high because few of the benefits of economic growth trickled down to the poor—that is, the growth elasticity of poverty was small. Every 1 percent of economic growth reduced poverty by only 0.7 percent in Africa, compared with a reduction of 2 percent elsewhere in the world (Bicaba et al. 2015). In Africa, economic growth benefited some people but left behind many others. Development has rarely been inclusive.

It is thus not surprising that there have been strong calls for the expansion of social assistance programs (e.g., Hanlon et al. 2010). These might not be able to eliminate poverty, but they can and do mitigate poverty and dramatically reduce extreme poverty. Social assistance programs have expanded in Africa, although the pace of this expansion is unclear. The international agencies that advocate expansion tend to talk up the pace at which expansion is actually happening, presumably in order to encourage laggards. In a celebration of cash transfer programs, the World Bank reported that the "enthusiasm for conditional cash transfer programs in other regions has spilled over into the continent . . . [M]any policy makers are excited about how cash transfers can be used to meet Africa's poverty and development goals" (Garcia and Moore 2012: xiii). More recently, the ILO reports "notable progress in the extension of social protection coverage" in Africa (2017: 119); "most African countries have made social protection a priority in their development strategies" and have adopted or are developing national social protection policies and plans (2017: 131). An inventory of social assistance programs (narrowly defined) counts more than 45 million people (i.e., about 5 percent of the population of sub-Saharan Africa) receiving a cash transfer as of 2015, through a total of 80 programs in 37 countries (see Hickey et al. 2019). Using a broader definition of social protection, the ILO estimates that 18 percent of the population of sub-Saharan Africa—220 million people—were covered in the senses of either receiving at least one cash benefit or contributing to a contributory social insurance scheme (ILO 2017). The World Bank, using an even more inclusive definition of social protection, estimates that about 20 percent of households across Africa benefit from some kind of social protection (World Bank 2018a). There are also many people across Africa living in peasant households who benefit from agricultural subsidy programs that function much like social assistance, as the Food and Agriculture Organization has noted (FAO 2017).

International agencies (as well as aid donors) have pushed strongly for social protection, not only placing it firmly on the policy agenda (von Gliszczynski and Leisering 2016) but also providing substantial funding and technical expertise. Large sums have been spent on study tours, seminars and other events to build coalitions of reform-friendly politicians and officials. In some cases, parallel quasi-state, nongovernmental, organization-based bureaucracies have been established. Reform was often "donor-driven" (Devereux 2010; Seekings 2021a). Yet across much of Africa it is the *absence*, or limited reach, of social protection that is most striking: whatever their policy documents proclaim, most national governments have resisted many reforms and been slow to implement the ones they have agreed to. This chapter argues that the ambivalence or hostility of political elites to the kinds of redistributive policies associated with the welfare state across much of northwest Europe is one factor that has informed the absence or slow pace of pro-poor social protection reforms. This attitude is rooted in the conservative ideology that predominates among political elites. Whatever their views on democracy and the role of the state in economic development, most members of the political elite distinguish between "deserving" and "undeserving" poor people, are averse to "dependency" on "handouts" and worry about the effects of government interventions (including social cash transfers) on productivity and morality. This does not entirely preclude pro-poor reforms. Across much of the region some members of the political elites recognize that the state should take over the responsibility for the poor (or, at least, the deserving poor) previously shouldered by kin or community.

This chapter does not argue that attitudes alone determine policy making. Some countries have extensive social protection despite the ambivalence of elites (and even citizens). Case studies of policy making suggest, however, that ideology does matter, in conjunction with other factors including material and institutional interests, and political and fiscal opportunities and constraints.[1] It is likely that

---

1. Many country case studies have been conducted under the auspices of two research programs, both funded by the UK's Department for International Development (DFID): the Legislating and Implementing Welfare Policy Reforms (LIWPR) project based at the

norms and values are more important for social protection than for many other public policies because of apparently deep-rooted beliefs about who is deserving of what and why.

## International Organizations, Norms and the Social Protection Agenda

The global social protection agenda has been driven primarily by international organizations, including not only UN agencies (especially the ILO and the UN International Children's Emergency Fund, UNICEF) and World Bank but also national development aid agencies (such as the United Kingdom's former Department for International Development, DFID) and even nongovernmental organizations (such as HelpAge International). The various organizations generally employ the same kinds of tactics to promote their preferred reforms, including research and publications, seminars and training courses, technical assistance in policy design and implementation, and funding—contributing more than half of the cost, on average, of social safety nets in Africa (Beegle et al. 2018). While they share an enthusiasm for reform and try to speak with one voice, these international organizations differ in their preferred models (von Gliszczynski and Leisering 2016). These differences reflect in part divergent norms and values (Seekings 2021a).

Two primary normative approaches—or ideologies—predominate within these international organizations. The World Bank's approach emphasizes poverty-reducing development. Social cash transfers and programs providing benefits in kind are seen as efficient mechanisms to raise productivity among the poor and to protect the poor against the kinds of shocks that deplete their assets and forestall development. Expenditure on social cash transfers thus constitutes an investment. The ILO, in contrast, focuses on rights. The ILO's Michel Cichon (2013) gushingly described ILO Recommendation 202 (on social protection floors) as the "Magna Carta" of social protection, referring to the charter of 1215 in which the then king of England recognized that at least some of his subjects had civil and political rights. ILO Recommendation 202 opened with a preamble that reaffirmed that "the right to social security is a human right" (ILO 2012). Whereas the word "right" appears almost 300 times in the ILO's 2017–2019 "World Social Protection Report" (ILO 2017), it appears only once in the main text of the World Bank's 2018 report "State of Social Safety Nets" (World Bank 2018b: 34).

Both approaches accommodate the concept of universalism but understand it in rather different ways (Leisering 2020). For the ILO, the right to social protection is a universal right—that is, an entitlement of all individuals across the world. For the World Bank, there are strong instrumental arguments for universal protection against the risks that impede poverty-reducing development. Both approaches are

University of Cape Town (South Africa) and the Effective States and Inclusive Development program based at the University of Manchester (UK).

normative in that they value the reduction of poverty, but the World Bank's support for (selected) social programs is instrumental rather than directly normative.

The ILO shares a broad normative approach to social protection with an array of other organizations such as UNICEF, DFID and HelpAge International. While there are differences between them, these organizations share an ideology of welfare rooted in the various strands of Western left-liberal and social democratic thought. This broad understanding of rights is also promoted by many scholars of social protection in Africa (and elsewhere) (e.g., Sabates-Wheeler et al. 2020).

This understanding of social protection has critics as well as adherents across Africa. When the "global" rights agenda is translated or vernacularized into African regional declarations, through deliberations in African regional fora, more attention is paid to the responsibilities that accompany rights, to the family and community as well as the individual, and to the supposed imperatives of development (Seekings 2021b). At the national level, many governments have adopted social protection strategies or other statements that suggest that they share the enthusiasm for social protection. In practice, however, many governments have been slow to implement most of the reforms recommended by international organizations. The concerns reflected in African regional declarations surface also in the anxieties of political elites at the national level.

## Elite Attitudes toward Social Protection

Political elites' attitudes toward social protection are rooted in their perceptions of the poor and their attributions of poverty. In Malawi, for example, Kalebe-Nyamongo found that elites (defined more widely than policy makers) view the poor as passive, dependent and fatalistic. Despite evidence of the positive effects of cash transfers on the poor, elites worry that such programs simply encourage laziness and "dependency" and therefore favor workfare (i.e., public employment programs) and supposedly developmental programs (such as microfinance) over cash transfers (Kalebe-Nyamongo and Marquette 2014). In interviews in a range of countries since 2014, political leaders and government officials repeatedly cite the mantra that people should "never get something for nothing."[2] In their view, social assistance ("handouts") generates dependency in that recipients lose the incentive or will to work, becoming lazy and dependent on the government. In this view, social protection undermines self-reliance—as opposed to development, which is understood as building self-reliance. In this normative worldview, work is the basis of desert (or deservingness).

---

2. This finding is based on research conducted for the LIWPR project in Ghana, Kenya, Uganda, Tanzania, Malawi, Zambia, Botswana, Zimbabwe, Lesotho, Swaziland, Mozambique, Namibia and South Africa. Many of the publications from this project are cited in this chapter.

The specter of dependency weighs heavily on elites in different parts of Africa, including among self-conscious modernizers. For example, the Kagame regime in Rwanda views the peasantry as undynamic and needing to be modernized. Poverty is seen as the consequence of a lack of determination. "If we can utilize the resources that God has given to us to good effect, we can eradicate poverty," Kagame told the country in 2000. "We would like to urgently appeal to the Rwandese people to work. As the Bible says, 'he who does not work should not eat'" (cited in Ansoms 2009: 297). This did not preclude social welfare reforms. The Kagame regime introduced a series of programs, in part because they appear to facilitate production and in part because they serve to legitimize what is essentially an authoritarian regime (Lavers 2019).

Conservative attitudes among national elites have often blocked or at least inhibited the efforts of international organizations to promote social protection. A clear example of this was Zambia in the 2000s. Faced with the dual challenges of drought and AIDS, the German aid agency Gesellschaft für Technische Zusammenarbeit and later DFID strongly supported pilot social assistance programs and encouraged and assisted the Zambian government to draft a "social protection strategy." The model prioritized cash transfers to "labor-constrained," ultra-poor households. Reforms were, however, strongly opposed by the influential minister of finance, Ng'andu Magande, who saw the poor as largely responsible for their own poverty and resisted any government interventions that were not clearly developmental. His views on the largely undeserving poor may have been extreme within his party, the Movement for Multiparty Democracy, but the party had been elected in 1991 in reaction against the failed statism (i.e., reliance on the state rather than on private initiative) of Zambia's previous governments (Kabandula and Seekings 2016). Under the Patriotic Front government elected in 2011, party leaders with social democratic tendencies expanded the reach of social grants, until they were pushed out of the party and government in 2015–2016 (Siachiwena 2016, 2017). Leading members of the major opposition party—the broadly liberal United Party for National Development—favored policies that expanded production over redistributive programs (Hallink 2019a). None of the major Zambian parties over this period showed consistent support for social protection.

In Uganda as well, donors—especially DFID—worked hard to move social protection up the government's agenda in the 2000s. The government was formally committed to poverty reduction. It implemented a number of relevant reforms: it abolished fees in clinics and primary schools and introduced school feeding programs and very modest programs for orphans and the disabled. In 2002, a Social Protection Task Force was established within the Ministry for Gender, Labour and Social Development. In 2006, DFID and the government signed an agreement to design and pilot a cash transfer scheme to address "chronic poverty." DFID-funded consultants worked closely with bureaucrats in the Ministry for Gender, Labour and Social Development as well as civil society groups. But, in 2007, the minister of finance blocked the proposed pilot cash transfer program. The minister expressed concern over long-term affordability. Underlying this concern lay a deep ambivalence about poverty-targeted cash transfers. The leader of the "technical assistance team" later explained that the initiative failed because decision makers "didn't see cash transfers as an answer to poverty, they saw economic growth and hard work and [the poor] getting off their backsides as the answer to poverty" (quoted in Grebe 2014: 17; see also Bukenya and Hickey 2019; Grebe and Mubiru 2014).

Tanzania's successive governments stand out for their lack of interest in social assistance. The government—controlled since independence by a single party, Chama Cha Mapinduzi—has consistently and strongly emphasized self-reliance, responsibility and hard work. The World Bank pushed for a Productive Social Safety Net project integrating workfare with cash transfers. It promoted its program as a "smart" safety net program that raises the productivity of the poor. The World Bank emphasized that poor people invested—rather than simply consumed—the benefits, expanding future production. The cash transfer component had developmental conditions attached, and program officials also emphasized that beneficiaries should "graduate" out of the program within three years (and therefore did not include any specific provision for the elderly through social pensions). They emphasized that these were not simply "handouts." In 2015, the government finally agreed to the countrywide rollout of the program to the poorest 10 percent of households, to be cofinanced by the government with the World Bank and other donors. At the same time, HelpAge International, DFID and the ILO promoted unsuccessfully the idea of a social pension. As of 2015/2016, however, the government was funding only 4 percent of the Productive Social Safety Net project: that is, much less than the 25 percent to which it had previously agreed. While newly elected President Magufuli emphasized hard work, the media reported cases of irregular beneficiaries (Ulriksen 2019; Ulriksen et al. 2018). Many—perhaps most—of the officials who implement the program hold the disparaging views of the "lazy" and "dependent" poor that are widespread within the Tanzanian middle classes (Green 2021).

In some countries in Africa (as in Europe), anxiety over dependency has become more prominent in part in response to the expansion of social assistance. In Botswana, the expansion of drought relief from the mid-1960s fueled concern that peasant farmers would become dependent on it and cease to farm. Anxiety grew as development rose in importance for the government: given that economic development meant rising productivity, dependency represented the failure of development. Anxiety about dependency became almost ubiquitous in Botswana by the 2000s. While poor people might have understood the necessity of drought relief, elites thought that it fueled the culture of dependency, causing rather than mitigating poverty (Seekings 2017). While government programs have considerable reach, benefits remain parsimonious in order, it is explained, to mitigate the risk of dependency (Seekings 2019a). In the 2010s, the government of Botswana repeatedly rejected calls from international organizations for new cash transfer programs to support poor families with children (Chinyoka 2018). The 2017–2023 National Development Plan called for programs that "empower" people rather than support them in ways that lead to dependency (Government of Botswana 2016). Even the more progressive opposition parties are generally conservative on social policy issues (Hallink 2019b).

In South Africa as well, the expansion of social grants fueled a backlash. The governing African National Congress (ANC) had always advocated development over welfare. In his inaugural presidential speech in 1994, Nelson Mandela himself had declared that his government would tackle the "scourge of unemployment" through creating opportunities to work, rather than through "handouts." The ANC aspired to build a developmental state, not a welfare state. In the late 1990s, it even considered abolishing programs that it inherited. In the early 2000s, it rejected calls for a basic income grant (Seekings and Matisonn 2012). As in Botswana, the expansion of social grants seems to have strengthened conservative criticisms, especially over the payment of grants to young mothers (on behalf of their children) (Moore and Seekings 2019). At an African Union meeting that was intended to promote social protection, South Africa's deputy-minister for social development warned that "the main challenge . . . was not to create a dependency syndrome among the population to the detriment of productivity" (AU 2015: 3).

Elite attitudes toward social protection are widely rooted in an anachronistic faith in the capacity of small farmers (i.e., peasant families) to support themselves through agricultural production and kin-based redistribution. Elites seem to have little appreciation of the extent of deagrarianization—that is, both the decline of smallholder agriculture and kinship obligations—across much of Africa (Bryceson and Jamal 1997). Even where urbanization has resulted in large urban populations, it is widely believed that people can support themselves and their families through informal work, even if for meager income. The mostly male elites also appear not to worry over how an emphasis on the family entrenches patriarchy and places a growing burden on women (Bryceson 2018). In some cases, prominent members of the elite see themselves as self-made men (or, less often, women) from ordinary backgrounds whose success is attributed to their hard work (e.g., Magande 2018; Kabandula and Seekings 2016). In other cases, people born into privilege in Africa (as elsewhere) may simply have little appreciation of the constraints on poor people, including especially poor women.

## Responsibility and the Possibility of Redistribution

The wide reach of conservative norms of self-reliance and non-state mechanisms for provision does not mean there is no normative basis for social protection among African elites. To varying extents, elites also subscribe to a concept of responsibility. Social and economic change means that the responsibilities previously effected through the family or community may now need to be assumed by the state. Whereas the anxiety about dependency was often rooted in an underestimation of deagrarianization, an ethic of state responsibility recognized that deagrarianization (and other factors) had transformed the capacity of local people.

In Botswana, the postcolonial state expanded public programs—initially of drought relief, later of general relief—on the basis that the new state needed to take over the responsibilities of traditional leaders. The country's first president, Seretse Khama (himself a traditional leader until effectively deposed by the British prior to independence), articulated a conservative ideology of responsibility as an integral component of a harmonious community (expressed through the Tswana concept of *kagisano*). Khama idealized rural society, demonized urban life, accepted inequality, emphasized self-help and denounced dependency. But he also emphasized social justice: "We cannot let the weakest go to the wall"; "the interests of the small man must be paramount"; "we must recognise our obligations to the under-privileged and help them to help themselves." His was a benign form of conservatism. Khama summed it up using a Tswana proverb: "A lean cow cannot climb out of the mud, but a good cattleman does not leave it to perish" (Khama quotes from Seekings 2016). After Khama's death, his ideology was institutionalized in the country's "Vision 2016," which promised that Botswana would become "a compassionate and caring society, offering support and opportunity to those who are poor, and including *all* people in the benefits of growth," including through a "social safety net for those who find themselves in poverty for any reason" (while avoiding a "culture of dependency") (Government of Botswana 1996: 8, 9, 25).

Guided by this ideology, the government of Botswana pioneered (in partnership with the World Food Programme) drought relief programs that ensured that very few if any Batswana died during the country's deep and protracted droughts. Drought relief programs evolved into the kinds of programs more usually understood as social protection, including social pensions for the elderly. The result was a conservative welfare state that combined broad reach with distinctively conservative features (parsimonious and often in-kind benefits, an emphasis on workfare and a reliance on family) (Seekings 2019a).

In South Africa, the ANC minister of social development in the 2000s, Zola Skweyiya, succeeded in expanding the reach of social grants in the face of skepticism among many of his colleagues. Skweyiya, like Khama, was the product of a mission-educated, Christian political tradition that was liberal on many issues but paternalistically conservative on others. Skweyiya lobbied for expanded provision of grants through a discourse of dignity and responsibility: the state had a responsibility to protect the dignity of its citizens through protecting them from extreme poverty, if they were unable to work; if they could work, then they must do so (and enjoy the "dignity of work") and not become "dependent" on social grants (Seekings 2020).

Reformers such as Khama and Skweyiya employed a discourse of responsibility, emphasizing that responsibility is reciprocal: the poor have their own responsibility to help themselves and others whenever possible through work. When poor people become "dependent" on the state, they are failing in their reciprocal responsibilities to help themselves (and others). In this view, dependency entails the denial of reciprocity as well as the failure of development. As Ulriksen and Plagerson (2014) have argued, concerns with rights and duties can be combined, for example, through social contract theory. The conservative social contract across much of Africa entailed reciprocal responsibilities between the individual and the community or society. The individual must work, and sometimes "show restraint and sacrifice" (as Khama put it); "nobody is allowed to starve," but it is "a matter of great shame for an able-bodied man who can help himself to try and rely on others for his livelihood" (quoted in Seekings 2016: 23–24).

## Popular Attitudes toward Social Protection

Solidarity with the poor is not easily achieved. Across much of the world, citizens often have a strong sense that some categories of poor people (especially the elderly, sick and disabled) are deserving but have (at best) mixed feelings about other categories (notably unemployed working-age adults and single parents) (see, e.g., Taylor-Gooby 1985; van Oorschot 2000, 2006). Popular attitudes toward poverty, inequality and social protection in Africa have not been examined deeply. Only for South Africa is there a substantial literature on perceptions of desert (but see Yeboah et al. 2016 and Abdulai et al. 2019 on Ghana). Moreover, it is quite complex to interpret popular attitudes: survey data on support for social protection show that responses depend on the precise question posed (Seekings 2007), and there is little detailed qualitative research.

In South Africa, which has by far the most widespread and most generous (or least parsimonious) system of social assistance, survey data suggest that there is strong support for social grants, including for raising the value of the benefits. At the same time, South Africans distinguish a clear hierarchy of perceived desert: the elderly and sick are considered most deserving, caregivers somewhat deserving and other working-age adults least deserving (Seekings 2008, 2010, 2019b). Qualitative research found that even unemployed young men were hostile to the idea that people like them should receive cash transfers from the state (Dawson and Fouksman 2020). One study of Ghana similarly found that there was widespread support for cash transfers (at least as an interim poverty-mitigating measure) but not for adults who were capable of work (Yeboah et al. 2016).

Both quantitative and qualitative research suggest that support for social grants among South Africans is conditional on the behavior of the recipients. Most respondents in two national surveys (in 2015 and 2018) agreed that young women who received the Child Support Grant spent too much on alcohol. Well over half (60 percent) of the respondents in the 2015 survey agreed that adults who were physically able to work should be required to do so in return for any money received from the government (Seekings 2019c). Grant recipients are subject to strong social pressure and potential stigmatization if they "misuse" their grants (Blake 2018; Hochfeld 2015; Hochfeld and Plagerson 2011; Kelly 2019). Similarly in Zambia, Schüring (2011) found a preference for conditionality among both urban and rural populations, especially among the better educated and better-off people, as well as among most government officials and members of parliament. Insofar as cash transfers are understood as a charitable gift—as found in one study of Ghana (Abdulai et al. 2019)—there is likely to be broad popular support for attaching the kinds of conditions to cash transfers as private individuals might attach to their own charitable gifts to others.

Popular attitudes might be inferred also from voters' responses to the promises made by parties and candidates during election campaigns. In Botswana, there is evidence that the provision of drought relief—which evolved into social cash transfers—was foundational to the incumbent Botswana Democratic Party's support base in rural areas from the mid-1960s (Gulbrandsen 2012; Seekings 2019a). In South Africa, however, there is little evidence that either receipt of a grant or conservative views has a significant direct effect on voting behavior (Graham et al. 2016; Seekings 2019c).

Social protection has rarely featured prominently in election campaigns. Even in South Africa, the ANC has been reluctant to emphasize heavily social grants in its formal campaign materials (although it is possible that activists emphasize them more heavily in their campaign speeches and other informal contacts with voters). Opposition parties have rarely taken the lead in proposing reforms. Even in Zimbabwe, where the opposition Movement for Democratic Change claimed to be "social democratic" and criticized the incumbent party strongly, it did not propose any specific welfare reforms (Chinyoka and Seekings 2016). Zambia's then opposition Patriotic Front did include a vague commitment to social protection in its 2011 election manifesto. After winning the election, the Patriotic Front did somewhat expand financial support for the hitherto donor-funded "pilot" social cash transfer program. In the following elections in 2016, one of the party's billboards proclaimed that more than 1 million people were benefiting from the social cash transfer program. But this particular poster was not used widely, with the PF preferring to emphasize other supposed achievements. Moreover, the Patriotic Front government proceeded to cut funding for social grants so that even registered beneficiaries failed to receive them (Siachiwena 2016, 2017).

Social protection did feature prominently in one election campaign, in Malawi in 2014. While it is not easy to identify the precise effect of the issue on the results, the outcome certainly does not suggest that championing social protection is a clear vote winner. The circumstances of the election were unusual, in that the incumbent president, Joyce Banda, had succeeded to the presidency only because of the death of her predecessor, Bingu wa Mutharika, and despite the fact that Mutharika had expelled her from his party before he died. Mutharika had established a strong brand for himself and his party (the Democratic Progressive Party) as the champion of farmers, to whom he provided heavily subsidized fertilizer and other inputs at considerable expense. Malawian voters favor government policies that strengthen their capacity to grow maize (van Donge 2005). Banda was compelled to build a new party and establish a new brand for it and herself. She chose to present herself as the champion of women and the poor through Malawi's nascent social protection programs. Banda spoke of "handouts" in positive terms but was strongly criticized by her opponents. Weighed down by a corruption scandal and a stuttering economy, Banda won just 20 percent of the presidential vote. The case showed that a pro-grant platform did not prevent a candidate or party winning some votes but was certainly not enough to offset other weaknesses (Hamer and Seekings 2019).

## The Covid-19 Crisis and Ideologies of Welfare

Covid-19 caused few deaths on the continent (except in South Africa and the countries of North Africa) in 2020 but massive economic disruption because of either national lockdowns or the collapse of international trade. The World Bank warned that Africa as a whole would slide into its first recession for 25 years, while the economies of Botswana and South Africa were expected to contract by as much as 10 percent. International organizations warned that the crisis was most acute for the urban poor, who could not fall back on subsistence agriculture and whose informal livelihoods were especially vulnerable to lockdowns. They ramped up their advocacy of an expansion of social protection (Gronbach and Seekings 2021).

South Africa saw at least one half of the total number of Covid-19 deaths across Africa as a whole in 2020. The crisis depressed an economy already in recession, resulting in a sharp rise in unemployment and widespread hardship. In response, the government expanded its existing unemployment insurance system, paid supplements to existing grant recipients and introduced a new emergency grant for adults with no other source of income. Together, these measures increased public expenditure on cash transfers from just over 3 percent of GDP to more than 5 percent of GDP, at a time when the government faced a deep fiscal crisis. The emergency social grant was the first paid to and for working-age adults, while the supplement to the child support grant was per caregiver and not for dependent children. Hitherto the government had touted workfare programs as its preferred instrument for supporting working-age adults, but workfare programs could not continue under lockdown conditions. The reforms were thus unprecedented in terms of expenditure, the number of beneficiaries and provision for working-age adults.

In South Africa, conservative ambivalence or hostility to social grants was suspended or overridden in the face of the Covid-19 crisis. An already extensive social protection system was extended further. Elsewhere in Africa, reforms to social protection were generally muted, despite pressure from international organizations. In Botswana, the government distributed food parcels but did little more. In Zambia, the PF government only resumed the payment of grants to existing registered beneficiaries when elections loomed in 2020-21. It continued to favor instead that funds would be directed to subsidizing small farmers. International organizations initiated and funded an emergency cash transfer program aimed at the urban poor, but its reach was very limited. In Botswana and Zambia, governments did what they were doing before the crisis, which did not entail significant expansion of cash transfers (Gronbach and Seekings 2021).

Even in the face of deep economic crisis affecting the urban poor especially, most African governments remained averse to extending social grants to able-bodied adults, even temporarily. In South Africa, despite renewed discussion of a basic income grant, it appeared that the emergency measures would be only temporary. Across most of Africa, including even South Africa, the conservatism of political elites, perhaps rooted in popular ambivalence, limits and shapes the expansion of social protection promoted by international organizations, sometimes on the basis of a quite different set of norms and values. Across most of Africa, payments to working-age adults remain viewed (with the exception of workfare) as the kind of government "handouts" that inhibit self-help, development, a conservative understanding of the social contract and hence social cohesion. In societies experiencing widespread and profound deagrarianization and urbanization, these ideological beliefs seem increasingly at odds with social and economic realities, but they remain powerful today.

Inequalities in the distribution of income or of opportunities persist or worsen because political elites tolerate or even prefer such inequalities and because poor people are unable to hold elites to account. Social protection offers a means to mitigate poverty and inequality, usually without addressing the factors that generate inequalities in the first place. Social protection remains limited across most of Africa, despite energetic advocacy by diverse international organizations (and their allies in civil society across Africa) because the political elites who wield immediate power over policy making have not been persuaded of the merits of such reforms. International organizations have generally wielded insufficient power over national governments to bend them to their will. Elite ambivalence or hostility to redistributive social protection policies thus constrains the extent to which poverty and inequality are mitigated. This is true even if or when such policies are likely to serve elite interests through strengthening a social contract that contains political dissent.

This chapter suggests that elites are sometimes constrained by their own norms, values and beliefs, and perhaps even by the norms and values that prevail in their societies more broadly. In the case of social protection it is not clear that the norms and values of elites across most of Africa are out of line with popular norms and values. Political elites might resist the expansion of social protection not only because they are ideologically opposed to it but also because they sense that there is insufficient popular clamor for such reforms. In those countries where competitive elections or the threat of direct action do serve to impose some limited accountability on elites, the slow expansion of social protection reflects not so much the absence of any elite accountability as the weakness of popular demand.

As this chapter has suggested, however, this does not preclude the expansion of poverty-mitigating social protection in Africa. Conservative beliefs around responsibility and the dignity of work can be reconciled with conservative forms of social protection, including workfare and conditional programs. Such programs are likely to be popular and politically advantageous to ruling elites, because they mitigate poverty and inequality in ways that are consistent with prevalent norms and values, legitimating the regime or consolidating electoral support.

## References

Abdulai, Abdul-Gafaru, Abdul-Bassit Abubakari and Jude Martey. 2019. "Is Social Protection in Ghana a Right?" *Development in Practice*, 29(8): 1064–1074.

Ansoms, An. 2009. "Re-engineering Rural Society: The Visions and Ambitions of the Rwandan Elite." *African Affairs*, 108(431): 289–309.

AU (African Union). 2015. "Social Protection for Inclusive Development: Draft Report of the Ministers' Meeting." *Paper presented at the first meeting of the Specialised Technical Committee on Social Development, Labour and Employment (STC-SDLE-1), Addis Ababa*, 20–24 April. Addis Ababa: African Union.

Beegle, Kathleen, Luc Christiaensen, Andrew Dabalen and Isis Gaddis. 2016. *Poverty in a Rising Africa*. Washington, DC: World Bank.

Beegle, Kathleen, Aline Coudouel and Emma Monsalve (eds.). 2018. *Realizing the Full Potential of Social Safety Nets in Africa*. Washington, DC: World Bank.

Bicaba, Zarobabel, Zuzana Brixiová and Mthuli Ncube. 2015. "Eliminating Extreme Poverty in Africa: Trends, Policies and the Roles of International Organisations." *ADB Working Paper No. 223*. Abidjan: African Development Bank.

Blake, Rosemary. 2018. "The Price of the Grant: The Social Cost of Child Support Grants for Female Caregivers and Their Extended Networks." *CSSR Working Paper 412*. Cape Town: Centre for Social Science Research, University of Cape Town.

Bryceson, Deborah Fahy. 2018. "Gender and Generational Patterns of African Deagrarianization: Evolving Labour and Land Allocation in Smallholder Peasant Household Farming, 1980–2015." *World Development*, 113: 60–72.

Bryceson, Deborah Fahy and Vali Jamal (eds.). 1997. *Farewell to Farms: De-agrarianisation and Employment in Africa*. Aldershot: Ashgate.

Bukenya, Badru and Sam Hickey. 2019. "The Politics of Promoting Social Cash Transfers in Uganda." In *The Politics of Social Protection in Eastern and Southern Africa*, edited by Sam Hickey, Tom Lavers, Miguel Niño-Zarazúa and Jeremy Seekings, 202–224. Oxford: Oxford University Press.

Chinyoka, Isaac. 2018. "Familial Child Welfare Regimes: The Case of Botswana." *CSSR Working Paper No. 430*. Cape Town: Centre for Social Science Research, University of Cape Town.

Chinyoka, Isaac and Jeremy Seekings. 2016. "Did the Participation of the Political Opposition in the Zimbabwean Government Between 2009 and 2013 Make a Difference to Cash Transfer Programmes?" *CSSR Working Paper No. 373*. Cape Town: Centre for Social Science Research, University of Cape Town.

Cichon, Michael. 2013. "The Social Protection Floors Recommendation, 2012 (No. 202): Can a Six-Page Document Change the Course of Social History?" *International Social Security Review*, 66(3–4): 21–43.

Dawson, Hannah and Elizabeta Fouksman. 2020. "Labour, Laziness and Distribution: Work Imaginaries among the South African Unemployed." *Africa*, 90(2): 229–251.

Devereux, Stephen. 2010. "Building Social Protection Systems in Southern Africa." *Paper prepared in the framework of the European Report on Development 2010*. Brussels: European Commission.

FAO (Food and Agriculture Organization). 2017. *FAO Social Protection Framework: Promoting Rural Development for All*. Rome: FAO.

Garcia, Marito and Charity M. T. Moore. 2012. *The Cash Dividend: The Rise of Cash Transfer Programs in Sub-Saharan Africa*. Washington, DC: World Bank.

Government of Botswana. 1996. *Vision 2016*. Gaborone: Government of Botswana.

Government of Botswana. 2016. *Draft National Development Plan 11, 2017–2023*. Gaborone: Ministry of Finance and Development Planning.

Graham, Victoria, Yolanda Sadie and Leila Patel. 2016. "Social Grants, Food Parcels and Voting Behavior: A Case Study of Three South African Communities." *Transformation*, 91: 106–135.

Grebe, Eduard. 2014. "Donor Agenda-Setting, Bureaucratic Advocacy and Cash Transfers in Uganda, 2002–13." *CSSR Working Paper No. 354*. Cape Town: Centre for Social Science Research, University of Cape Town.

Grebe, Eduard and John Bosco Mubiru. 2014. "The Politics of Welfare Policy-Making and Cash Transfers in Uganda." *CSSR Working Paper No. 353*. Cape Town: Centre for Social Science Research, University of Cape Town.

Green, Maia. 2021. "The Work of Class: Cash Transfers and Community Development in Tanzania." *Economic Anthropology*, 8(2): 273–286.

Gronbach, Lena and Jeremy Seekings. 2021. "Pandemic, Lockdown and the Stalled Urbanization of Welfare Regimes in Southern Africa." *Global Social Policy*, 21(3): 448–467.

Gulbrandsen, Ørnulf. 2012. *The State and the Social: State Formation in Botswana and Its Precolonial and Colonial Genealogies*. New York: Berghahn.

Hallink, Courtney. 2019a. "Liberalism as a Manifestation of the Ideals and Values of Zambia's Southern Province: The United Party for National Development and the Promotion of Self-Reliance through Social Welfare." *CSSR Working Paper No. 437*. Cape Town: Centre for Social Science Research, University of Cape Town.

Hallink, Courtney. 2019b. "Defending Negative Freedoms: Liberalism as a Response to the Rising Authoritarianism of the Botswana Democratic Party." *CSSR Working Paper No. 439*. Cape Town: Centre for Social Science Research, University of Cape Town.

Hamer, Sam and Jeremy Seekings. 2019. "Social Assistance, Electoral Competition, and Political Branding in Malawi." In *The Politics of Social Protection in Eastern and Southern Africa*, edited by Sam Hickey, Tom Lavers, Miguel Niño-Zarazúa and Jeremy Seekings, 225–248. Oxford: Oxford University Press.

Hanlon, Joseph, Armando Barrientos and David Hulme. 2010. *Just Give Money to the Poor: The Development Revolution from the Global South*. Sterling, VA: Kumarian Press.

Hickey, Sam, Tom Lavers, Miguel Niño-Zarazúa and Jeremy Seekings. 2019. "The Negotiated Politics of Social Protection in Africa." In *The Politics of Social Protection in Eastern and Southern Africa*, edited by Sam Hickey, Tom Lavers, Miguel Niño-Zarazúa and Jeremy Seekings, 1–41. Oxford: Oxford University Press.

Hochfeld, Tessa. 2015. "Cash, Care and Social Justice: A Study of the Child Support Grant." PhD Thesis, University of the Witwatersrand, South Africa.

Hochfeld, Tessa and Sophie Plagerson. 2011. "Dignity and Stigma among South African Female Cash Transfer Recipients." *IDS Bulletin*, 42(6): 53–59.

ILO (International Labour Organization). 2012. *R202—Social Protection Floors Recommendation*. Geneva: ILO.

ILO (International Labour Organization). 2017. *World Social Protection Report 2017–19: Universal Social Protection to Achieve the Sustainable Development Goals*. Geneva: ILO.

Kabandula, Abigail and Jeremy Seekings. 2016. "Donor Influence, the Minister of Finance and Welfare Policy Reform in Zambia, 2003–11." *CSSR Working Paper No. 395*. Cape Town: Centre for Social Science Research, University of Cape Town.

Kalebe-Nyamongo, Chipiliro and Heather Marquette. 2014. "Elite Attitudes towards Cash Transfers and the Poor in Malawi." *DLP Research Paper No. 30*. Birmingham: Developmental Leadership Programme, University of Birmingham.

Kelly, Gabrielle. 2019. "Disability, Cash Transfers and Family Practices." *Critical Social Policy*, 39(4): 541–559.

Lavers, Tom. 2019. "Understanding Elite Commitment to Social Protection: Rwanda's Vision 2020 Umurenge Programme." In *The Politics of Social Protection in Eastern and Southern Africa*, edited by Sam Hickey, Tom Lavers, Miguel Niño-Zarazúa and Jeremy Seekings, 95–121. Oxford: Oxford University Press.

Leisering, Lutz. 2020. "The Calls for Universal Social Protection by International Organizations: Constructing a New Global Consensus." *Social Inclusion*, 8(1): 90–102.

Magande, Ng'andu Peter. 2018. *The Depths of My Footprints: From the Hills of Namaila to the Global Stage*. Atlanta, GA: Maleendo.

Moore, Elena and Jeremy Seekings (eds.). 2019. "Social Protection, Intergenerational Relationships and Conflict in South Africa." *Critical Social Policy*, 39(4): 513–621.

Sabates-Wheeler, Rachel, Nikhil Wilmink, Abdul-Gafaru Abdulai, Richard De Groot and Tayllor Spadafora. 2020. "Linking Social Rights to Active Citizenship for the Most Vulnerable: The Role of Rights and Accountability in the 'Making' and 'Shaping' of Social Protection." *European Journal of Development Research*, 32(1): 129–151.

Schüring, Esther. 2011. "Preferences for Conditioning and Being Conditioned— Experimental & Survey Evidence from Zambia." *UNU-MERIT Working Paper 2011-46*. Maastricht: Maastricht University and United Nations University.

Seekings, Jeremy. 2007. "The Mutability of Distributive Justice Beliefs in South Africa." *South African Review of Sociology*, 38(1): 20–44.

Seekings, Jeremy. 2008. "'Just Deserts': Race, Class and Distributive Justice in Post-Apartheid South Africa." *Journal of Southern African Studies*, 34(1): 39–60.

Seekings, Jeremy. 2010. "Racial and Class Discrimination in Assessments of 'Just Desert' in Post-Apartheid Cape Town." In *Discrimination in an Unequal World*, edited by Miguel Centano and Katherine Newman, 63–87. New York: Oxford University Press.

Seekings, Jeremy. 2016. "'A Lean Cow Cannot Climb Out of the Mud, but a Good Cattleman Does Not Leave It to Perish': The Origins of a Conservative Welfare Doctrine in Botswana under Seretse Khama, 1966–1980." *CSSR Working Paper No. 387*. Cape Town: Centre for Social Science Research, University of Cape Town.

Seekings, Jeremy. 2017. "The Discourse of Dependency and the Agrarian Roots of Welfare Doctrines in Africa: The Case of Botswana." *Sozialpolitik.ch*, 2(2.4).

Seekings, Jeremy. 2019a. "Building a Conservative Welfare State in Botswana". In *The Politics of Social Protection in Eastern and Southern Africa*, edited by Sam Hickey, Tom Lavers, Miguel Niño-Zarazúa and Jeremy Seekings, 42–67. Oxford: Oxford University Press.

Seekings, Jeremy. 2019b. "The Conditional Legitimacy of Claims Made by Mothers and Other Kin in South Africa." *Critical Social Policy*, 39(4): 599–621.

Seekings, Jeremy. 2019c. "Social Grants and Voting in South Africa." *CSSR Working Paper No. 436*. Cape Town: Centre for Social Science Research, University of Cape Town.

Seekings, Jeremy. 2020. "Reformulating the 'Social Question' in Post-Apartheid South Africa: Zola Skweyiya, Dignity, Development and the Welfare State." In *One Hundred Years of Social Security: The Changing Social Question in Brazil, India, China, and South Africa*, edited by Lutz Leisering, 263–299. London: Palgrave.

Seekings, Jeremy. 2021a. "International Actors and Social Protection in Africa, 2000–2020." In *Handbook of Social Protection in Development*, edited by Esther Schüring and Marcus Loewe, 492–507. Cheltenham: Edward Elgar.

Seekings, Jeremy. 2021b. "The Vernacularisation of Global Rights Discourses and Social Protection in Regional African Arena." *Global Social Policy*, 21(2): 215–233.

Seekings, Jeremy and Heidi Matisonn. 2012. "South Africa: The Continuing Politics of Basic Income." In *Horizons of Reform: Basic Income Solutions around the World*, edited by Carol Pateman and Matthew Murray, 128–150. London: Palgrave Macmillan.

Siachiwena, Hangala. 2016. "Policy Reform in Zambia under the Sata Presidency 2011–2014." *CSSR Working Paper No. 390*. Cape Town: Centre for Social Science Research, University of Cape Town.

Siachiwena, Hangala. 2017. "The Politics of Welfare Policy Reform in Zambia after the Death of Sata in 2014." *CSSR Working Paper No. 403*. Cape Town: Centre for Social Science Research, University of Cape Town.

Taylor-Gooby, Peter. 1985. *Public Opinion, Ideology and State Welfare*. London: Routledge and Kegan Paul.

Ulriksen, Marianne. 2019. "Pushing for Policy Innovation: The Framing of Social Protection Policies in Tanzania." In *The Politics of Social Protection in Eastern and Southern Africa*, edited by Sam Hickey, Tom Lavers, Miguel Niño-Zarazúa and Jeremy Seekings, 122–147. Oxford: Oxford University Press.

Ulriksen, Marianne, Flora Myamba and Constantine George. 2018. "External Influence and (Shifting) Elite Commitment to Social Protection in Tanzania." *Paper presented at conference on Building Social Protection Systems in the Global South: Different Trajectories and the Influence of External Factors*, Bremen, Germany, June.

Ulriksen, Marianne and Sophie Plagerson. 2014. "Social Protection: Rethinking Rights and Duties." *World Development*, 64(C): 755–765.

UN (United Nations). 2015. *The Millennium Development Goals Report*. New York: UN.

van Donge, Jan K. 2005. "The Farmer's Perspective: Values, Incentives and Constraints." In *Starter Packs: A Strategy to Fight Hunger in Developing Countries? Lessons from the Malawi Experience 1998–2003*, edited by Sarah Levy, 117–128. Wallingford: CABI.

van Oorschot, Wim. 2000. "Who Should Get What, and Why? On Deservingness Criteria and the Conditionality of Solidarity among the Public." *Policy and Politics*, 28(1): 33–48.

van Oorschot, Wim. 2006. "Making the Difference in Social Europe: Deservingness Perceptions among Citizens of European Welfare States." *Journal of European Social Policy*, 16(1): 23–42.

von Gliszczynski, Moritz and Lutz Leisering. 2016. "Constructing New Global Models of Social Security: How International Organizations Defined the Field of Social Cash Transfers in the 2000s." *Journal of Social Policy*, 45(2): 325–343.

World Bank. 2018a. "ASPIRE: The Atlas of Social Protection—Indicators of Resilience and Equity." Washington, DC: World Bank. https://datacatalog.worldbank.org/coverage-social-protection-and-labor-programs-population-0.

World Bank. 2018b. *State of Social Safety Nets 2018*. Washington, DC: World Bank.

Yeboah, Felix, Michael D. Kaplowitz, John M. Kerr, Frank Lupi and Laurie G. Thorp. 2016. "Sociocultural and Institutional Contexts of Social Cash Transfer Programs: Lessons from Stakeholders' Attitudes and Experiences in Ghana." *Global Social Policy*, 16(3): 287–308.

## Part IV

A New Social Contract: Alliances for
Transformative Change

# Chapter 11

## OTHERING AND SOLIDARITY IN TWENTIETH-CENTURY AGRARIAN CALIFORNIA

### LESSONS FROM CROSS-SECTOR ALLIANCES FOR PROGRESSIVE POLITICAL CHANGE

Antonio Roman-Alcalá

*Introduction: Crisis and Continuity in the Contemporary US Context*

In the contemporary United States, economic, social, political and environmental crises abound: opiate addiction and eviction epidemics, climate change–induced droughts and floods, resource extraction conflicts (particularly fossil fuels), increasing unaffordability of health care, racist structures that subject some to premature death (especially at the hands of police), the desiccation of rural communities and an extraction of wealth upward to the richest. All these have been compounded by the 2020 Covid-19 pandemic. While there is much that appears as *new* in these crises, seeing them as *novel* can obscure a deeper continuity in the country's life and politics. Existing crises emerge from previous trajectories of inequality, oppression, and environmental exploitation and degradation, and Covid-19 should be seen as having exacerbated—rather than generated—such trajectories.

In similar ways, Donald Trump's surprise election and presidency can be seen as contiguous with history. Rather than a break with the past, Trump's politics extended neoliberal assaults on the poor, the working class and the environment. Rather than a completely new policy agenda, the Trump administration brought new lows and frightening extremity to an existing neoliberal playbook. That playbook combines rhetoric against the state and elites with policies that leverage or strengthen the state in key areas (e.g., security, borders, surveillance, bailing out industry, deregulation as regulation) while enhancing the extractive resource gains of elites. A key ramification of this approach is to further insulate state policymaking from nonelites, prohibiting policy change that could truly address compound crises. Like tracing the continuity of Trump with previous policy trajectories, we also must acknowledge the uncomfortable continuity of nonelite politics in the racism, sexism and xenophobia that have long characterized domestic US politics. Trump's authoritarian political agenda relied on this regressive nonelite lineage which, combined with the crises engendered in part by neoliberalism, works to build resentment among (and rally consent of) an ostensible populist majority behind a strong man to protect them.

This is not to say that the US electoral populace is irredeemably reactionary. We cannot easily separate out racial resentment and economic degeneration as motivating factors for individual vote choices (Edelman 2019). However, we can say that a long history of social inequalities and racialized thinking provides an essential backdrop to understanding the political moment of Trumpism. That is because Trumpism, like other regressive political movements before it, has utilized "Othering" to divide an already stratified populace and build power. "Othering," as defined by powell and Menendian (2016: 17), is "a set of dynamics, processes, and structures that engender marginality and persistent inequality across any of the full range of human differences based on group identities." Trump's common scapegoats—immigrants, Muslims, Black people, feminists and Leftists—are constructed to be "Others" and threats to the social order. To accomplish this Othering, Trumpian politics must enroll many nonelites into a political project to vilify these out-groups in the name of "the people," thus relying on the synergy of top-down and bottom-up forces. Importantly, Othering is a process found in various forms of oppression, marginalization and inequality, but it is neither about one particular axis of these (e.g., race, gender, class), nor is it a concept that gives preference to one or the other forms.

Considering that Trumpist politics relies on Othering, it seems insightful to inquire into how social movements have sought—successfully or not—to counter their own Othering. This includes asking how and if these movements have acted with solidarity. Solidarity can be thought of in two senses. The first more simple sense is of working together: solidifying internal group ties through mutual support. The second sense is of working across difference, and this latter definition is my focal interest in this chapter. Many movements and theorists have posited working together across lines of difference (e.g., race, class, gender) as a key factor in movement success against injustice (Barber 2014; Brent et al. 2015; Constance et al. 2014). Accordingly, it is key to understand how and why movements do or do not act in solidarity to counter Othering.

To understand the potential of solidaristic movements to overcome Othering dynamics, and to take lessons for other countries, we need to examine historical examples of Othering/solidarity dynamics in the United States and within its movements of "Others." I use food and agrarian movements as a lens to see this process for a number of reasons. First, food and agricultural movements are inherently linked to issues of the interface of human beings and nonhuman nature. This makes ecological questions as present and unavoidable as social questions. Second, food and agricultural movements are linked to many social sectors, especially those who have been so often Othered in society, such as immigrant workers, people of color and Indigenous inhabitants. Finally, as an engaged researcher with roots in food movements, I seek to produce scholarship that is actionable, and insights from these cases will be valuable to both future organizing and research efforts.

## Outline and Method: Case Histories

Unpacking this dynamic of Othering and solidarity requires a historical view. There is no way to understand how oppression works in the moment or how countering current forms of power *might* work, without tracing a long arc of struggle. As such, I focus here on a handful of sectors—Indigenous people, farmworkers, Black agrarians and agrarian environmentalists—whose struggles are emblematic, yet also often underexamined. The sectors should be seen in their full and rich histories and relationally (less as separate sectors and more as overlapping and co-constituted). However, owing to space limitations, I can only provide basic outlines of these histories, offering vignettes upon which theorizing about Othering and solidarity may be based. I have also simplified by focusing on California, which offers movement histories from all the above sectors.

My selection of cases is directed by "strategic sampling" and "illustrative/evocative sampling" considerations (Mason 2002: 123–125, 126–127). As a subset of strategic sampling, "theoretical" sampling entails selecting your categories and focuses of analysis with regard to your theoretical interests and emerging frameworks; your samples are chosen for their relevance in revealing dynamics of importance to your theories. Hence, my case selection was driven by whether and how historical agrarian and rural movements exhibit "certain contexts or phenomena [that] have a special or pivotal significance in relation to [my] research question" (Mason 2002: 124). These contexts encompass the diverse social positions and histories of multiple kinds of Others, and these diverse and multiple histories enable comparisons that develop my arguments. Meanwhile, cases are selected based on their evoking or illustrating key themes or relationships or processes in a particularly compelling way—without necessarily making claims of representativeness of the larger sample. The vignettes thus offer a sense of the deep diversity in people, processes and outcomes. Instead of endeavoring a transhistorical and over-deterministic reading of one or the other group's histories, this approach can appreciate the contingencies and nuances vis-à-vis processes of countering Othering and acting in solidarity.

In the sections that follow, I first provide some historical background of both the national and Californian contexts. Then, through twentieth-century vignettes involving the aforementioned sectors, I show how the sectors have responded to Othering through three overall strategies: *assimilation*, *valorization* and *differencing*. Finally, I conclude with lessons about these strategies and their relations to dynamics of Othering and solidarity.

## Histories of Relevant Sectors of Others

Contrary to the view that the United States has always had an identity as a "white" society, whiteness was created over a long and fraught period during which racial inventions helped to solidify and maintain property relations, including chattel enslavement of Blacks and the continued expropriation of Indigenous people from their lands (Omi and Winant 1986; Roediger 2017). In a sense, matters of landscape have always been racialized but not always in the same ways (Mitchell 1996). From Indigenous people who have maintained traditional land management practices against all odds, to those migrant settlers whose ethnic identity transitioned from specific (e.g., Irish, Italian, Polish) to generic ("white") as they "pioneered" new landscapes, to escaped or freed formerly enslaved people, many different groups have been and continue to be active in rural and agrarian issues. These histories are not anomalies or irrelevant, as farmers not identified (at the time) as white have continually shaped US agrarian development through contributions of labor, culture, values and biocultural knowledge (e.g., Bandele and Myers 2017; Carney 2002).

Indigenous people in the United States are one such nonwhite group, although they should not be seen as monolithic. For instance, though associated with rurality, over half of Indigenous people have led urban lives for generations (Fixico 2000). One scholar argues for recognizing differences within original Indigenous experiences of encounter and therefore that one narrative cannot define them all:

> The Americas were and are home to a great many different nations and tribes who have often had dissimilar experiences depending upon their location, the period of contact, who they had contact with, and the various strategies of confrontation and/or accommodation each group adopted. . . . [N]ative responses to contact varied and evolved over time based on previous experience, contingent circumstances, and individual actors. (Alvarez 2016: 4–5)

We know, for instance, that some tribes allied with colonists to subjugate other tribes, and this occasionally provided the crucial resources for colonization's success (e.g., Taraval 2015). Acknowledging heterogeneity, we might justifiably describe California's post-colonization Indigenous history as one of violence, displacement, forced assimilation and ongoing invisibilization and marginalization (Lindsay 2015). As the state came into being, Californian policy targeted all tribes for extermination and removal, as seen in the notorious scalping payments offered by governments to vigilante settlers (Johnston-Dodds 2002). Languages have been lost or nearly lost and with them much of the knowledge of human interaction with the environment (or what many Indigenous would call their "relations") in specific places. Luckily, science has begun to acknowledge the historical management of the Californian landscape by Indigenous tribes:

> First, we stress that California is blessed with Indigenous populations who generated many unique cultural traditions centering around pyrodiversity economies—specific kinds of practices employed by complex hunter-gatherers that emphasize diversity and flexibility in their engagement with food and nonfood resources. . . . Second, we need to stress the close interaction that California Indians maintained with the natural world. . . . The basic principle of pyrodiversity economies is not to transform the natural world into a humanly constructed artifact, but rather to enhance the diversity, productivity, and

availability of the wild resource base by complementing and working with ongoing natural ecological processes. (Lightfoot and Parrish 2009: 143–145)

This approach contrasts with agriculture, and capitalist agriculture in the modern era in particular, as the latter is guided by a focus on productivity and profit. Much of agricultural production (aside from commodity crops such as corn and soybeans) requires heavy amounts of hand labor, particularly the harvesting of seasonal and quickly ripening fruits and vegetables that form a large part of California's cropping patterns, and this labor tends to fall to those who will accept or can be forced into accepting low rates of pay (Daniel 1981). Indigenous, Chinese, Filipino, Japanese and other ethnic groups have played this important role as agricultural laborers at various points in Californian (and US) history. In fact, scholars of Californian agrarian development have pegged exploitable migrant labor as indispensable to that development (Mitchell 1996); unlike areas of the United States with a substantial "family farming" sector, Californian agriculture was capitalist from its early years (Walker 2004). Latinos (ethnic groups coming from Central and South America), and especially migrant Latinos, are now the dominant source of wage labor in agriculture. This dominance is not incidental: the Bracero program was a US policy that from 1942 to 1964 enabled farm owners to import a pliable labor force from Mexico, deportable once no longer needed (see Cohen 2011). The program's false promises to workers of fair pay and decent working conditions, along with its overtly racialized structure and enormous profitability, did not create—but certainly reinforced—the grower class' expectation that they would be entitled to low-paid wage laborers indefinitely. Before, during and since the program, farm owners stoked racial divisions between workers, sometimes successfully, though not always. Filipinos were successfully convinced to break Latino-based strikes (Mitchell 1996: 125), while in 1903 Mexican American field workers stood up for Japanese coworkers, whom bosses tried (unsuccessfully) to exclude from labor contract negotiations (Street 1998). Farm owners used many methods to undermine labor agitation, including stoking multiple intra-working-class divisions through public relations campaigns that pitted racial resentment, religious fervor and a defense of "family values" against farmworker organizations, collaborating with state officials and agencies, and deploying their identity as "farmers" to gain public sympathy despite their obviously dominant class position (Olmsted 2015).

California's farm owners have for decades relied on agrarian imaginaries of hardworking family farmers as stalwarts of egalitarian democracy to defend their interests and reap profits. As it has emerged over US history, such agrarianism is in actuality linked to colonization, private property and white supremacy (Carlisle 2013). This link emerges through the ideal of the male yeoman farmer, owner of his land and head of his patriarchal household. As tamer of the land (and those who used to live on it), he was the shock troop for westward expansion. The ideal of the propertied agrarian steward of land has long been used to defend existing private property relations, which are extremely unequal still, with whites owning around 98 percent of farmland (and men owning most farms). Critiques of this agrarianism legacy continue and include critiques not only of elite growers but also of ostensibly progressive food movements (e.g., Bradley and Herrera 2015). Today's food movements, it seems, are too white (Slocum 2007) and too embedded in neoliberal approaches (Guthman 2008) to make substantial change. Though it would stand to reason that today's critiques (and critics) of the industrial capitalist food system have many origins, the food movement has largely been linked to white, consumer, middle-class and reformist aspirations. This, however, seems to be changing more recently, as scholarship and popular attention are increasingly focused on more marginalized sectors: food workers, low-income consumers, Indigenous communities and people of color (e.g., Alkon and Guthman 2017; Sbicca 2018).

Black agrarianism in particular is of paramount importance in the development of alternative ways of being in rural spaces and in the development of strategies to counter Othering. Against governmental neglect, outright dehumanization and state-sanctioned, citizen-driven violence, Black agrarians have developed pioneering methods of cooperative structures for organizing food production, financing and consumption (Nembhard 2014), and political organizing for defense and social change. Having stood at the bottom of a US racial hierarchy involving many and rotating Others, Black people's forms of struggle—particularly in agrarian contexts—are particularly generative of relevant insights for strategies to counter Othering (see Davy et al. 2017; Penniman and Snipstal 2017). And it is to an early Black-led project to found an agricultural community that we now turn.

### Assimilation as Liberation?

The town of Allensworth, California, was established as a Black-led land development project, founded by Colonel Allen Allensworth and four close allies in 1908 (Cox 2007). Colonel Allensworth agreed with Booker T. Washington's vision of liberation: "that the Negro as an efficient worker could gain wealth and that eventually through his ownership of capital he would be able to achieve a recognized place in American culture" (Du Bois 1940 [1967]: 61). As an advocate of this vision for Black liberation, Allensworth was committed to education and an entrepreneurial spirit by which Black people might advance themselves into full rights and participation in Western civilization. As a response to Othering, this strategy may be called *assimilation*. According to some accounts, a main reason for founding the town was to influence white society and how it judged Blacks, asserting that Blacks could become an accepted part of society as well (Cox 2007). In theory, creating a new "colony" owned and managed by Blacks would generate autonomous wealth and capacity while signaling Blacks' ability to participate in the American project at large. An assimilation approach can also assume that building wealth through landownership and agriculture—"Africans' blueprint for economic independence" (Davy et al. 2017: 42)—would provide a foundation upon which to combat oppression by providing a base of support for efforts to make political change.

The history of Allensworth offers lenses into the limits of assimilation as a strategy. For one, the very alliance with a white-owned, urban-based capitalist land development firm, which arranged the original land purchase and was slated to provide irrigation water to the town, was to prove fatal for the effort to found the town:

> Allensworth's prosperity peaked in 1925 and after that date the lack of irrigation water began to plague the town. Irrigation water was never delivered in sufficient supply as promised by the Pacific Farming Company. . . . As a result, town leaders were engrossed in lengthy and expensive legal battles with the Company, expending scarce financial resources on a battle they would not win. (Mikell 2017)

Second, Allensworth's efforts came up against more integrationist perspectives on Black liberation held by urban Blacks in cities such as San Francisco and Los Angeles:

> In keeping with Colonel Allensworth's idea of self-help and self-reliance programs, city leaders in 1914 proposed to establish a vocational education school. . . . Although it received support for a state funding appropriation from Fresno and Tulare County representatives in the California State Senate and Assembly, the proposal was defeated by the entire state legislature. (Mikell 2017)

Allensworth's efforts to achieve state support for their school failed in part because of opposition from integrationist Blacks, who saw the town's efforts to advance themselves as Blacks *separate from white society, but through alliance with white politicians* as a threat to the long-term vision of equal rights within the institutions of white society (Cox 2007: 9).

Allensworth's example shows that on its own assimilation is an incomplete strategy against Othering. Success is not just a matter of working together across differences but also *who* works together and *on what terms*. As we see with the town's "development" of stolen Indigenous land, in partnership with a colonial enterprise, these latter questions matter for forms and outcomes of solidarity. Moreover, lack of ideological unity (in this case regarding education and its relation to the strategy of integration) can reduce the likelihood of solidarity within a sector. There is also the more fundamental question of whether assimilation is worthwhile, given the brokenness of hegemonic society's institutions, as alluded to by Black civil rights icon Martin Luther King Jr. when he said: "We have fought hard and long for integration, as I believe we should have. . . . But I've come to believe we're integrating into a burning house."[1] Sectors are not monolithic, nor

---

1. This quote is attributed to King by Harry Belafonte, a close friend of King's, civil rights activist and well-known entertainer, who met with King shortly before his assassination.

do they hold the same politics over time, and these differences provide sources of tension in efforts to counter Othering.

## *Valorization: The Vital Self-Worth of the Other*

Allensworth sought to improve the image of Blacks, directing this effort toward "changing white sentiment" (Cox 2007: 30). "Valorization" *can* result in external recognition, but it is motivated first by affect, on personal and intracommunal levels within a sector of Others—that is, it is about "we." This is the sense in which I use *valorization*. If assimilation could be described by the statement "We (Other) are just like you (in the hegemonic position)," valorization would claim "We are valuable, *because of who we are, as we are.*"

The creation of the American Indian Movement (AIM) in the 1970s was a pivotal moment in US Indigenous peoples' valorization, in response to centuries of Othering. AIM was active in California, dramatically launching its efforts through the 1969 occupation of Alcatraz Island in the San Francisco Bay. Through AIM, Indigenous identity was reclaimed, refashioned and revitalized. AIM gathered all tribes into a common project of asserting the right to exist, of recognizing and exposing past and present injustices (particularly those perpetuated by the US state) and revalorizing Indigenous identity, particularly by revitalizing Indigenous traditions, ceremonies, land and resource management practices, and storytelling. Though the movement was largely crushed by federal suppression, its effects were profound:

> before AIM, Indians were dispirited, defeated and culturally dissolving. People were *ashamed* to be Indian. . . . [Now] you find young Indians all over the place who understand that they don't have to accept whatever sort of bullshit the dominant society wants to hand them, that they have the right to fight, . . . that in fact they have an obligation to stand up on their hind legs and fight for their future generations, the way our ancestors did. (AIM leader Russell Means, quoted in Churchill 2003: 181)

Internal valorization is supported by external validation, such as how science has validated Indigenous wisdom as it pertains to food systems, as described by Lightfoot and Parrish (2009: 147):

> Native Californians were able to maintain strong cultural traditions and successful economies for thousands of years. They handcrafted small-scale economies that were tailor-made to the specific environmental parameters of local places. . . . This emphasis on local, small-scale enterprises that are ecologically sensitive may be prudent for us to consider in developing sustainable food economies in California today.

Indeed, Indigenous people are already acting on the suggestion, working to advance food sovereignty throughout the so-called North America, as tribes revitalize old food traditions, recultivate old seed varieties, continue (or deepen) practices of wide-scale ecological management, and reintegrate tradition and ceremony into ways of gathering, preparing and sharing food (Coté 2016; Daigle 2017). One example from California is the Karuk tribe (described further in the next section), organizing to regain traditional land and fisheries management rights and practices.

Since the mid-nineteenth century, the many Others composing California's farm labor workforce struggled for rights, pay and dignity but rarely did they make appeals to valorization. These struggles varied in character—some revolutionary, others reformist; some parochial, others interethnic—but ultimately none achieved substantial transformation of the state's exploitative labor regime. It was not until the 1960s and 1970s—during a period of cultural revalorization among various ethnic groups, an ascendant and dynamic socialist Left, and an increasing legitimacy for civil and human rights—that something like success was seen (Ganz 2009; Shaw 2008). The United Farmworkers Union (UFW) pioneered a form of union organizing that achieved wage gains and policy changes, and launched its founder Cesar Chavez into prominence as a national figure. The emphasis on Mexican American culture—seen in the predominant use of Spanish in organizing, the folk songs sung at rallies, the official flag's display of a Mexican Eagle symbol and the description of the union as "*La Causa*" (the Cause)—shows how UFW utilized a strategy of valorization. But it only succeeded because it worked in solidarity with others: students, clergy, multiple ethnic groups of (farm and nonfarm) workers, politicians and Left activists from differing ideological and class positions. Coming up against the entrenched power of farm owners, the UFW mobilized this wide array of allies and used novel tactics of farm product boycott, leveraging consumer and working-class power from cities across the country. A prime example of this solidarity work is found in the UFW's relations with Black liberation movement groups of the time, notably the Black Panther Party (BPP), whose nationwide chapters mobilized to support the UFW's boycotts (Araiza 2014). The BPP was an urban-based revolutionary organization founded on internationalist-socialist (rather than ethnic nationalist) principles but was firmly grounded in an articulation of valorized Black history and identity.

Perhaps ironically given its urban constituency, the BPP's politics, strategy of armed self-defense, name and logo were inspired by Black liberationists in rural Lowndes County, Alabama (Anderson 2007). Clearly, in struggles against discrimination and oppression, differences between rural and urban (or between the post-slavery US South and the ostensibly less racist North) are sometimes less important than they seem. These efforts were linked through not only similar experiences of anti-Black Othering but also lineages of countervailing rural and agrarian identity and practices. To this day, as Bandele and Myers (2017: 20) remind us, "Africans in America . . . are still surviving, struggling to retain their land, agrarian roots, and memory of communal beliefs about land ownership and caring for nature." These memories and communal ways of being have provided resources for generations of cooperative and resistance movements, both rural

(Davy et al. 2017; Penniman and Snipstal 2017) and urban (Akuno and Nangwaya 2017).

Importantly, just because a movement uses valorization does not mean it forecloses possibilities for assimilation. The UFW in particular offers examples of this, in the ways that it (especially in later years) incorporated its leadership into mainstream Democratic Party politics, playing insider politics instead of organizing at the grassroots and dumping money on candidates while losing grassroots participation as individual activists lost the sense of the union as a movement and became disillusioned by its increasingly top-down leadership (Ganz 2009). The UFW at times also played into anticommunist and anti-undocumented immigrant sentiments—supporting (even if inadvertently) existing forms of ideological and nationalistic Othering (Guthman, 2017; Shaw 2008). And as has been pointed out by sociologists (e.g., Pulido 2006) and farmworker organizers (e.g., Bacon 2017), Latinos can, like any sector of Others, reproduce unjust social relations as they assimilate, for instance by becoming farm owners who exploit labor to make a profit. For valorization to go beyond assimilation, it must surpass identity politics and effectively enroll different groups in a common cause, to build strength in unity beyond (self)valorization or (relatively) individualistic-capitalistic forms of assimilation. This brings us to the third strategy for countering Othering: "differencing."

## Differencing: An Essential Complement to Solidarity

The bootstraps modality of Allensworth (and the concomitant potential that workers of all stripes pursue only narrow-horizoned assimilation) has long been opposed by more revolutionary Black liberationists such as the BPP, whose anticapitalist perspective linked the liberation of Black workers to the liberation of the entire working class globally. The BPP's "intercommunal" approach, like that of other internationalist socialists, sought to create a common movement from disconnected struggles by emphasizing the antagonism between "Us" (workers) and "Them" (the capitalist class). This approach echoes calls for "Left populism," as in the work of Ernesto Laclau (2005) and Chantal Mouffe (2018). Laclau's formulation of populism relies on a collective antagonism, brought together through a "chain of equivalences" linking diverse demands, against a common enemy that refuses to accommodate them. A key aspect to such Left populism is its (re)creation of "the people" around this chain, the act of naming the people being a constitutive act. A socialist concept of working-class struggle can build into a Left populist strategy insofar as it links disparate struggles beyond class terms. In turn, a Left populist strategy parallels but is not equivalent to the strategy of differencing. Differencing can be thought of as a process by which a new "We" is created but without obscuring the differences contained within this new "We." It unsettles (and in Left forms expands) categories of identity and political community, without necessarily displacing the valorization that sustains self-worth in those existing positions or categories of identity. It demands neither that

Others become assimilated to hegemonic politics nor for them to validate their political claims only through existing self-categorization (valorization).

Differencing unsettles categories, not disclaiming or reifying identity but reshaping it in relation to both close and distant others. The passion that drove so many people to volunteer years of their life for the UFW was linked to *"La Causa"*—a defined identity as a movement. During the UFW's heyday, a perception emerged that diverse national (and even international) struggles in actuality constituted *one* capital-"M" Movement, encouraging broad participation and ambitions. Identity as a movement supports acts of solidarity, while acts of solidarity build identity as a movement. The BPP's revolutionary intercommunalism similarly built up collective identity from diverse ethnic groups in the United States, crafting a revolutionary movement identity among various marginalized ethnic workers (Sonnie and Tracy 2011). In this intercommunal work, BPP supported the UFW, while the UFW also returned that support as the party moved into electoral politics. The BPP's successful alliance with UFW can be contrasted with Black Nationalist groups that refused alliances with other ethnic groups; in the 1970s, groups that previously supported UFW withdrew their support as they moved in nationalist directions (Araiza 2014). That era's movements at times took valorization too far: owing to Blacks' position at the bottom of the US racial hierarchy, Black struggle was often given priority, while Asian Americans (who participated widely in some of the most notable struggles of that era) saw their marginalization unappreciated, because they were seen as being higher up on the racial hierarchy (Pulido 2006).

Differencing can also occur at smaller or less all-encompassing political scales. The Karuk tribe of northern coastal California have been working for decades to remove dams from the Klamath River, which have been profoundly detrimental to the lifecycle of the salmon, upon which the tribe depends (Hormel and Norgaard 2009). Built during California's rush of modernist development, the dams now serve non-Indigenous and Indigenous communities alike with drinking water and electricity. The Karuk have had to generate Western scientific forms of knowledge, including by having tribal members trained in Western science programs at reputable universities, in order to validate their traditional methods of land management. In order to reclaim its role in the rural ecology, the tribe has had to negotiate with the federal government, white ranchers and many other dam resource-related groups in order to create a common understanding that can lead to the removal of the dams (and has achieved some success; see Kober 2018). The Karuk thus built a new and expanded identity as "watershed stakeholders" that transcended Indigenous/non-Indigenous boundaries, which simultaneously revalorized their cultural worldview and tangibly improved their base of economic survival. In addition, the tribe has developed alliances with researchers from non-Indigenous backgrounds. Considering a history of colonial, extractive and exploitative forms of research, Indigenous people have rightfully been skeptical of researchers interested in studying them. As such, Karuk developed principle-based partnership rules, in order to protect their sovereignty while codeveloping new knowledge of service to both social justice and ecological ends (Karuk and UC Berkeley Collaborative 2021).

At the scale of California, but with larger ramifications, was the story of National Land for People (NLP). Formed through the 1960s and 1970s, and led by George and Maia Ballis, the NLP involved farmers, farm workers, consumers, lawyers and others in a struggle for democratic reallocation of farmland against "the Biggies": large-scale agribusiness and its political enablers. NLP acted variously "as a lobby, advocacy group, and community/farm alliance that ran a food coop and organized a network of farm suppliers" (Welch 2017: 237). But its main battle was over the Newlands Reclamation Act. The act was

> passed in 1902 to fund large irrigation projects for 16 states in the American west, [and] stipulated that federally funded water could only be used by landholders who owned 160 acres of land or less. However, for decades, large, corporate farming enterprises, as well as the Bureau of Reclamation charged with enforcing the law, were ignoring this restriction. National Land for People used the information they had gathered and maps they had produced to bring a bill to the Senate to force the Bureau to enforce the Reclamation Act's excess land law and break up the large farms and sell them in small parcels to farm workers. (Ballis and Ballis 2011: 3–4)

NLP nearly succeeded in forcing agribusiness to break up its concentrated landownership of California's agricultural heartland, using a combination of strategies. It organized tours that brought Californian residents, citizens and legislators face to face with the valley's agrarian dysfunctions, in the process "lacing together environmental concerns; the anti-Vietnam War movement; criticism of US imperialism; the civil rights struggle; fear of corporate power; and demands for a pesticide-free, unprocessed 'health food'" (Welch 2017: 235). Welch (2017: 237) explains further how

> the NLP sought to create a development model for a reimagined Central Valley. . . . [T]hey collected information on farmworkers and others who might want to farm their own land and generated guides to small scale farming . . . [gathered] information to feed the publication of newspaper articles and production of film documentaries . . . [and] worked to support existing small farms, to recruit farmers like Berge Bulbulian, an Armenian grape grower with 150 acre farm on the Valley's east side, and outreach to former farmworkers like UFW organizer Jessie de la Cruz, who belonged to a small cooperative farm. The Board of the NLP was headed by Bulbulian and included representatives not only of Armenian growers and Mexican farmworkers, but also of African American and Asian farmers. (Welch 2017: 237)

From this base of activists, NLP found an attorney willing to take on the Biggies in court. Surprisingly, their 1976 lawsuit against the federal government succeeded, forcing the US Department of the Interior to create new rules in compliance with the Reclamation Act (Welch 2017: 237). Efforts by agribusiness organizations and sympathetic politicians to undermine implementation of the rules, however, continued until the 1980s, when the Reagan administration passed updated legislation to change the act. By raising the acreage limit nearly six times and removing the key requirement that farmers reside on their acreage, this law change took away the foundation of NLP's central strategy.

Rallying various sectors against an articulated enemy, NLP addressed the state head-on, where what looked like success quickly turned to defeat. Likewise, UFW's initial successes dissipated in the face of agribusiness power and a state complicit with a low pay, seasonal labor regime. Unequal distribution of land and water resources (as in NLP's case) and exploitable migrant labor (as in UFW's) are necessities for existing systems of agriculture and power in California and are not easily changed. As this history shows, however, differencing strategies laden with acts of solidarity get closest to something resembling success.

## Conclusion: Differencing Our Way to Emancipation?

All the above-discussed movements, including even those focused on assimilation, utilized support from groups outside their own: solidarity is ubiquitous, though not always with progressive effects. Collective action and strategic alliances are key features of nonelite efforts to upend long-term power imbalances. Efforts by elites to undermine working-class solidarity through divide-and-conquer Othering are similarly constant, but nonelite responses vary, failing to follow any apparent determinative mechanism. Considering that the most relatively successful movements surveyed here have encompassed (or at least worked alongside) anticapitalist elements—which enable an expansive and oppositional formation of "we"—we might at least propose that working against ideological Othering of those holding anticapitalist views is an indispensable though formidable task for movements of Others (especially given the weight of anticommunism in US history). Given that debates between nonelite people of similar interests about *how* to achieve change are a key place where solidarity breaks down, the tension between the obvious need to engage institutions for immediate reform (or to assimilate in order to thrive) and the less obvious need for an expansive vision (of both the horizon of emancipation and "the people" included therein) must be navigated carefully. For instance, to the extent that reform efforts "[take] the present structure of the farming economy in California for granted" (Mitchell 1996: 181), they limit the vision of what new worlds may be possible and who may be included therein.

Assimilation offers the promise of easy wins and wealth creation, especially when it involves control of land and resources but can undermine solidarity without a necessary complement of communal and intercommunal tenets. Valorization brings an essential assertion of human value and the right to self-determination and provides cultural resources through lineages of ancestral strategies for resistance and survival. While it may be readily accessible and generative, valorization cannot alone build ever-larger movements and must be combined with differencing in order to avoid undermining cross-sector solidarity. Differencing is the least concrete strategy, regarding immediate needs, and is especially difficult, because working across differences and creating (new) common identities are no easy task. Yet differencing is essential, as it generates new affective and organizational resources for broad ambitions to take root and blossom. Differencing brings the creation of new political communities to the task of countering Othering and in so doing keeps alive the possibilities of acting in (and experiencing) an ever-enlarging spiral of solidarity. Forces for Othering can absorb tendencies toward assimilation and valorization (for instance, elites today celebrate meritocratic, assimilationist ideas of social advancement and non-threatening "lean-in" forms of identity politics). But elites are harder pressed to divert or subvert energies of differencing, making differencing the pivotal strategy. Movements to counter Othering should thus seek a combination of assimilation, valorization and differencing strategies but with emphasis on differencing.

# References

Akuno, Kali and Ajamu Nangwaya (eds.). 2017. *Jackson Rising: The Struggle for Economic Democracy and Black Self-Determination in Jackson, Mississippi*. Montreal: Daraja Press.

Alkon, Alison H. and Julie Guthman (eds.). 2017. *The New Food Activism: Opposition, Cooperation, and Collective Action*. Oakland: University of California Press.

Alvarez, Alex. 2016. *Native America and the Question of Genocide*. Lanham, MD: Rowman & Littlefield.

Anderson, Erica L. 2007. "Lowndes County Freedom Organization." *Black Past: An Online Reference Guide to African American History*. http://www.Blackpast.org/aah/lowndes -county-freedom-organization.

Araiza, Lauren. 2014. *To March for Others: The Black Freedom Struggle and the United Farm Workers*. Philadelphia: University of Pennsylvania Press.

Bacon, David. 2017. "Unbroken Connection to the Land: An Interview with Farmworker Activist Rosalinda Guillen." In *Land Justice: Re-imagining Land, Food, and the Commons in the United States*, edited by Justine M. Williams and Eric Holt-Giménez, 154–173. Oakland: Food First Books.

Ballis, George and Maia Ballis. 2011. "National Land for People Collection." *Online archive of California Special Collections Research Center*. Fresno: California State University at Fresno. http://pdf.oac.cdlib.org/pdf/csuf/spcoll/National_Land_For_People.pdf.

Bandele, Owusu and Gail Myers. 2017. "Roots!" In *Land Justice: Re-imagining Land, Food, and the Commons in the United States*, edited by Justine M. Williams and Eric Holt-Giménez, 19–39. Oakland: Food First Books.

Barber, William. 2014. "Looking Back & Moving Forward, Together." *Keynote address made at the FarmAid Conference*, Raleigh, North Carolina, 11 September. https://www .farmaid.org/issues/roots-and-vision/looking-back-and-moving-forward-together/.

Bradley, Kathleen and Hank Herrera. 2015. "Decolonizing Food Justice: Naming, Resisting, and Researching Colonizing Forces in the Movement." *Antipode*, 48(1): 97–114.

Brent, Zoe W., Christina M. Schiavoni and Alberto Alonso-Fradejas. 2015. "Contextualising Food Sovereignty: The Politics of Convergence among Movements in the USA." *Third World Quarterly*, 36: 618–635.

Carlisle, Liz. 2013. "Critical Agrarianism." *Renewable Agriculture and Food Systems*, 29(2): 135–145.

Carney, Judith A. 2002. *Black Rice: The African Origins of Rice Cultivation in the Americas.* Cambridge, MA: Harvard University Press.

Churchill, Ward. 2003. *Acts of Rebellion: The Ward Churchill Reader.* New York: Routledge.

Cohen, Deborah. 2011. *Braceros: Migrant Citizens and Transnational Subjects in the Postwar United States and Mexico.* Chapel Hill, NC: University of North Carolina Press.

Constance, Douglas H., Marie-Christine Renard and Marta G. Rivera-Ferre. 2014. "Alternative Agrifood Movements: Patterns of Convergence and Divergence." *Research in Rural Sociology and Development*, 21: 313–322.

Coté, Charlotte. 2016. "'Indigenizing' Food Sovereignty. Revitalizing Indigenous Food Practices and Ecological Knowledges in Canada and the United States." *Humanities*, 5(3): 57.

Cox, Beatrice R. 2007. "The Archaeology of the Allensworth Hotel: Negotiating the System in Jim Crow America." Master's Thesis, Sonoma State University.

Daigle, Michelle. 2017. "Tracing the Terrain of Indigenous Food *Sovereignties*." *Journal of Peasant Studies*, 46(2): 297–315.

Daniel, Cletus E. 1981. *Bitter Harvest: A History of California Farmworkers, 1879–1994.* Ithaca: Cornell University Press.

Davy, Dānia C., Savibaka Horne, Tracy Lloyd McCurty and Edward J. Pennick. 2017. "Resistance." In *Land Justice: Re-imagining Land, Food, and the Commons in the United States*, edited by Justine M. Williams and Eric Holt-Giménez, 40–60. Oakland: Food First Books.

Du Bois, William E. B. 1940 [1967]. "Science and Politics." In *The Progressives*, edited by Carl Resek, 43–62. Indianapolis and New York: Bobbs-Merrill Company. Originally published in *Dusk of Dawn* (New York: Harcourt Brace & Co., 1940).

Edelman, Marc. 2019. "Hollowed Out Heartland, USA: How Capital Sacrificed Communities and Paved the Way for Authoritarian Populism." *Journal of Rural Studies*, 82: 505–517.

Fixico, Donald. 2000. *The Urban Indian Experience in America.* Albuquerque: University of New Mexico Press.

Ganz, Marshall. 2009. *Why David Sometimes Wins: Leadership, Organization, and Strategy in the California Farm Worker Movement.* New York: Oxford University Press.

Guthman, Julie. 2008. "Neoliberalism and the Making of Food Politics in California." *Geoforum*, 39(3): 1171–1183.

Guthman, Julie. 2017. "Paradoxes of the Border: Labor Shortages and Farmworker Minor Agency in Reworking California's Strawberry Fields." *Economic Geography*, 93(1): 24–43.

Hormel, Leontina M. and Kari M. Norgaard. 2009. "Bring the Salmon Home! Karuk Challenges to Capitalist Incorporation." *Critical Sociology*, 35(3): 343–366.

Johnston-Dodds, Kimberly. 2002. *Early California Laws and Policies Related to California Indians.* Sacramento, CA: California Research Bureau.

Karuk and UC Berkeley Collaborative. 2021. *Practicing Píkyav: A Guiding Policy for Collaborative Projects and Research Initiatives with the Karuk Tribe.* Berkeley, CA: Karuk and UC Berkeley Collaborative.

Kober, Amy S. 2018. "Plan Released for Klamath River Dam Removal: Important Milestone for the Most Significant Dam Removal and River Restoration Effort in History." Washington, DC: American River. https://www.americanrivers.org/2018/06/plan-released-for-klamath-river-dam-removal/.

Laclau, Ernesto. 2005. "Populism: What's in a Name?" In *Populism and the Mirror of Democracy*, edited by Francisco Panizza, 32–49. London: Verso.

Lightfoot, Kent G. and Otis Parrish. 2009. *California Indians and Their Environment: An Introduction*. Berkeley and Los Angeles: University of California Press.

Lindsay, Brendan C. 2015. *Murder State: California's Native American Genocide, 1846–1873*. Lincoln: University of Nebraska.

Mason, Jennifer. 2002. *Qualitative Researching* (2nd Edition). London: Sage.

Mikell, Robert. 2017. "The History of Allensworth, California (1908–)." *Black Past: An Online Reference Guide to African American History*. http://www.blackpast.org/perspectives/history-allensworth-california-1908.

Mitchell, Don. 1996. *The Lie of the Land: Migrant Workers and the California Landscape*. Minneapolis, MN: University of Minnesota Press.

Mouffe, Chantal. 2018. *For a Left Populism*. London: Verso.

Nembhard, Jessica G. 2014. *Collective Courage: A History of African American Cooperative Economic Thought and Practice*. University Park, PA: University of Pennsylvania Press.

Olmsted, Kathryn. 2015. *Right Out of California: The 1930s and the Big Business Routes of Modern Conservatism*. New York: New Press.

Omi, Michael and Howard Winant. 1986. *Racial Formation in the United States: From the 1960s to the 1980s*. New York: Routledge and Kegan Paul.

Penniman, Leah and Blain Snipstal. 2017. "Regeneration." In *Land Justice: Re-imagining Land, Food, and the Commons in the United States*, edited by Justine M. Williams and Eric Holt-Giménez, 61–74. Oakland: Food First Books.

powell, john a. and Stephen Menendian. 2016. "The Problem of Othering." *Othering and Belonging: Expanding the Circle of Human Concern*, 1: 14–40.

Pulido, Laura. 2006. *Black, Brown, Yellow and Left: Radical Activism in Los Angeles*. Oakland: University of California Press.

Roediger, David. 2017. *Class, Race, and Marxism*. London: Verso.

Sbicca, Joshua. 2018. *Food Justice Now! Deepening the Roots of Social Struggle*. Minneapolis, MN: University of Minnesota Press.

Shaw, Randy. 2008. *Beyond the Fields: Cesar Chavez, the UFW, and the Struggle for Justice in the 21st Century*. Berkeley and Los Angeles: University of California Press.

Slocum, Rachel. 2007. "Whiteness, Space and Alternative Food Practice." *Geoforum*, 38(3): 520–533.

Sonnie, Amy and James Tracy. 2011. *Hillbilly Nationalists, Urban Race Rebels, and Black Power: Community Organizing in Radical Times*. Brooklyn: Melville House.

Street, Richard. 1998. "The 1903 Oxnard Sugar Beet Strike: A New Ending." *Labor History*, 39(2): 193–199.

Taraval, Sigismundo. 2015. "1734: Indian Rebellion." In *Lands of Promise and Despair: Chronicles of Early California, 1535–1846*, edited by Rose Marie Beebe and Robert M. Sekewicz, 85–90. Tulsa, OK: University of Oklahoma Press.

Walker, Richard. 2004. *Conquest of Bread: 150 Years of Agribusiness in California*. New York: New Press.

Welch, Cliff. 2017. "National Land for the People and the Struggle for Agrarian Reform in California." In *Land Justice: Re-imagining Land, Food, and the Commons in the United States*, edited by Justine M. Williams and Eric Holt-Giménez, 228–242. Oakland: Food First Books.

# Chapter 12

## BUILDING NETWORKS, BRIDGING DIVIDES?

### ORGANIZATIONAL EXPERIENCES OF PAID DOMESTIC WORKERS IN URUGUAY AND PARAGUAY

Raquel Rojas Scheffer

*Introduction*

Around 18 million people work in the domestic services sector in Latin America, equaling around 7 percent of the workforce of the region and 14.3 percent of the female workforce (ILO 2019). This makes domestic work one of the most important occupations for women in many Latin American countries. Yet despite its high share of the labor market, this occupational group has been historically discriminated against, both in law and in practice. In this respect, labor codes tend to mandate lower salaries and benefits for domestic workers, as well as longer working hours (Barbagelata 1978; Valiente 2016). Only since the mid-2000s has this occupational field started to gain political attention and recognition worldwide. In this context, from 2006 onwards, many Latin American countries modified their laws to guarantee more rights to domestic workers (Blofield and Jokela 2018).

That said, the resulting situation varies from country to country: in many, domestic workers are still guaranteed few rights regarding wages, working hours or access to social security (Soto 2017), and even when they are legally granted the same rights as any other wage worker, enforcing the law remains a major challenge. The vulnerable situation of domestic workers became even more evident during the Covid-19 health crisis. According to International Labour Organization (ILO) estimates, by mid-2020 around 70 percent of domestic workers in Latin America had been affected by quarantine measures, leading to unemployment, reduction of working hours or loss of wages (UN Women et al. 2020). This situation, combined with little or no social protection, has caused many domestic workers to be left with insufficient or no income to support themselves and their families. It has also made clear that despite having won legal protection, domestic workers must still actively fight to guarantee their enforcement.

But why was it so difficult for domestic workers to organize and fight for their rights in the first place? The answer to this question can be found by taking a closer look at this occupational group and its characteristics. Domestic work has historically been perceived as women's terrain and naturalized as an activity that women can do because of their "innate caring faculties" (Gutiérrez-Rodríguez and Brites 2014: 1). By this logic, domestic tasks would not require any specific qualifications, being thus considered inferior to other forms of work (Chaney and Garcia Castro 1989; Federici 2010; Gutiérrez-Rodríguez 2010). To this day, domestic work is an almost entirely female occupation—according to the ILO (2015), at the regional level, about 93 percent of domestic workers are women— and one of the most precarious occupations in terms of informality and low wages. In addition, domestic workers are generally situated at the point where the most vulnerable ends of the axes of gender, class and race/ethnicity converge. For example, in countries with a high immigration rate, there is a large number of migrant domestic workers; and where the population of Indigenous people or Afro-descendants is elevated, they tend to be overrepresented in the domestic services labor force (ILO 2015). The interplay among these axes of stratification triggers disempowerment and inequality, particularly in the workplace, a site marked by unequal relations of power between domestic workers and their employers (Bernardino-Costa 2014; Gutiérrez-Rodríguez 2010).

Furthermore, paid domestic work involves working within a household, in an otherwise private and isolated setting that does not offer the possibility to meet with other workers. At the same time, it is particularly difficult for the state and its institutions in charge of regulating the relations between employers and employees to control the working conditions of domestic workers. In this occupational setting, where family life and workplace overlap, it is common for employers not to see their households as a site of employment (Hondagneu-Sotelo 2001) and to claim that the domestic worker is "just like one of the family" (Anderson 2000; Hondagneu-Sotelo 2001; Parreñas 2015; Young 1987). All this makes it highly difficult for domestic workers to be seen and see themselves as subjects of labor rights, making collective organizing to demand better working conditions a remarkably difficult task.

Notwithstanding the difficulties, domestic workers organize and not in isolation. On the contrary, they build networks with other actors and construct transnational coalitions to increase their strength and chances of achieving their goals (see Boris and Fish 2014, 2015; Goldsmith 2013a; Mather 2013; Pape 2016). In analyzing collective action of domestic workers in Paraguay and Uruguay, this chapter establishes a dialogue between literature on social movements and social inequalities. Drawing on the specificities of domestic work, I discuss how structural and contextual particularities shape the organizational experiences of domestic workers and the networks they build with different types of actors. The intersectional analysis highlights that while the confluence of inequalities in the experience of domestic workers can compound discrimination, it can also lead to political agency, allowing the creation of alliances with other actors that have similar interests and struggles. However, the intersectional character of domestic workers' struggles can result in tensions within the alliances, which, if not addressed properly, can have a negative effect on the outcomes of collective action.

## Intersectionality and Network Building

Domestic work has historically been considered women's work and "reproductive" (and thus nonproductive) labor. In this context, its role in the production of value has been concealed (Dalla Costa and James 1975; Federici 2010), while work carried out in the "public sphere of the market" is seen as totally detached from the reproduction of life. Men's and women's work are thus presented as parallel worlds, hiding the close relationship and interdependency between capitalist production and care, and granting value to one—which deserves a wage—while denying it to the other.

This link between gender and domestic work has proven to be strong and persistent. Several studies have shown that even when both members of a heterosexual couple work outside the home and a third person is hired to do the housework, the woman is still the one in charge of organizing and supervising everything related to it (Federici 2010; Hondagneu-Sotelo 2001; Rollins 1985). At the same time, the domestic worker hired is almost always a woman and one that frequently belongs to an economically, racially, ethnically or religiously subordinated social group (Anderson 2000; Gutiérrez-Rodríguez 2010; Hochschild 2000; Lan 2006). Different axes of inequality converge in the experience of domestic workers in a paradigmatic case of intersecting inequalities.

The term "intersectionality" was popularized by Kimberlé Crenshaw, who used it to describe the way in which racism, class oppression and patriarchal relations interacted with each other, generating discrimination and inequalities (Crenshaw 1994). An intersectional analysis is one that highlights that the axes of stratification mutually construct one another, in the sense that class relations are also shaped by gender and ethnic dynamics, and vice versa (Anthias 2008). Along this line, an intersectional approach also questions the homogenizing dimension of categories such as class, race and gender, highlighting internal differences within groups.

Analyzing domestic work from this perspective makes visible how class-, gender- and race/ethnicity-based discrimination is crystallized within this group, affecting the position domestic workers assume in society. This can be seen from an economic perspective—domestic work is globally one of the lowest paid forms of labor (ILO 2015)—and also considering its political or cultural dimensions: despite the centrality of domestic work for the reproduction of society and its huge incidence in the labor market, this occupation has historically been undervalued, and domestic workers have not had enough power to make their claims heard, at least not until the last decade. In this sense, all dimensions are interrelated and affect each other in a reciprocal way. As Gutiérrez-Rodríguez (2010: 15) points out, the lower value attributed to domestic work is not only rooted in the belief that domestic labor is a nonproductive activity but also "because those doing this work are feminized and racialized subjects considered as 'inferior' to the hegemonic normative subject."

At the same time, however, the dynamics of these axes of stratification can mobilize political will, allowing for activism and organizing (Collins 2000). Thus, an intersectional analysis of paid domestic work not only focuses on the production of disempowerment but also highlights the possibility of political agency and the production of political subjects (Bernardino-Costa 2014).

Because of the characteristics of domestic workers—their position in the social structure, mediated by different axes of inequality—labor, feminist, ethnicity-based or migrants' organizations are potential allies of the sector. However, engagement from these groups does not come naturally. Organizations advocating for labor, women's or migrants' rights do not tend to regard the situation of domestic workers as their priority (Blofield 2012; Blofield and Jokela 2018; Tilly et al. 2019). This can be interpreted in terms of what Kurtz (2002: xvi–xvii) calls "lowest-common-denominator" politics: in the name of unity, social movements tend to organize around the common injustice that everyone is said to share, disregarding those affected by intersecting inequalities. For example, trade unions have historically framed their claims in terms of class and from a gender-blind perspective, which has tended to prioritize the interests of male workers and/or those working in the formal sector (Britwum et al. 2012; Gottfried 2013). Similarly, feminist organizations did not focus on domestic workers rights until recently. Previous research (Bunster and Chaney 1985; Chaney and Garcia Castro 1989; Goldsmith 2001) has highlighted the distrust of domestic workers toward feminist groups and organizations of women professionals, who in turn rely on household workers in order to pursue their professional or activist activities. This means that while the intersection of inequalities enables political agency that can resonate with various potential allies, it does not automatically translate into the creation of coalitions.

To describe the alliances that domestic workers build, I draw on the concept of Networks of Labor Activism (NOLA), developed by Zajak, Engels-Zandén and Piper (2017), to identify activist groups that "are neither solely connected to the position of labour in production processes, nor wholly reliant on the soft and discursive power of advocacy coalitions" (Zajak et al. 2017: 899). These networks have two distinct but related characteristics. First, they involve cross-border strategizing, having activists from different countries working together. Second, they involve cross-organizational networking that brings together different types of actors. While addressing labor-based struggles, the NOLA concept also makes space for other ways of organizing, different from traditional trade unions. Thus, it includes other types of organizations—such as nongovernmental organizations (NGOs)—that have supported the claims of women workers in the informal economy for decades (Kabeer 2015). In the cases addressed in this chapter, this means considering the action of organizations *of* domestic workers (i.e., their own associations and trade unions), organizations working *with* domestic workers (e.g., local NGOs) and organizations that make claims *on behalf of* domestic workers (e.g., multilateral organizations). Rather than analyzing them separately, the aim is to focus on their joint work, their interactions and their relationship with each other.

Although cooperation between different organizations is seen as something desirable, their different focus and strategies can lead to fractures and conflicts (Zajak et al. 2017: 904). In this sense, even if these networks are expressions of solidarity, components of rivalry and competition can still be found within them.

Zajak and her colleagues stress that the structure of the network of labor activism is affected by the characteristics of the workers they are trying to defend. It is here that the bridge between both perspectives—intersectionality and networks of labor activism—can be seen. My main argument is that the position of domestic workers in the social structure will have an impact on the actors with whom they relate and the type of relationships they build. At the same time, drawing on the cases of Uruguay and Paraguay, I intend to show how contextual particularities also influence the way domestic workers organize and, to a certain extent, the results they can achieve.

Combining an intersectional approach with the analysis of collective action makes the relations of inequality within the networks of activism visible, pointing out hierarchies of power that can be contested and subverted or legitimized and reproduced.

### In the Vanguard: The Case of Uruguay

Uruguay was the first country in Latin America to pass a broad reform on domestic workers' rights, following the victory of the Frente Amplio (a left-oriented political coalition) in the national elections for the president and the parliament, held in October 2004. The government itself encouraged the collective organization of domestic workers: already in his inaugural speech, the newly elected president Tabaré Vázquez stated that they were planning to change the law in order to guarantee more rights to domestic workers (Mazzuchi 2009) and that they would introduce a tripartite negotiation procedure for this sector to set wages and other benefits, known in Uruguay as Consejos de Salarios (Wage Councils). These bargaining procedures bring together workers' and employers' representatives of each occupational sector who, with the government as the mediator, set the working conditions for their branch of activity.

In this context, the gender department of the Plenario Intersindical de Trabajadores-Convención Nacional de Trabajadores (PIT-CNT, Inter Trade Union Plenary-National Workers' Convention), the Uruguayan national trade union confederation, made a call to all domestic workers to reactivate the Sindicato Único de Trabajadoras Domésticas (SUTD, Single Domestic Workers' Union), the domestic workers' trade union that had been active between the decades of 1980 and 1990.

Before the end of 2005, the SUTD had been reactivated, and in 2006, Uruguay approved a law guaranteeing domestic workers the same rights as any other wage worker. But fulfilling the governmental promise of the bargaining procedure proved to be more complicated, since finding an actor that could represent all households that hire domestic workers was not an easy task. After failed negotiations with some employers' organizations, the responsibility was finally assumed by the Liga de Amas de Casa del Uruguay (LACCU, Uruguayan Housewives' and Consumers' League). Finally, in August 2008, the tripartite bargaining council met for the first time, and by the end of the year, they had signed their first agreement that stipulated an increase in wages and other benefits. To achieve this, the SUTD worked closely with the PIT-CNT, maintaining a strong identification with the trade union confederation as one of the SUTD representatives expressed: "When we go out, both abroad and here within our country, when we say we are SUTD, we are also SUTD PIT-CNT. We have a first name and a last name. And that last name has a lot of value for us."[1] To be sure, the support of the PIT-CNT was more than symbolic: the confederation provided the SUTD with an office in their premises to hold their meetings, funds for traveling to different points of the country to promote their activities and recruit new members, as well as with legal advice and professional support for their participation in the wage councils.

The Universidad de la República, the main national university in Uruguay, also played a vital role. Joint projects from the School of Law provided legal advice to the SUTD and the LACCU, respectively. Other schools like Social Work and Psychology also implemented projects with the SUTD, helping them to organize (see Brenes et al. 2012). But, surprisingly, the LACCU, the counterpart of the SUTD in the wage councils, was fundamental in helping domestic workers to gain more rights. Although some actors attribute the great success of domestic workers in the wage councils to the lack of housewives' experience in collective bargaining, it was the capacity of the LACCU to see their own claims reflected in the claims of domestic workers which helped the SUTD to achieve such good results. As I have argued elsewhere (Rojas Scheffer 2021), the LACCU saw the struggle of domestic workers for labor rights as a first step that could help them achieve their own main objective, namely, the recognition of the work of housewives as worthy of rights such as social security or retirement.

Besides the SUTD, there exist and existed other organizations dedicated to fighting for domestic workers' rights. The role of the feminist NGO Cotidiano Mujer is worth mentioning. This organization had been working on the issue from 2006 onwards and had tried to maintain a different focus than the union in order not to overlap with their work. Thus, Cotidiano Mujer became involved in projects addressing migrant domestic workers, who generally do not have the time to participate in the trade union's meeting (held on Fridays), as they tend to live in the household they work for and only have time off on Sundays.[2] The SUTD and Cotidiano Mujer worked together in joint activities, especially during the first years of the SUTD (2005–2010). Over time, however, tension grew between the two, until they eventually parted ways. A representative of Cotidiano Mujer explains what happened: "We were working mainly with migrant workers

1. All interviews conducted in Spanish by the author, between October and December 2016, in Montevideo (Uruguay) and Asunción (Paraguay).

2. The SUTD tried to be receptive to this criticism. By 2016, they were also holding meetings on Thursday evenings, and by 2018, also on Tuesdays. In spite of this, the fact that they were not offering services on Sundays was still an impediment for many live-in domestic workers.

that were not part of the trade union because we understand that the union is the responsible institution [for representing domestic workers and their claims related to labor rights]. Despite this, some conflicts arose."

In 2011, internal problems within the SUTD produced a cleavage that resulted in the division of the organization. The faction that left the SUTD decided to work directly with Cotidiano Mujer, but after a couple of years, they suffered another split. Some workers of the parting group decided to start a parallel trade union. The main claim of this new group, which adopted the name Trabajadoras Domésticas sin Fronteras (Domestic Workers Without Borders), was that the SUTD did not consider the situation of migrant domestic workers.[3] Nevertheless, the SUTD remained the main organization of the sector—representing domestic workers in the wage councils—while Trabajadoras Domésticas sin Fronteras had only a marginal presence. This is related to the close relationship of the SUTD with the PIT-CNT (the sole trade union confederation) and the labor movement's history in Uruguay, where the existence of a unified confederation is its main feature and pride (Padrón and Wachendorfer 2017).

But even though the PIT-CNT was a key ally of the SUTD and a strong advocate of domestic workers' rights, this does not mean that relations between them were always easy. PIT-CNT members had to get used to the presence of a new and markedly atypical actor. One of these atypical features was the composition of the SUTD, as an exclusively women's organization seeking to partake in a predominantly male world. It should be noted that the Uruguayan workers' movement—represented by the PIT-CNT—has been widely criticized for the scarce participation of women in positions of power (Padrón and Wachendorfer 2017). Furthermore, the presence of domestic workers forced those leading the confederation to shift sides on the worker–employer relationship, confronting them with their role as employers. Along this line, members of the SUTD mentioned cases of trade unions' representatives who hired domestic workers but did not comply with their contribution payments to the workers' social security.

The relationship between domestics' workers' allies—particularly labor and feminist organizations—has also had some difficulties. This was the case in 2010, when a conflict regarding the participation of Uruguayan labor delegates in the 99th International Labor Conference in Geneva came to light. That year, preliminary discussions about the international regulation of domestic work took place, and while the SUTD insisted on sending a member to Geneva to take part in the conference, the PIT-CNT argued that none of them were ready for such a task and decided to send a representative of one of their departments instead. Some members of the SUTD, the Uruguayan feminist movement and organizations of domestic workers from other countries argued that this decision proved that the PIT-CNT had a "paternalist and sexist attitude" (Goldsmith

---

3. According to official data from the Ministry of Labor and Social Security, only 2 percent of domestic workers in Uruguay were born in other countries (MTSS 2017).

2013a, 2013b: 8). Members of the PIT-CNT, in turn, rejected the criticism of the feminist movement, stating that labor demands had nothing to do with gender issues: "For me it is a contradiction that comrades claim equal opportunities and rights then discriminate against themselves and say, 'but we are women.' Come on, this is a class problem! So, for me, this is not a gender issue" (former PIT-CNT leader).

Despite some occasional disagreements such as the ones mentioned earlier, the network of activism fighting for domestic workers' rights in Uruguay proved to be highly successful. A year later, in 2011, members of the SUTD participated in the 100th International Labor Conference, at which the Domestic Workers Convention (No. 189) was passed. This event represented not only a victory for the sector but also an important recognition for Uruguay, whose experience in this regard was considered one of the "best practices from across the world" (ILO 2010: 18). Uruguay was not only the first country in the region to legally recognize all labor rights for domestic workers, but its government also implemented innovative strategies to perform inspections without violating the privacy of households while putting into place high sanctions for employers who did not comply with the law (Goldsmith 2013b; Palomeque 2019).

The positive evolution of domestic workers' rights in Uruguay was possible, thanks to the confluence of many factors: the strength of the labor movement, the active support of the national government, the push of the feminist movement, the involvement of the university and the participation of a counterpart—the LACCU—that legitimized the process. Once reorganized, the SUTD became the protagonist but continued to have the support of various organizations.

### Paraguay's Decade-Long Struggle for Equal Rights

The organizational process of domestic workers in Paraguay was quite different. Without strong support from the government and immersed in a social context marked by the weakness and high fragmentation of the labor movement, domestic workers started to organize with the help of a feminist NGO, the Centro de Documentación y Estudios (CDE, Center for Documentation and Studies), which got involved in the issue through ILO-funded projects.

Paraguay had a domestic workers' trade union in the 1980s, the Sindicato de Trabajadoras Domésticas del Paraguay (SINTRADOP, Paraguayan Domestic Workers' Union), but its role was minimal and it finally disbanded in the 2000s. In this decade, the first organization of domestic workers that emerged was the Asociación de Empleadas del Servicio Doméstico del Paraguay (ADESP, Paraguayan Association of Domestic Service Employees). In around 2008, the CDE was working on a research project entitled "The Life of Domestic Workers" and began conducting focus groups. This is how many domestic workers from impoverished areas around Asunción, the capital city, met for the first time and recognized that their problems were similar. They decided to create the ADESP, which by 2009 was working as a legally constituted association.[4] It is noteworthy that they organized as an association and not as a trade union, even if their main objective was gaining labor rights for the sector. When asked about this decision, one of the representatives told me that they did so because they were not familiar with trade unions and because they did not know that a domestic workers' trade union had existed in the past.

This appeared to be the necessary impulse that the SINTRADOP needed to reorganize. This union, which at that time was a member of the Central Nacional de Trabajadores (CNT, National Workers' Union), one of the many trade union confederations in the country,[5] recommended work in 2009. A couple of years later, another large national trade union confederation, the Central Unitaria de Trabajadores-Auténtica (CUT-A, Authentic Sole Workers' Union), also decided to work in this area, helping to organize domestic workers in the south of the country—in the Itapúa department—through an ILO-funded project. This is how the third domestic labor rights organization in Paraguay, Sindicato de Trabajadoras Domésticas de Itapúa (SINTRADI, Itapúa's Domestic Workers' Union), emerged in 2012.

As mentioned previously, although having support from different organizations could be seen as something positive, it can also lead to tensions and conflicts. In this respect, in my interviews in Paraguay I heard expressions such as "the best way of demanding labor rights is through trade unions and not through NGOs" or "in this country NGOs are replacing trade unions and stealing prominence and funding from them." From a different perspective, other actors told me that "this issue was never a priority on the agenda of trade union confederations" and that "domestic workers don't want to be swallowed by the trade union confederations' structure; they want to have their own voice."

Despite the conflictual situation between the main allies, all three domestic workers' organizations—ADESP, SINTRADOP and SINTRADI—worked together from the beginning of this process. They organized joint demonstrations and public hearings, and worked together on the draft of the domestic workers' law, which was approved in 2015. This law introduced new rights and better conditions for the sector, such as an eight-hour workday, social security, maternity leave and paid holidays. However, the main demand of domestic workers—the right to a minimum wage with the same terms as any other wage worker—was not included in the law. For sure, their situation improved—the minimum wage for the sector increased, going from 40 percent of the legal minimum wage to 60—but domestic workers

4. On 8 July 2018, around 10 years after it was founded, the ADESP became an official trade union, Sindicato de Trabajadoras del Servicio Doméstico del Paraguay (SINTRADESPY, Paraguayan Union of Domestic Service Employees).

5. Unlike Uruguay, the labor movement is extremely fragmented and debilitated in Paraguay. For a country with a remarkably low union density—5.7 percent or around 106,444 workers, according to Ovando Rivarola (2021:16)—there are 10 national trade union confederations. For an analysis of the crisis and stagnation of the Paraguayan labor movement, see Lachi and Rojas Scheffer (2017) and González Bozzolasco (2021).

were not satisfied with the result. That said, far from interpreting this as a defeat, this experience showed them that their efforts were producing tangible results, and they continued working together on different campaigns, lobbying activities and demonstrations. Finally, in June 2019 and after years of struggle by organized domestic workers, their right to the minimum wage was legally recognized.

Unlike the Uruguayan case, the Liga de Amas de Casa del Paraguay (LAC-Py, Paraguayan Housewives' League) publicly opposed the new law and especially the increase in the minimum wage for domestic workers. As a LAC-Py representative told me in an interview, they believe that since most domestic workers lack previous working experience, it would be unfair to pay them a minimum wage; wages should rather be negotiated between the parties. Now, even if the Housewives' Organization in Paraguay (LAC-Py) has the same objective as the homonymous group in Uruguay (LACCU)—that is, winning retirement rights for housewives—they do not see a connection between the demands of domestic workers and their own struggle. Furthermore, highlighting ethnic and cultural differences between these groups,[6] one interviewee defined domestic workers and housewives as belonging to "different universes," reinforcing the differences between them and justifying the undervaluation of the work performed by paid domestic workers (see Rojas Scheffer 2021).

Even though obtaining equal rights took domestic workers longer, the approval of the new law in 2015 was regarded as a huge victory for the sector, especially considering that poor working conditions of paid domestic workers were seen as something "natural" in Paraguay (González and Soto 2009; Soto and Ruiz Díaz Medina 2014). The support of national actors—such as the CDE, some governmental branches, human rights organizations and union confederations— was essential. However, probably more important was the backing of multilateral institutions such as the ILO and UN Women. As already mentioned, the mobilization of domestic workers in Paraguay began after the CDE decided to conduct research on this subject. The first projects—and many more that came later—were funded by the ILO and UN Women. This funding not only supported research and publications but also helped domestic workers organize, providing them with material resources for staging demonstrations, attending meetings and taking part in training courses to learn how to present their claims in political settings (Rojas Scheffer 2019).

The support of the transnational allies was not only material but also symbolic. In contrast to Uruguay, in Paraguay the discussion about changing the law to guarantee more rights for domestic workers was only taken seriously after the ILO Convention 189 was adopted in 2011. The recognition of domestic work as work, and as such entitled to rights just as any other occupation, marked a milestone for domestic workers, locally and globally. This legal instrument approved by an

---

6. In Paraguay, a large proportion of domestic workers have a background of rural– urban migration (Heikel 2014; Soto 2014). Their cultural identity differs from the one that predominates in the capital, the more obvious difference being their mother tongue, the Guaraní language (in urban areas, Spanish is the most spoken language).

institution with the legitimacy to set basic principles and rights at work, made up of representatives from governments, workers and employers, helped to legitimize the claims of household workers and opened new opportunities in the domestic sphere (Keck and Sikkink 1998; Sikkink 2005).

Compared with the Uruguayan case, the Paraguayan experience was not as successful. The process began later, the government and the labor movement were less present and there were sectors that strongly opposed the domestic workers' campaign for more labor rights, such as the LAC-Py. However, domestic workers managed to position themselves as actors with advocacy capacity and made significant progress in terms of rights. The support of the network of allies, together with domestic workers' mobilization capabilities, has been fundamental to achieve this end.

## Contrasting the Cases: Interaction of Different Contexts and Actors

Despite some similarities between Uruguay and Paraguay, in particular their small size in terms of population, geography and economy, they differ profoundly in social and political aspects. For example, the left-oriented Frente Amplio stayed in power for three consecutive periods in Uruguay (from 2005 to 2019), promoting policies in response to workers' demands. And while Paraguay also took part in the so-called pink tide—the shift in Latin America that brought more pro-labor left-wing governments to power between 1999 and 2016—its experience ended abruptly after a crisis that removed the president from office a year before the end of his mandate.

The organizational process of domestic workers and the way in which their demands were included in the national agenda also differed in several regards. In the case of Uruguay, the country with the strongest labor movement in the Americas (with a union density of 30 percent, according to the ILO [see ILO n.d.]), it is not surprising that domestic workers decided to organize within the national trade union confederation. The deeply rooted Uruguayan union culture and the proximity of the workers' movement with the Frente Amplio government (Padrón and Wachendorfer 2017) created a highly favorable context for domestic workers to seek and find support in this actor. The Paraguayan process, in turn, was markedly different. Faced with a weakened and atomized union movement, domestic workers found in a feminist NGO their main ally. And although a few years later the labor movement began to show interest in this issue, their involvement was less determined and surrounded by greater tensions.

The first Paraguayan domestic workers' organization emerged as an association and not as a trade union. This is linked, again, to the labor situation in the country, in which unions are fragmented and do not enjoy as much social recognition as in Uruguay. The greater support of feminist organizations in Paraguay also influenced the way domestic workers presented their claims, framed as demands of *women* workers. The leading participation of domestic workers' groups in demonstrations organized on International Women's Day and other feminists' events contrasted with their absence on more labor-related activities, such as First of May celebrations. Conversely, in the case of Uruguay, the identification with the workers' movement—to carry "PIT-CNT" as a last name, to quote an SUTD representative—was much stronger.

The differences in the time it took for the process to result in new and egalitarian labor legislation are also worth mentioning. Whereas in Uruguay only about a year went by between the constitution of the SUTD and the new law, in Paraguay the process spanned over 10 years. In the same vein, the number of demonstrations and public events staged by domestic workers was much higher in Paraguay. Lacking institutionalized mechanisms, such as the bargaining councils in Uruguay, domestic workers in Paraguay had to take to the streets many times to make their claims heard.

As the cases show, identifying as a union versus an association, appealing to class versus gender solidarity or opting for strategies of dialogue versus confrontation are not decisions taken lightly or arbitrarily. On the contrary, they reveal a series of complex relationships, the result of strategic decisions and perceived opportunities according to the local context and participation of different partners.

Similarly, the interaction between the different scales of action (national and transnational), common to both cases, has had different effects. When Convention No. 189 was discussed and later adopted by the ILO, Uruguay had already gone through a broad legal reform and had negotiated two collective bargaining agreements with the domestic workers' union. In Paraguay, on the other hand, the adoption of Convention No. 189—together with projects funded by multilateral institutions such as the ILO and UN Women—was the starting point of the legal reform process. Thus, while the organization and achievements of domestic workers in Paraguay could not have been realized without the implementation of multilateral cooperation projects and the approval of international regulations, in Uruguay the process was initiated and supported mainly by domestic actors. Moreover, the Uruguayan experience was presented as a model for the rest of the world when discussing the ILO Convention.

The contrast between the cases also reveals how the way in which inequalities are approached and perceived locally can affect the support that domestic workers find in other actors who, although situated outside the network of activism, have common interests. The examples regarding the relationship between domestic workers' and housewives' organizations have drawn attention to how the perception of cultural and ethnic differences—and the meaning attributed to them—is linked to a greater or lesser distancing from housewives in relation to the demands of domestic workers.

In sum, even though the creation of networks has been a central strategy in both countries, their specific conformation differs from one case to another.

## Concluding Remarks

The position that domestic workers occupy in the social structure gives rise to a clear asymmetry of power in their relationship with their employers, reducing their ability to negotiate and claim rights in the private sphere. Yet the categories of class, gender and race/ethnicity can become elements of political action and mobilization in the public sphere (Bernardino-Costa 2014). The intersection of axes of inequality produces thus an ambivalent effect, oscillating between subjugation and emancipation, making it possible to turn categories of discrimination into vectors of political agency and giving rise to a common language that opens channels of communication with potential allies.

Domestic workers connect with actors with whom they share an interest in subverting power hierarchies, be they based on regimes of gender, class, ethnicity and/or citizenship. Thus, the network of activism built around the demand for more rights for domestic workers brings together different types of organizations. This distinction is observed either considering their organizational form (unions, associations, NGOs, multilateral organizations, government institutions, universities, etc.), their collective identities (labor, feminist or migrant movements, academic group, etc.) and their level of action (local, national, transnational). This great variety implies advantages but at the same time presents important challenges. The cases analyzed have provided evidence in both directions; that is, they have demonstrated elements of integration and tension, making clear the ambivalence and contradictions of the highly complex process of constructing alliances between structurally and ideologically diverse actors. Processes of integration and their positive effects are clearly observed when analyzing the organizational, legal and practical advances in the struggle for rights of domestic workers, as well as when considering the emergence of various organizations in the sector, the adoption of international regulations and the promulgation of laws at the national level. At the same time, it cannot be ignored that a deeper analysis reveals cleavages and conflicts that have taken place within the networks, paradigmatically between the feminist and labor movement, but also with migrant organizations or even between different domestic workers' organizations. These dynamics point out underlying lines of conflicts that need to be overcome, or at least addressed, for forming a successful coalition.

An essential point to understand the complex relations within the networks of activism for domestic workers' rights in Uruguay and Paraguay is related to the fact that most of their allies—members of trade unions and the feminist movement, academics, government representatives and staff of multilateral organizations with a local presence—hire domestic workers. Although as organizational representatives they identify as allies, personally they are confronted with their position as employers. This situation could end up perpetuating unequal relationships within the network of activism, yet it can also lead to greater commitment to subverting social hierarchies. Thus, in line with the feminist slogan of "the personal is political,"[7] activists from both Uruguay and Paraguay strongly positioned themselves in both spheres—individual and collective,

---

7. This phrase was popularized by the publication of an essay written by feminist Carol Hanisch, which appeared under the title "The Personal Is Political" in the anthology *Notes from the Second Year: Women's Liberation* in 1970.

private and public—recognizing their dual participation as employers and allies and reconciling both roles, advocating for labor relations within a framework of respect and guaranteeing labor rights. This points out that the differences among actors do not disappear when a coalition is formed; they remain present, although the reproduction of inequalities can be mitigated or subverted.

On a similar note, these cases highlight the necessity of constructing an intersectional practice within coalitions and social movements. Regardless of the specificity of the group, different members will be affected by different axes of inequalities, and none of them is more important than another. Opting for a "lowest-common-denominator" politics (Kurtz 2002), far from representing all constituents, marginalizes those that need support the most. In other words, without an intersectional approach, social movements and advocacy groups could end up benefiting some members of the group at the expense of others.

Now, even if this chapter has pointed out many conflicts and tensions among different actors within the network of activism for domestic workers' rights, it has also touched upon unlikely alliances, such as the case of the housewives' organization in Uruguay. Despite great differences between them and domestic workers, housewives recognized that they had a common objective—the recognition of domestic labor, paid or unpaid, as work worthy of rights—and were able to identify themselves with domestic workers' claims, overcoming class differences and (at least temporarily) dissolving the boundaries between them.

To be sure, tensions will more likely be the constant within coalitions and any type of advocacy groups. But actors can decide to focus either on the differences or on the unifying aspects of their struggle, on reproducing inequalities or on mobilizing equality-enhancing reforms. The case studies have shown that despite underlying tensions, different groups can work together and achieve important goals. Now, for the coalition to last, those differences need to be recognized and addressed. An intersectional approach, far from denying the existence of differences, takes them into consideration, seeking for unity without uniformity.

## References

Anderson, Bridget. 2000. *Doing the Dirty Work? The Global Politics of Domestic Labour*. London: Zed Books.

Anthias, Floya. 2008. "Thinking through the Lens of Translocational Positionality: An Intersectionality Frame for Understanding Identity and Belonging." *Translocations: Migration and Social Change*, 4(1): 5–20.

Barbagelata, Hector Hugo. 1978. *Derecho del Trabajo II: Los Contratos de Trabajo y sus Modalidades*. Montevideo: Fundación Cultura Universitaria.

Bernardino-Costa, Joaze. 2014. "Intersectionality and Female Domestic Workers' Unions in Brazil." *Women's Studies International Forum*, 46: 72–80.

Blofield, Merike. 2012. *Care Work and Class. Domestic Workers' Struggle for Equal Rights in Latin America*. University Park: Pennsylvania State University.

Blofield, Merike and Merita Jokela. 2018. "Paid Domestic Work and the Struggles of Care Workers in Latin America." *Current Sociology*, 66(4): 531–546.

Boris, Eileen and Jennifer N. Fish. 2014. "Domestic Workers Go Global: The Birth of the International Domestic Workers Federation." *New Labor Reform*, 23: 76–81.

Boris, Eileen and Jennifer N. Fish. 2015. "Decent Work for Domestics: Feminist Organizing, Work Empowerment, and the ILO." In *Towards a Global History of Domestic and Caregiving Workers*, edited by Dirk Hoerder, Elise van Nederveen Meerkerk and Silke Neunsingen, 530–552. Leiden: Brill.

Brenes, Alicia, Maite Burgueño, Macarena Gómez, Laura González and Ana Martínez. 2012. "Barriendo la Invisibilidad: Sistematización del Proceso de Trabajo con el Sindicato Único de Trabajadoras Domésticas." In *Apuntes para la Acción II: Sistematización de Experiencias de Extensión Universitaria*, edited by Leticia Berrutti, María José Dabezies and Gabriel Barreto, 207–232. Montevideo: UdelaR.

Britwum, Akua O., Karen Douglas and Sue Ledwith. 2012. "Women, Gender and Power in Trade Unions." In *Labour in the Global South: Challenges and Alternatives for Workers*, edited by Sarah Mosoetsa and Michelle Williams, 41–64. Geneva: International Labour Organization.

Bunster, Ximena and Elsa M. Chaney. 1985. *Sellers and Servants: Working Women in Lima, Perú.* New York: Praeger Publishers.

Chaney, Elsa M. and Mary Garcia Castro. 1989. *Muchachas No More: Household Workers in Latin America and the Caribbean.* Philadelphia: Temple University Press.

Collins, Patricia Hill. 2000. *Black Feminist Thought: Knowledge, Consciousness, and the Politics of Empowerment.* New York and London: Routledge.

Crenshaw, Kimberlé. 1994. "Mapping the Margins: Intersectionality, Identity Politics and Violence against Women of Color." In *The Public Nature of Private Violence*, edited by Martha Albertson Fineman and Rixanne Mykitiuk, 93–118. London: Routledge.

Dalla Costa, Mariarosa and Selma James. 1975. *The Power of Women and the Subversion of the Community.* Bristol: Falling Wall Press.

Federici, Silvia. 2010. *Calibán y la Bruja: Mujeres, Cuerpo y Acumulación Originaria.* Madrid: Traficantes de Sueños.

Goldsmith, Mary. 2001. "Un Puente Maltendido: Feminismo, Trabajo Doméstico y Servicio Doméstico en América Latina." *Paper presented at the XXIII International Conference of the Latin American Studies Association*, Washington, DC, 6–8 September.

Goldsmith, Mary. 2013a. "Los Espacios Internacionales de la Participación Política de las Trabajadoras Remuneradas del Hogar." *Revista de Estudios Sociales*, 45: 233–246.

Goldsmith, Mary. 2013b. *Negociación Colectiva y las Trabajadoras Domésticas en Uruguay.* Cambridge: Women in Informal Employment: Globalizing and Organizing.

González, Maridí and Lilian Soto. 2009. "Avances en los Derechos de las Trabajadoras del Hogar en Paraguay." In *Buenas Prácticas en Derechos Humanos de las Mujeres. África y América Latina*, edited by Estefanía Molina and Nava San Miguel, 139–150. Madrid: Universidad Autónoma de Madrid.

González Bozzolasco, Ignacio. 2021. *Las Organizaciones Sindicales en Paraguay: Un Panorama General sobre su Situación, Composición y Estrategias de Incidencia.* Asunción: Friedrich-Ebert-Stiftung.

Gottfried, Heidi. 2013. *Gender, Work, and Economy: Unpacking the Global Economy.* Malden: Polity Press.

Gutiérrez-Rodríguez, Encarnación. 2010. *Migration, Domestic Work and Affect: A Decolonial Approach on Value and the Feminization of Labor.* New York: Routledge.

Gutiérrez-Rodríguez, Encarnación and Jurema Brites. 2014. "Feminization of Labor. Domestic Work between Regulation and Intimacy." *Women's Studies International Forum*, 46:1–4.

Heikel, María Victoria. 2014. *Trabajo Doméstico Remunerado en Paraguay*. Asunción: International Labour Organization.

Hochschild, Arlie Russell. 2000. "Global Care Chains and Emotional Surplus Value." In *On the Edge: Living with Global Capitalism*, edited by Will Hutton and Anthony Giddens, 130–146. London: Vintage.

Hondagneu-Sotelo, Pierrette. 2001. *Doméstica. Immigrant Workers Cleaning and Caring in the Shadows of Afluence*. Berkeley, CA: University of California Press.

ILO (International Labour Organization). 2010. "Provisional Record." International Labour Conference, 99th Session. Geneva: ILO.

ILO (International Labour Organization). 2015. *Panorama Laboral América Latina y el Caribe 2015*. Lima: ILO.

ILO (International Labour Organization). 2019. *Panorama Laboral América Latina y el Caribe 2019*. Lima: ILO.

ILO (International Labour Organization). n.d. *Country Profiles Database*. Geneva: ILO. Accessed 9 March 2021. https://ilostat.ilo.org/data/country-profiles/.

Kabeer, Naila. 2015. "Women Workers and the Politics of Claims-Making in a Globalizing Economy." Working Paper No. 2015-13. Geneva: United Nations Research Institute for Social Development.

Keck, Margaret E. and Kathryn Sikkink. 1998. *Activists beyond Borders. Advocacy Networks in International Politics*. Ithaca: Cornell University.

Kurtz, Sharon. 2002. *Workplace Justice: Organizing Multi-Identity Movements*. Minneapolis: University of Minnesota Press.

Lachi, Marcello and Raquel Rojas Scheffer. 2017. *Diálogo Social, Contratación Colectiva y Tripartismo en Paraguay*. Asunción: Arandurã.

Lan, Pei-Chia. 2006. *Global Cinderellas: Migrant Domestics and Newly Rich Employers in Taiwan*. Durham: Duke University Press.

Mather, Celia. 2013. *¡Sí, lo Hicimos!. Cómo las Trabajadoras del Hogar Obtuvieron Derechos y Reconocimiento a Nivel Internacional*. Cambridge: Women in Informal Employment: Globalizing and Organizing.

Mazzuchi, Graciela. 2009. *Las Relaciones Laborales en el Uruguay de 2005 a 2008*. Documento de trabajo núm. 6. Geneva: International Labour Organization.

MTSS (Ministerio de Trabajo y Seguridad Social). 2017. *Trabajadoras Domésticas en Uruguay*. Montevideo: MTSS.

Ovando Rivarola, Fernando. 2021. *Nuevas Formas de Empleo en Paraguay. Cambios en el Mercado de Trabajo y Desafíos en el Campo Sindical*. Asunción: Friedrich-Ebert-Stiftung.

Padrón, Álvaro and Achim Wachendorfer. 2017. "Uruguay: Caminos Hacia la Construcción del Poder Sindical." *Nueva Sociedad. Sindicatos en transformación (Estrategias para crecer—Número especial)*, 62–86.

Palomeque, Nausícaa. 2019. "Negociación Colectiva y Perspectivas sobre el Trabajo Doméstico en Uruguay Según las Trabajadoras, las Empleadoras y el Estado." In *La Mesa está Servida. La Lucha de las Trabajadoras Domésticas en Argentina, Brasil, Paraguay, Perú y Uruguay*, edited by Lilian Celiberti, 133–161. Montevideo: Articulacíon Feminista Marcosur-Cotidiano Mujer.

Pape, Karin. 2016. "ILO Convention C189—A Good Start for the Protection of Domestic Workers. An Insider's View." *Progress in Development Studies*, 16: 189–202.

Parreñas, Rhacel Salazar. 2015. *Servants of Globalization. Migration, and Domestic Work* (2nd Edition). Stanford: Stanford University Press.

Rojas Scheffer, Raquel. 2019. "De Asunción a Ginebra. Trabajo Doméstico Remunerado y Redes de Activismo Laboral en Paraguay." In *Giros Espacio-Temporales. Repensando los Entrelazamientos Globales desde América Latina*, edited by Diana Suárez, Luis Aguirre, Carolin Loysa, Brenda Sánchez and Joanna Moszcynksa, 47–64. Berlin: Edición Tranvía.

Rojas Scheffer, Raquel. 2021. "Same Work, Same Value? Paid Domestic Workers' and Housewives' Struggles for Rights in Uruguay and Paraguay." *Current Sociology*, 69(6): 843–860.

Rollins, Judith. 1985. *Between Women: Domestics and Their Employers*. Philadelphia: Temple University Press.

Sikkink, Kathryn. 2005. "Patterns of Dynamic Multilevel Governance and Their Insider-Outsider Coalition." In *Transnational Protest and Global Activism*, edited by Donatella della Porta and Sidney Tarrow, 151–173. New York: Rowman & Littlefield.

Soto, Lilian. 2014. "Trabajo Doméstico Remunerado en Paraguay: Información para el Debate." Asunción: CDE-UN Women.

Soto, Lilian. 2017. "Las Trabajadoras del Hogar Remuneradas en el Cono Sur. Lucha y Superación de Exclusiones Históricas." *Cuaderno Nº 1, Igualdad de Género*. New York: United Nations Development Programme.

Soto, Lilian and Natalia Ruiz Díaz Medina. 2014. *Trabajadoras Domésticas Remuneradas. Aprendizajes para la Acción*. Asunción: CDE and ONU Mujeres.

Tilly, Chris, Georgina Rojas-García and Nik Theodore. 2019. "Intersectional Histories, Overdetermined Fortunes: Understanding Mexican and US Domestic Worker Movements." *Gendering Struggles against Informal and Precarious Work (Political Power and Social Theory, Vol. 35)*, edited by Rina Agarwala and Jennifer Jihye Chun, 121–145. Bingley: Emerald Publishing.

UN Women, ILO (International Labour Organization) and ECLAC (Economic Commission for Latin America and the Caribbean). 2020. "Trabajadoras Remuneradas del Hogar en América Latina y el Caribe Frente a la Crisis del COVID-19." *Brief v 1.1*. Santiago: UN Women, ILO, ECLAC.

Valiente, Hugo. 2016. *Las Leyes sobre Trabajo Doméstico Remunerado en América Latina*. Asunción: Centro de Documentación y Estudios and ONU Mujeres.

Young, Grace Esther. 1987. "The Myth of Being 'Like a Daughter.'" *Latin American Perspectives*, 14(3): 365–380.

Zajak, Sabrina, Niklas Engels-Zandén and Nicola Piper. 2017. "Networks of Labor Activism: Collective Action across Asia and Beyond. An Introduction to the Debate." *Development and Change*, 49(5): 899–921.

## Chapter 13

## INFORMAL WORKERS CO-PRODUCING SOCIAL SERVICES IN THE GLOBAL SOUTH

### POLITICAL STRATEGY TOWARD A NEW SOCIAL CONTRACT?

Laura Alfers

*Introduction*

Social services—for example, health and education, among other areas of social policy—have long been considered key to the promotion of an egalitarian agenda. Whether or not services feed into such an agenda, however, is also dependent on how they are provisioned. In particular, the question of who should bear the main burden of provision is always a topic of hot debate: Is it the state, the private sector, nongovernmental organizations, communities and/or individuals? While there is widespread consensus that each of these actors have a role, there is much discussion about the allocation of responsibility. It is a debate that has been central to questions of rising inequality and what constitutes the appropriate response to it. This chapter is concerned with how informal workers' organizations have become involved in health service provision—something that is often termed "co-production." Debates on the co-production of services within social policy have been dominated by the debate about the shifting of responsibility onto poorer women, overburdening them with unpaid care work and low-paid work.

This chapter examines the tension between this concern and a less considered aspect of co-production: the way it is being used by organizations *as a political strategy*—as a means by which to shift relations of power between the state and poorer informal women worker-citizens—to influence the shape and nature of policy, and ultimately to reimagine a social compact for the twenty-first century. It focuses at the level where national or local social policies and practices of the state meet the ground, and where these are contested, engaged with and transformed by informal workers. The study draws from empirical case studies of two organizations of informal workers—the Self Employed Women's Association (SEWA) in Gujarat, India, and HomeNet Thailand. Both organizations are part of the Women in Informal Employment: Globalizing and Organizing (WIEGO) global network.

The research on which this chapter is based was conducted before the health and economic crisis occasioned by Covid-19, but it is now perhaps more relevant than ever. It addresses the critical issue of health provision, the weaknesses of which have been sorely exposed by the virus, exploring some of the tensions implicit in the building of health systems that are responsive to grassroots needs and realities. It is a reflection on service provision more generally, key to breaking cycles of inequality and poverty that will undoubtedly worsen in the aftermath of the crisis. It is also a reflection on the ways in which organizations of the poor work to shift power dynamics—something that will be central to realizing an agenda that really "builds forward better" for the majority of the world's people in the wake of the crisis.

### *Shifting of Responsibility, Informalization and Co-Production*

In 1989, Caroline Moser posed a differentiation between women's "practical" gender interests and their "strategic" gender interests. She argued that development projects and programs could only be considered feminist if they went beyond women's pragmatic needs and challenged structural gender inequalities. Similarly, Chant and Sweetman (2012) draw a line between "political action," which challenges gendered social structures through the "transformation of the laws, politics and practices" (and which can truly be defined as women's empowerment), and "pragmatic action," which while often being very welcome to local communities, continues to uphold the gendered order of society. While neither of these authors directly address the issue of social service provision, there is an implication that programs reinforcing women's unpaid (or low-paid) care work in the community as a way in which to fill gaps in state provision would address practical or pragmatic concerns. They would not, however, necessarily be thought of as empowering unless they were simultaneously transforming gendered norms.

When it comes to the provision of social services, this feminist literature has also intersected with a more mainstream political economy critique that focuses on the informalization of public sector work. In the health and care sectors, a common response to the roll-back of public provision has been to outsource to the private sector, including to nongovernmental organizations. Increasingly, there is also a reliance on the work of cadres of (mainly women) "volunteers"— especially in the health and care sectors—whose role is to extend state health or care services into the community but with no employment contracts and little or no pay or job security. This type of work—which falls outside the confines of formal employment—is not only argued to increase women's marginalization through intensifying their care responsibilities but also "generally theorized as a key component of a neo-liberal privatization agenda that erodes both the public sector and the rights of workers employed within it" (Samson 2015: 2).

A central argument that has emerged from trade unions (and indeed from many such community workers themselves) is that such work should be formalized. By this, it is meant that community health and care workers should become public sector employees, paid at least the minimum wage and have access to the superior social security provisions that are often attached to employment in the civil service. In this way, it is argued, the relations of power that perpetuate women's marginalization would be challenged—women's essential work in the community would be valorized through a decent wage and the public sector social services bolstered by the creation of decent waged employment (Glenton et al. 2010; Palriwala and Neetha 2009).

This approach does, however, sit in tension with alternative currents of left and progressive thinking about public provision in the global South, something that could perhaps be thought to draw more strongly on a postcolonial vision of both work and public sector provision, and even ideas implicated in what is commonly referred to as the solidarity economy. Two scholars—both largely engaged in urban policy debates—in particular have attempted to complicate the narrative discussed earlier.

The first of these is Diana Mitlin (2008), who discusses the issue of co-production in the context of urban service delivery. Co-production here is defined as the joint production of services by citizens and the state, something that has long been a subject of academic interest in both the global North and South. Much attention has been paid to co-production in terms of its effectiveness in promoting citizen participation and improving service provision. While there are justifiable concerns about the shifting of responsibilities from state to communities, it has also been shown that co-produced services are not necessarily less expensive for the state and may be a more effective form of provision particularly in relation to services that require behavior change—something that state bureaucracies are not best equipped to deal with (Mitlin 2008). Mitlin's key point, however, is that there is a form of co-production of urban services (housing, water, sanitation) that has emerged in the global South, driven largely by organized groups of the urban poor. She argues that to see this as a purely pragmatic activity is to miss the point that co-production is also a form of political action "through which the organized poor may . . . consolidate their local organizational base and augment their capacity to negotiate successfully with the state" (Mitlin 2008: 340). Using examples from the international movement Shack/Slum Dwellers International, Mitlin (2008) shows that in the context of weak states and inaccessible private provision, grassroots organizations are managing to build relationships with more powerful institutions, and through their work with the state, shift the relations of power and influence state policy and practice in their own interests. In these terms, co-production can be thought of as both pragmatic/practical and political/strategic action.

Melanie Samson (2015) is the second scholar who has provided a somewhat different perspective on the role of informal workers in urban service provision. Her concern is with the inclusion of waste pickers into urban solid waste management. Samson (2015) argues that while the inclusion of informal waste workers into urban systems may be a consequence of the informalization and privatization of the local state, it cannot always be thought to be so. For example, in India, Brazil and Colombia, cooperatives of waste pickers have negotiated their own inclusion into waste management systems in a way that has improved their working conditions and stabilized and/or improved their incomes (Samson 2015). In these cases, the inclusion of waste pickers into urban systems cannot be thought of as a withdrawal of public provision, but rather as a broadening of the conception of public provision in a way that responds to the context of the global South.

Both Mitlin and Samson are, however, clear that not all these processes can be thought of as progressive as opposed to a regressive shifting of responsibility and state withdrawal. For Mitlin, the key conditions under which co-production is progressive are (1) when it is driven and initiated by grassroots movements themselves (i.e., it is not a top-down process), (2) when it is not motivated by income generation so that co-production becomes akin to a public–private partnership, (3) the grassroots organizations are able to maintain autonomy from the state—"the objective is not to develop a model to be passed over to state employees" (2008: 352)—and (4) the grassroots organization maintains a political objective of increasing citizen control of the state. For Samson, what differentiates the inclusion of waste pickers into solid waste management systems (which does have an income-earning element) from a standard public–private partnership is (1) the fact that waste pickers are providing a service (recycling) that has generally not been provided by municipalities in the global South before (hence this is not the informalization of previously formal jobs), (2) inclusion is driven by grassroots organizations of waste pickers themselves, (3) their motivation is not only to improve incomes but to transform the nature of the state and (4) their working conditions and incomes improve rather than worsen through inclusion.

### *Lok Swasthya SEWA Mandali and the Shakti Kendras*

The Lok Swasthya SEWA Mandali (LSSM) was founded as a cooperative in 1990 in order to provide health services to the members of India's Self Employed Women's Association (SEWA)—a trade union of almost 2 million informally employed women based in Ahmedabad, Gujarat. Aside from the provision of health services, LSSM also aims to provide greater economic security to the community health workers who make up the cooperative. In 2016 it had close to 2,000 shareholders managed by a board of 15 elected directors (Desai and Chatterjee 2018). As a cooperative, LSSM is unique in its focus on the provision of a social service rather than on market-based production. The fact that it is owned and operated by the health workers and generates its own income also distinguishes it from the majority of nongovernmental public health service provision in India, which either relies on voluntary work or is subsidized by grants from external donors (Desai and Chatterjee 2018).

For many years, India's public health system was infamous for its lack of resources (with government spending of less than 1 percent of GDP), poor quality of care, lack of frontline health workers and a bureaucratic mode of operation. Poorer citizens, including informal workers, have learned to distrust the system, often preferring to bankrupt themselves seeking private health care as an alternative. It was in this context that the LSSM first began to operate, attempting to bring affordable health care closer to SEWA's members by providing basic preventive and promotive health services, organizing diagnostic health camps suited to the working hours of informal workers and linking workers to any entitlements that did exist (health insurance for the poor, for example). Since the implementation of the National Rural Health Mission in 2005, public health provision has expanded and improved, particularly in rural areas. Primary health care (PHC) services were bolstered and the position of Accredited Social Health Activist (ASHA) was instituted in order to strengthen the frontline provision of sexual and reproductive health services (Saprii et al. 2015).

As the role of the state has expanded under subsequent health missions, LSSM has developed new ways of working in fulfilling its mission not to replace public health services but to continue to fill the gaps in provision. While continuing its basic health promotion and prevention services, there is now also a much stronger focus on working with the state to ensure that the public health services on offer actually reach informal workers. In 2015, SEWA's Social Security Team in Gujarat began to adapt a model of working originally developed by SEWA in Delhi and Madhya Pradesh, called the SEWA Shakti Kendras (SSKs). Whereas before health workers would give out information about public services and schemes, now they adopt an approach called "follow the worker" (Interview with SSK Team Leader, Ahmedabad, April 2018). This entails accompanying workers throughout the entire process of accessing public entitlements: providing information, filling out forms, helping workers to get documentation ready, and accompanying workers when they submit forms, collect cash benefits and/or access health services. Only once an entitlement or treatment has been received successfully by the worker do the health workers consider the job completed. Data on the impact of the SSKs in Gujarat is not yet available. However, evaluations of the SSKs operating in Delhi and Madhya Pradesh suggest that they can help large numbers of poor workers to better access health services. There are now 23 SSKs operating in five states of India (Gujarat, Uttarkhand, Rajasthan, Bihar and Murshidabad). In Delhi, during the year 2015/2016, 69,000 workers visited the SSKs, and nearly 67 percent of those people received benefits as a result. It is estimated that the 5,023 referrals to the public health system that year saved poor families 411,520 rupees (just over USD 6,000) in costs that would otherwise have been spent on private health care providers.[1]

In order to "follow the worker" and ensure that either benefits or treatment is received, it is necessary that community health workers are empowered to engage with the state effectively. One way in which LSSM has consistently approached a basic level of empowerment is through its cooperative structure. Within the public health system, community health workers—all of whom are women—are firmly situated at the bottom of a heavily bureaucratized hierarchy that pays poorly and demands much. "If you want anything done at grassroots level, from data collection through to vaccinations, you just grab an ASHA and make them do it," says Mirai Chatterjee, director of SEWA's Social Security Team. In this context, as Chatterjee and her coauthor (Desai and Chatterjee 2018) point out, community

---

1. Data provided by SEWA Delhi and SEWA Madhya Pradesh (SEWA 2017).

health workers effectively become employees with no rights or decision-making power. The cooperative structure, on the other hand, is based on the idea of community health work as collective action—decisions about priorities, work plans and activities are taken jointly by the cooperative members. This is an empowering process for the community health workers, who are drawn from SEWA's membership (LSSM 2018), and it is not surprising to hear that SEWA's health workers regularly turn down coveted government jobs so that they can remain with the cooperative: "I wouldn't take a job from the government instead of SEWA. . . . We've all been offered opportunities, but I never would. . . . I've learned so much here, . . . there just isn't any way my self-confidence would be the same" (SSK Leader, Jalalpur, April 2018).

Key to the work of the SSKs, however, is that they are not only about the individual empowerment of health workers. They also serve as a platform to develop a relationship between LSSM and the state. Establishing this relationship has been far from easy, mainly because of the power differentials that exist between the Indian state and its poorer citizens (Gupta 2012). An important part of establishing this relationship has therefore been about evening out the terms of engagement. Within this process, the generation and uptake of knowledge has played a central role.

Multiple departments are involved in the provision of both social security and social services, both of which have an impact on access to health care. In order to "follow the worker" through the system, SEWA's health workers have had to study and understand the system better. They have had to learn which departments are responsible for which services, which forms and documents are necessary to apply for which benefits[2] and whom in each department should be contacted to ensure the best services for the workers. Mapping that information—a time-consuming job because very little of this information is official, written down or accessible in any way—was the first step in the process.

Community health workers then had to be empowered to use the information collected during the mapping. Initially, health workers were accompanied by their supervisors on "exposure visits" to government departments and public health services so that they could establish personal contacts with officials. This was not something that came easily to many of the women, who were comfortable interacting with their own community members but found it difficult to interact with state authorities. "I cried the first time I had to go and talk to a government official," said Ranjanben, who worked as a health worker on the first pilot round

2. The number of documents needed to access benefits in India is astounding. In some cases, a person seeking to access a benefit could be asked to produce the following: an aadhar card (the national unique identifier), election card, ration card, Below Poverty Line (BPL) certificate (there are three different grades of BPL), income certificate, caste certificate, birth certificate, marriage certificate and proof of age certificate. If the benefit is a cash grant, evidence of a bank account is needed. Understandably, documents have themselves become a barrier to access for many poorer Indians.

of the SSKs in Gujarat. Slowly, relationships were built through repeated exposure visits, and the confidence of the health workers to communicate with officials has improved to the point where they are able to operate independently: "Our community health workers now understand the public health system. . . . All these lower caste women are not scared anymore—they can just march into a health center and sit down as if they own the place, rather than waiting outside to be told to come in" (Mirai Chatterjee, Director, SEWA Social Security, April 2018).

The SSK model builds on the improved confidence of the health workers to engage in a number of strategies which are aimed at influencing the operation of public health services on the ground. With their greater confidence and ability to engage with the state, many of the health workers have become respected members of their communities. This means they are regularly nominated to serve on local health committees. For example, SEWA now has several representatives sitting on the Rogi Kalyan Samiti (RKS, patient welfare committees), which are given a small lump sum each year by the government to spend on community health activities. Their positions on the RKS have meant that the SEWA health workers are able to influence the way this money is spent and to ensure it does in fact directly benefit community members.

The health workers also make a concerted effort to maintain the relationships they develop with government officials, which can be challenging because of the high staff turnover rate. Nevertheless, whenever a new official arrives, the health workers move in to introduce themselves, providing regular reports of their activities to the medical officers (MOs) who staff PHC centers, following this up with consistent personal contact. "We used to give the medical officers our reports in the old days, but they never read them," says an SSK supervisor in Pathan-ni-Chali in Ahmedabad. "I think that's changed because now we're always around, always talking about what we do." The SEWA team is also careful to point out the mutual benefits that can come from working together:

> When we first started working we got no support from the ASHAs, . . . but after a year we've started to build a relationship with them. We told them we weren't going to complain about them, that we wanted the same things as them, that we could help them and that they could also help us. (SSK Supervisor, Pathan-ni-Chali, April 2018)

The result is that SEWA community health workers increasingly find themselves being called in to provide assistance to public health officials—from MOs down to frontline health workers. This allows them influence over the process of implementation and delivery of health services and activities and means that their members are more likely to benefit from what is on offer. "Often I have to call in [a SEWA health worker] to help us run our health and nutrition days," said the manager of an urban health center in Rajiv Nagar in Ahmedabad. "Government needs help to reach people. Truthfully, we really don't have any idea how to do this and the SEWA workers really help us there." On the other hand, ASHAs in this area have also started to help make connections between SEWA's health workers and the public health system, aiding the types of relationships which further enable SEWA to influence the process of public health implementation.

SEWA also continues to offer its own health promotion and prevention services, as well as running health camps where workers can access basic diagnostic services before being referred onwards to the health system. This provides a service to workers, but it also has another motivation: "This is about instilling a different health behavior. It's about getting members to understand the importance of check-ups, and to actually use the public health system to do this. We're trying to counter the negative view people have of the public system" (SSK Supervisor, Shiheshwari Nagar, Ahmedabad).

Building trust with the public health system isn't always easy, particularly if people are then let down by poor care or medicine stock-outs, but SEWA sees this process as important. "The more people start to use the public system, the more they are able to start demanding things from it" (SSK Supervisor, Shiheshwari Nagar, Ahmedabad).

### HomeNet Thailand and the Local Health Funds

Founded in 1997, HomeNet Thailand (HNT) has worked across the country to organize workers, mainly women, engaged in the home-based production of goods and now has a membership of approximately 6,000 informal workers. One of HNT's main concerns around which it has organized workers is health. They were one of nine civil society networks in Thailand who joined forces with public health professionals in the early 2000s to push for the implementation of the well-known "30-Baht" and later Universal Coverage (UC) Scheme (Nitayarumphong 2006). The 30-Baht health scheme allowed all Thai citizens to access a basic package of health services for a payment of 30 baht (approximately 1 US dollar). The 30-Baht payment was later scrapped in favor of a fully free public health service, now known as the Universal Coverage Scheme. This is in many respects a model of inclusiveness (see Alfers and Lund 2012), and HNT plays an active role in the many mechanisms for public participation that characterize the scheme, including being represented on the National Health Security Office (NHSO) Board. Many of its members also serve as volunteer health workers, of whom there are about 800,000 active across the country (Kowitt et al. 2015).

One aspect of the UC Scheme that HNT has been unsatisfied with, however, is the operation that is known as Local Health Funds (LHFs). The LHFs operate at local level, are partly funded by the NHSO and municipalities, and are governed by a board that includes representatives from the health system, the municipality and the community. They have been set up to fund community health services across four dimensions—health promotion, preventive health, rehabilitation and out-of-hospital progressive treatment. One of the key goals of the LHFs is to foster a form of co-production between grassroots "people's organizations" and the primary health care system. Organizations can put in a proposal to the LHF for a health-related activity, which they then carry out with the assistance of the local PHC unit and the health volunteers. "While rehabilitation and progressive treatment are best handled by PHCs, we realized that people's organizations do much better than the government health system when it comes to promoting the behavioral changes that are needed for preventive health" (NHSO District Director).

The problem is that people's organizations, including organizations of informal workers, have not been accessing the LHFs, to the extent that the NHSO is now considering cutting the LHF budget. Where the money is claimed, it is largely through proposals submitted by PHC units, often with little real input from community members. "In 2016 the Director of the PHC Unit, who is very respected here, decided that a good health intervention would be to get the community to grow its own organic vegetables," said an HNT member. "We had the training, and we also had a follow up training. . . . They even bought in trainers from the Department of Agriculture. But after the end of the activity nobody went on to grow organic vegetables" (Toddy Palm Growers in Song Khla Province, August 2018). "This story shows the problem," says Suntaree Saeng-Ging from HNT:

> The PHC Director thinks it's a good project. He proposes it and calls for comment, but no one is really empowered to give a proper comment, and he has already set out the terms of engagement. The project is not coming from the people themselves. And people give up on things when they haven't initiated it themselves.

The question then is: Why haven't people's organizations been accessing funds that are intended for them? "There are several problems," says Saeng-Ging. First, many people's organizations do not actually know about the LHFs, and quite often this serves local political interests who can then direct the funds toward their own interests and patronage networks. Second, even when people's organizations know about the funds, they are both afraid of interacting with government officials and intimidated by the idea of writing and submitting a proposal. "The biggest problem for us is that we are so afraid of approaching the municipality," said a garment producer from Pattani Province. "I honestly thought that if we submitted a proposal, they would just throw it in the bin." Third, there is a feeling—related to the process of writing the proposal—that health issues should be left to health experts. "I am really unconfident in writing issues, and in academic issues. This makes me think the proposal should be left to the experts like the PHC director. Health issues need experts, not ordinary people" (Toddy Palm Grower, Song Khla Province). Often this idea is reinforced by health professionals themselves: "The PHC staff tell us it's better for them to design the health activities—we shouldn't be coming up with any ideas ourselves. As health volunteers we should just be the implementers and as informal workers we should just be the beneficiaries" (Toddy Palm Grower, Song Khla Province).

Through its project on improving access to LHFs, HomeNet Thailand has been working to change this situation. They have provided information, training and proposal writing support to 26 informal worker organizations across the country. The project came about because of HNT's frustration with the way the funds were being managed. "Really it isn't good enough what the local state is doing. You can't just tell people that a fund exists—you have to be proactive especially when you know that people are going to struggle to write the proposals" (Suntaree Saeng-Ging, HomeNet Thailand, August 2018).

The project has also tried to disrupt the idea that it is only health professionals—not health volunteers or informal workers—who can develop health interventions: "Our work is to try and change what is normal. By supporting worker organizations to make their own applications, it's not the PHC writing the proposal and informal workers being the target group anymore. Now informal workers are able to write the proposals themselves" (Suntaree Saeng-Ging, HomeNet Thailand, August 2018).

The training sessions developed by HNT have involved technical information and support, but they have simultaneously also involved training on political strategy. "Good technical proposal writing is important, but it is not enough. The workers also have to understand how power works so that they can be powerful too" (HNT Southern Provinces Regional Coordinator). The power dynamics around the LHFs operate on several different levels, and informal workers are trained in how to engage on multiple levels. The fact that the LHF funds come under the purview of elected figures such as the mayor and deputy mayor means that informal worker groups have had to use the electoral system to demand the fair implementation of the LHFs. But they have also had to learn to develop relationships with the LHFs and engage in politics in less overt ways. "It is really important for the worker organizations to develop personal connections with the LHF committee members. We teach them how to develop these relationships, to get in touch with these people, to let them know who they are" (HNT Southern Provinces Regional Coordinator). This has certainly been beneficial for the informal worker organizations in Pattani Province. "This was the first time we'd heard anything about informal workers," said the local mayor. "It's now a lot clearer to us that their work and their health are closely related. . . . I want to see how far they can go with this, and then perhaps we can start extending to other informal worker communities in the province."

The process of training and proposal development has had an important impact on the informal worker organizations. Fifty percent of the organizations that have gone through the HNT trainings have received (or will receive) government funding to carry out health activities designed by themselves for their communities and organizations. This has resulted in both personal and collective empowerment. "After going through this process, it feels like we are able to have good ideas and to achieve our goals," said one of the garment workers from Pattani Province. She pointed out as well that the process had had a beneficial impact on her organization, which had served as a very concrete concern around which to organize. "This process has really helped strengthen the garment workers. Every time we had a meeting about the health project, most of the members would actually come—they really care about it."

However, not all the organizations have been able to take advantage of the situation, illustrating some of the more difficult aspects of co-production. The organization of rice millers in Song Khla decided after the training not to submit a proposal. "After we developed the proposal we just got so busy with work," said the leader of the organization. "Actually, the grant would feel like a bit of a burden. . . . If we were successful it would take all of our time to organize this activity, and it takes us away from work."

## Co-Producing Social Services: Challenging Power in the Interest of a More Equal World?

"Our bodies are our only asset," say SEWA's members, and for this reason good health is essential to maintaining income security (LSSM 2018). The two case studies presented earlier give a brief overview of how two membership-based organizations (MBOs) of informal workers are involved—to a greater or lesser degree—in the co-production of health services. Both organizations are working with public health services to extend the provision of the all-important preventive and promotive health services to their members by their members, in the hope that this will ensure not only good health but also more stable incomes. This is intensive work for both SEWA and HNT. Leveling the playing field between state and citizen takes a large amount of resources, both human and financial, and it relies heavily on the work of women in the community, which, as the HNT example showed, can sometimes be a real problem. Is it really sustainable to expect MBOs to take on this role? Is this strategic action or is it serving pragmatic needs? In Samson's terms, is this a narrowing of the public sphere through a reliance on social movement action, or is this potentially a redefinition of the public?

To answer these questions, it may be useful to think through the work being done by these organizations through the criteria laid out by both Mitlin (2008) and Samson (2015) for determining whether co-production can be thought of as progressive. Merging the two sets of criteria leaves us with the following.

In order for co-production to be thought of as progressive, it must:

1. provide a service not yet provided by the state (or not best provided by the state), so that it cannot be considered a withdrawal of the state;
2. be driven by grassroots organizations from the bottom up, not the top down;
3. be engaging in a political process to transform the nature of the state/have an objective to increase citizen control of the state;
4. improve working conditions for informal workers, rather than worsen, through the process of co-production.

Criterion No. 2 is easy to judge—in both cases this has been driven by grassroots organizations from the bottom up. It can also be argued in relation to Criterion No. 1 that in both cases the organizations are either providing services that are not offered by the state or are not best offered by the state. In India, the ASHAs link workers with the grassroots and the public health system, but only in relation to sexual and reproductive health. LSSM's health workers attempt to "fill the gaps" by providing linkages and services in other areas that are important to informal workers: non-communicable diseases, occupational health and safety and mental health. Similarly, HNT's specific focus has been to encourage their members to apply to the LHFs to fund occupational health and safety activities.

In both cases as well, state officials themselves have made the case that social movements are better equipped than the government to do the work of reaching out effectively to the grassroots than the government. There are differences. Thailand has a relatively well-resourced and effective primary health care system. The feeling is still, though, that to promote health behavior change, it is necessary to work with communities themselves—it cannot only be the state involved. In India, however, Akhil Gupta's (2012) ethnographic account of the workings of state bureaucracy shows how state-run social services provide very different outcomes than the Weberian ideal would suggest (Weber 1947).[3] In this case it is perhaps related to the idea that it is only organizations that can somehow subvert the bureaucracy (and allow state officials to do the same), thereby ensuring a more consistent standard of care reaches the ground.

Criterion No. 3 links the feminist debates highlighted earlier in the chapter regarding pragmatic versus strategic or political work. While both SEWA and HNT engage in more traditional forms of policy advocacy, their work on the ground could easily be classified as a pragmatic form of service delivery. This would, however, miss the point that while, for example, the SSKs do indeed have very pragmatic aims, the *ways* in which they achieve these aims are profoundly political. They challenge established and often gendered relations of power between poor workers and the state from the bottom up. In doing so, they are attempting to transform the nature of the state and citizens' control over it. There are a number of ways in which this is true.

First, as Michael Lipsky (1980) observed in his work on what he called "street-level bureaucrats," state policy is not only made in formal policy-making settings. Lipsky argued that it is often frontline public employees who are tasked with the implementation of public policies who in effect make policy. They are often under-resourced, subject to public pressure, and the structure of their work makes it impossible for them to carry out policies as officially mandated. The solutions they develop in this context become the real policy, argues Lipsky, and thereby street-level bureaucrats become policy formers rather than just implementers (Hupe and Hill 2007). The fact that both LSSM and HNT have worked to develop relationships with frontline government workers, and used those relationships to shift the way in which health programs are implemented, can therefore be thought

---

3.  Weber argued that bureaucracies were a superior way of organizing the state because they ensure a basic standardization of service provision. In the Indian context, Gupta shows that it is the bureaucracy of the state itself that creates the conditions for highly uneven service provision outcomes.

of as a form of strategic action to shift policy as well as ensuring service delivery. Here the line drawn by Moser between pragmatic and strategic action is blurred.

Second, both organizations are engaged in processes to transform ideas about community health workers/volunteers. Hierarchies within the public health system often reinforce the class and gender structure of society, allowing poor women workers little decision-making power and/or autonomy in their work. LSSM has been working to change this idea through their cooperative structure and empowering their health workers to engage more confidently with the health system. Through their training courses, HNT is trying to shift the idea of health volunteers as only the implementers of ideas developed by PHC staff by encouraging them to develop their own ideas for health activities.

Third, by bringing poorer workers into closer contact with the health system and even providing their own health services, both LSSM and HNT are engaging in a process of conscientizing workers to the idea of state-provided health care. Holland (2018: 556) argues that "in many unequal societies important welfare programmes exclude the poor, which dampens the poor's support for redistribution." The corollary to this is that in order to develop the widespread support necessary to expand public provision, it is necessary to ensure that people are coming into contact with social programs. In this case, programs that serve practical needs by bringing public health services closer to the previously excluded may also be doing political work to increase support for public provision.

Criterion No. 4 is more complicated, and here the differences in context are important. In Thailand, health volunteers are paid a small stipend of 600 baht (approximately USD 20) per month by the state to cover transport costs but are considered volunteers, not paid workers. In general, informal workers who become health volunteers do the work for non-monetary reasons. It is considered to be part of the "service-minded" tradition, rooted in Buddhist philosophy, and the reward is respect and a higher status within the community (Kowitt et al. 2015). However, it is largely women who take on this role, and as the example of the rice millers showed, this can add to their burden of care and detract from their income-earning work. Overall, while the Thai volunteer program is considered by the World Health Organization to be a model of community health provision, it may not be the best example in situations where community health work is being thought of as a way to enhance women's income security.

Here the Indian example may be more relevant. One of LSSM's central goals has been to provide a steadier income to its health workers. For their work they not only earn an income from SEWA, but they also supplement this through selling the cooperative's products: health insurance coverage and ayurvedic medicines. In 2016, the ILO released its global research about cooperatives providing care services. It found that the co-production of care services through cooperatives can be an effective way to both create decent work opportunities for women and provide responsive community-based care (Matthew et al. 2016). Financing the incomes of the health workers is a challenge for SEWA, however, and it is here that the state could play an important role in providing public financing. Mirai Chatterjee from SEWA believes that in the Indian context, where cooperatives are common, co-producing health services in this way would be a solution to current human resource challenges within the health system (Interview with Mirai Chatterjee, August 2018). This is not a cheap option, she insists—cooperatives would need to receive financing from the state, as well as generate their own resources—but it would be a cheaper, more realistic and more effective option than training doctors to perform the grassroots community health functions that they are ill-suited to perform.

## Conclusion

Power—and who holds it—is at the center of current discussions about what the world will look like in a post-Covid era. Already civil society groups are mobilizing globally to challenge the status quo and bring about a more equitable recovery (ITUC 2020; Oxfam 2020; WIEGO 2020).[4] These big campaigns set on a global stage are critical to shifting power dynamics. At the same moment, we should not forget the everyday groundwork that is needed to translate policy change into real change. Shifting power relations requires multiple strategies, and the often less glamorous actions at the frontline of the state-society relationship are just as critical as global and national policy campaigns. Central to this is the work of grassroots organizations that build the relationship between the state and the people, empowering their members to engage in that relationship more fully. Including such organizations in recovery initiatives—whether it is the strengthening of health systems or the rebuilding of local economies—will help to ensure a more equitable recovery.

There is, of course, also the very real danger that, as declining state incomes manifest in the wake of the crisis, austerity measures will be implemented, impacting the public provision of services and shifting responsibility onto individuals and civil society organizations to fill the gaps. This is certainly something to guard against. At the same time, it must be realized that, in some cases, collaboration between the state and civil society may be strengthening inclusive public provision and widening rather than narrowing the public sphere. Such collaborations can represent a political strategy by organizations of the poor to shift uneven power dynamics and may be pointing toward a future where an engaged citizenry actively participates in social provisioning. This is a model that has shown itself to be critical to some of the most effective responses to the Covid-19 pandemic (Vijayanand 2020) and should be seen as a critical part of (re)building the social contract in the wake of the crisis.

4. Some examples include the International Trade Union Confederation's campaign for a global social protection fund, Oxfam's People's Vaccine Alliance and WIEGO's Informal Workers are Essential Workers campaign.

## References

Alfers, Laura and Francie Lund. 2012. "Participatory Policy Making: Lessons from Thailand's Universal Coverage Scheme." *WIEGO Policy Brief No. 9*. Cambridge, MA: Women in Informal Employment: Globalizing and Organizing.

Chant, Sylvia and Caroline Sweetman. 2012. "Fixing Women or Fixing the World? 'Smart Economics,' Efficiency Approaches and Gender Equality in Development." *Gender & Development*, 20(3): 517–529.

Desai, Sapna and Mirai Chatterjee. 2018. "The SEWA Lok Swasthya Mandali: A Dual Experiment in Organizing and Service Provision in Gujarat." In *Redefined Labour Spaces: Organising Workers in Post-Liberalised India*, edited by Sobin George and Shalini Sinha, 208–225. London and New York: Routledge.

Glenton, Claire, Inger B. Scheel, Sabina Pradhan, Simon Lewin, Stephen Hodgins and Vijaya Shrestha. 2010. "The Female Community Health Volunteer Programme in Nepal: Decision Makers' Perceptions of Volunteerism, Payment and Other Incentives." *Social Science and Medicine*, 70: 1920–1927.

Gupta, Akhil. 2012. *Red Tape: Bureaucracy, Structural Violence and Poverty in India*. Durham and London: Duke University Press.

Holland, Alisha. 2018. "Diminished Expectations: Redistributive Preferences in Truncated Welfare States." *World Politics*, 70(4): 555–594.

Hupe, Peter and Michael Hill. 2007. "Street-Level Bureaucracy and Public Accountability." *Public Administration*, 85(2): 279–299.

ILO (International Labour Organization)/WIEGO (Women in Informal Employment: Globalizing and Organizing). 2018. *Cooperatives Meeting Informal Economy Workers' Child Care Needs*. Geneva: ILO.

ITUC (International Trade Union Confederation). 2020. *ITUC Campaign Brief—A Global Social Protection Fund Is Possible*. Brussels: ITUC.

Kowitt, Sarah D., Dane Emmerling, Edwin B. Fisher and Chanuantong Tanasugarn. 2015. "Community Health Workers as Agents of Health Promotion: Analyzing Thailand's Village Health Volunteer Programme." *Journal of Community Health*, 40: 780–788.

Lipsky, Michael. 1980. *Street Level Bureaucracy: Dilemmas of the Individual in Public Services*. New York: Russell Sage Foundation.

LSSM (Lok Swasthya SEWA Mandali). 2018. *Our Bodies Are Our Only Asset: The Story of the Lok Swasthya SEWA Mandali*. Ahmedabad, India: LSSM.

Matthew, Lenore, Simel Esim, Susan Maybud and Satoko Horiuchi. 2016. *Providing Care through Cooperatives: Survey and Interview Findings*. Geneva: International Labour Organization.

Mitlin, Diana. 2008. "With and Beyond the State—Co-production as a Route to Political Influence, Power and Transformation for Grassroots Organizations." *Environment and Urbanization*, 20(2): 339–360.

Moser, Caroline. 1989. "Gender Planning in the Third World: Meeting Practical and Strategic Gender Needs." *World Development*, 17(11): 1799–1825.

Nitayarumphong, Sanguan. 2006. *Struggling along the Path to Universal Care for All*. Nonthaburi: National Health Security Office.

Oxfam. 2020. *People's Vaccine*. Oxford: Oxfam International. https://www.oxfam.org/en/tags/peoples-vaccine.

Palriwala, Rajni and N. Neetha. 2009. "Paid Care Workers in India: Domestic Workers and Anganwadi Workers." *UNRISD Research Report No. 4*. Geneva: United Nations Research Institute for Social Development.

Samson, Melanie. 2015. "Forging a New Conceptualization of 'The Public' in Waste Management." *WIEGO Working Paper No. 32*. Cambridge, MA: Women in Informal Employment: Globalizing and Organizing.

Saprii, Lipheko, Esther Richards, Puni Kokho and Sally Theobald. 2015. "Community Health Workers in Rural India: Analysing the Opportunities and Challenges Accredited Social Health Activists (ASHAs) Face in Realising Their Multiple Roles." *Human Resources for Health*, 13(95).

SEWA (Self Employed Women's Association). 2017. *Unpublished Data on Impact of Shakti Kendra's in Delhi and Madhya Pradesh*. Mimeo.

Vijayanand, S. M. 2020. *Kerala's Management of Covid-19: Key Learnings*. New Delhi: Ideas for India.

Weber, Max. 1947. *The Theory of Social and Economic Organization*. London: Collier Macmillan Publishers.

WIEGO (Women in Informal Employment: Globalizing and Organizing). 2020. *WIEGO Network Global Solidarity Platform*. Manchester: WIEGO. https://www.wiego.org/COVID19-Platform.

EPILOGUE

ONENESS VERSUS THE 1 PERCENT

ECONOMIC POLARIZATION AND THE THREAT TO FREEDOM

Vandana Shiva

*This book concludes with an epilogue by Vandana Shiva, radical scientist, environmental activist, tireless advocate for women's, peasants' and farmers' rights and one of the world's most prominent global thought leaders. The text is based on a keynote speech delivered at the 2018 UNRISD conference "Overcoming Inequalities in a Fractured World: Between Elite Power and Social Mobilization" and further elaborated in her book written with Kartikey Shiva,* Oneness vs. the 1%: Shattering Illusions, Seeding Freedom *(New Delhi: Women Unlimited, 2018). We invite the reader to read the epilogue as complementary to the book's narrative, as it ties together the many threads developed by the different contributors to this book into one compelling argument: true freedom and a world in harmony with nature are incompatible with the economy and ideology of the 1 percent. Vandana Shiva's concept of Earth Democracy is a powerful vision for a better future based on unity with planet Earth and our common humanity.*

## Economic Polarization and the Rise of the 1 Percent

Economic polarization and inequality have divided humanity into the 1 percent and the 99 percent. The 1 percent economy is a glaring and brutal expression of economic inequality. But it is not just a system of economic inequality. It also has implications for the planet, for society, for democracy. Economic polarization also contributes to social and political polarization, with intended and unintended consequences for social cohesion, political democracy and ecological sustainability.

The 1 percent symbolizes a system of thought and an intellectual paradigm. It is based on a worldview of separation and extermination—separation of humans from nature, of humans from humans, and fragmentation and dismemberment of ecosystems and communities through constructed divisions, which I refer to as walls in the mind. It is based on reducing everything to a commodity to be bought and sold for profit.

In 2010, 388 billionaires controlled as much wealth as the bottom half of humanity; this number dwindled to 177 in 2011, 159 in 2012, 92 in 2013, 80 in

2014, 61 in 2016, 43 in 2017 and 26 in 2018. In 2018, billionaires increased their wealth by USD 900 billion, that is, 2.5 billion a day (Oxfam 2018, 2019), and during the Covid-19 crisis, by July 2020 they increased their wealth by 27.5 percent (UBS Group AG 2020).

Thomas Piketty in his landmark book *Capital in the Twenty-First Century* (2013) warned that the rise of the 1 percent will take us back to the days of nineteenth-century inequality—that is, the days of the robber barons. As summarized by Johnston (2014):

> The top 1 percent of Americans raked in 95 cents out of every dollar of increased income from 2009, when the Great Recession officially ended, through 2012. Almost a third of the entire national increase went to just 16,000 households, the top 1 percent of the top 1 percent. . . . The income changes for the vast majority are just as revealing. The bottom 90 percent saw their average incomes rise 8.8 percent in 1934 over the prior year, while in 2012 the same statistical group had to get by on 15.7 percent less than in 2009.

This economic polarization is not a natural phenomenon. It is engineered through processes of corporate globalization implemented through structural adjustment programs and free trade agreements over the past two decades—beginning with the North American Free Trade Agreement and the World Trade Organization (WTO), established through the Uruguay Round of the General Agreement on Tariffs and Trade in Marrakesh in 1994—as well as the imposition of neoliberal economic philosophy. It is based on new forms of colonization.

The processes of deregulation and wealth accumulation include privatization of public goods and services and enclosures of the commons. Such enclosures lead to dispossession of the commoner, destruction of livelihoods and erosion of people's rights. Wealth grows through dispossession, creating poverty.

### *"Free Trade" as Freedom for the 1 Percent and Unfreedom for Nature and People*

"Freedom" has become a contested term. When we use "freedom" we refer to people's freedom to live and have livelihoods, to have access to vital resources—seed, food, water, land, health, education, knowledge, work, creativity and communication. Freedom to know and freedom to choose. For us, freedom is in the commons, through "commoning," the constant conserving, protecting, reclaiming and reinventing of the commons, the constant resistance to the enclosures of our commons. And we refer to the freedom of the Earth and all her beings. From the Earth's freedoms flow our freedoms, because we are of the Earth, we are the soil, we are the seed.

For corporations, "free trade," which is corporate globalization, is the freedom to destroy the Earth's ecological fabric, the fabric of people's economies, the fabric of societies. "Free trade" rules are written by corporations to enlarge their freedom to commodify and privatize the last inch of land, the last drop of water, the last seed, the last morsel of food, the last knowledge, the last information, the last data, the last imagination, the last freedom.

Democracy includes economic democracy. The dictatorship of the 1 percent kills economic democracy. What is referred to as "free market democracy" is in fact an oxymoron. The freedom to profit at the cost of nature and society by deregulation and dismantling of laws to protect the environment, human rights and workers' rights cannot coexist with the freedom of nature and people. Aristotle differentiated between *oikonomia* (the origins of the word "economy"), "the science or art of efficiently producing, distributing and maintaining concrete use values for the household and community over the long run," and *chrematistics*, "the art of maximizing the accumulation by individuals of abstract exchange value in the form of money in the short run" (Daly 2010: x). By redefining economy as the art of making money by any means, all laws for the protection of the rights of people and nature that were carefully evolved by Indigenous cultures and democratic societies are being dismantled. Freedom of people and nature has been replaced by "free trade," both during colonizations of the previous centuries and in today's recolonization.

"Free trade" is doublespeak. It is about an end to truly free trade between independent producers exchanging and selling goods at fair and just prices. "Free trade" is a corporate invention for forcing unfair, unjust, unfree trade to establish monopolies. International trade is not an invention of the West as is often said. In fact, the East India Company was created in 1600 to usurp the trade of which India was the hub. In 1600, India accounted for 23 percent of the global economy (Tharoor 2016: 9), while Britain held a mere 1.8 percent. But over two centuries of British rule, India was turned into a land of hunger and poverty, with India's global manufacturing exports falling from 27 percent to 2 percent (Tharoor 2016).

As Shashi Tharoor (2016) points out in the *Era of Darkness*, "the British proclaimed the virtues of free trade while destroying the free trade Indians had carried on for centuries, if not millennia, by both land and sea" (252).

"Free trade" is not just about how we trade. It is about how we live and whether we live. It is about how we think and whether we think. It is about how we choose and whether we have choices. In the last two decades, our economies, our production and consumption patterns, our chances of survival and the emergence of a very small group of parasitic billionaires have all been shaped by the rules of deregulation in the WTO agreements.

Freedom to extract, exploit and exclude is being called "free trade" in our times. Creating markets by destroying people's freedoms is at the heart of the rules of globalization, enshrined in the WTO Rules, which are written by corporations, for corporations. Free market means the person with the most money is free to do whatever pleases his pocketbook.

One of the greatest consequences of the rise of "free trade" has been the transformation of food from a right to a commodity. The corporations behind these trade agreements attempt to take away farmers' freedoms to save their seeds and exercise their seed sovereignty. They attempt to take away our food freedom by dumping toxic food, junk food, genetically modified organisms (GMOs) and destroying our local ecological agriculture and food systems.

Various trade agreements, pushed into existence by corporations, are wreaking havoc on our health, livelihoods, communities and planet by shutting down local industries and replacing them with large-scale operations for export, criminalizing local small-scale producers and businesses in favor of reducing competition for international corporate chains, destroying the diversity of plant varieties, which is vital to nutrition as well as climate resilience, placing intellectual property restrictions on agricultural traditions on which many farmers have long relied for their livelihoods, and promoting the unchecked use and development of GMO crops and hazardous agricultural practices.

One of the greatest culprits in these injustices is Monsanto,[1] the agricultural conglomerate behind the drafting of the Trade Related Aspects of Intellectual Property Rights (TRIPS) agreement. A representative from Monsanto stated that they were the "patient, diagnostician, physician" all in one in drafting the TRIPS agreement (Shiva 2014), and the "disease" they diagnosed and sought to cure was that farmers saved seeds. The cure was that farmers should be prevented from saving and exchanging seeds by defining these fundamental freedoms as a crime (Shiva 2014).

Through the TRIPS agreement, Monsanto attempted to claim seeds as their "invention" and own seeds as "intellectual property" through patents with the aim to make massive profits through the collection of royalties. We have seen the consequences of these illegitimate corporate-defined "property" rights with the driving up of seed prices: 300,000 farmer suicides are evidence of this institutionalized genocide. Thankfully, through mobilizing the people against this corporate hijacking, we ensured exceptions were written in the TRIPS agreement, and India wrote a law clearly stating that plants, animals and seeds are not human inventions and hence not patentable.

In order to cement their power, global corporations and those who own and control them are trying to define corporations as having personhood through Investor–State Dispute Settlement systems, which are secret tribunals in which corporations and investors can sue governments that act according to their constitutional obligations to protect the interest of their citizens.

In effect, the new "free trade" agreements are an attempt to substitute real human beings with the fiction of corporate personhood. They are trying to replace our constitutions with dispute settlement systems they control. They are trying to replace our democracies with secret agreements and secret courts controlled by the .01 percent super-wealthy who hide behind corporations as their masks to take over our lives and freedoms.

Deregulation of the economy through so-called free trade and neoliberalism thus has consequences beyond trade. Consolidation and spread of corporate power, and the undermining of the real economies that nourish and sustain people, is one

---

1. Monsanto was acquired by the German multinational Bayer in June 2018.

impact. In addition, on a deeper level, one of the most significant shifts has been the emergence of financial power over the real economy, as well as the destruction of the real economies of nature and society. Another major consequence has been a mutation in politics, with representative democracy moving rapidly from "of the people, by the people, for the people" to "of the corporations, by the corporations, for the corporations." Worse still, the concentration of economic power in the hands of a small group of unelected, unaccountable individuals translates into political power to influence governments, laws and policies, and shape the future of our food and health and the future of the planet.

The project of globalization based on freedom of corporations and the power of the wealthy also creates new threats to life on earth and to social harmony and peace. The concentration of economic power and destruction of local economies create unemployment, displacement and economic insecurity. The insecurities are used by the powerful to divide societies along racial and religious lines. Fragmentation and disintegration of societies are intimately linked to the extractive economic model of wealth accumulation by the few.

Deregulation of corporate invasions into our daily lives is also becoming a direct threat to democracy and autonomy of the people. Corporations such as Google and Facebook are taking away our freedom to be our autonomous selves and members of real communities. Through the invasion of digital tools of surveillance, manipulation and control into our daily lives, they are robbing us of our freedom to know and choose.

These trends toward ecological and social breakdown are being accelerated by the dominant economic model, which is based on limitless extraction and non-sustainable exploitation of nature's resources, and society's wealth.

The time is ripe for a planetary freedom movement that defends and protects the freedoms of all beings from the 1 percent, especially the .01 percent, who would expand their empires, expend with life on earth and humanity, and extinguish our freedoms to live and thrive.

## Corporate Globalization as Recolonization

The 200 years of the construction of the mechanical mind that suited the purposes of both colonialism and industrial capitalism—extracting resources, labor and wealth, and in the process destroying nature and economies—went hand in hand with the rise of anthropocentrism. It also went hand in hand with the construction of capitalist patriarchy, as I have written in *Staying Alive: Women, Ecology and Development* (Shiva 1998) and (with Maria Mies) *Ecofeminism* (Shiva and Mies 2014). Today's 1 percent build on these constructions. This worldview exhibits a hyper-anthropocentrism, objectifying nature at the deepest level, falsely claiming not just mastery over the Earth but now having the illusion of being "creators" of life and life's processes. And the masters of the universe decide who will live and who will die, who is expendable, who will be enslaved, what we will think and whether we are allowed to think, and how we will choose and whether we can make choices free of control and manipulation.

The story of the 1 percent as told by the 1 percent is also a retelling of history. It includes an erasure of the links between today's super-rich and yesterday's robber barons. It includes a forgetting of the processes of colonization, and enclosures of the commons, which continue to be used by the 1 percent to appropriate the wealth of others. It presents those who are stealing our wealth and enclosing the commons through new forms of colonization as achievers and "innovators."

There are old instruments and new ones that are being used by the new kings of the 1 percent and their empires to control the resources of the planet and the lives of people, rob them of the wealth they create, and subvert and undermine sovereignty from the personal to the political, and local to global levels, and destroy the political and cultural diversity that is the true expression of freedom.

While the old and new colonizations share these colonizing patterns, they differ in their tools and their reach and their impact. The design of the economy based on the paradigm of neoliberalism, globalization, deregulation and privatization has been shaped by the rich and powerful in order to extract nature's wealth and social wealth people create. The neoliberal economic paradigm is an attempt at recolonization and re-establishment of corporate rule through the use of old instruments of conquest, control and wealth extraction in a new form accompanied by deregulation. Today's global economy is based on reinvention of the project of colonization, with the colonizers creating a historical narrative that writes laws and rules to steal others' land, resources and wealth. What the papal bull of 1493 was to colonization, free trade agreements, corporate deregulation and new tools of genetic engineering and digitalization are to the twenty-first century.

### New frontiers

The colonizer sees a new frontier, the possibility of making a new colony from life, the land, resources, cultures, knowledges, wealth, experience, behavior of others. The first colonizers constructed the assumption of *terra nullius*, empty lands, to claim the land and territories of colonized people. In contemporary times, the biotechnology and chemical industries have constructed the assumption of *bio nullius*, empty life, to steal seeds, genetic resources and Indigenous resources, and engage in biopiracy.

The digital giants and surveillance capitalists such as Google, Facebook and Microsoft have constructed the assumption of *mente nullius*, empty minds, to mine our minds and thoughts, extract data from our behaviors, manipulate our actions, choices and relationships, and in turn capitalize on their access to our minds, feeding the economic and political machines it has started to control.

The assignment of property rights to every idea, every living being, and every aspect of nature's processes and social communication functions as an extractive industry of theft of resources and people's commons. The newness in our times is the carving out of new "colonies," including lifeforms and living organisms, our biodiversity, food and health, our bodies and our minds, our knowledge and our histories, our relationships and friendships, and our communications and our choices by creating new tools, new legal constructs, new dependencies, new enslavement, new inadequacies, new empires and new dictatorships.

In today's colonization, the new frontier and new territory that the chemical and biotechnology industries are seeking are the inner processes of nature's creative work and Indigenous knowledge of biodiversity.

For the digital giants, "the dark data continent is your inner life, your intentions and motives, meanings and needs, preferences and desires, moods and emotions, personality and disposition, truth telling or deceit" (Zuboff 2019: 255).

## Civilizing missions and new religions of technology and money

The colonizer constructs a "civilizing mission" to justify the takeover and theft of our land, our lives and now our minds and experiences. The brave new world of the 1 percent is actually the old, brutal, violent world of colonization as the "civilizing mission," of the liberation of the "savage" and "barbarian" through the religion of the church 500 years ago, and through the religion of the new church of the 1 percent today. It is recolonization in modern garb. But then as now, exterminating the diversity of life, cultures, knowledges, economies, sovereignties and democracies is the objective. Piracy is still the method.

The robber barons of today rule the worlds of information technology and finance, which are converging in the digital economy. At the end of 2016 we witnessed how the digital economy was violently imposed on India through a "cash ban." Those without smartphones and credit cards were overnight rendered "barbarians," needing to be tamed and "civilized" through "digital literacy." The word "smart" encapsulates the civilizing mission of the digital barons, who simultaneously define our freedom, our sovereignty, our autonomy, our real lives lived without the trappings of their digital slavery as "dumb." Citizens who live lives of freedom and cultures that self-organize through communications and exchange without the "smartphone" or the "smart device" are the new barbarians who need to be civilized through coercion.

The civilizing mission needs a religion and "barbarians" who stand opposed to it. The religion in the colonization of old was Christianity. In today's colonization, technology and money, which should be means to higher ends and governed by values and ethics, have been elevated to become ends in themselves. They have been elevated to be the new religion.

Dharma, the right action and right livelihood, is replaced by the Adharma of money-making and technology development for profit and control, without taking into account its impact on nature and society. And with human meaning, worth and value reduced to money-making, the unethical and unjust wealth accumulation by the 1 percent is made the measure of human superiority, needing no ecological and ethical evaluation in the framework of our duties to nature and society.

The billionaires and the tools they impose to make more money are the new emperors, popes and merchant adventurers. "Technology" has been mystified and raised into a new religion to subjugate and control. "Innovate" is rooted in the Latin *innovare*, which means to renew. It has been reduced to mechanistic invention, erasing the living worlds of nature and society on which it builds to construct "emptiness" as a license to conquer. "Technology" and "innovation" have become the new words for the "civilizing mission." But as Shoshana Zuboff (2019) cautions us, we must not equate the puppet (technology) with the puppet masters (the corporations).

### The tools of empire

Then as now, the pen has long been a mighty tool of colonization. With his pen, the colonizer declares rights and ownership over other people's land and resources, minds and knowledge, without their permission. These documents are used to claim discovery, invention and ownership, and dispossess the original inhabitants of that land. Laws are written overriding local and national laws and policies, including customary Indigenous laws based on rights of Mother Earth (Pachamama, Vasundhara). Earth laws, laws of the Seed, cultures of sharing and self-provisioning are made illegal and criminalized. Earth cultures are destroyed and the culture of conquest and mastery over nature based on separation from the Earth is imposed. Monocultures of the mind are imposed with exclusive promotion of one religion in early colonialism and one mechanistic reductionist paradigm since the rise of industrial, patriarchal capitalism. Knowledge totalitarianism is created, criminalizing Indigenous and ecological knowledge, including seed breeding, traditional health systems and local economies, which Gandhi referred to as "swadeshi."

A map is made to carve out the colony and the domain of control. In the first colonization, geographical maps were created of colonized territories without any knowledge of the land, its people or its cultures. As Tharoor writes, "The map is an instrument of colonial control" (2016: 157). As William Hicks, former British home secretary, stated in 1928, "We conquered India by the sword, and by the sword we shall hold it. . . . We went with a yardstick in one hand and a sword in the other" (cited in Tharoor: 173). Quantifying to appropriate resources, knowledge and culture go hand in hand with the violence and coercion of the sword or the gun.

In the current colonization, genomic maps of living organisms are created without any knowledge of biodiversity, its self-organization, its cultural and biological evolution or cultures associated with it. Psychographic maps of people's relationships, choices, preferences, behaviors are made possible through tech companies such as Google and Facebook.

### Privatizing the commons

Commons of nature and society that sustain life and freedom are enclosed and privatized, and resources that belong to the people such as seeds, land and water are rebranded as private property. By usurping people's common rights through privatization and intellectual property rights (IPR), a rent economy is created based on the collection of taxes/revenues/royalties. In contemporary times, this rent economy includes the creation of a private "taxation" system to rob wealth from the people through privatization of public and common goods such as health, education, knowledge, information, transport, energy, justice and water services.

Resources of the commons and labor of uprooted, enslaved people are exploited through setting up linear extractive economies to produce globally traded commodities and destroy local circular economies. People are forced to buy what they could have produced themselves—their seeds and food, their health and knowledge, their communications and culture. Exploitation of nature and people is one process. As Cecil Rhodes, who played a key role in the colonization of today's Zimbabwe—which until the country's liberation was called Rhodesia— stated frankly, "We must find new lands from which we can easily obtain raw materials and at the same time exploit the cheap slave labour that is available from the natives of the colonies. The colonies would also provide a dumping ground for the surplus goods produced in our factories" (cited in Gibbs 2017: 116).

The corporations use consolidation, cartelization, corruption and IPR to establish monopolies and increase the prices of goods and services that people buy, and depress the prices of goods and services that people produce and supply, thus creating super-profits for Big Money, collapsing incomes and earnings for working people and destroying the economic diversity that creates real wealth.

The linear, extractivist, commodified system creates ecological waste and pollution and social waste in the form of displacement, dispossession and disposability. Nature knows no waste. Sustainable cultures know no waste.

Today's raw materials include the seeds and genetic resources of farmers and Indigenous people, and our experiences, relationships, thoughts and behaviors, which are rendered into "data." As Shoshana Zuboff (2019) writes in *The Age of Surveillance Capitalism*, we are the new "raw material."

## How the 1 Percent Is Polarizing Society and Hijacking Democracy

There are multiple levels and processes through which the 1 percent, which has dispossessed people and polarized society economically, is also polarizing society culturally and politically.

Dispossessing people of their resources, livelihoods and jobs creates vulnerability. This vulnerability is predated on creating "divide and rule" policies, pitting people against each other along lines of religion, race, ethnicity, gender, and other identities and characteristics. New tools of digital technology, artificial intelligence and machine learning are being deployed globally to shape through advertising not only our consumption but also our political choices. The same tools of manipulation that are driving consumerism through targeted advertising are driving election outcomes through targeted political advertising.

As Shoshana Zuboff writes, "Weaponized innovations have become the envy of every political campaign, and more dangerously, of every enemy of democracy" (2019: 281).

The 1 percent has used its money and its technologies, their tools of power and control, to genetically engineer electoral democracy, further destroying all freedoms of nature and of 99 percent of humanity. The media, including social media, has become the medium for the hijacking of democracy. Tweets and TV shows alike provide the spectacle as well as the raw material for political manipulation. Participation is being replaced by spectatorship, or worse, manipulated responses through "emotion analytics" and "sentiment analytics." Propaganda and advertising have always targeted the unconscious mind as an instrument of power and control. Big data enterprises work to extract our most intimate thoughts and communications to manipulate people's behavior both to make money and to engineer a politics of hate to divide and rule (Zuboff 2019).

As the *Newsweek* article "How Big Data Mines Personal Info to Craft Fake News and Manipulate Voters" informs us, "big data artificial intelligence and algorithms designed and manipulated by the folks at Cambridge have turned our world into a panopticon, the 19th century circular prison designed so that guards, without moving, could observe every inmate every minute of every day" (Burleigh 2017). The same tools were used to influence Brexit and the US elections. As the article in *Newsweek* reported, Facebook sold people's private data to Cambridge Analytica, which in turn used its algorithms (artificial intelligence) to analyze the data and create political campaign messaging. Voters who had privately on Facebook favored racist sentiments, white supremacy, resentment of refugees, anti-Semitism and virulent misogyny were targeted with dark ads. Psychological algorithms could amplify these sentiments and spread a contagion and virus of hate. In the United States, four types of hatred identified through Facebook exchanges were amplified through targeted political advertising. According to *Newsweek*, "finding and provoking people who hate immigrants, women, blacks and Jews is not hard to do with Facebook's various tools." This manipulation and amplification of indicators of hate then influenced the election outcome.

Hate is not an essential or intrinsic human trait. It is cultivated through external inputs. Without the new and invisible divide and rule policies through manipulation using psychographic profiling and micro-targeting through digital technologies, people would cultivate solidarity and cooperation, and organize as autonomous citizens and communities to act democratically to protect the planet and their human rights and freedoms.

The economy of limitless greed of the 1 percent is maintained through a politics of engineered hate, using the same tools of extraction and colonization that have created the 1 percent. These tools are also being used to maintain their power and expand their new frontiers and new colonies in our lives and our minds.

And the pattern is global. The faces, like masks, might be different. But the show is one. The delusion of democracy is being used to crush and criminalize people's movements in defense of the Earth and people's rights, and to divide societies through hate and fear.

The money machine, dedicated only to the 1 percent and the corporate forms behind which they hide, also use the money they have accumulated by stealing society's common wealth, to undermine democracy by directly financing elections, appointing leaders who will continue writing laws and rules to steal more from society.

### Corporate personhood and the hijack of democracy by the money machine of the 1 percent

In the rule of the 1 percent, representative democracy mutates from being of the people, by the people, for the people, into of the corporations, by the corporations, for the corporations. The electoral machine has become an appendage to the money machine. Its purpose is no more people electing people's representatives to protect the common good and public welfare. Its purpose has become to install corporate representatives to promote corporate interests, dismantle all protections for people and the planet, and bypass constitutions, creating structures of absolute, unaccountable power.

New "free trade" agreements have introduced investor–state dispute settlement clauses which allow "investors," that is the corporations, to sue governments if governments make policies and laws that cut into their profits. This process has now reached the absurd level of the delusion of democracy, with corporations claiming to be persons and money being their "speech."

In 2008, Citizens United, a conservative political action committee with major funding from the Koch brothers, challenged the US Federal Election Commission—which regulates the funding of election campaigns and campaign communication—for their attempt to stop Citizens United from airing a documentary critical of Hillary Clinton because it was too close to the election. In a landmark 4–5 ruling, the US Supreme Court ruled that prohibiting independent political spending is a violation of free speech protected by the First Amendment, overturning long-standing restrictions on election spending, even though four judges argued that the First Amendment protects only individual speech. As the Center for Public Integrity stated, the Citizens United decision in effect was saying "spending is speech and is therefore protected by the Constitution—even if the speaker is a corporation" (Dunbar 2018).

By replacing real people who need protection of their rights through regulation from the predatory and undemocratic behavior of Big Money and Big Corporations with the fictitious construct of a corporation as a "person" and the capacity to spend money as "free speech," in effect human rights have been undermined, and democracy has been hijacked.

In her book *Dark Money*, Jane Mayer (2016) follows how Big Money and the billionaires stole democracy. She focuses particularly on the Koch brothers and calls them the "Standard Oil of our times" (2016: 5). Over many years, the Koch brothers funded the fundamentalist ideology committed to destroying the "statist" paradigm, while they depended on the government for tax cuts, permits, licenses and deregulation. What they were really assaulting was people's rights. They want the Bill of Rights to be reduced to "just a single right, to own private property." Mayer has described this as "free market absolutism" in which, in the words of political theorist Isaiah Berlin, "Total liberty for the wolves is death to the lambs" (2016: 156).

Even though "less government" is the slogan of the neoliberal rule of the 1 percent, or .01 percent, they require more government, not less, to grab people's resources, enclose and privatize the commons, create police states and militarize societies. Without state invasion into farmers' lives, seed as commons cannot be enclosed to create "intellectual property rights" for Monsanto. Without the US government and the Government of India declaring a war on cash, the digital giants could not enclose the economic commons of people's economies in which cash circulates, instead of being extracted into the global financial system to generate rents for those who control it. Without forced digitalization through state policy and public funds, surveillance capitalists could not invade into our daily lives, extract our thoughts and experiences, and create an information empire. Without the militarized power of the state, the continuous resource and land grab to feed the limitless appetite of the global money machine would not be possible.

People in their self-organized systems of people's economies can do without a centralized state. The 1 percent need the strong arm of a centralized state to impose their violence on society.

A "free market" is the freedom of the 1 percent to destroy the planet and people's lives, destroy people's freedoms and undermine real democracy. The destruction of economic democracy practiced by and for the people is enabled through the rush of both deregulation of corporate activities and overregulation, policing and criminalization of ordinary people's lives to create new colonies.

Autonomy is self-organized regulation by the self, embedded in ecological and social networks. Heteronomy is control and regulation by others. Corporations want to destroy the self-organization and autonomy of living beings and human communities through a combination of deregulation for themselves, and surveillance and control of society. As Shoshana Zuboff observes, "surveillance capitalists must use all means available to supplant autonomous action with heteronomous action" (2019: 308); "The new global means of behavioral modification that we see under construction at Facebook and Niantic represent a new regressive age of autonomous capital and heteronomous individuals, when the very possibilities of democratic flourishing and possibilities and human fulfilment depend on the reverse" (2019: 320).

## Earth Democracy for Living Economies and Living Democracies

We are living in times in which the very basis of life and freedom are threatened. Freedom is the essence of the human spirit and the spirit of all beings. It is the self's urge to evolve to one's full potential, based on a deep consciousness of the interconnectedness and interdependence of all life within the Earth family, the human family, our communities. We are ecological beings, we are social beings. And our full social and ecological freedoms are based on both the duty to care for our relations and rights that flow from our duties to the Earth and to our human families, including our ancestors who came before us and the seventh generation to come.

Freedom is self-organization. Self-organization, *autopoesis*, allows the thriving of biological and cultural diversity. Lack of freedom externally imposes uniformity and control. *Allopoesis*, external organization and control, does not cultivate freedom.

Because we are not isolated, atomized particles but interconnected beings, freedom is not atomistic. It is relational, it is interconnected. Human freedom is indivisible from the freedom of the Earth and the rights of all her beings. Humans are less free when they destroy nature and nature's rights. Human freedom is a continuum, including the freedom of all colors, faiths, genders, cultures.

We are part of one humanity. One part of humanity trying to increase its freedoms at the cost of others is also an illusion of freedom. Atomized freedom as well as freedom of the 1 percent is unfreedom for humanity.

Self-organization contributes to evolution of distinctiveness and diversity. Freedom is diversity. Diversity and democracy are inseparable. And unity in diversity is the condition for peace, sustainability and justice.

Diversity is true freedom and true democracy. Democracy is participation. And since participation is embodied, not disembodied, participatory democracy is lived and living democracy. It cannot be imposed from a distance. According to Gandhi, "True democracy cannot be worked by twenty men sitting at the center. It has to be worked from below by the people of every village" (1948).

Self-organized interconnectedness is based on diversity and different beings interacting with each other in mutually beneficial ways. Without difference, and diversity, there is no sharing, no exchange, no giving. Sameness, uniformity, monocultures, external imposition and centralized control of economic or political powers are violence against the self-organizing, interacting capacity of living beings and living cultures.

As Marder reflects, "life is 'living with'—cohabitation in a community mediated not by the immutable bonds of a common essence but by the non-essential difference inherent in existence" (2013: 50).

We are at a critical threshold in the evolution of the planet and our evolution. Ninety-three percent of vegetable varieties have been lost, and more than 90 percent crop diversity has been pushed to extinction by the monocultures of the mechanical mind. This is a moment where we need to rejuvenate biodiversity in our farms and fields, in our kitchens and plates, in our cultures and knowledges, in our minds and our choices, to address the biodiversity crisis, the climate crisis, the health crisis, the crisis of corporate control over our food, thoughts, minds, behavior and decision making. Conservation and care for biodiversity is what we are being called to dedicate ourselves to.

In *Earth Democracy*, I wrote:

Earth Democracy enables us to envision and create living democracies. Living Democracy enables democratic participation in all matters of life and death—

the food we eat or do not have access to, the water we drink or are denied due to privatization or pollution, the air we breathe or are poisoned by. Living democracies are based on the intrinsic worth of all species, all peoples, all cultures; a just and equitable sharing of this earth's vital resources, and sharing the decisions about the use of the earth's resources. (Shiva 2005: 6)

Since we are members of the Earth family, real freedom has to be freedom for all beings. It cannot be the enlargement of freedom of the powerful at the cost of freedoms of others. Freedom for humans at the cost of nature (the central premise of anthropocentrism) does not just take away the rights of other beings; it also destroys human freedom by destroying the conditions of our lives. Anthropocentric freedom is both an illusion and a violation of the rights of Mother Earth.

The principles of self-organization and self-determination that inspired freedom movements of the past are more relevant than ever. The seeds of democracy lie in finding a new unity in and through nature, in and through our common humanity, while simultaneously seeking our deepest sense of self in an interconnected and generous universe. Solidarity, courageous compassion and fierce defense of our diverse sovereignties and freedoms are our powers to resist the colonization by the 1 percent.

This is what I call "Earth Democracy."

## References

Burleigh, Nina. 2017. "How Big Data Mines Personal Info to Craft Fake News and Manipulate Voters." *Newsweek*, 6 August.

Daly, Herman. 2010. "Foreword." In *What Matters? Economics for a Renewed Commonwealth*, edited by Wendell Berry, ix–xiv. Berkeley, CA: Counterpoint.

Dunbar, John. 2018. *The "Citizens United" Decision and Why It Matters*. Washington, DC: Center for Public Integrity.

Gandhi, Mahatma. 1948. *Harijan*, 18(1): 519.

Gibbs, Thomas. 2017. *Why the Dalai Lama Is a Socialist: Buddhism and the Compassionate Society*. London: Zed Books.

Johnston, David Cay. 2014. "Trickle-up Economics." *Al Jazeera*, 23 March.

Marder, Michael. 2013. *Plant-Thinking: A Philosophy of Vegetal Life*. New York: Columbia University Press.

Mayer, Jane. 2016. *Dark Money: The Hidden History of the Billionaires behind the Rise of the Radical Right*. New York: Penguin Publications.

Oxfam. 2018. *Reward Work, Not Wealth*. Oxford: Oxfam GB.

Oxfam. 2019. *Public Good or Private Wealth*. Oxford: Oxfam GB.

Piketty, Thomas. 2013. *Capital in the Twenty-First Century*. Cambridge, MA: Belknap Press.

Shiva, Vandana. 1998. *Staying Alive: Women, Ecology and Development*. London: Zed Books.

Shiva, Vandana. 2005. *Earth Democracy: Justice, Sustainability, and Peace*. Cambridge, MA: South End Press.

Shiva, Vandana. 2014. "Foreword." In *Grassroots Post-Modernism: Remaking the Soil of Cultures*, edited by Gustavo Esteva and Madhu Suri Prakash, ix–xiii. London: Zed Books.

Shiva, Vandana and Maria Mies. 2014. *Ecofeminism*. London: Zed Books.

Tharoor, Shahi. 2016. *An Era of Darkness: The British Empire of India*. New Delhi: Aleph Book Company.

UBS Group AG. 2020. *Riding the Storm: Market Turbulence Accelerates Diverging Fortunes*. Zurich: UBS Group AG and PricewaterhouseCoopers Switzerland.

Zuboff, Shoshana. 2019. *The Age of Surveillance Capitalism: The Fight for a Human Future at the New Frontier of Power*. New York: Hachette Book Group.

# INDEX

Page numbers in **bold** refer to tables; page numbers in *italics* refer to figures; 'n.' after a page number indicates the footnote number.